HOW MUSIC HELPS
IN MUSIC THERAPY AND EVERYDAY LIFE

Music and Change: Ecological Perspectives

Series Editors:

Gary Ansdell, Director of Education, Nordoff Robbins Music Therapy, UK
Professor Tia DeNora, Department of Sociology & Philosophy, HuSS,
University of Exeter, UK

Series Advisory Board:

Kenneth Aigen, Temple University, USA
Jane Davidson, University of Western Australia
Timothy Dowd, Emory University, USA
Lucy Green, Institute of Education, UK
Lee Higgins, Boston University College of Fine Arts, USA
Raymond MacDonald, Edinburgh University, UK
Mercédès Pavlicevic, Nordoff Robbins, UK
Even Ruud, University of Oslo, Norway
Brynjulf Stige, University of Bergen, Norway
Henry Stobart, Royal Holloway, University of London, UK

Music and Change: Ecological Perspectives, is a cross-disciplinary, topic-led series
for scholars and practitioners. Its aim is to explore the question of how, where and
when music makes a difference. If music is a dynamic ingredient of change, what
are the processes and mechanisms associated with music's powers, and how can
ecological perspectives help us to understand music in action? Book proposals are
welcome in any of the following areas: healthcare, social policy, political activism,
psychiatry, embodiment, mind and consciousness, community relations, education
and informal learning, management and organizational cultures, trauma, memory
and commemoration, theories of action, self-help, conflict and conflict resolution,
the life course, spirituality and religion, disability studies, palliative care, social
criticism, governance, resistance, protest, and utopian communities.

Forthcoming titles in the series:

Music Asylums: Wellbeing Through Music in Everyday Life
Tia DeNora

Musical Pathways for Mental Health
Gary Ansdell and Tia DeNora

How Music Helps
in Music Therapy and
Everyday Life

GARY ANSDELL

ASHGATE

Published by
Ashgate Publishing Limited
Wey Court East
Union Road
Farnham
Surrey, GU9 7PT
England

Ashgate Publishing Company
110 Cherry Street
Suite 3-1
Burlington, VT 05401-3818
USA

www.ashgate.com

British Library Cataloguing in Publication Data
A catalogue record for this book is available from the British Library

The Library of Congress has cataloged the printed edition as follows:
Ansdell, Gary.
How Music Helps in Music Therapy and Everyday Life / by Gary Ansdell.
    pages ;   cm. – (Music and Change: Ecological Perspectives)
    Includes bibliographical references and index.
    1. Music therapy. 2. Music – Psychological aspects. I. Title.
    ML3920.A78 2014
    615.8'5154–dc23   2013019343

ISBN   9781409434146 (hbk)
ISBN   9781409434153 (ebk-PDF)
ISBN   9781472405715 (ebk-ePUB)

Printed and bound in Great Britain by
TJ International Ltd, Padstow, Cornwall.

Contents

List of Figures

Series Preface

This book represents volume two of a three-volume book 'triptych', the outcome of a six-year interdisciplinary study of Community Music Therapy. The research focused on mental health and wellbeing within the context of a centre supporting people with mental health challenges. The project was a collaboration between this centre, Gary Ansdell and Sarah Wilson from the music therapy charity Nordoff Robbins, UK, and Tia DeNora at Exeter University, UK.

The set of books was inspired by the idea of a visual triptych – a three-panel painting where the first and third panels fold inwards to reflect upon the main, centre panel. Two complementary books by DeNora (Volume 1) and Ansdell (Volume 2) represent the two 'side panels'. They aim to develop grounded theory of music as a medium of wellbeing in therapy and everyday life (arenas that, the authors show, cannot be fully distinguished from each other). This topic is addressed from the complementary perspectives of the two authors' professional and theoretical backgrounds – as a sociologist and music therapist respectively. A third co-authored volume forms the main panel, refracting and further developing understandings and perspectives from the two 'side panel' volumes. The overall structure of the three books is:

- **Volume 1** – *Music Asylums: Wellbeing through Music in Everyday Life*, in which DeNora considers the question of how music offers forms of asylum. Music 'asylums' may offer respite (from pain or distress), but they can also involve collaborative transformations of social worlds. The book draws upon DeNora's work as a cultural sociologist with a longstanding interest in music in action.
- **Volume 2** presents Ansdell's complementary perspective, drawing on his twenty-five years of experience working as a music therapist and researcher. *How Music Helps in Music Therapy and Everyday Life* presents an ecological framework for understanding the key continuities between the specialist area of music therapy and people's more everyday experiences of how music promotes wellbeing.
- **Volume 3** – *Musical Pathways for Mental Health*, co-written by Ansdell and DeNora. A wide range of methods of data collection and analysis are used in this single-case study to explore how collective musical activity helps the participants of a Community Music Therapy project, at a centre supporting people with mental health challenges, forge pathways into greater wellbeing.

One doesn't think about 'music', but one can think according to music, or in music, or musically, with 'music' being made into the adverb that refers to a way of thinking.

Vladimir Jankélévitch – *Music and the Ineffable*

ℭ

I am concerned primarily with what music is, and not what it is used for. If we know what it is, we might be able to use and develop it in all kinds of ways that have not yet been imagined, but which may be inherent in it.

John Blacking – *How Musical is Man?*

ℭ

Music is something in itself, but not for itself.

Victor Zuckerkandl – *Man the Musician*

ℭ

Between your availability to experience whatever happens (what I call aesthetic openness ...) and the desire to change the world (an active responsibility for the littlest things) there is no break or reversal.

John Cage – *For the Birds*

Preface

Music triggered a healing process from within me. I started singing for the joy of singing myself... and it helped me carry my recovery beyond the state I was in before I fell ill nine years ago... to a level of wellbeing that I haven't had perhaps for thirty years....

These words, Cleo's, were broadcast in a BBC Radio 3 programme on the role of the arts in healthcare in 2008, and then quoted a few months later in a debate at the House of Lords, when Lord Howarth was trying to galvanise the government to support such work. This was one of many recent signs that the relatively unsung work of music therapy in the last fifty years is finding a wider public understanding and appreciation. Cleo told me how important it was to her that people were finally listening to patients' experiences of how music makes a difference to their health and wellbeing.

Working as a music therapist for twenty-five years now has shown me just how personal music is, how musical people are, and how much music can often help. When I began this work, it was often difficult to explain how 'music' and 'therapy' fitted together. But more recently I've found that the idea that music helps is increasingly part of everyday knowledge. When a friendly taxi driver asks me what I do, and then wants me to explain what music therapy is, I say, 'What do *you* think it is?', and wait. Many then tell me stories about how they've noticed that their baby is soothed by music, or how singing with an elderly parent who has dementia is better than talking, or simply that they deal with their own stress when driving by selecting particular music. I say, 'Yes, you've got it, that's like music therapy!' (The worst follow-up question I've had yet is, 'What's your real job, then?')

I think I was about eight when I first noticed that music helped people. My cub-scout group were visiting a local old people's home to sing Christmas carols and I was playing the piano. I remember seeing a woman gently weeping, and somehow realising that there was something interesting and important in how, although she looked sad, the music seemed good for her. Recently I was taking part in a music group for people with serious mental health difficulties. A man sang a song with great charm and I watched the tears fall down a woman's face as she listened. After the singer finished, he asked the woman if she was okay, and she said 'Thank you, that was one of my favourite songs, you sang it beautifully... it made me cry, but I feel better now'. Interestingly, the man told me later that he felt better too, because his music had been able to help someone. The group also felt better because they'd witnessed this.

I've seen so often how music offers something to people challenged by all kinds of problems and in very different situations. Music helps in many ways. It seldom just soothes: it also enlivens and motivates; calls forth emotions and movements; joins people together, but also sometimes gives them a haven away from others, or helps them transcend both their situation and themselves. That something so seemingly everyday as music can be so powerful and effective can seem puzzling. Why does a man who says he wants to die also want to sing? Why does a ninety-year-old woman in pain still want to dance? Why can a child recently removed from a traumatic conflict situation be coaxed into playing a drum with a music therapist, and suddenly look free and happy for a while?

Many cultures around the world (and most throughout history) would have less difficulty understanding how music helps. For them, people, music, healing and wellbeing fit together in an everyday and obvious way – linked to personal, social and spiritual practices. But is this not also true somewhere for most of us – even if the modern world has buried or denied this knowledge for a time? At some level, most of us instinctively turn to music to make (and remake) our personal and social worlds, regardless of our health or situation.

౮

The challenge of getting public appreciation and support for those music therapists, community musicians, teachers and performers who help others through music is related to an equal challenge of understanding *how* music helps, and how to best communicate and act on this understanding.

Something that hampers this quest is our current way of thinking about music itself. Aged eight, I think I instinctively understood something about people and music, and the reason I later went on to study music at university was to learn more. But here (in the early 1980s) I found a way of explaining music that had largely forgotten people and society. Music was approached as an object, and we tried to understand how music worked by studying the internal structure of the scores of great composers, or the history of styles. But this approach didn't touch the questions I really wanted to address: Why are people musical? What is music, that people love it, attach to it, dedicate themselves to it, help change the world with it? How do people do personal and social things with music? These were all non-questions to most academic inquiry then. A second factor that has distorted our view of music is its rapid commercialisation and professionalisation in the last century in the West. People have increasingly seen music as a product, and a musician as a special, talented person. In short, 'real music' is something you buy rather than do, and 'pieces' of music are sacrosanct, to be heard but seldom touched.

Luckily, I came across music therapy soon after university, and the Nordoff–Robbins tradition, in which I trained, provided a humanly satisfying perspective for thinking about people, music and wellbeing. It gave me a place to ask questions about music within real-life settings, and to learn about how music helps from the courageous and inspiring people I met, and continue to meet, through my practice. But I still lacked the more formal support of a different way of thinking systematically about music and people. Certainly there were possibilities in music psychology in the 1980s, but its focus was very 'internalist' at this stage – seeking underlying mechanisms of music perception and cognition, but seldom coming out of the laboratory to see how people actually used music in real-life situations. Ethnomusicology had some of the answers, had I looked more carefully, but its focus seemed too culturally distant at the time. Music therapy as a discipline was still at the stage of borrowing its theory from other more respected (but non-musical) fields such as psychotherapy or behavioural psychology. Puzzlingly, it gave little serious attention to how its core material, music, offered its help.

I wrote a book in the early 1990s called *Music for Life*, in which I tried to make sense of some of my early experiences as a music therapist, focusing on the specific ways in which music seemed to be working within the cases I described. But somewhere I still lacked a theoretical key for conceptualising the relationship between people, music and situations in the ways that my practical music therapy work was nudging me towards. Tantalising new material in scholarly disciplines started showing up during the mid-1990s. One newcomer was loosely called 'New Musicology' and consisted of an interdisciplinary synthesis of overlapping currents from ethnomusicology and music anthropology, pop and jazz studies, performance studies and cultural theory. It went some way towards putting people back into the music, and exploring music as active and embedded in culture and society. It even sometimes showed an interest in music therapy. Unfortunately, this material was something of a false dawn for what I was searching for. Closer inspection showed how this newer thinking had inherited the older musicological bias of focusing first on musical texts and pre-composed pieces and how these somehow represented or reflected aspects of psychological and social life. As sociologists reviewing this work quipped, it might be new musicology, but it was old sociology. The theoretical fit for music therapy as I was trying to understand it was still not quite right. More promising was a developing ecological perspective on people, music and realworld situations, popularised in a rightly celebrated book by Christopher Small (1998) called *Musicking*. This encouraged us to think of music not as an object but as an activity (hence the gerund 'musicking'), which is about creating a system of relationships between sounds, people, and places, in order to enhance personal, social and cultural needs. A second crucial theoretical epiphany followed from a chance occurrence with another book, and then its author. In 2000, I found a then newly published copy of the music sociologist Tia DeNora's groundbreaking book *Music in Everyday Life*. Here was the kind of theory I'd really been looking for, and I overran three stops on my train devouring it. DeNora focuses on music in action and builds a view of music that is about real people, in real places, doing things with and through music in their everyday lives. She shows how music is a dynamic 'workspace' for how people move, think, remember, make sense of who they are, regulate their bodies and minds – and generally pursue personal and social wellbeing. DeNora has gone on to do equally pioneering work in developing a social–ecological perspective for music therapy/

music and health, and I've been fortunate enough to work with her on some of this during the last ten years.

As has happened to me several times, a fresh theoretical perspective helped me to realise what my practical experience had been trying to tell me for years. I'd been involved for some time in broadening traditional music therapy through a movement called Community Music Therapy. This involved reopening the artificial divide that had set in between music therapy and other forms of everyday music making, and also nudging music therapy towards a more psycho-sociocultural view (and away from its over-individualistic and 'internalist' tendencies). Theoretically this suggested that, if I were to understand more about how music specifically helps people in music therapy, I'd need to stop thinking about music therapy separately from music in everyday life. There's rather a smooth continuity between the two. Music therapy is certainly a skilled professional enterprise – music therapists train for years and develop enormous expertise. But how music offers its help within music therapy is very little different from how it does so within the various situations of everyday life. Understanding music therapy is a continuation of the project of understanding how music helps in general over a wide range of areas of human need. This book is an exploration of this basic continuity, and its implications.

ಬಾ

The structure of the book, and the blend of voices in it, shows how I've attempted to trace this continuity of music's help. You will find three sets of 'informants', who I think of as 'voyagers', 'locals' and 'scholars'. 'Voyagers' are the brave souls who show directly, or report back, something about how music helps from their journeys through illness and personal and social challenge. Mostly these are clients from music therapy – either from my own work or from that of colleagues – presented in a highly disguised form (though I hope their essence comes through). These examples show music helping within some relatively extreme situations – where music can often be seen to make a dramatic difference, and where we can see its 'effects' especially clearly. The second group, the 'locals', stay at home, as it were, when reporting on their relationships to music and how it helps them. I see their role in this book as partly 'talking for' others who can't report in detail about their musical worlds or musical experiences. The locals give something of a baseline of everyday musical experience with which the sometimes more dramatic and non-ordinary experiences of the voyagers can be compared and contrasted. The locals group consists of twenty-one people I've met over the years who were willing to be interviewed in some depth about their musical worlds and musical experiences. At one level, these people are quite varied: listeners and players in classical, rock and jazz idioms; therapists and teachers; a pop biographer.[1] That half of them are also music therapists is not surprising, since those who follow this professional path are often motivated by strong experiences of how music

---

[1]   See the Appendix for more details about the 'locals'.

has helped them in their own lives. My opening question to the locals was, 'How would you characterise your relationship with music?' We had a conversation about music and life from there. The third group consists of the 'scholars', interdisciplinary informants I've mostly never known, but who have inspired and influenced me through their ideas. I've selected material from them based not on a single disciplinary loyalty, but because an idea matched or further illuminated an emerging phenomenon shown up by the voyagers and the locals.

Overall, my attempt is to 'triangulate' these three perspectives in order to find an orientation to how music helps. I realise that sometimes the voices may not always fully align. But this reflects the overall dialogical spirit of the book, not attempting to force agreement but to further a conversation engaged in by many people, from many angles.

ɕɔ

To avoid disappointment, a word about the title: *How Music Helps*. There are two ways of reading 'How?' – either as, 'In what ways?' or as, 'By what means?' Mostly I pursue the first of these, my aim being to set out 'on the table' the various ways I've seen music help people – and to arrange these so as to see better how they connect up and are continuous with each other. This is not to search for a final theory, but hoping for a more inclusive or 'synoptic' view of the territory.

The other sense of 'How?' – as in, 'By what means is music able to help in this way?' – is a more directly explanatory one. And here I want to be careful not to overclaim. If you are in search of a causal, scientific explanation of the underlying mechanisms of how music 'works' (in terms of acoustics, brain processes, or anything else), this is probably not the book for you.

It's now assumed by many that the ever-increasing work from neuroscience on music and the brain will provide a satisfactory explanation of how music works for us. I have several reasons for avoiding much reference to this field. The simplest relates to my own shortcomings – I'm far from an expert on this complex level, and it's certainly not an area that merits amateur treatment. I take heart from the fact that, even for the experts, we are in the early days of understanding exactly how the brain and music relate. The current texts couch most of their statements in a tentative form of 'perhaps' or 'could be'. When there are aspects of this perspective that are directly relevant, however, I certainly make use of them, and would encourage readers to make their own connections. A second aspect of my caution relates to a basic tension between a neuroscientific view and the ecological perspective that I explore and champion. A critical counter-argument is currently developing in relation to what Raymond Tallis (2011) has called 'neuromania', the belief that explanations from neuroscience will provide sufficient and complete explanations of complex human behaviours. But to put it crudely: brains don't make music, people do! – and moreover, only people immersed within the ecology of their everyday situation of cultural and interpersonal meaning systems, social actions and relationships. A similar caution applies to current attempts to form an evidence base for music therapy and other music and health practices through

randomised experimental trials. These necessarily leave all of the process of
the work in the famous methodological 'black box'. However, without further
understanding of just *how* music helps, it's probably not very likely that costly
trials that try to prove *that* it works will be very fruitful. Both music therapy and
the music and health movement are aware of the lack of a grounded theory of
the process that aligns well with what clients and other beneficiaries actually
experience as helpful.[2]

Tia DeNora (2013) suggests that what's needed is more attention '"in the
middle" of music, right inside the otherwise black box' in situations where music
is helping. This involves being 'in the middle' of both the place and the time of
musical transformations – witnessing and understanding the *where* and the *when*
as key dimensions of *how* music helps. My book aims to contribute to this project
through a detailed account of this 'middle' territory seen from the dual perspective
of the voyagers and locals.

How Music Helps forms part of the book triptych *Music, Health & Wellbeing*,[3]
a set of related books in which Tia DeNora and I outline a more 'ecological'
perspective on music, health and wellbeing – a concept that I hope will make
more sense as this book progresses. For now, think of it as a quest to see and
hear the pattern which connects people, music and situations. We suggest that
music doesn't have some magical power in itself, but rather that what music can
uniquely do shows up *between* people, *within* situations, and *about* specific local
needs and possibilities. Music comes to life and quickens others only within and
amongst a musical ecology. I explore how music's specific features, properties,
qualities and processes form the foundation of music's help in four key areas of
a musical ecology: the creation and maintenance of *musical personhood, musical
relationship, musical community* and *musical transcendence*. I suggest that these
domains provide a broad framework for thinking about how music helps with
basic human needs – for anyone, anywhere.

The central questions (which I've carried with me for my entire career as
a music therapist) are, What does 'musical' mean in relation to human needs?
What is this basic reciprocity between people and this thing we call 'music'?
This 'adverbial perspective' could also be put the other way: What is it about
personhood, relationship, community and spirituality that's musical? Both the
sections of this book and many of the chapter and sub-section titles keep taking us
back to thinking musically about people, their situations and predicaments – and
the 'musical solutions' that can emerge.

---

[2]   See Ansdell and Meehan 2010; Maratos, Crawford and Procter 2011. Raw, Lewis,
Russell and Macnaughton (2012) describe the lack of a theoretical framework for the arts
in health as a 'hole in the heart' of the field.

[3]   With DeNora (2013), *Music Asylums: Wellbeing through Music in Everyday Life*,
and Ansdell and DeNora (in preparation), *Musical Pathways for Mental Health*, part of the
new Ashgate Music and Change Series.

༄

Here are three final caveats to what you will read. The first concerns how my title could suggest that music always helps. This is clearly untrue, as a growing list of its uses in torture and warfare demonstrates (Pieslak 2009). I think the simple point is that music is morally neutral. It can harm in the same way that it can help. But its harmful potential detracts nothing from how it can help – this simply alerts us to the intentions and actions of the people who use it. Its potency to work for 'both sides' rather shows up its essential power as a medium. We must be mindful of our uses of it.

The second caveat is related to the currently fashionable 'instrumental' understanding of music, suggesting that it is merely a convenient tool for repairing health or society. We can and do certainly use music as a means, but paradoxically its help often only arrives when it is seen and experienced first and foremost as an end in itself. The too-prevalent idea of a 'musical pill' devalues and reduces the phenomenon. Music is no more (or less) powerful than the people who appropriate it within particular circumstances, and is thankfully a more complex and often more anarchic phenomenon than people at first imagine. So I want you to be clear from the outset that my title *How Music Helps* is no endorsement of using music as a straightforward panacea for personal and social problems. On the other hand, if we can understand more about what music is from exploring what it does, it may yield further and subtler help than we currently imagine.

The third caveat relates to a possibly confusing flip between 'music' and 'musicking'. Is music an object, an activity, or a place of refuge? Is it a noun or a gerund or, as 'musical', an adjective? Take it as all of these for now. This terminological ambivalence is symptomatic of the interesting territory that a consideration of music in action and situation reveals.

༄

I've written this book from a music therapist's perspective, but not exclusively for music therapists. I tend to speak to both amateur and professional musicians involved in broader musical/social work, people who appreciate how music addresses human needs within their work as teachers, community musicians, development workers, church musicians or choir conductors. Often these musicians are looking for ways of thinking more deeply about what happens in their work, and how to take it further. A problem has been that most books about music therapy are written largely for music therapists, and in the last fifty years the music therapy field has spun a bewildering variety of complex theories in search of illumination or legitimation. These are often less than useful to musicians outside this specialist field. So this is not a book about music therapy in the usual professional sense (or, indeed, aiming to represent a complex professional field in any comprehensive way). It's rather a personal perspective coming *from* music therapy towards a broader consideration of music's help. I hope this is useful to other practitioners and scholars whose work also spans people, music, illness, health and wellbeing. I hope it provides some orientation to how we can all help music help people.

Most of all, I want to reinforce an insight that the pioneer music therapists Paul Nordoff and Clive Robbins came to fifty years ago through their work, an insight that echoes down the centuries and across the continents: to understand the ways in which music helps is also to understand how we relate to it, step into it, love it, share it – and how it still remains central to human flourishing.

GARY ANSDELL
London, July 2013

Acknowledgements

My practical, intellectual and imaginative work with the triumvirate of Rachel Verney, Mercédès Pavlicevic and Tia DeNora has inspired, informed, corrected and supported this book. I owe its roots to many other inspirations. David Aldridge first introduced me to an ecological perspective on music, people, health and illness. Trygve Aasgaard, Ken Aigen, Even Ruud, Brynjulf Stige, Simon Procter, Stuart Wood, Jane Davidson, Eric Clarke, John Meehan and Jeffrey Kittay directly expanded and challenged my thinking on music therapy in relation to key interdisciplinary perspectives. Music therapists Felicity North, Richard Sanderson, Oksana Zharinova-Sanderson, Sarah Wilson, Harriet Powell, Simon Procter, Stuart Wood and Fraser Simpson especially inspired me with their music therapy work in relation to themes of this book. My generous 'local' informants illuminated so many angles of the subject and provided me with wonderful stories that they have generously allowed me to draw on. Thank you to Adam, Simon, Ben, David, Tony, Rachel, Ken, Alan, Diane, Matthew, Christina, Jane, Richard, Mercédès, Fraser, Oksana, Oliver, Michael, Nigel, Peter and Susanna. I hope it's clear from the text that most of all it's my clients to whom I owe the most in terms of inspiring both my work and my thinking. They know most about music's help.

I want to thank the following people who have helped this book shape up and arrive: Tia, Mercédès, Heather, Brynjulf, and an anonymous reviewer for Ashgate for reading drafts and giving spot-on feedback. Thanks also to several people from Ashgate who have helped this book appear. Heidi Bishop was enthusiastic and supportive from the beginning, and continued to be so when Tia DeNora and I cheekily expanded our proposal from a 'triptych' to a whole series. Also at Ashgate, Felicity Teague copy-edited with skill and tact, and Kirsten Weissenberg shepherded the book through editing and production so well. Nearer home I thank Keith for the long-term task of either dispelling writer's gloom or deflating grandiosity by occasionally pointing out, 'It's only music therapy!'

Finally, thanks to Nordoff Robbins, the music therapy charity, and its former chief executive Pauline Etkin for long-term support of my work, and for granting a sabbatical to complete this book. Some of the work was done in the New York Public Library, whose staff kindly allowed me the scholarly peace of the Wertheim Room.

A Note on Referencing

I'm conscious of all of those whose work underpins this book, but whom I do not quote or reference. As Emerson wrote, our debt to others is so massive, and our own addition to a field is so rare and insignificant. I'm aware of the debt – but I had to make a particular decision for this book, which is the first of the 'practice track' volumes of Ashgate's new Music and Change series. Our intention is to address a broader audience through some of these volumes, blending practice and the latest theoretical and research perspectives in an accessible but scholarly informed way. Consequently I have reduced ongoing academic referencing in an attempt not to over-clutter the text. I mostly cite only the direct sources I've used, and use footnotes where additional references or comments are needed. Much of the content, however, inevitably rests on previous work by many colleagues, who I hope will forgive me for not always detailing the complex lineage of some ideas. When fretting about the style of this book, an odd incident occurred, which Jung would have called a 'meaningful coincidence'. A book came to my mind called *Counselling for Toads* – which charmingly puts forward counselling theory in the guise of a *Wind in the Willows* spoof. As I climbed up the steps to a London rail platform thinking of this book, the first person I set eyes on was reading… *Counselling for Toads*. I had my answer!

A Note on Confidentiality

The material in this book comes from a range of sources. The 'locals' have seen and approved the material used from their interviews. The 'voyagers', who come from my practice as a music therapist over many years, have mostly been anonymised and heavily disguised to ensure confidentiality. A few have not wanted to be disguised in this way, but even here I've been careful that this does not compromise others' confidentiality.

For Rachel Verney, co-author of what matters here

Introduction
Music's Help

You can't separate culture and clinic.

James Hillman[1]

'Just wait here a few minutes,' says the nurse. 'She's putting on her lipstick.'

I know my friend Christina is going to be fine as soon as the nurse says this. If she is still keeping up appearances, the operation has clearly gone well. And indeed, as I go into her hospital room, there is Christina in her trademark bright red lipstick, sitting up in bed. Though battered and bruised from her recent brain surgery, she is recovering already. On her bedside table is a portable CD player with small speakers. Wafting gently over the room is the distinct music of John Tavener, one of the so-called 'holy minimalists'. Christina's room feels a bit like a chapel, with this otherworldly music and the weak autumnal light filtering through closed blinds. The atmosphere is respite for me too – I feel like staying there in the calm. But a ten-minute visit is enough for Christina today.

A few months later, we talk more about how music helped her in those early days of recovery.

❧

Christina: *Two days after the operation, I needed music. I'd only brought two CDs with me to the hospital, both with music stemming from the Orthodox faith – Arvo Pärt and John Tavener.*

I saw them as 'good-for-me music', and I chose these particular pieces – Tabula Rasa and Fratres – because there are big blocks of sound with simple descending gestures, all quite simple, nothing too dramatic, or with too big an emotional charge, or too thick a texture, which I'd have found confusing. Because I found myself literally disorientated at this time – because with just one ear working[2] my brain was trying to reconstruct my soundworld. It was as if the music was like a gyroscope, turning and moving in an orbit with 360-degree movements, but at the same time having a direction, which I absorbed at a time when I had no sense of what was upright, what was floor level.

---

[1]   Hillman 1983, p. 149.

[2]   In order to remove Christina's tumour, the surgeon had to cut the auditory nerve in one ear.

ꙮ

A few days after we talk about this, Christina sends me a postcard with a picture of the fox telling *Le Petit Prince*, 'The only things you learn are the things that you tame'. Christina writes that her thoughts on music during her convalescence seem very muddy, and in particular she feels the gyroscope idea needs expansion. She cites the OED definition of gyroscope: 'wheel spinning fast to preserve equilibrium of thing in which it is fixed':

> *I felt at that time like a thing without gravity or direction, which was contained only by the faster spinning in space of the music. It was the musical path that gave me equilibrium. The spatial property of music seems all the more bizarre given that my hearing is monophonic now. But despite this flatness of my equipment... just the one ear, music implied depth – in both senses of the word. Perhaps the relative movement in music implies a three-dimensional world: up– down, side-to-side, back-and-forward....*

She signs off the card with, 'Please, let's talk more about this...'.

ꙮ

We do this a few weeks later. Christina and I have always talked about music and our love of it since the first days we went up to London on the train together as teenagers on Saturdays, to the Junior Department of Trinity College of Music. We've always been musical friends, and I'm worried that Christina's operation will spoil music for her. But something more complex is happening to her relationship with music. The next time we meet, Christina explains:

> *Prior to the operation, when I was getting sick my balance was poor – it felt as if I was seeing the world through a hand-held camera – jagged, but I knew what was where.... Then after the operation I had no idea how to be upright and music was like this 'gyroscope' to find upright. So I used the music to orientate me – as well as providing a pleasurable sound, another world than the one immediately around me. And when the music was turned off, I couldn't turn it off in my inner ear: I had the descending patterns of Fratres going on... I found it spooky to begin with, I thought, 'I hope it doesn't stay there for ever!'*
>
> *But I also found then that I had 'musical hand-rails' somehow: very much a feeling of giving me balance, that I could make spaces. Yes, that's it, it was giving me a spatial sense: the world around me again had up and down... depth as well. Certainly it helped reconstruct a world with three dimensions at a time when I had a faulty reading of them. So I appropriated music to orient me in space... and also, beyond the properties of the music itself – though I'm not sure you can distinguish this – there's the place where the music was recorded, which I've always felt very sensitive to. You can feel the space where it originated. And I felt the spaces of this music were nice spaces, large... they didn't make me feel*

small or hemmed in. They were expansive and allowed me to grow, like in a cathedral or a big Victorian railway station....

Since my operation I've had the experience of the movement of music reinforced. I've been extremely sensitive to everything in my environment – especially sound and music. When I heard music I liked, there was an involuntary movement. Feet would start trembling and wobbling, and then their movement would become rhythmic. At first I was embarrassed, then I thought, 'Oh, just let it happen!' Any music I didn't instantly like I just turned off immediately. If the music didn't evoke a resonance – this was the test of whether I liked it or not at this stage.

⁊ဠ

Christina and I still go to concerts together. Some are clearly more pleasurable for her than others. At a concert in a church with just Arvo Pärt's latest choral music, we're both in seventh heaven. Then a few months later we go to a performance of *Tristan und Isolde* at the Royal Opera House. I'm in seventh heaven, but I see Christina soon reaching for her ear protectors!

Like many people who've had brain trauma, Christina has had to rebuild her world, starting from not only the orientating coordinates of her physical world, but also the coordinates of her emotional and aesthetic world – finding how her tastes, pleasures and tolerances have changed:

I think I now listen to a Beethoven symphony with the ears of someone living in about 1800! It's absolutely shocking! Because I've now got primitive ears, learning to make new connections with sound... so music has a different impact on me now. I have different reactions, different associations. So my musical taste has changed, certain music actually hurts me now. That's so sad, because it's wonderful music that I've enjoyed in the past, but now it creates a tinnitus effect, which distorts it. This is mostly pop, especially that with the thick Phil Spector texture, it's awful to listen to now! I just can't take it – I feel stupid in a way, as if I can't discern sound any more. By that I mean how I follow a musical line, with notes and phrases having meaning, not just being atoms of sound, but intelligible. A lot of pop is just fragments for me now, it's indigestible. But, as you'd imagine, I can still do Bach and Mozart... their music is very easy to discern.

Christina's musical identity has shifted, and by contrast I'm aware how static my own relationship to music is. I'm sad to see the rift in Christina's longstanding love affair with music, but I'm pleased at how she compensates by beginning a foundation course in drawing, turning to the pleasures of the eye:

I don't need to physically listen to music so much now. I realise how much music I've internalised, it's held in my memory. So I don't really have to listen to the St

Matthew Passion, bits of it will come into my mind in moments of involuntary recall. Silence is often a lot better for me now….

ᚱᚩ

'I think music is a very powerful thing,' Louis tells me at the beginning of our first music therapy session. 'You can use music for good purposes, like here… but equally music can be used to make people anxious. And as my brother says, Hitler liked Wagner!'

This ambivalent statement stems from bitter experience for Louis. From childhood, music had been central to his life. He learned to play the cello, played a lot at school, and then, as he developed his professional life, he became an avid concert goer. Then, in his late twenties, his world collapsed.

A severe psychotic breakdown disrupted both his career and his relationship with music. He tells me how music started becoming part of his illness and how some of the worst points for him in the recent year have been strangely associated with music. When listening to his CDs, 'the music became a jumble of the sounds and voices from my head,' he tells me. He also remembers playing his cello to a friend and suddenly finding swear words coming out of his mouth at the same time as the music – sacred and profane mixing together. This became so distressing to Louis that he stopped any contact with music. 'Music was spoilt for me,' he says. For several years, he has neither played nor listened to music.

It's important to Louis now that I understand how music has 'two faces' for him: the enchanted and the desecrated. Music is bound up not only with his identity and hope, but also with some of the most frightening experiences of his life. He's in a psychiatric hospital at the moment, trying to put his life together again. The voices have stopped, but Louis is seriously depressed and anxious, especially about time. He worries about the future as well as the present, as he finds himself lapsing into a frozen, passive state where time almost stops.

It's understandable that, as we chat together in the music therapy room, Louis is also anxious about what might happen in music therapy. His relationship with music is fraught and complex. It is both precious and feared. Can he trust himself, or me, with it?

Louis is brave and gives himself to what must be a difficult process for him. He begins improvising on percussion instruments, and then sings his favourite songs from the shows. At his penultimate session fifteen weeks later, Louis spontaneously improvises a sung ode to music, accompanied by me on the piano. It poignantly expresses how something in his relationship with music has healed again.

Our Relationships with Music

Christina and Louis, two musical 'voyagers', found that their relationship to music changed significantly as a result of their health crises. The 'locals' I interviewed mostly had less dramatic stories to tell, but they also gave complex and passionate answers to the opening question of my interviews: *How would you characterise your relationship with music?*

> **David:** It's certainly absolutely central to my life… there's a sort of presence of music inside me. Music's fundamental to me… literally, it feels to me as I've got older that it's the thing I most 'stand upon'…. It's mainly a very active relationship. And it *does* feel like a relationship….

> **Susanna:** Certainly a very deep relationship… it's sort of personal, in that when you're listening to music you know it's in you already – so you're both hearing it outside yourself and at the same time in your head…. Either listening to music or playing it, it's sort of part of you, but it doesn't encroach somehow. I was going to say that there's also a sense of detachment in my relationship to music – it doesn't overwhelm me – but this is also a characteristic of a good relationship anyway – there's an intimacy, but with each person staying themselves… and yet there's a deep relationship between the two.

> **Simon:** As a lover! And I can't believe I'm the only person who says that! Because music both supports who you are, and what you want to be… and also what you want to feel.

> **Adam:** I was going to say friend and companion… I feel like music's been something that's held my hand throughout my life. Music became a sanctuary… but if we animate it a bit more to become a person… I think that hand holding is something important. Emotionally I had something that understood me, as much as I understood 'it'. That I could spend time with 'it', and in a solitary way, just me and music.

> **Diane:** Very intimate… complex… evolving constantly… I'm thinking of a song I once wrote: *'Music's been a friend to me… a lover and a family… something to believe in… Music is my friend….'*

These people take for granted that their relationship with music is like that with another person. But it's surely strange that something seemingly as abstract as music is experienced so personally; that for some people I interviewed, it's the most important 'person' in their lives. This 'music person' is described as a lover, friend or companion who is intimate and understanding. But then there's often a dimension that goes beyond normal human relationships. Music is described both as someone with whom you're intimate and as an intimate space that is somehow (as Susanna describes) simultaneously 'in you', and you 'in it': 'you're both hearing it outside yourself and at the same time in your head…'. Adam describes it first as 'a sanctuary', then decides to animate this, with music holding his hand.

The locals I interviewed were not, I think, unusual in describing their musical relationships as personal. One of the things people most often spontaneously say to me as a music therapist is, 'I love music!' The vocabulary they use is that of relationships. Through talking about music, these people also talk (perhaps inevitably where love is concerned) of difficulties, phases and transitions; of endings, reunions, of failure, loss and hope.

Many of the locals went on to locate the seeds of their relationship with music, often evoking a scene from their history that linked people with a location, occasion, objects and type of music. Mercédès, for example, remembers living in Rome as a young girl and being given a small record player by her parents:

> **Mercédès:** I have this memory of lying on my tummy, listening to this record that told Mozart's life, with bits of his music. There was something very private, very warm, precious, mysterious about his music. And somehow my whole being resonated with Mozart's music. It was a very intimate relationship, and I think that's where my experience of music as a highly intimate relationship comes from. It was more than listening, it was a thrill, a being altered by this thing… and an experience of myself in a different way… it was the joy of finding what it was that made my spirit vibrate, something like that, yes.

Christina speaks of her relationship to music as 'religious', explained, she says, by how in her childhood music was part of the ongoing tug of family culture between a Catholic mother and a Protestant father. However, when I ask Matthew about his relationship to music, he laughs and says, 'In a word, obsessional!' For him, it's always been about making music himself, mastering it technically, and cultivating a close relationship with the instrument that allows him to do this (Matthew talks of having to take his oboe on holiday as a child, as he couldn't bear to be parted from it). For Matthew and others, musical relationships have served as guides and orientations to future life: 'Every time I come back to the question of what I should do with my life,' says Matthew, 'the answer is the same… make music!' For Simon, on the other hand, music helps to clarify the narrative of his past. He says at the end of his interview: 'I think what I've described in relation to music are the milestones of my life. I'm quite surprised it's so clear cut!'

Other locals told me that their relationship with music was a multiple one that developed and changed over time. This potential complexity of the 'music-as-person' metaphor again highlights its similarity with its real-life model. Music as an evolving relationship through time can act not only as a companion and guide, but also as a mirror and witness to a life and its course, helping reflection on 'who and where we are', and where to go next.

The 'music-as-person' metaphor is complex. We can have the ambiguous experience of not just being in a relationship to music, but also sometimes being 'in' it, or alternatively 'it' being in us. Adam tells me that this gives him the reassuring sense 'that I'm me, but I'm also more-than-me… because I'm connected to life, and to other people'.

Our relationships to music therefore have similarities to, but also some key differences from, the everyday relationships we have with other people. A convergence between the stories of the 'voyagers' and the 'locals' comes when, often quite soon into their characterisation of their relationship to music, they start to talk about how music helps – either themselves or others. Music's power and its help often go together:

> **Christina:** I still think music's so powerful. I'll tell you another story. When I was in Russia, I made it my business to see how people survived terrible situations. Some people had lived in very compromising positions – they bore the scars. I asked one friend, who I considered a consummate escape artist, 'How have you done it? How have you survived?' He had two answers: to feel that you were loved by somebody, and music. He'd always used music to help him – to transform his mood, or to feel nourished, or energised. For me too at that time... things were a bit grey, I was a bit lonely, I realised simply how music could give you communion with others here and now, communion with the past, and less fear of the future.

Music Lovers and 'Music Needers'

That we often call people 'music lovers' is no surprise given that the vocabulary people use to talk about their relationship to music is often one of attraction and passion, attachment and obsession, choosing and testing, pleasure, surrender, support, ambivalence, and so on. The sociologist Antoine Hennion (2001, 2003) makes the observation that this discourse of attachment is shared by those describing their religious, aesthetic, sexual or addiction experiences. People devoted to each of these often seek transformation or transcendence through a close attachment to a charged or potent thing (animate or inanimate) towards which they combine passion and connoisseurship with need and potential help. Hennion also points out that other more moderate types of 'lovers' share the same connoisseur behaviours – 'wine lovers', for example.

Musical amateurs tend to be especially passionate – an *amateur* being, of course, literally someone who 'does it for love'. Professional musicians may also love music, but it's amateurs who usually talk about it most ardently. What Hennion's observational and interview research with many music lovers usefully adds to this general characterisation of passionate attachment is that it's the *acts of love* towards music that are key to understanding the process of music loving. It's not that some 'musical object' arrives and transports the listener or player, but rather that there's an active and gradual cultivation of music, which offers itself as a fluid and flexible partner within specific social situations. The relationship evolves through repeated meetings, with help from varied media and resources (recordings, rehearsals, concerts, conversations, study, and so on). The lover therefore cultivates her receptivity to music – which sometimes transports her only because she's prepared and waiting. A similar pattern can be found with wine connoisseurs and with those attached to more harmful substances and their rituals.

The amateur's rewards are pleasure, engagement, interest and absorption, and the challenges that come from serious connoisseurship. Hennion's (2001) and Tia DeNora's (2000, 2003) studies of people interacting with music in their everyday lives show how taste, aesthetic pleasure, and other personal and social benefits are usually intertwined. We saw this pattern earlier in how David, Mercédès, Susanna, Adam and Diane described a variety of pleasurable and helpful outcomes from their relationship with music. Perhaps Matthew and Simon edge towards something slightly different, in that they express more of a *need* to keep in contact with music. The stories of Christina and Louis show a different level of reliance on music, because of how it helps with key existential needs at a particular point in their lives.

I suggest we imagine these different shades of relationship with music not as discrete types, but rather as a gradual continuum stretching between 'music lovers' and 'music needers'. Whilst music lovers primarily extract pleasure from music, music needers seek a relationship with music in order to meet more basic human needs. But the two basic designations apply not primarily to persons, but to situations: 'lovers' can become 'needers' when times get tough; 'needers' can revert to 'lovers' as situations improve.

౬⌒

The stories people tell me as a music therapist tend to highlight the qualities of ambiguity and intensity that often accompany that passionate attachment to music of those who find themselves both 'music lovers' and 'music needers'. The continuum between these types was illustrated in a study I did with psychiatrist John Meehan, in which we explored the accounts of people receiving music therapy in an adult psychiatric unit (Ansdell and Meehan 2010). We were interested in the benefits for patients who continued for more than ten sessions. Interviews with nineteen people showed how their experiences of music therapy often linked with their longstanding relationship to music, at whatever level this was or had been.[3] When these people talked about music therapy, they often told a story that interleaved an account of their general relationship with music with aspects of both their illness and their health, as if these three strands naturally belonged together. One patient said, for example:

> *Music's always been a very important thing to me. But during this period of depression I found that I couldn't listen to any music for a long period of time – for, like, over a year. And it's been nice to feel that I can again here [in music therapy]. Because music's very emotion provoking, and here you can really experience that, but in a safe environment. But because I always did enjoy*

---

[3]   These close relationships to music mostly did not involve people being in any sense what Western culture calls 'musicians' (that is, people trained to produce music), but 'music lovers' in the sense used earlier.

*music, it can make me feel better again... it can put me back in touch here with
how it could make me feel better... and when I was at school I was very musical...
but you lose touch with all that when you're ill.*

We called such accounts 'music–health–illness narratives'. These mostly fell into
a three-part structure of: (i) an identified pre-illness relationship to music, and its
usually positive role in their life, leading to (ii) how illness has disrupted their
relationship with music and their use of it as a helping resource, ending with (iii)
how music therapy has started to re-establish their relationship to music, such that
it can be helpful again.

Both the form and the content of these narratives confirmed for us that music
therapy with these patients was often experienced as 'continuous' with their
previous and ongoing relationship with music in their everyday life.

ଏଠ

Jessica was one of several people over the years who have quoted to me the line
from the song 'American Pie', 'The day the music died'. She went on to explain:

*Music used to be absolutely central to me – I couldn't live without it. I had music
on everywhere, I'd sing in the bath, I'd sing everywhere. And then at a certain
point in my life, a very bad point... it simply stopped, there was no music at all.
And at this moment something in my spirit died too. It was like going into a
tomb.*

For Jessica, this loss of music came just before she became mentally ill again,
following some terrible happenings in her life. Illness came, and music left. It took
many years for it to come back again, but when it did her spirit came back again
too, she said.

Hannah had the opposite experience. This time, it was she who'd left and
music that had stayed. Her depression got so bad, she said, that one day she simply
walked out of her house:

*I started sleeping on the streets, curled up, and I stayed on the streets for ten
years! I can't reason with it, I was just unwell and I simply hardly noticed – there
was an almost complete absence of feeling, I was numb as if I was dead. But
when I heard music, from anywhere, coming from someone's radio... I'd just
stop and listen. If you're on the streets you can't just turn on your own music,
you have to wait for it. Music reminded me that I was alive. Most of the time I
didn't feel alive, I didn't respond to people. But music reminded me that I could
respond – I think that music is one of the best ways that you can reach people.
It can set you on the road to being healed.*

Both of these women experienced a different kind of rift in their relationship with
music, caused by circumstance and illness. Music therapists often meet people

whose relationship with music has become damaged, disrupted or troubled in some way. Whilst music remains central to their lives, it is often a relationship that includes struggle, ambivalence, resistance or sadness. A milder ambivalence tends to be found in relation to the associations people have with music or musicking within their life. Sometimes making music has been part of a competitive world of parents' expectations, or unsatisfactory professional work, or it is associated with painful memories of unhappy childhoods, failed relationships or bereavement.

People's 'music–health–illness narratives' chart the complexity of their relationship with music. A music therapist needs to understand this. But part of this understanding is just how often people's core relationship to music often remains sound and whole, even if everything else around this seems disrupted or damaged. This basic attachment to music is often a key resource for people to locate what is still healthy in themselves and others.

This was one of the key discoveries of music therapy pioneers Paul Nordoff and Clive Robbins (1971, 1977), who in the late 1950s observed how the very isolated autistic and disabled children they worked with often seemed first to make a relationship with the music that was newly in their lives, and only then (typically some time later) begin to build a personal relationship with the therapists. These children did not, of course, have the kind of cultivated relationship with music that many of the 'voyagers' and 'locals' have. But perhaps what they did have was a more basic and 'natural' relationship to music, one that could equally serve as a platform for music's helping them, albeit with the aid of the therapist. They were, that is, instinctive 'music needers', who, in many examples that Nordoff and Robbins report, subsequently became young 'music lovers', finding not only help but real pleasure and joy in making music with other people.

Music and Healing

I recognise him from the music therapy group on the ward the previous week. He'd been there for the first time and was mostly quiet and withdrawn. But I remember catching his eye at a point in the session, and wondering whether the situation was too much for him. I meant to speak to him afterwards but had been distracted by someone else, and he'd vanished.

A few days later, I'm in the music therapy room, a floor down from the wards. A patient hasn't turned up, so I'm playing for myself from a book of Mozart opera arias. The door to the room is open, and I hardly notice when he quietly slips in and sits down. Something about him makes me simply carry on playing. He seems to be listening intently, living through the music. Again I notice that the music seems almost too much for him to bear, so I don't play for too long before lapsing into silence.

'Mozart... beautiful... play some more please.... Can you play Schubert?'

I play *An Die Musik* – Schubert's ode to music's help – and tears roll down his cheeks. 'Such strong music,' he says. He asks me to play Beethoven next, and

I manage the opening section of the 'Moonlight Sonata' by memory, but then falter and bring the music to a somewhat premature close.

'Do you know the story of that piece?' he asks. 'Some woman had lost her child and was trapped in mourning. Beethoven was called to play for her. He improvised music that became that piece you played, and finally she cried... all the sadness came out... and she was made better... I could listen to that music all day.'

Then he got up and left, as silently as he'd arrived.

That's a nice story about Beethoven, I think to myself; *strange I've not heard it before*. It's a shameful fact that working in a psychiatric context has meant that I sometimes question the factual truth of patients' statements almost by habit.

Only days after this incident, I'm browsing in the music section of the bookshop in London's Festival Hall. My eye catches on a new book, Maynard Solomon's *Late Beethoven: Music, Thought, Imagination* (2003), in particular the final chapter, 'The Healing Power of Music', where I find the exact story the man had told me:

> After the death of her three-year-old son in 1804 Dorothea von Ertmann[4] found herself unable to weep – and she was additionally troubled by Beethoven's failure to offer his condolences in person. Some years afterwards she told her niece, 'I could not understand at all why he did not visit me after the death of my beloved only child.' Apparently he had some reluctance to come to her house, and finally – reportedly at her husband's urging – he invited her to his own home. According to Felix Mendelssohn's account, when Beethoven sat down at the keyboard, his only words to his bereaved friend were 'We will now talk to each other in tones.' He played for more than an hour until, as she said, 'he told me everything, and in the end even brought me comfort.' (Solomon 2003, p. 230)

ꝏ

This chance echo between Vienna in 1804 and a contemporary psychiatric unit reminds us that 'modern' music therapy is neither a new practice nor a new idea. Forms of musical healing can be found throughout history, and are still alive in both professional and traditional practices across the world. Cultural beliefs and practices modify how the music and healing theme sounds in any given time or place, but look closely at most music making and some aspect of health, illness or wellbeing almost always shows up.

Across History...

Over the centuries in the West, one of the most common answers to the question, 'Does music heal?', has been, 'The Greeks thought so.' In *Music as Medicine: The History of Music Therapy since Antiquity* (2000), the historian Peregrine Horden suggests that this historical legitimation is rather like the trick a small army plays,

---

[4]   Dorothea von Ertmann had been a former pupil of Beethoven, and was a leading exponent of his keyboard music, the dedicatee of his piano sonata in A, op. 101 of 1816.

sending a few soldiers round and round in front of the enemy to give the illusion of a large force. Just a few classical theories and anecdotes that link music to healing effects are endlessly recycled, and can still be found in current music therapy texts – for example, the stories of King David or Orpheus.

Perhaps more consequential is a foundational dichotomy between a metaphysical theory of musical healing, and a more physical and ecological one.[5] These two foundational theories derive in turn from who we might consider (continuing the military metaphor) as the two great generals of classical thought – Plato and Aristotle. Their contrasting views provide the pre-history of most approaches to music therapy today. For Plato (through Pythagoras), musical healing is spiritual and direct, based on a belief in the basic correspondence between the 'music of the spheres' (*musica mundana*) and the *musica humana* of our earthly soul. Musical healing involves the re-harmonising of the human soul in relation to the cosmic order. The 'translation' of this more perfect order comes into the body via the varying characters of the musical modes (their ethos) and the body's characters (its humours). Though it's a powerful idea, historians can find almost nothing about how this may have translated into practice. In contrast, Aristotle was sceptical about Plato's musical metaphysics. His more earthbound view was that music enhances wellbeing by helping to provide what we'd now call a 'therapeutic environment' – though for the Greeks it may have been more of a case of providing 'wine, women and song'. This perspective led to an ongoing tradition of exploring how music helps in illness prevention and rehabilitation, rather than claiming that music directly causes the cure.

Studies of 'musical healing' in subsequent periods through 2500 years show how these two basic theories alternate and compete in various ways: that is, either the claim that music *directly* heals (by whatever means), or that it more *indirectly* creates psychosocial conditions that address and support basic human needs, and through this promote healing. A key point that emerges from the scholarly studies is that 'music therapy' in pre-modern times was often more a scholar's idea than an applied practice – especially in relation to most mainstream medical traditions. Music therapy was, it seems, always on the fringe, even in historical times. There are a few interesting exceptions to this. A form of music therapy seems to have been institutionalised within what we would now call psychiatric hospitals in the Caliphate in mediaeval times. Here, music was played to patients in the service of restoring their wellbeing, part of the creation of a therapeutic environment that also included gardens with fountains. Overall, however, historians clearly strain to find concrete examples of 'music therapy' actually being practised, rather than its theory being repeated. It could have been, of course, that those who practised did not write about it (an issue with music therapy even today).

---

[5]   All of the material in this section can be explored in more depth through the various scholarly chapters in Horden 2000.

Across Culture…

Tareq looks thoughtful at the end of his music therapy session. Then he says,

> *Doing this… it reminds me of when I was a child in the south of Iran… my mother took me to these groups… there were people shaking with some kind of sickness – which people said came from the evil spirits. And there was this music… I can hear it now… this bagpipe instrument and drums… and some kind of dance. There were people going into the rapture, getting the evil spirits out of you… and getting relief. I saw people doing this, dancing and moving the body, and some sort of relief is coming… I remember as a child I was excited to see this dance, to hear this music…. But I was also afraid!*

I think how closely this resembles how Tareq spontaneously described his music therapy process to me just a few weeks ago – that despite his problems, despite his inability to talk about them yet, relief had come for him through drumming, and through finally managing to make genuine contact with another person through making the raw and energetic music we improvised together. The tradition of the shamans?

అ

The Guardian reports on a revival of traditional Arabic music therapy in an intensive care unit of a modern hospital in Istanbul. A picture shows the anaesthetist playing a *yaylı tambur* (a stringed instrument) and the professor of surgery the *ney* to a patient wearing an oxygen mask who has just undergone heart surgery. These modern medical practitioners relate their work directly to the ancient practices of music therapy in mediaeval hospitals of the Arab world, describing how 'there is a different *makam* [musical mode] for every illness'. But they report as well that 'we also play for our colleagues who are on a break. That way everybody is cared for'.

అ

Another scholarly collection of essays – Penelope Gouk's (2000) *Musical Healing in Cultural Contexts* – shows how the music-healing theme is equally constant across most cultures. Comparative anthropological studies have found strong similarities between traditional music-healing traditions from Siberia, North America, Indonesia, Australia, Central Asia and South America. Generally these fit well with a broad 'shamanistic' model – where a natural link is forged between music, magic and medicine. As Ted Gioia argues in *Healing Songs*, 'the shaman is the quintessential music healer', integrating music healing within a wider ritual context of dramatic communal transformations of body and soul (2006, p. 56).[6] The key point that Gouk and other writers on cross-cultural practices emphasise is how music's 'healing power' only becomes potent as part of a broader ecology of people, places and cultural practices. The catalytic effect of musical materials and activities is nested within a local and cultural understanding of the body, soul and spirit, sickness and health, individuality and community, the role of the healer and the role of the to-be-healed.

Accounts of how 'modern' music therapy has developed in the last fifty years have tended to bypass this almost universal cross-cultural music-healing tradition. Partly this is because most non-Western indigenous traditions are aural ones, lacking the key formal texts of the 'classical tradition'. It is also perhaps because of how non-Western traditions have been associated with corrupted selective borrowings by 'New Age' systems, and are therefore considered risky as models of music therapy for scientific healthcare contexts. But there's no doubt that indigenous traditions of music healing have increasingly caught the popular imagination, and have helped to focus awareness of how music links to health and wellbeing in ways we Moderns have mostly forgotten, but which other cultures show so readily. These traditions also often exemplify a seamless ecological blend of individual and communal practices, and of the use of lay and semi-professional 'music therapists'. Or, to put it another way, they highlight how separating out music and healing from the everyday communal maintenance of collective wellbeing makes little sense.

Music and Illness

The development of 'modern music therapy' in the West[7] during the last century is a modest episode in comparison, though it reveals how historical and cultural forces keep shaping both practice and theory (Tyler 2000, 2002; Edwards 2008). The rise of capitalism, professionalism, and state-directed institutions of health and social care gave music new sites for practice and new roles for musicians. A condition of the medical establishment's sponsorship and protection, however, was that musical practices aligned themselves with the medical model and its current treatment theories.

We could take a colourful experiment in a London hospital in the 1890s as symbolic of the birth of modern music therapy, and as a hint to its future fate. A priest called Frederick Harford founded the Guild of St Cecilia, a band of 'musician healers' who hid themselves behind screens to perform specially composed music to patients on hospital wards. They later experimented with how the newly invented telephone might transmit the music to other hospitals. The satirical magazine *Punch*

---

[6]   For accounts of the 'shamanic tradition', see chapters 3, 4, 5 of Gioia's *Healing Songs* (2006).

[7]   In the late-modern era, 'Western' models and practices of music therapy have also globalised to most continents during the last thirty years.

ridiculed this work, and the *British Medical Journal* suggested that Harford's guild had 'worked somewhat fitfully and aimed too high'. This project, and the professional reaction it received, previews some key aspects of music and healing as it developed within twentieth-century contexts: working alongside the medical profession, experimenting with how music and medicine relate in contemporary professional and social contexts, organising training and research, seeking legitimation, and battling to define the line between fringe and mainstream practice.

The literature concerning the relationship between music and healthcare settings in the period 1890–1940 (Edwards 2008) charts an ongoing pattern of well-intentioned projects where musicians worked in hospitals, innovated practices, and tried to account for their successes within the dominant treatment models of their institutions. Jane Edwards sums up the overall verdict on this period as being that music therapy (in whatever guise) was often considered 'neither sufficiently musical nor sufficiently medical'. Other musicians often criticised the standards of music making, while doctors criticised the lack of theory or research. The professional labels they tried – *medical musician, musical aide, hospital musician, music worker, musical therapy, musico-therapy* – show the ongoing problem of finding the right conceptual niche and professional validation, even when their work itself was understood and appreciated by patients and staff.

The mostly medical sites in which these musicians worked through the twentieth century shaped this era as one of 'clinical music therapy'. Psychiatric asylums, 'special hospitals' and clinics provided the key venues for music's being played to patients and categorised as recreation. A key stimulus for the further professional and academic development of music therapy came in the United States during the Second World War, when new hospitals were built to cater for thousands of physically and emotionally wounded veterans, staffed by people keen to experiment with new approaches to rehabilitation. Musicians responded to this call, using music to work with the veterans and their psycho-social needs, rather than just entertaining them. This in turn stimulated training, research, and professional organisation. The era of professionalism and institutionalisation of music therapy began, followed by similar moves in the UK and Europe from the 1950s onwards.

Between 1960 and 2000, music therapy began to stabilise internationally as a practice, discipline and profession (Barrington 2008; Darnley-Smith and Patey 2003). Music therapists were now skilled musicians who trained professionally in music therapy (often at postgraduate level) and became health professionals working in medical, social care and special education settings. Music therapists were free to experiment and develop their techniques in response to their clients' particular needs and the working traditions of the treatment contexts. For example, music therapists in the UK working with children with profound disabilities developed a flexible improvisational approach that used music to foster communication and develop active musical participation. In psychiatric hospitals, music therapists responded to patients' social and cultural deprivation by organising music listening groups and communal musical events.

Music therapists in many countries enjoyed a halcyon period between 1970 and 2000, when they found paid work, professional recognition and public interest. They embarked on training and research and secured a near-professional monopoly in state services[8] – one, I might add, that they well deserved, given that few other musicians during this period were willing to work in the back wards of psychiatric hospitals, or with children with severe disabilities.

Music therapy theory during this time was largely shaped by the medical model, with its humane yet individualistic and pathology-based concept of working primarily with symptoms. Music and healing increasingly had to accommodate itself into the subtly different but symbolically important frame of 'music and illness'. To work 'therapeutically' therefore came to mean that the music therapist concentrated on an individual and his/her problems, and helped foster positive changes in relation to symptoms or behaviour. Sessions were therefore mostly individual, private, and little concerned with culture and context. This was true whether the underlying theory aligned with a psychotherapeutic approach (in Europe from 1970s on) or a more behaviourist model (in the United States).

At the end of this impressive period of professional development, we see that the pre-modern notion of 'music healing' has been replaced by the more modest concept of 'music therapy', as an adjunct to medical or psychological treatment. 'Musical cure' or 'transformation' within a cultural context has been replaced by the 'musical exploration' of problems as defined by a psychological or medical theory. Increasingly, it seemed that the communally recognised and tangible benefits of music were being replaced by the professionally defined mysteries of therapy. In this process, music itself often lost its allure and potency through its conversion to the non-musical theories and working practices of generically defined 'therapy'.

Of course, during this period some individual therapists struggled to fit transformative experiences with patients into this rational, individualistic and pathology-based thinking. Paul Nordoff and Clive Robbins developed the Nordoff–Robbins approach partly as a reaction to what they saw as the dominance of non-musical theories in the early phase of modern music therapy. Instead, they encouraged music therapists to keep their music therapy practice and thinking *musical*, and to consider themselves as musicians first and foremost, as working in a broad and creative way to bring music's help to people and their communities. Such 'music-centred' work showed how well music can locate and develop what is still healthy in a person or a situation, despite illness or deprivation.

Not all musicians who worked with people in this era thought of themselves as music therapists. 'Community music' was also developing along a looser professional pathway, working more within social or mainstream educational settings, leaving

---

[8]   In 1996 in the UK, music therapy became accepted as a state-registered profession, with the professional title 'music therapist' legally protected (as with doctor and lawyer) in exchange for increasingly regulated training and professional organisation. Other countries are in varying stages concerning this process.

the healthcare arena to music therapists.[9] Community music has mostly resisted being institutionalised or professionalised, choosing to keep its independence in order to pursue a more radical political agenda of cultural democracy (originating in the European 'community arts movement' of the 1960s to the 1970s). Community musicians typically did project work with underprivileged or at-need communities, organising workshops and performance events that encouraged maximum musical participation, often focusing on communicating a current social or political agenda. A yet further strand of musical–social work has been that of 'outreach' workers from mainstream cultural establishments, such as orchestras and opera houses, who have engaged with areas of the community for both social and fundraising agendas.

Overall, this professionalised era has certainly succeeded in reaching many more people in real need of music's help. Public interest and approval of music therapy has progressively increased, and external critique has been rarer. It's interesting, therefore, to note music historian Ted Gioia's recent withering evaluation of this modern phase of music therapy, when he writes 'how cautious and stodgy the profession of musical healer has become' (2006, p. 135). For him, music therapists have sold their soul in the process of becoming healthcare professionals. Music therapy has translated the grandeur and uniqueness of traditional 'music healing' into either a quasi-medical treatment or an academic metaphor. For Gioia, modern music therapy is neither musical nor ecological enough. Music itself has become relegated to a side show of the therapeutic process, and is failing to reach out to the broader community and its needs. But this critique is frankly rather late – for by the mid-2000s, the exclusive reign of the professional music therapist was in any case largely over, and the formulation of 'music and illness' was transforming instead to a broader and more ambitious interdiscipkinary vision of 'music and wellness'.

Music and Wellness

In keeping with its historical pattern, the music-and-healing field seems again to be reconfiguring – this time in relation to shifts in practice, thinking and policy characteristic of late modernity in the West. Structural changes in health, social care and special education systems in many societies since 2000 have led to services moving from institutional and medical settings to community-based provisions that often draw on a broader range of social and cultural resources. Related to this shift, the former dominance of the medical model is increasingly being challenged by psycho-sociocultural models of health and wellbeing that take seriously service users' views on what best helps them. The increasing de-institutionalisation of health and social care has led to traditional expertise needing to accommodate both commercial models and lay forms of self-help.

---

[9] Until fairly recently, this work was under-studied and documented formally or academically, based more on an informal and aural method of transmission. Higgins 2012 is probably the first comprehensive scholarly account.

Music therapists and others working musically with people are adapting their work and thinking in the light of these new factors. The Community Music Therapy movement (Stige and Aarø 2012; Ansdell and Stige, in press) has successfully advocated a broader social practice supported by a psycho-sociocultural theory on music and wellbeing.[10] But, interestingly, the late modern period has also seen music therapy travel on a professional trajectory in just the opposite direction within services still sponsored within traditional medical systems. In response to the increasing challenge by the evidence-based movement, a sub-discipline called 'Music Medicine' aims to develop focused musical interventions for specific medical problems that can be objectively evaluated for their effects and success (Dileo and Bradt 2005). A final strand of this postmodern landscape features a bewildering variety of non-professional 'alternative music therapies' that promise healing and therapeutic effects through music. These range from the quasi-scientific Tomatis method, or the 'Mozart effect', to transplanted world music healing traditions in New Age packaging. While professionals have tended to distance themselves from this area, the free market has happily stepped in with 'proprietary practices' of music healing' (Stige 2010, p. 303).

Is this plurality a welcome diversity or a risky cacophony? If there's a lesson from exploring the historical and cross-cultural perspective on the music-and-healing theme, it's that this current situation may be no different from that of previous eras in some ways. Music therapy as a historically located and culturally constructed phenomenon has always aligned with shifting needs, local situations, politics and ideology.

The latest incarnation of the music-and-healing theme is an emerging international field of 'music, health and wellbeing'.[11] This is attempting to create a more comprehensive and inclusive identity by pooling the traditions of music therapy, community music, music education and other socio-musical practices. Theoretically, it is an interdisciplinary blend of the varying themes of music studies, music therapy, music psychology, ethnomusicology, music sociology, public health, neuroscience, and music education. A hopeful sign is that overall this new field is advocating a more ecological conception of health and wellbeing in relation to musical involvement – giving equal attention to individuals, groups and communities, and to the social, cultural and musical specifics of their local situations. Music's help is being seen not just as treatment or therapy, but also as a natural part of health prevention and promotion, conflict resolution, and social development work.

Another key aspect of this new configuration is the increasingly fluid interface between professional, amateur and lay expertise. The popular media today highlight how much the link between music and health is becoming accepted. Interest in choirs and live music is growing rapidly, but with the added message that they

---

[10]   See Part V for more on Community Music Therapy.

[11]   The title of this hybrid movement is far from settled at present (especially internationally). For some evolving formulations and discussions of this area, see MacDonald, Mitchell and Kreutz 2012; Bonde 2011.

are good for us, not just enjoyable. Musical self-help, amateur music making and professionally mediated musical–social work are all recommended. Brynjulf Stige (2002) has suggested the inclusive term 'health musicking' to encapsulate this broad notion of participating in music in the service of any health agenda. Today, it seems we are all becoming experts in how music helps.

The perennial music-and-healing theme is sounding again in a new way. This gives us the chance to think how a broad spectrum of 'music's help' can meet the current complex needs of people and places. This will involve acknowledging people's own capacity to mobilise their own 'music therapy' within social and cultural contexts. But at the same time we need to understand how and why access to music's help can be prevented and limited by circumstances such as illness, disability, deprivation and injustice. This is where the range of professional and semi-professional facilitation of music's help comes in, in addition to a necessary attention to wider issues of access, ethics and justice.

The music, health and wellbeing movement is perhaps currently at the beginning of a timely rethinking of these practical, theoretical and political dimensions of music's help. The territory is new in some ways, but grounded in a perennial and ancient homeland.

Music's Help: In Music Therapy and Everyday Life

A man I don't recognise stands at the door of the music therapy room holding a battered trumpet. I ask him whether he wants to come in and play something. He ignores my invitation, but says,

> *The doctors tell me I'm sick because of my illness, but I tell them, it's because I'm not in tune. Music gets me back in tune. Against music... all of science... all of technology... it's nothing! Music is in everything... in how my body moves... in how my speech comes out. It's music that gets me back in tune. Everyone needs music therapy today!*

I nod – clearly all he needs from me at this moment. He turns and walks away.

ॐ

Let's take this story allegorically. This man could represent the perennial tradition of music and healing I've sketched in this Introduction. He's a music lover and a music needer. His close relationship with music is key to his identity and to his healthy functioning at physical and spiritual levels. Now he's a wounded Orpheus with his battered trumpet – but somehow his relationship with music includes both his illness and his health. His belief system links his healing with being 'tuned' again – perhaps becoming 'in tune' again with himself, others, and his cultural and social ecology.

However, he stands on the threshold of the music therapy clinic, not sure he wants to take up my offer to have therapy in this setting. 'Everyone needs music therapy today!' he says. But here, now, with me, a professional music therapist? He's ambivalent.

⅋

His ambivalence about music therapy in its current professional uniform has increasingly been mine too. This book is an attempt to look at the question of music's help from a more inclusive perspective. I try to trace the continuities between music's help in our everyday lives, and those situations where 'specialist help' is offered by music (in my case through my work as a music therapist). To put this as a simple question, *How is music's help in music therapy the same as in everyday life?* (But also, *How is it different?*)

The six parts of this book take us through a possible framework for answering these questions. I suggest that whoever we are, wherever we are, and in whatever situation we find ourselves, music has some basic similarities in relation to our core human needs and possibilities. Parts I to VI explore in a mostly cumulative fashion how:

I. We find ourselves necessarily within the immediate physical, social and cultural ecology of musical worlds. We make our place, and take our part within these – using their resources and opportunities to furnish a personal musical lifeworld (or where this is difficult, are helped to do so by others).

II. Within 'music's world' we actively create, give and share musical experiences – through which the specific features and helpful properties of music show up for us through our direct personal engagement with them.

III. Discovering ourselves and others as musical persons helps in recognising, developing and sustaining personhood, and elaborating musical identities and roles through musical experiences, actions and reflections.

IV. Cultivating and developing musical relationship offers helpful ways to connect, communicate, experience companionship, and enter creative dialogues with others.

V. Fostering musical community offers helpful ways for people to belong together, collaborate, show hospitality and celebrate their collective identity.

VI. Forms of musical transcendence can take people out of themselves, and beyond themselves during musicking, and can bring epiphanies that reveal spiritual aspects of people, the world, and the 'world beyond'.

This sequence is disappointingly linear when unfolded like this, whereas in real life all of these dimensions would naturally interpenetrate and support each other in different ways, at different times, in different places, and for different people. An ecological perspective, however, suggests that we think of these 'dimensions' of music's help only ever as part of a particular and dynamic ecology of place and circumstance, where musical people, musical things and musical situations come together in particular and often helpful ways, assembling our musical worlds.

PART I
Musical Worlds

Music is a world. Every one of us has his own experiences in that world. There are endless depths, infinite varieties and facets of musical experience for the listener, the student, the performer, the composer, and for the therapist....

Paul Nordoff and Clive Robbins

Music is a resource – it provides affordances – for world-building.

Tia DeNora

Chapter 1
Musical Ecologies

> What does it mean when this performance takes place at this time, in this place, with these participants?
>
> Christopher Small[1]

Emerging Musical Worlds

Sesha lives in a well-designed community home with five other adults with profound physical and cognitive disabilities. Her father Jeffrey[2] shows me how nicely thought out the physical and visual surroundings are, but how problematic the auditory environment is for someone like Sesha. We listen. Background recorded music (and its volume) is chosen by care staff. Jeffrey says he can see that it's often not to any of the residents' tastes. A further background 'soundscape' consists of food blenders whizzing, a TV left on, a hoover, someone's habitual moaning. Because of the residents' various challenges they become a captive audience to these unwanted sounds, whilst their musical worlds remain deprived.

A day later, I have a quite different experience of Sesha's relationship to music when I visit the family home where Sesha is staying for the weekend. The last section of Beethoven's Ninth Symphony fills a large room with high-quality sound through high-quality speakers. Sesha seems powerfully involved with the music, following the contours of energy and excitement. Her father sits beside her, sometimes taking her hand and allowing Sesha to pump it up and down, not exactly in time with the music, but in close sympathy with the music's energy coursing through her. Together they enjoy the music, and take pleasure in each other's pleasure.

ಬಿ

On a Saturday evening, I go to London's Wigmore Hall with my old friend David for a song recital by the baritone Thomas Hampson. The venue is an exclusive one, the tickets are rare, and I'm only there because David books early. I find the plush antique environment reassuring: it somehow reflects back to me an ideal image of myself as a connoisseur – socially and culturally competent (though,

---

[1]   Small 1998, p. 10.

[2]   Jeffrey Kittay is also an academic who has pursued an interdisciplinary study of sound environments and music in relation to people with special needs. See Kittay 2008. I use Kittay's concept of 'captive audience' from this publication.

tellingly, I identify less with the audience, most of whom are considerably older than me). Such concerts are part of how David and I meet socially, and there's now a satisfying history to our sharing pleasure together this way.

The atmosphere is formal, and people's conduct follows the reassuring rituals of a classical concert. An announcement is made – 'Please, no coughing' – as a recording is being made that night, and people concentrate and mostly inhibit expressive movements, save in the right places. All attention is on the performer, as people savour the musical icons (Schumann and Wolf) that Hampson brings to life, and the qualities of his voice and interpretation. In the interval people, drink wine and along with social gossip talk of the music rather as if it too were a fine wine – a matter of refined taste and judgement. Thomas Hampson sings beautifully, and after long appreciative applause he pledges to come more often 'to this shrine to the art of music'.

ℂ

People are chatting, laughing, joking... cups clatter, chairs and tables scrape, a short buzz of feedback comes from an amplifier as an electric guitar tunes up to notes from a piano....

A guitar fiddles around with fragments of riffs and scales, bending notes Blues-style, then a gentle harmonica emerges from the blend, leading to a few minutes of loose dialogue between harmonica and guitar....

Across these sounds, a sharp voice chimes: *'Did you know it was Sally's birthday yesterday!? Did you? Did you?'* It pierces the atmosphere, then disperses rapidly....

Attention returns to the music as the piano produces a sequence of jazz chords – bits of this and that, tryings-out, soundings... and the guitar recognises the chords and joins in... as does the harmonica, but in the wrong key. *'E flat? No? B flat... got you!'*

Then unexpectedly there's a lull in conversation and people are listening, and the players orientate to their newly focused audience, swiftly choosing a song. The piano offers an introduction and the singer leads with authority....

'I Left My Heart... In San Fran...cis-co...', his voice stylishly curling over the room, commanding attention. There's a slight discrepancy between singer and pianist over the tempo, but soon all the players fall in with the singer, weaving their own melody lines and rhythmic elaborations into the mix. Within a few phrases, the chatting crowd turns into a listening audience – there's a gathering of attention and focus, someone quietly whistles, a few people sing snatches of the melody they know....

We've just sat through the first five minutes of a drop-in music session in a café for people with enduring mental health problems. Extraordinary music happens here each week.

ℂ

I walk into a small park in Shanghai, an oasis of calm in an urban jungle where all types and ages of people are strolling through. Under a fixed shelter at the confluence of a number of paths, a group of about twenty elderly people are singing. I sit on a nearby bench and listen for half an hour.

There's a leader, but also a constant flow of suggestions both from members of the choir and from their ever-changing audience. The singers occasionally look at song-sheets but seem to know most of the repertoire by heart. This has the casual feel of a regular event. They seem relaxed and enjoying themselves, interacting quite casually with people around them. A man asks me whether I'm enjoying it, and I ask him what they are singing. 'They're old-timers,' he explains. 'They like the old revolutionary songs of their youth.'

There's a nice spontaneous sense to their singing, and it has a 'porousness' that somehow catches (and responds to) the flow of the park's life around them. A nurse positions an elderly lady in a wheelchair in front of the singers, and soon she suggests a song and they willingly perform it for her. She taps her hand on the armrest of her wheelchair. Later a baby catches the attention of one of the women singers, and she turns to sing to the baby, who responds noisily. Then all of the other singers also orientate towards the mother and baby, who receives an entire choir's performance for a minute.

¿

Here are four very different stories of people and music in particular situations. Do they have anything in common? Are they all performances? How can we think further about what's happening?

Traditional approaches to thinking about music would typically zoom in or zoom out to understand more about each scenario. For some scholars, the micro-level is key. A musicologist might zoom in to the internal structure of the 'musical objects' yet be less interested in the people involved. A music psychologist might, in contrast, be interested in how Sesha listens to music as a cognitive achievement of her mind and brain. An acoustician might be interested in how loud a cough in the Wigmore Hall needs to be to spoil the evening's recording. A 'critical sociologist', in contrast, might take the opposite strategy of zooming out from the event in order to explain how music and concerts relate to broader social structure, illustrated by how David and I banked further 'cultural capital' to reinforce our already privileged social position by attending the classical concert. And a philosopher might reflect on Thomas Hampson's comment about 'this shrine of music' and what music is as a phenomenon to be worshipped in this way.

In this chapter, I shall suggest an alternative way of thinking about such musical situations, neither just zooming in or zooming out, but taking a third perspective that music sociologist Tia DeNora (2000, p. 4; 2011b) has called a *meso*-level of analysis[3] – one that tries to steer a middle way between micro-musical detail and

---

[3]   '[M]eso-level studies focus on what emerges between actors and conditions of action (and on the processes of this emergence). How, in other words, do scenes, perceptions,

broader non-musical abstractions. 'Meso' means 'middle' or 'intermediate', and it aims to stay looking, listening and thinking *in situ*, in the middle of the musical action. It follows and observes people and music within particular situations and their unique conditions – sometimes zooming in or zooming out, but mostly listening and watching from that crucial middle distance that allows us to see where, when and how musical action emerges and takes shape.

To understand more about the scenarios with which I began this chapter from a meso-perspective, we need to compare how people, music and situations interact by asking: *When? Where? Who? With what? With whom?* We then see how each scenario involves…

- …*a particular place* – inside a home, care setting, concert hall, café, park… all of which have specific atmospheres, functions and typical activities, conventions, and patterns of how people move in, through and out of them…
- …*at a particular time* – either regular times that signal a ritual-like accumulation, or unique one-off events, or domestic times (Sesha and Jeffrey mostly listen after dinner), or the formal duration of a concert…
- …*with particular people* – including their abilities and disabilities, their history and inherited culture, their personal preferences, talents, habits of action and practice, thoughts and memories, ways of presenting and 'performing themselves', their needs, and their gifts for others through and with music.

To these dimensions we can add three more key factors – that the people involved are all:

- …*using particular things* – both musical things (organised sounds, songs from a specific repertoire, instruments, CDs and audio equipment) and non-musical things ('props' that match or support the occasion – such as tea cups or wine glasses, food, chairs and tables, stages, canopies, costumes etc.)…
- …*involved in particular relationships* – long term or just established, real or historical, ideal or actual…
- …*becoming part of the action* – nobody is really 'just listening' – all are doing something in some way.

For all their differences of type and scale, the four scenarios show musical worlds taking shape in relation to exactly where people are, what they are doing at that time, and what resources they have to hand. Reciprocally, people can be seen as shaping themselves and their relationships within these emerging musical worlds,

---

situations, and actors get "composed" in ways that perform both the figure and the ground of action?' DeNora 2011b, p. 312

exploiting the possibilities they offer. Music is always something between and amongst. Making music is making social life.

Musicking: An Ecological Perspective

Thinking about music in this way is to take a broadly ecological perspective. Although this concept is more familiar today in relation to the natural world, it makes a lot of sense to think of human social and cultural life as ecological too. The Greek origin of *ecology* combines *oikos* – the household – with *logos* – word, or in a more philosophical sense the order, principle or 'logic' of something. Thinking ecologically means exploring how people manage to live together more or less successfully within both their natural and their social environment. Recent movements such as 'community psychology', 'health psychology' and branches of sociology have increasingly used an ecological metaphor to explore how people thrive and sicken, adapt and develop in relation to their ever-changing physical, social and cultural environment.

Certain key principles are common to both natural and human ecologies. The most important of these is that everything in an ecology is connected and interdependent. Ecological relationships are often embedded or nested inside each other, a concept represented by the 'Russian dolls' model.[4] Individual people, for example, are part of family structures, which in turn are nested within a local community, and so on – up to 'macro-structural' levels of government. A change at one level of an ecology ripples up or down to influence the others. A second key principle is that ecologies work through a subtle interdependence and exchange between living and non-living things and processes. Whilst each entity normally keeps its own boundary and identity, it is also porous and in continual interaction and transaction with other things around it. Processes of communicating, collaborating, improvising and recycling are key to keeping an ecosystem flexible, resilient and sustainable.

A meso-level of analysis helps us to see these ecological principles in action within musical situations. It means attending closely to how music is part of a complex process of interdependent interactions between people, practices and things within a particular place. We could see a 'musical ecology' in terms of the original Greek sense of household management – as one of the sub-systems that helps to make and keep our broader social world habitable.

એ

---

[4] The model originates with Bronfenbrenner. See Nelson and Prilleltensky 2005, p. 71. For an application to Community Music Therapy see Stige and Aarø 2012.

Christopher Small's (1998) concept of *musicking* (popularised through his book of that name) elegantly portrays such an ecological perspective on music[5] – although, interestingly, he does not specifically name it so.[6]. In a sense, Small's concept was old news. For decades, ethnomusicologists and anthropologists have been reporting how music is woven into everyday social life in traditional cultures. But this perspective had largely not filtered through to the mainstream. Thinking about music in our own culture has been obsessed until very recently with the idea of music as an object to be venerated, or sold as a product, or performed by talented others up on a stage. Each of these moves music away from its more mundane place in everyday life.

Small writes of how he struggled for years to get satisfactory answers for himself to the traditional 'big questions': *What is the meaning of music? What is the function of music in human life?*

> It is easy to understand why those are the wrong questions to ask. There is no such thing as music. Music is not a thing at all but an activity, something that people do. The apparent thing 'music' is a figment, an abstraction of the action, whose reality vanishes as soon as we examine it at all closely. (Small 1998, p. 2)

A certain cognitive reframing has taken place in music scholarship and popular opinion in the last ten years, helped by Small's use of the gerund *musicking* to clinch this idea. His definition of musicking is provocatively wide and liberal:

> To music is to take part, in any capacity, in a musical performance, whether by performing, by listening, by rehearsing or practicing, by providing material for performance (what is called composing), or by dancing. (p. 9)

This implies that

> [t]he fundamental nature and meaning of music lie not in objects, not in musical works at all, but in action, in what people do. It is only by understanding what people do as they take part in a musical act that we can hope to understand its nature and the functions it fulfils in human life. (p. 9)

Musicking for Small is a 'thinking-tool' for exploring the ecology of any musical act or situation, towards which we need to address the key question,

---

[5]   The music educationalist David Elliott 1995 produced a similar 'praxial' concept using the term 'musicing', though with some important nuances that differ from Small. See Ansdell 2004 and Elliott and Silverman 2012 for applications to music and health.

[6]   Small does, however, extensively use Gregory Bateson's 1985 ecological theory as an acknowledged influence on his concept of *musicking*. He gives no clue as to why he doesn't use a more explicit ecological vocabulary.

What does it mean when this performance (of this work) takes place at this time, in this place, with these participants? … or to put it more simply, we can ask of the performance, any performance, anywhere and at any time, *What is really going on here?* (p. 10)

In his book, Small analyses a typical Western classical concert in terms of this last question, and shows that, far from its just being about the 'music itself', 'it is the relationships that it brings into existence in which the meaning of a musical performance lies' (p. 10).

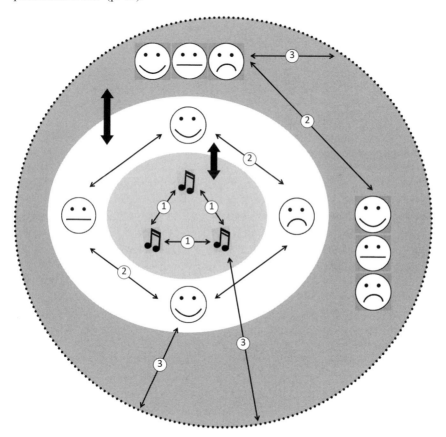

Figure 1.1   The ecology of relationships in musicking

In Figure 1.1[7] I've tried to encapsulate Small's suggestion that any musical event can be understood as a complex ecology consisting of the interaction of three core dimensions:[8]

1. ***Tone Relationships*** between sounded tones[9] within the musick(ing) – both as defined by a musical text (or from musicians' memories) and as experienced by those performing and listening.
2. ***People Relationships*** between (a) individuals (e.g. players and each other; audience and each other), or (b) groups of people (e.g. between players and audience, or different audience groups).
3. ***Situational Relationships*** between (a) sounds/tones, individual people, groups of people, , and (b) the physical setting – its size, acoustic, and the social and cultural meanings it has.

As if this set of relationships is not complex enough, Small tells us that this is just the beginning of the story. These basic relationships between people, things and practices are, as in any ecological system, amplified by further relationships between the relationships (so-called second-order relationships). How, for example, do the relationships between the tones as specified in the score or in musician's memories relate to individual people's musical experiences? How do these tone relationships affect the social relationship between the players and the audience? How do the relationships between the sounds and the building affect the relationships between people within it?

Then there are relationships between relationships between relationships, and so on, until it's simply too complicated to talk about! Small's point, however, is that at some level we nevertheless *hear* and experience this relational and ecological complexity within musicking. And we find this complexity humanly compelling not as an abstract mathematical pleasure, but because we intuitively sense how musicking is a ritual that enacts and symbolises the overarching pattern of ideal relationships that we want and need in our personal and social lives. Small writes:

> Such ideas held in common about how people ought to relate to one another of course define a community, so rituals are used both as an act of affirmation of community ('This is who we are'), as an act of exploration (to try on identities to see who we think we are) and as an act of celebration (to rejoice in the knowledge of an identity not only possessed but also shared with others). (Small 1998, p. 95)

---

[7]   The arrows show relationships, the numbers and letters the different types of relationships (as suggested by the categories 1–3 above).

[8]   The labels for the three categories of relationships are mine, not Small's.

[9]   The precise difference between sounds and tones will be explored in Part II. Think of tones as 'musicalised sounds' for now.

Taking Small's perspective seriously requires us to acknowledge that the smallest sound or musical gesture is potentially related to the overall outcome; to see how everything is connected within a musical ecology, for good or ill. Musicking is therefore necessarily both an aesthetic and an ethical matter.

℘

We can now revisit the scenarios that opened this chapter in the light of Christopher Small's understanding that the meaning of any musical performance lies in the relationships that it brings into existence. The musical world that we see emerge within each vignette comes from the complex interaction and interdependence between *tone relationships*, *people relationships* and *situational relationships*. Each unique musical ecology shows up both needs and potential, both history and happenstance.

The first vignette presents a private domestic scene where an intimate encounter emerges only when the tone relationships of Beethoven are projected into the acoustic in such a way that Sesha can latch on to them. Father and daughter then form a relationship to these particular sounds in this particular place, and at precious moments share their experience and pleasure within an interpersonal relationship.

David and I walk away satisfied from the concert, having again refreshed our friendship through this repeated ritual, obtained aesthetic pleasure, and perhaps reinforced our social and cultural identity. This all comes through a public and conventional occasion of musicking that is refracted through our personal experience and history in a way that seamlessly blends together a complex series of relationships between place, occasion, repertoire, performer and audience members. David calls it a 'shared private experience'.

The afternoon session at the café is part of a semi-public musical world where the sounds of the musicking enhance the social space and connect it with the world outside. For some people there, it provides the only opportunity they have in the week to have social experiences and to demonstrate their musical talent to others. For others, it's something they just chance upon and find pleasurable and sociable.

Lastly, the park in Shanghai is the scene for a completely public event in which a group of people finds companionship and satisfaction through performing a repertoire of songs together. The music helps them to rekindle a collective social and cultural identity through its nostalgic evocation of a previous era, whilst their performance also creates social connection with others in the immediate present within this fluid locality.

Christopher Small would probably suggest that, if we dig a little deeper into these vignettes, we might discover a further crucial dimension of relationships that concerns politics and values. What, for example, can we say of Sesha's 'rights to music' in relation to the exclusivity of the Wigmore Hall concert? How do the non-verbal 'messages' about values and worldviews that are communicated through any of the musical styles and performances affect people's relationships to each other? What message are the elderly Chinese people conveying (intentionally or not) through their performances about their society today? Does the musicking of the people in the mental health centre liberate or further constrain them?

'Musical worlds' are at once individual, social, historical, temporal, aesthetic and political. A musical world is not something that stands 'outside' of us, and that we just 'step into'. Rather, it's a case of how we can draw 'musical things' and musical processes into the interpenetrating personal and social worlds that we constantly build and maintain for ourselves. Music helps when there's a good fit between what music can provide, and what we need in a given situation.

Musical Affordances

Someone is playing Irish fiddle music this Saturday morning. It suddenly catches my attention. Lively sounds seep up through the air shaft and into my apartment through a small window. Is it live or recorded? No matter; I imagine the movements of a young red-haired man playing this music. It taps my foot; my ear follows the windings of its melodic line; and somehow this frees my mind from the rather dogged concentration of writing this book. I breathe easier as my body latches onto its repetitive phrases, and it delivers a nostalgic image of the Irish pub on the corner of my London street (which I never go to), and the Irish countryside I've never visited. It pleases me, shifts my mood, enhances my morning.

Does 'it' do all these things? If not, what am *I* doing too?

ొ

Late Friday evening on the New York subway, an old man sits on a crate, playing folk music on a fiddle. The feet of a hoodie ten metres from him start doing Irish line-dance steps – it looks almost involuntary. Two Puerto Rican guys next to me parody the style with body movements and laugh. They look to me to support their view – which I don't. As I walk along the platform, my legs find a new spring in their step, and then I get the feeling the fiddle player notices this, and imperceptibly changes the timing of his next phrase so that we momentarily come into musical contact over two lines of railway track, just before the next car thunders in....

Does 'it' do all these things? If not, what are *we* doing too?

ొ

Is it possible both to accept Christopher Small's campaign against turning music into an idealised object and to keep a place for definable 'musical things' and their influence? The useful concept of *affordances* from ecological psychology helps us to find a crucial halfway house here. Thinking about *musical affordances* gives a way of specifying and situating what music uniquely offers, and how it does this within situated action. This notion is key in a trend that sees music as an ecological phenomenon, where people recruit and set in motion situated musical things and processes – or are recruited and set in motion by them.

I shall approach this idea of musical affordances by asking three slightly unconventional questions: *How many things is music? Where is music?* and *How do we do (other) things with musical things?*

How Many Things is Music?

What if we changed the conventional question, 'What *is* music?', to, 'How *many things* is music?' After all, if you asked most people to point to something musical, they might choose a CD, a book of sheet music, an iPod, a singer performing live, a guitar, an opera house, or a picture of a composer – or they might just sing a single tone. They would naturally, that is, select musical things from their own musical world. A philosopher might take issue with this, saying that these all miss the 'music itself', most of the choices being ways of mediating or reproducing music. But perhaps the non-philosophers have a point too in how they intuitively understand something about the pragmatic and everyday nature of 'musical things'.

But isn't thinking about 'musical things' just what Christopher Small was trying to wean us away from? The musicologist Lawrence Kramer suggests that the nicely titled 'Thing Theory' makes a helpful clarifying distinction here – between *objects*, which are distanced, fixed and inanimate, and *things*, 'which are open-ended, semi-animate, intimate forms that become what they are as we become what we are. Their consistency is neither completely objective nor subjective, but an unstable and fluid blend of both' (2011, p. 186).[10] Being a thing or an object, that is, depends on our relationship to it, and our use of it. Kramer begins his exploration of 'musical things' with an ecological analogy:

> You treat music like a houseful of things, from a jug to a piece of dolomite to a Styrofoam cup ... You ask whether you feel at home there, and why, and which things draw you closer and which shut you out or defamiliarize your surroundings. You consider which entities must consent to act as objects so that others can act as things.... (p. 188)

A musicologist can name and think about musical objects, but 'objecthood is just a role they can play if required. Around the house ... they are things' (p. 186) where they blend in and take their place within the 'gathering' of a real-life, personal musical situation. So a 'musical thing' can be anything from a musical interval, or the rhythmic hook of an Irish jig, to the phrase of a famous song, or a whole symphony. A musical thing can also be a so-called mediator of the structured sounds – a violin, CD, written musical text, live performance, someone's opinion about the latest band, a musical idea from 200 years ago, or a wordless rhythmic

---

[10]   Zuckerkandl, however, was already writing about musical things in *Man the Musician* 1973: '"Thing" stands here for everything that is not an "I", whether it is material or spiritual, an object or a state of mind, a feeling or an event' p. 41.

movement or gesture. They all take their place within the dynamic ecology of relationships that comprise musicking.

Does this not fit in better with how we often experience and informally think about music if we are not on duty as musicologists or acousticians? Music is most often a fluid gathering of many things together, rather than a single object we isolate, and then concentrate on exclusively. One of the key qualities of musical things, and the creative musical processes they get caught up in, is precisely their constant mutability, ambiguity and fickleness. They change identity according to who they are with, or what they are currently doing. Kramer therefore suggests musical things have an 'ontological openness': 'Their meaning can change their being; they are always susceptible to becoming something else altogether, to being themselves without being the same old thing' (p. 187).

'Music', that is, could perhaps be more usefully thought of as plural – as many things for many people and occasions. We can still have our musical objects and products when we need to name them (Beethoven's Ninth, 'Yesterday', a Blues mode, a CD...), but all of these singularities can also forget themselves and fold back into the complex flux of musical action and situation.

As an example of this way of thinking about music, let's return to one of the scenarios, and to how this particular occasion of musicking for Sesha and Jeffrey is a gathering of many 'musical things', such as:

- still-living traces of Beethoven's musical thinking that became the score of the Ninth Symphony, that allowed the Berlin Philharmonic players to record it in 1978, that allowed a CD to be made in order to be played in upper New York for Sesha and Jeffrey to listen to that afternoon in 2007 through...
- ...a state-of-the-art sound system matched perfectly with the airy, resonant acoustic of their home to give a quality sound experience that conveyed...
- ...the particular tone relationships that Jeffrey appreciates as the Ninth Symphony, that Sesha recognises and remembers as these dynamic-sounding forms that make sense, and that transmit energy and excitement and beauty... especially just this phrase, this musical moment between bars x and y... which allows daughter and father to share musical form, time and energy, which they communicate to each other through gestures and looks.

Likewise, 'musical things' for the other three scenarios above include: performers, songs and their histories, song sheets, musical scores, programmes with Lieder texts, instruments, voices and their qualities, ears listening and bodies swaying to music, tapping toes, stages and canopies, sounds' qualities, stylistic figurations and forms, interpretations, improvisations, clapping, dancing, connoisseurship, interval talk about music and people, shifts of thought and feeling during and after the music stops, reports, reviews, memories, analyses, pleasures...

This list ranges anarchically over the usual fences that are put up to keep 'purely musical things' (tones and their formal relations, and possibly the media for projecting these through voices and instruments) apart from 'non-musical things' (almost anything else!). Such pragmatic gatherings are what Tia DeNora (2011a) calls an *aesthetic ecology*, which she defines as 'a cluster of people and their relations to and with each other, as well as materials and settings, situated vocabularies, symbols, values, patterned ways of doing and – importantly – happenstance' (p. xi). Unexpectedly, that is, we often come across just the kind of musical things we need for this situation, just now.

Where is Music?

How do we tune into, or pick up, these musical things? How do they make sense to us? How do we know what to do with them?

Traditional theories from psychoacoustics and cognitive psychology have portrayed our reception of music as something rather internal and passive. The mind processes sounds like a computer processes information. But some music psychologists have increasingly felt that this perspective is too limited, and have developed an alternative ecological theory of music perception that better matches our active and more external involvement in musical worlds (Clarke 2003, 2005, 2011; Windsor 2012). Eric Clarke (2005) suggests that we think of musical perception more as a specific case of how we actively orientate ourselves in general to our environment. Like a digital radio scanning for the clarity of signals, our aural apparatus tunes in to what can be heard, and latches onto this feature in order to explore it. Any sound to some extent specifies its source and certain key things about it. We instinctively 'bend our ears' towards sound events, asking (non-consciously) the key questions, What's going on here? Where exactly? What do I need to know about it? What can I do *with* it? Our aural perception tunes us into our world, flagging up current dangers and opportunities. We keep listening because we need to keep making sense of our world and joining in with what's happening.

Understanding music is more, then, than just the acoustic functioning of our ears or, if the sound is more complex, the cognitive sound processing of our brains (though it relies on both). The important additional factor from an ecological perspective is that it is *me* listening here and now, a particular person in a particular context, with a particular history and capability, purposes and needs. I find myself part of the 'sonic ecology' that surrounds me. This is physical, but also social, cultural and political.

The tradition of ecological psychology has a long history of exploring the active reciprocality between organisms and their natural environments. In his pioneering work on animals, James Gibson (1979) described what he called the *perception–action cycle*. This proposed that organisms don't just passively 'receive' perceptual information, but rather they 'act towards' it, with the consequence that we can usually see a two-way reciprocal process between the searching out that the organism makes, and the appearing to it of the key features of its environment. That is, organism and environment are always coupled together in a personal, dynamic and interactive way. Perception is designed to lead us towards action; and, reciprocally, action guides us towards what interests, or what is helpful to us in our environment.

Gibson made up a word to encapsulate this theory: *affordance*.[11] The everyday word 'afford' means 'to yield, give, provide, allow', so an 'affordance' suggests the value of things in our environment (their properties, qualities, structure, etc.) in relation to our abilities to perceive, use, interpret or act with them. It's this qualification that Gibson critically adds to the picture of perception and understanding. An affordance is always relational, rather than something either intrinsic (in the object) or subjective (in the organism). An affordance is always part of our action in the real world.

For example: a flight of steep stairs affords rapid spatial ascent and descent to an able-bodied human – but to any horse, 'human steps' are not a good affordance for this need. A blade of grass affords landing to a bee, but not to a person; a chair affords not only sitting on relative to a table, but also standing on to change a light bulb, or to fend off a lion. But then, change the material the chair is constituted of – say, to flexible rubber – and it affords contemplation as an art object, perhaps, but not sitting on. Alternatively, change my perceptual capability (should I lose my sight, for example), and such visual art affords me very little.

To measure the stairs objectively gives little clue to their affordance until you know the mutual relationship between stairs and stair user. So importantly, affordances are relative to who and where you are, what you are like, and what you need or want to accomplish. The wrong kind of thing can frustrate or resist a course of action. So what we pick up in the world is indeed based on our perceptual mechanisms (we are hardwired to attend to size, shape, colour, texture, density, animation, and so on). But the broader human realm brings affordances that are not just physical but also socio-cultural – the assembled relationships between people, things and signs. These assemblages, however, only become truly present and meaningful within particular events and situations, when we become sensitive to engaging with the possibilities they offer us to do or know something. Some affordances we detect and attune to instinctively, as ours for the taking. Some we need to be educated about – by parents and by our cultural heritage – in order to identify them, and use them.

Musical affordances follow this logic. They are 'actionable musical things' within our immediate environment. Music is a special case of general aural perception in some ways. It is possible to attend to sounds as only sounds, consciously limiting their significance only to the tone relationships, whilst ignoring all the information they specify – such as, for example, a performers' voice, where they are, who they are, how they sing tonight, and so on. (This is to attend only to the central area of the schema in Fig. 1.1.) But an ecological perspective

---

[11]   That is, the word 'afford' is real, whilst Gibson made up the noun 'affordance' for his specific technical purpose. In this sense, the original dictionary definition has migrated from 'provide', 'yield' or 'make available' to 'suggest' or 'invite'.

would argue that in real life we seldom listen this way. We are usually aware of a more complex set of ecological relationships in play when we are musicking – both in our heads, and between us and others within a musical occasion.

Eric Clarke writes that 'music affords dancing, worship, co-ordinated working, persuasion, emotional catharsis, foot-tapping, and a myriad of other activities of a perfectly tangible kind' (2005, p. 38). These possibilities flow as action consequences from the direct perceptual pick-up of properties and qualities of music at all levels of a musical ecology. This might involve: types of sound and timbre; the structural features and patterns of tones, rhythms, metres, forms and genre; meanings linked to history and cultural convention; and so on. But each time it is the personal and social *context* that regulates how the affordance tells you, simultaneously, what is 'going on' musically, and what you can *do musically* in relation to what's going on.

For both the vignettes that head this section I asked, 'Does "it" do all these things?', followed by, 'If not, what am *I*/are *we* doing too?' By 'it', I mean, of course, 'the music', conventionally conceived – the idea that somehow 'the power of music' causes things to happen in us. I hope that this discussion of 'music things' and musical affordances helps us to nuance this assumption. 'Music' is not simply a single entity 'out there', but rather a particular gathering of specific but circumstantial musical things. These gatherings can usually be specified in terms of the fairly precise properties, qualities, features and histories that make up music's potential affordances for given people in given situations.

Where is music? It's where the action is. Music taps my foot in the Irish jig, but only because it matches what my foot can physically do on a flat floor, and how it catches its willingness to be tapped because of my need just then for distraction, quickening, and a little human company. For as Gibson (1979) commented, for humans it is other people who are the richest source of affordance, and who provide most of what we really need.

Music only comes to us as we go towards it. We find and join its sounds, tones, chords, rhythms, styles, genres; we find instruments and the people moving their arms and legs to play them, and the acoustics of the places they are/were in; we perhaps also find the emotions, attitudes and ideologies of the composer, improviser or performer; we locate our own memories, reactions, preferences; and, perhaps most importantly, we find our own musical needs and desires here and now through our moving towards and into what these very sounds as music offer us.

How Do We Do (Other) Things with Musical Things?

The music sociologist Tia DeNora also uses the idea of affordance in her influential book *Music in Everyday Life*. '[T]o speak of "what music makes possible"', writes DeNora, 'is to speak of what music "affords" … to suggest that it is a material against which things are shaped up, elaborated through practical and sometimes non-conscious action' (2000, pp. 45–6). DeNora uses the ethnographic strategy of following people around and observing them in musical action, or asking them to give detailed accounts of how they use music in particular contexts, when doing particular things. From these detailed case studies, she developed a more precise way of thinking about how music gets 'into' action, and once there how it 'works'.

For example, one of DeNora's key case studies explores how recorded music features in a women's aerobics class. The instructor selects recorded music strategically for different phases of the session. Different tempos and energy levels are needed, as well as ways in which the women can become more conscious of their body states at crucial points. The opening warm-up phase of the class needs conscious slow stretching; the middle section needs motivation for increased pace and energy, forgetting the body; lastly, the 'come down' section towards the end requires the women to relax and bring back full consciousness to their body. DeNora's analysis shows how the musical affordances of the exercise tape offer something specific for all these practical requirements.

Traditional explanations might have evoked some power in 'the music itself' that 'made' these physical and psychological effects happen for the women. And indeed, there are certain key objective features of the changing music in terms of its character, speed, melodic trajectory, texture, etc. But as we've argued above, these features do not mechanically act on a passive body; rather, the beneficial effect relies on how the women also bring themselves (and whatever they are trying to do at that particular moment) 'towards' the musical affordance, such that a helpful effect emerges *between* music and action, and *between* action and context. The women pick up and use the affordances the music offers in relation to the action in which they are involved.

In order to stress this active aspect, DeNora suggests a second, complementary notion of *musical appropriation*. If an affordance is a 'musical offering' then an appropriation is a 'musical grasping', a person's ability to take what's offered, and to adapt and work with it for some immediate purpose (though, again, not necessarily consciously). Some affordances will only 'stand out' perceptually in relation to what a person can do with them, or does *to* them. It is the individual and their situation that defines what music can offer:

> It is only through this appropriation that music comes to 'afford' things, which is to say that music's affordances, while they might be anticipated, cannot be pre-determined but rather depend on how music's 'users' connect music to other things; how they interact with and in turn act upon music as they have activated it. (DeNora 2003, p. 48)

Whilst musical affordances might be most obvious when linked with physical action such as aerobics or running, exactly the same process can be seen happening in very different areas of human purpose or need. Music also affords shifting emotional states, remembering, concentrating, creating or clarifying identity, enhancing personal relationships, socialising, or finding 'the spiritual'. In each of these areas, you can see people actively working with the particular features or properties that music offers in order to create a personal linkage between musical

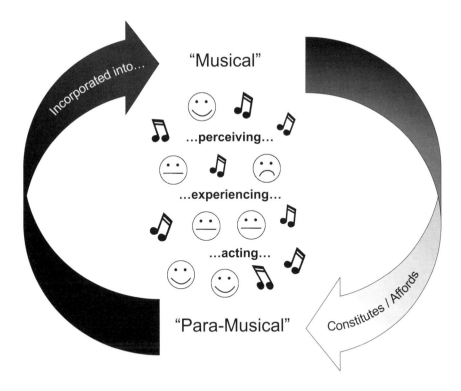

Figure 1.2   DeNora's model: when the 'paramusical' takes shape in relation to the 'musical'

things and 'other things'. We can therefore only know what a musical affordance is by witnessing its action consequences for a particular person or situation.

   An analytical dilemma when thinking about 'music's help' has been to show a convincing link between specifically musical activities and the 'extra-musical' benefits they afford. DeNora approaches this problem by suggesting that

> [m]usic comes to afford things when it is perceived as incorporating into itself and/or its performance some property of the extra-musical, so as to be perceived as 'doing' the thing to which it points. Music is active, in other words, as and when its perception is acted upon, and this circularity is precisely the topic for socio-musical research into music's power. Thus, music is more than a structural 'reflection' of the social. Music is constitutive of the social in so far as it may be seen to enter action and/or conception when things take shape in relation to music. (DeNora 2003, p. 57)

DeNora suggests here how seemingly 'non-musical other things' (such as movements, emotions, communications, identities, events) take shape in relation to seemingly 'purely musical things' (sounding forms and their performances). It will perhaps be useful here to find an alternative to the phrase 'extra-musical', as this gives the wrong impression that things are either 'totally musical' or 'extra-musical' (that is, 'outside' the musical). Instead, we want to understand the more oblique relationship between those phenomena that we perceive as specifically 'musical' and all of those actions and activities that 'go with' these. The term '*para*-musical' has been suggested for this latter 'go-with' class of phenomena (Stige, Ansdell, Elefant and Pavlicevic 2010, pp. 297–9). 'Para' as a prefix suggests 'besides', 'alongside', on the border, or connecting through or between (Cobussen 2008, p. 7). The realm of the para-musical covers the full range of the 'more-than-musical' phenomena – be these physical or mental, individual, relational, social, or political.

DeNora (in the previously quoted passage) suggests a fundamental circular process where: (i) para-musical things are somehow incorporated into musick(ing), and consequently (ii) the musical is subsequently seen to afford and constitute the para-musical, as Fig. 1.2 illustrates.

In this model, music is far from being a physical stimulus leading to predictable outcomes. It 'acts', rather, only 'in concert' with the material, cultural, social and political environments in which it is located – where the musical and para-musical can seldom be separated. This illuminates how we must explore *where* music is performed, perceived, experienced, acted and reflected upon in order to understand *how* it serves as a resource for us through its gathering together of musical things, people and events.

This all highlights a crucial aspect for exploring music's potential help for people. If music, as a key cultural resource, does not 'do' this help by itself, its beneficial appropriation must either be learned or facilitated by others – not 'done for' people, but somehow 'brought closer' in such a way that appropriation is possible. To make such facilitation successfully requires an understanding of the subtleties not only of what music can offer, but also of how it can be taken and used by people. This in turn means that we need to understand how music takes its place, or could take its place, within people's lives as a whole – how, that is, musical worlds interface with the full complexity of the everyday world.

Chapter 2
Musical Lifeworlds

Affordance: what things furnish, for good or ill.

James Gibson[1]

Ivor: *Coming into music has been quite unexpected, especially in my seventies! But it's opened up my world, it's opened lots of doors. It's made me socially a lot more alive, because I meet more people, and if I give them some pleasure through my singing, well it gives me a great uplift to do that. It's been very helpful, you know. Mind you, there's a lot of work attached to it, practising and rehearsing and all that. But I don't mind doing that, you know. So music's made a lot of changes in my life... it's added a lot to my life to be able to sing....*

Our Human Worlds

Each of us inhabits the unique space and perspective of our human world. It changes shape, quality and meaning according to our current experience of it. This in turn depends on factors such as our age, health and ability, the circumstances we're in, the past we've had, the future we expect, the current needs we have, and the resources we can access. But all of this is certainly not to say that 'our world' is only some 'internal world'. As we discussed in the previous chapter, the ecological view is that we're always involved in the external world through a constant interchange with the physical, social, cultural and political ecology. But this is necessarily experienced and lived from our uniquely individual perspective. Our world flows out from the core of our personal experience, and it flows back to this core, defining what and how it is for us to be in the world, here and now.

The pioneer sociologist Edmund Husserl (1935/1970) called this unique human world the *lifeworld*[2] – better expressed, perhaps, in a more active sense, as our *livingworld*. Husserl wanted to emphasise how a human world is not just physical and objective, but a unique first-person space of experience and meaning that has a something-that-it-is-like quality for us at any moment. Our lifeworld is the embodied, continuous yet taken-for-granted background against which we experience the actions and meanings of our lives. Here we are persons, not bodies; other people are our relations; and we draw in 'things' that become affordances from the material world. So this personal lifeworld is far from autonomous or

---

[1] Gibson 1979, p. 127.

[2] From Husserl's original term *Lebenswelt*.

solipsistic. It is totally dependent on our being a contributing part of a larger shared social and cultural world, the 'community of minds', in Raymond Tallis's nice expression (2011, p. 93).

This sociological perspective meshes usefully with the ecological model of the organism–environment reciprocality we explored in the previous chapter. An affordance, you will remember, has both an objective aspect to it (a slope really has a gradient, a sound a frequency), but these properties are real and effective for us only in relation to our personal fit with what they offer at a particular time, place and event. In the same way, our lifeworld is externally real, yet personally tailored and experienced. Its physical and social reality appears to us only as we access, shape and find a path through it to our future. But our ability to navigate our lifeworld in this way is strongly influenced by both our past and the current circumstances of the present. An ecological perspective therefore adds the important questions, 'How habitable is our lifeworld?' and, 'How can we maintain and enrich it, for ourselves and others?'

A 'musical lifeworld' is therefore a musical ecology assembled, experienced and described from a first-person perspective. To understand a musical lifeworld is to see how a person lives in and makes a path through their 'musical world' – being shaped and shaping its forms and opportunities; using its resources, and fashioning them to fit in with their emerging needs and projects, whilst also joining together with others to expand its boundaries.

Like the lifeworld, a musical lifeworld is continuous with the shared physical and sociocultural world, but unique in being shaped by the personal history of our unique attachment to music, our current access to it, and our engagement with it. As such, a musical lifeworld is one way of viewing a very personal life that is nevertheless thoroughly embedded in the wider physical, social and cultural ecology.

How Music Furnishes a World

James Gibson remarked that by 'affordance' he meant how the environment *furnished* a world for an animal, providing what was needed to make life habitable in a particular niche. An ecological perspective on the lifeworld shows how something similar often happens with us all. We creatively adapt to our situation by furnishing a corner for ourselves to feel safe and comfortable in, but also to form a base to branch out from and to entertain others.

ക

Ivor is in his early seventies when he starts going to weekly lessons with an opera singer. He is now in his early eighties and spends at least an hour each day practising and preparing for future performances.

Ivor and I first meet at a music project I'm running in the lively café of a centre for people with mental health problems. The format of this group is a cross between an open-mic session and a music therapy group, and on this particular day energy and concentration is flagging. At just this moment an elderly gentleman walks in, opens his briefcase, takes out the sheet music of 'Some Enchanted Evening', which he puts in front of me at the piano, clears the microphone out of the way, and prepares to perform. I've never seen him before and I'm a little puzzled by the confidence with which he launches into both the place and his performance. However, when Ivor sings with a polished and powerful voice supplemented by a theatrical delivery, everyone in the café falls silent and a few jaws drop as he commands the room and moves to the song's climax. He gets a wonderful reception and has come fortnightly to the group for the last five years, bringing two prepared songs each time.

ട്ര

When I interview Ivor about his musical life and his participation in the group, the coordinates of his musical world begin to emerge. He found out about the café music group by chance through talking to the centre's manager in a pub. Since coming, it seems, however, that the group's been something of a watershed for Ivor's renewed confidence and purpose in life. Whilst Ivor doesn't have a mental health problem, he does say to me once, 'London is a very lonely place sometimes, you know.... It does me good to think that I'm some use to people.' He continues:

> I was at a loose end... I mean, at my age you don't get many opportunities, they're very rare... and it's a sort of urge for me... I was feeling inadequate, or not at my best.... You feel as though you're sort of useless... no use to myself, no use to anybody else, you know. But it's different when you stand up there and perform. You see faces looking up at you, and you hear the applause at the end.... It's being appreciated for what you do....
>
> I remember one woman grabbing hold of me, giving me a kiss. Saying, 'Oh, you do make such a difference to us.' Even a man did that when I sang 'Old Man River'. Which is a rather emotional song, isn't it? The words, you know. Where he sings, he's tired of living, scared of dying. And he says, show me that stream called the River Jordan, the long stream I long to cross. And I was serious faced all through it, because it's a very serious song. But when I got to that, I lifted my face up and smiled a little, with thought of seeing the River Jordan. Bit of acting. And at the end, I can't remember who it was, I've not seen him recently, since, leapt onto the platform and gave me a big hug [laughs]. And I was really touched, actually.

Ivor then makes an interesting link to how he thinks about people at the centre:

> ... because they think nobody cares about them sometimes, don't they? ... you know, 'Everybody's forgotten about us, nobody bothers about us, we're just numbers... you're not a person, you're an un-person.' But if somebody comes along and treats you like a person, and stands up and sings for you, or plays the piano for you, that makes a difference. I'm sure it does. I can sense that

sometimes. Because I've had a lot of put-downs in my life... pushed around, rejected.... Nobody wants you for what you've got to offer, you know. And you feel sort of worthless or inferior. So I understand what they feel like. So if it helps those people, it also helps me, you see?

Ivor thinks of his musical performances as something that he gives to others, but he clearly receives something vital back too. This particular sympathy Ivor has for others finds a place within his musicking, and how he understands what it means for others. He describes himself gradually getting more confident in the situation over the years. People talk to Ivor in the interval, mostly about their love of music and its place in their lives. The way he talks about this, it seems that Ivor is surprised by his effect on people. He tells me that he notices the effect of certain songs on people:

I was singing 'I'll See You Again' by Noel Coward... and she was crying a little when I was singing that song. I suppose she remembered... it reminded her of her husband or something. And I said, 'I hope I didn't upset you', and she said, 'No, it was very nice, don't worry about that, you know.' And, a similar thing happened when I sang 'Night and Day'... one of the ladies came up to me and said, 'Oh, that brought back so many memories, I do love hearing it,' she said, you know. So, well, tears....

Ivor is sensitive to what songs mean for people, what genres might be suitable for this particular group and their range of tastes. He also puts considerable effort into making his performance a quality one, out of respect both for the music and for the people he's singing to. He sources new repertoire, rehearses it with the help of his weekly singing lessons, and tries it out on the group: 'If it's something they really like, I might do it again sometime later on... it's sometimes difficult to guess... not always that easy...'.

There's also a reciprocal influence of this particular musical community on how Ivor's performance changes over the years, moving from a classic 'stand-and-deliver' style to the more participatory and collaborative practice that's characteristic of the afternoon overall. He'll typically sing a song through once, then step forward towards the 'audience' and invite everyone to join in. He also increasingly both permits and enjoys the backing of an *ad hoc* band that can be a bizarre mix of electric guitar, bass guitar, piano, violin and accordion. He even copes when the other musicians 'swing' a song (as against his more classical 'straight beat' style).

ଚଉ

Ivor comes back from New York with something to tell me about a further development in his musical life. He's always liked the piano bars in New York, but he had never considered singing there himself. This time he felt different:

I was feeling rather down at heel that evening, so I went to the bar in the hotel, thought, I'll have a couple of drinks, might make me feel better, and I listened to this bar pianist playing, quite close up, and got into conversation with a guy next to me who turned out to be an airline pilot. Telling me about all his travels and all that. And quite suddenly he said, 'Do you sing?'

I don't know quite what made him ask that, but the piano player leaned across and said, 'Where are you from?' and I said, 'I'm English, I come from London.' And this man said, 'He sings.' You see, well, she said, 'Come round here and sing for us.' So, I went round, and did 'My Heart Stood Still', which is a Rogers classic. I sang it, and they liked it. 'Do something else,' she said. So I did. The place was crammed with people! There was a very smartly got-up woman leaning on the bar, and I sang 'Some Enchanted Evening'. And she sat there looking moved, and she gave me a couple of kisses afterwards. And that's how it's all started in New York....

Ivor goes a few times each year to New York. He's also asked to sing at events back in London through the mental health network he's increasingly known within. So much has happened for him between seventy and eighty: 'It just goes to show, you're never really too old for all sorts of things!' he tells me. Ivor still sings every two weeks at the café group. At eighty-four, he says that it keeps him going.

೮

Ivor shares his physical world with millions of other Londoners, but his lifeworld is unique to him and his situation as a man in his eighties, with his particular personality, talents and challenges; his unique history with its successes and disappointments; and his attachment to music – which has unexpectedly returned to Ivor's life and flowers during his retirement years. But, of course, this doesn't just happen. We also see Ivor's considerable conscious efforts to bring music and its help closer.

Although his newly passionate attachment to music begins relatively late, Ivor draws on the accumulated cultural learning and skills of a long life to help furnish a habitable musical world. As with any effort to 'make a home', Ivor works simultaneously on a number of fronts, assembling and drawing into action an ecology of musical things, people and occasions. Firstly, he assembles a repertoire of musical materials (idioms, songs, performance styles) that help define his niche and that afford musical things to work on. He then invests time and energy into learning, practising, and immersing himself in the technical aspects of music and its vocal performance, training himself physically and using a singing teacher to help him reach the standard he's set for himself. He then finds places to perform in and musical people to perform with. Some events become regular, others are one-offs – but all afford a gradual broadening of his musical world. Through performing, Ivor also builds a variety of social experiences and ongoing social relationships as para-musical benefits. Not only does he see his performing as giving, but he also receives much in terms of self-identity, social acceptance, and self-esteem.

Ivor's story illustrates well the ecological idea of musicking we've been exploring: how he crafts and sustains for himself a personal 'musical lifeworld' that is nevertheless coextensive and interdependent with the social and cultural resources and networks of the surrounding musical world. Performing music forges musical–social pathways and networks for Ivor to other places and groups of people who then offer conviviality, companionship and support. In short, musicking furnishes Ivor's world just perfectly for his current needs.

However, for all his courage and effort, Ivor's success in furnishing his world through music is still dependent on the wider social and cultural infrastructure that supports his activity and recognises his needs. As for all of us, there is an ongoing precarious balance between what the physical, social and cultural world potentially offers, and our ability to successfully access these resources.

Music and Health Ecologies

In the late 1950s, Paul Nordoff and Clive Robbins began their pioneering music therapy work with severely disabled and autistic children whose lifeworlds were narrow and limited. Their creative and improvisational way of working was probably the first attempt within such therapeutic care to fully enter into the children's musical world (however impoverished), rather than just playing some nice music 'over' them from an adult's perspective, as was mostly the practice at that time. Instead, Nordoff experimented in how to creatively improvise music that was unique for each child, there and then – tailoring the character and qualities of what he played to what he perceived both of their character and of their answering responses (however minimal these were). This might mean establishing an initial tempo or tone-world for a child, and then varying a sequence of tones within a mode, or quickening the pace, or adding a harmonic nuance as the situation developed. The children's unexpected sensitivities to tone, rhythm or melody were a revelation to Nordoff. He and Robbins wrote of how these children showed them that 'music is an enormous world to live in and to work in' (in Aigen 1996, p. 12). Music was not just something to play: it could often be 'inhabited' in a profound way when what it offered matched what these socially and emotionally deprived children most needed.

During the following years, Nordoff and Robbins explored how best to help establish musical worlds for such children to live and work in. This meant learning how to prepare and allow 'musical things' in this musical world to afford 'para-musical' things that were most necessary to their life and difficulties: contact, relationship, expression, collaboration, performance. Through listening and attuning carefully to each child, they found how they could coax them into a shared musical world where they felt more at home yet were also increasingly involved with other people and the broader world of their musical culture. What could subsequently happen in this musical world helped to reach beyond or behind the children's problems, and to elicit previously unseen potential.

Nordoff commented that the world that music opened up for these children is 'the only world we can conceive that can meet the variations of pathology as one sees them in any individual' (in Aigen 1996, p. 12). Music's world, he believed, offers a world of different, often compensatory experience. To put it at its simplest, from their therapeutic work with hundreds of children with many severe challenges Nordoff and Robbins found how many important things can be done 'in music' that can simply not be done 'outside music'.

Stepping into music's world in this way gave the children new access to a range of musical affordances that in turn opened up their musical lifeworld for them. Importantly, when these children could really trust to live in their newly opened-up musical worlds, these proved capacious and flexible enough to accommodate the complex and often paradoxical ecology of their illness and health, limitations and potential. Because they felt at home in music, therapeutic change was possible.

ಐ

It is becoming more common to talk of 'health ecologies', which Arthur Frank introduces as follows:

> Health ecology poses the question, participation in what? What is the network of connections that the ill person participates in? How does disease originate in a network of connections, and how must healing involve recognizing the person's place in this network? *Ecology*, as it pertains to health, is another word for the moral necessity of dialogue … of people acting with the awareness that their lives are lived wholly on the boundary with others. (Frank 2004, p. 68)

Like *musicking*, Frank reminds us that *healing* is a verb, not a noun; a shared activity, not a possession. A more ecological understanding of health, illness and wellbeing is currently developing that sees health and wellbeing as performed and relational. It is performed in the sense that it is something that we do not passively 'have', but actively pursue, cultivate, take part in, accomplish (on many different levels – physical, psychological, social); and relational in the sense that health emerges not 'within' but *between* us and things, people and ways of thinking about our world. As Tia DeNora writes,

> Putting performativity and relationality together and understanding both in terms of how affordances are appropriated in action, it is possible to understand 'health' as an identity that is achieved (performed) within an environment or ecological setting. For its accomplishment, performance draws on resources that are to be found distributed within that environment, such as objects, practices, attitudes, and postures. In this sense performance emerges *in relation* to resources within an environment. (2011b, p. 310)

Being 'healthy', 'ill' or 'disabled' is therefore a state or condition that partly depends on the environment in which you find yourself. Or, to put it the other way around, a change in the ecology of this environment can mean a change in either objective health state, or the subjective sense of being healthy. This highlights that, whilst health and illness have key physical dimensions, this is only the beginning of any adequate account of them. We also need to attend to the total ecology of health and illness, and how they come to be constructed, maintained or undermined by social and cultural factors. For example, a person with mobility problems is disabled or not in relation to the resources they can access to keep mobile. If a social environment is built where non-verbal communication is valued then people with learning disabilities are less 'disabled'.

Our understanding of both illness and healing should include our ability to imagine the network of connections of which a person is part, and how these contribute to supporting or undermining the help they need to achieve a level of wellbeing, even if the objective condition of their health does not change. Most of all, as Frank comments, we need to recognise the difficulty 'people who are ill or disabled have staying in networks of participation, and participating on terms that are meaningful to themselves and are recognized as meaningful by others' (2004, p. 64).

Here is where an understanding of musical worlds and musical lifeworlds can interface with health ecologies. What we could call 'music and health ecologies' are where health and wellbeing can be seen as musically influenced and managed. As we've seen in the vignettes in this and the previous chapter, whilst the processes of musical ecologies may be similar, the ways in which they interface with musical lifeworlds are complex and individual. Ivor can appropriate the musical affordances he needs more immediately than Sesha, whilst the other examples show a range of ability to identify, access and appropriate the healthy fruits of musical participation. This highlights the social, cultural and political dimensions of what music and health ecologies entail in practice.

This idea of music and health ecologies usefully focuses our attention on what Arthur Frank calls the moral forms of dialogue – contact, recognition, communication, collaboration – that underwrite any 'health ecology'. Given the right conditions and access, sensitive musicking can often foster these dialogical necessities amazingly well. This is well illustrated by Cleo, who after a year of struggling with a particularly severe episode of her mental illness describes the process as follows:

> *It's a bit like a plant... it's under the earth... you've sown a seed in the ground, and it's germinating... but you have no idea what's going on there, because it's invisible. But once that shoot comes up through the earth, you can begin to see things visibly growing... so if you take that year of my life... and you consider that I'm a little shoot... [laughs]... and I've actually appeared... visibly... and I'm developing a bit here and there... with a little bit of water and a little bit of sunshine... you know... it's part of a whole context [...] [S]o it's this [participating*

in the music project]... that gives me the platform for me to come out of myself...
to emerge... that's the best way I can put it... and, um... and this is actually
hugely important to me... it's not just through music... it's through personal
confidence... being able to go up to a microphone and sing... to get myself back
into mainstream life... and it's all helped... it's probably been the single most
therapeutic catalyst... for my recovery... that I can actually name... and I really
mean that!

Passing Over into Music?

Sitting on the back row of the hall, listening to the New York Philharmonic play Bruckner's Seventh... I just catch the aura of my split-second passing over into the music, when figure and ground shift from its being 'over there' to my being 'within it'. Is it my imagination, or did everyone in the hall pass at exactly the same time?

ॐ

Before ending this chapter, we need to acknowledge a potential paradox that emerges from the 'musical worlds' theme we've been developing. Music seems to build 'a world of its own', but it's one that interfuses freely with our everyday world. It seems often to lead us into a different world of purely musical experience, whilst at the same time linking this to many 'para-musical' aspects of our lives, and ultimately to some core sense of ourselves as dwelling within the lifeworld (that itself is perhaps musical in some way).

'Music is a world,' state Nordoff and Robbins, describing how the children they worked with seemed often to step into this alternative world of musical experience, and become someone different there, where their lifeworld is richer, more extensive and habitable. But if we're not careful, this can be confused with the seemingly similar sentiment that music is 'a world of its own', transcending the everyday and sometimes messy world of human action and circumstance. As we've seen, often the opposite is true – musicking is a *return* to action and interaction. This is not, of course, to say that at times music can be an important refuge from the harsh realities of everyday life, a source of asylum and consolation (DeNora, 2013). But seen from an ecological perspective, this very asylum seeking through music is actually a very practical and worldly affordance of music and musicking, and a perfectly understandable form of everyday musical use (as we'll see further in Part VI).

So our everyday intuition that stepping into music takes us 'somewhere' qualitatively different can be true without this meaning that we travel to a 'musical realm' that is hermetically sealed off from everyday life. Rather, as the lifeworld flows into the musical world, so the musical world flows back into the lifeworld. The musical and the para-musical form a natural ecological interchange. At certain times, we can almost feel the air thin as we step into music, but this is the experience of a subtle and almost indistinguishable border crossing, not the cut-

and-dried 'this or that' of a boundary. We can end up in music, but not be quite sure how we got there. Nevertheless, we can feel our lifeworld suddenly musicalised in an equally mysterious way. As Tia DeNora writes,

> This passing over into music, this musical mediation of action, is often observable, often known to self as a feeling or energy state. It is also a local phenomenon, something that occurs in the here and now of action's flux, as actors interact with music's presence in an environment or social space. (2000, p. 159)

This worldly yet mysterious presence of music within human action and interaction is what Nordoff and Robbins were trying to convey in their very practical reports of the people they worked with in music therapy. They asked the simple but profound question, *What can you be or do 'in' music that you can't be or do 'out' of it?* This question led them to describe the realm of the *musical–personal*, where we enter music's world as it reciprocally comes towards ours. If we can 'pass over' into this musical–personal realm, we can begin furnishing a musical world to feel at home in, and to share with others through musical relationship and community.

 This is perhaps why we are so attached to our musical worlds – they can help us find a place and a path alongside others.

PART II
Musical Experience

I maintain that the world of music is a world of human experience....

John Blacking

Experience is the result, the sign, and the reward of that interaction of organism and environment which, when it is carried to its full, is a transformation of interaction into participation and communication.

John Dewey

Experience is not something that happens in us. It is something we do. Experience itself as a kind of dance – a dynamic involvement and engagement with the world around us. To study the experience, we must study the dance.

Alva Noë

Chapter 3
The Music of Experience

At its height experience signifies complete interpenetration of self and the world of objects and events.

John Dewey[1]

Where do you stop, and where does the rest of the world begin? There is no reason to suppose that the critical boundary is found in our brains or our skin.

Alva Noë[2]

[Music] is the space which, instead of consolidating the boundaries between within and without, obliterates them.

Victor Zuckerkandl[3]

No Boundary?

Adam: I never really got into the theory of music... the nuts and bolts of it. I didn't really care about that stuff. OK I had to learn it, but it wasn't what pulled me into music. Even now, it's just information for me, but it's never what music is for me... which is about becoming so involved with it that you can go into places where you usually can't....

But at the same time I guess I think music is outside of me too. Yes, the music for me is always personalised – I have a subjective experience of it, which I can't ever deny. I can't just say, 'There's music over there which I'm listening to'... I'm always having some interaction... some transaction with it; I don't necessarily think of it 'there', and I'm 'here'. It's a paradox, because it does feel like it's something 'out there', but equally it feels in me at the same time. I feel there isn't a boundary between me and music – it's a kind of mysterious thing in that way; that music's not seen, just heard, yet I'm having this strong experience with it. I think it's magic! The inner and the outer fused... there's no boundary....

℞

---

[1] Dewey 1934, p. 22.

[2] Noë 2010, p. 67.

[3] Zuckerkandl 1956, p. 339.

Rachel: I see myself standing at the piano, terribly small, I couldn't see the keys yet, just the edge of the key coming down. I remember suddenly finding that I could create a tune I knew! It must have been *Baa Baa Black Sheep* or *Twinkle Twinkle Little Star*, I think... I remember being totally absorbed by this. I knew this tune and suddenly this tune that was in my head, I could make it happen on the piano. The point was the sound, and the fact that I could do it... or, rather, that it could be done. And the truth that I intuited this time was I think that there's a structure in sound which is both outside me and inside me! And then a whole new world opened up. This truth is deeply inside my work as a music therapist. And this is why I think I understood what pioneer music therapist Paul Nordoff said – because I've always known this about sound and music being both inside and outside....

෨

Adam and Rachel report spontaneous and intuitive ways of thinking about musical experience that make practical sense yet go against standard assumptions. Experience is supposed to be located somewhere inside us, but for both Adam and Rachel it is more complicated than this. Adam experiences music both 'going inwards' and being 'outside' – personalised *and* objective. He eventually reconciles the paradox by saying that his experience of music has 'no boundary', the inner and the outer being magically, mysteriously fused. Rachel's discovery is likewise that the music is both in her head *and* outside her in the world. But as with Adam, this realisation about musical experience is not just a philosophical one, but part of finding out what she can *do* within her emerging world, using music as an early discovery tool. The consequence of discovering that music is both inside and outside is, as Rachel says, that 'I could do it... or, rather, that it could be done' – that is, it opens up a pathway for her becoming more active and creative in her world.

What's common to these two stories is that music is a way for Adam and Rachel to experiment with the relationship between 'inside' and 'outside' through something they do with music (and that music does reciprocally with them). They find through this practical experience with music that something can be created and controlled, and they come to the intuitive or more conscious understanding that there is indeed 'no boundary' between inside and outside, but rather, as Adam says, 'I'm always having some interaction... some *transaction* with it'.

Perhaps Adam's and Rachel's musical experience is showing something more general about personal experience – that, contrary to how we often talk and think about this, it is neither 'inside' nor 'outside' us, but *between and among*. Also, that experience is not passive; rather, it is something we do when acting in and interacting with the world around us. This interaction includes other 'things' like music, but also other musical people.

෨

Mary has no speech, and significant physical problems have left her body twisted and her movements slow and laborious. But her beautiful large brown eyes are expressive and mobile as they search mine out. I've composed a very simple song for Mary, with just a single melody line. As I sing this, I hold out a small Greek bell for her:

Mary... listen to the bell... [C–C...G→F→E→F→G....⁴]

I wait with the bell poised. Mary slowly looks at me, looks at the bell, and then with what seems like enormous effort she moves a stiff hand sideways and nudges the bell, which clangs loudly. She smiles broadly and laughs. I repeat the same line, and Mary hits the bell again at the end of the phrase, smiles, and laughs again. The next lines of the song reduce the phrase to a repeated two-note motif in a downward melodic sequence, sung to the word 'LISTEN!' – followed by a charged pause for Mary to add the bell each time:

LISTEN! ... *[G→A]* .... **RING**... ☺ *LISTEN!* ... *[F→G]* .... **RING**... ☺ *LISTEN! [E→F]*...
RING... ☺ *LISTEN!* ... *[D→E]* .... **RING**... ☺

Finally, the full first line repeats again to complete the little song, and Mary is bang on cue for the final bell, arching back in her chair in excitement and effort as she plays.

More than the heroic effort she makes to play the bell, what's magical and disquieting to me is how Mary listens. She clearly follows the structure of the song and attends closely for the precise moment in it that calls for her hand to reach out and strike the bell. But more than this, I also have the sense of Mary's living through the melody of this song, then taking the musical invitation to add her part in just that musical time and space. I also feel her sensing my living through this melody as I sing it, sharing musical time and space with me. A musical experience has been given and received (both ways), something that connects us closely for these minutes.

ॐ

Mary was one of the first clients I worked with as a music therapy student, and she introduced me to the puzzle of the musical experience of others. How did I really know that Mary had a 'musical experience', or that it resembled my own? And, as Paul Nordoff asked about his own music therapy with people like Mary, 'Is what I am giving this child a musical experience?' (in Robbins and Robbins 1998, p. 22). If musical experiences can be 'had', can they also be 'shared', 'given' and 'taken'?

The simplest way to approach these questions would be for me to directly ask the person I was making music with, 'What was that like for you?', and they may have been able to tell me about their side of the experience (though it's notoriously

⁴   Where C is the tonic of the key.

difficult to put experience into words). But Mary couldn't tell me. She did, however, show me something very relevant to understanding another's musical experience. The philosopher Wittgenstein wrote in one of his occasional comments about people and music how understanding a musical phrase (or playing it with understanding) is similar to understanding someone's facial expression. He asks:

> how would you know that someone else was having this kind of understanding and what prompts you to say that he is having a particular experience? For that matter, do we ever say this? Wouldn't I be more likely to say of someone else that he's having a whole host of experiences? Perhaps I would say, 'He's experiencing the theme intensely'; but consider how this is manifested (Wittgenstein, in Scruton 2009, p. 35).

What prompted me to think that Mary was having a musical experience? I think that I instinctively followed Wittgenstein's suggestion: I considered how it was *manifested* in her musicking, rather than by guessing what was 'inside' Mary's head. I understood something about her musical experience from her changing facial expressions in those moments, and how her explicit musical action of playing the bell made sense in relation to my own actions and my own subjective experiences, to which I *did* have first-person access. As I tracked Mary's responsive expressions (visually and aurally), it was clear to me how Mary and I were jointly 'following a musical phrase with understanding' – which is also to say, we were sharing a musical experience in some way because of how our paths of musical action meaningfully aligned.

ଙ୍କ

Adam, Rachel and Mary introduce us to some of the puzzling questions about experiencing music: *Where is it? What is it like? Can we share it?* They show how music can cross and play with the boundaries that normally define 'inside', 'outside' and 'between'. If these boundaries are more permeable than we might think, this does not mean that everything merges, or that our musical experience is not our own or 'like something' for us. Rather, it shows how experience is not always limited to our personal consciousness, nor just created from it. As such, musical experience is naturally something shareable and giveable.

The Complexities of (Musical) Experience

The 'locals' I interviewed talked in two basic ways about their musical experience. Firstly, they told me about their musical knowledge or craft as something that they'd accumulated, and that they draw upon when needed. As David said to me, 'It's slowly developed, my experience of music… through twenty-five years of listening… to the point where I think of my life as full of music'. People also told me about particular experiences, often beginning, 'I had this experience…', and then going on to describe a significant musical moment and how it had influenced their lives. Such experiences sometimes led them to reflect on what they thought music was really like (which included telling me that musical experience can't be put into words).

These two ways of using the word 'experience' follow everyday English grammar. Experience means either something personal we accumulate (as in, 'After thirty years, I'm an experienced pianist'), or something more immediate and particular that we undergo in the present, and that leaves a vivid impression (as in, 'I had this extraordinary experience this morning!').[5] The word and concept 'experience' has a rich and complex etymological history that the anthropologist Victor Turner suggests conveys in its essence 'a journey, a test (of self, of suppositions about others), a ritual passage, an exposure to peril or risk, a source of fear' (1982, p. 18).

This more dramatic sense of 'experience' became the root of two seemingly contradictory theoretical traditions in modern intellectual history. Firstly, there is *experiment*, where a scientific stance is taken to testing a phenomenon from a third-person perspective, keeping it something objective and 'over there'. But there is also *experiential*, which characterises a way of understanding things from a first-person perspective by living through how they make a subjective impression on us, body and mind. What the two forms do share is the common empirical ideal of exploring phenomena by using the senses, rather than relying on magical or purely theoretical means. But they also epitomise a long-term dualism in Western thinking – splitting objective, mental, rational knowledge from its supposed subjective, embodied and feelingful opposite.

Wavering between objective and subjective perspectives, 'experience' has retained its place in everyday discourse, but it has all but disappeared for several decades from many academic fields. For many scholars in the physical and social sciences, 'experience' became an outdated and redundant term that was tainted by the fuzziness of introspection and subjective description of earlier methods that cognitive psychology and neuroscience had worked hard to supersede.

Serious thinking about music has generally followed this trend towards making theories of music as objective and factual as possible. A brief informal survey I made of the indexes of a pile of classic texts within music studies suggests how far 'musical experience' has simply disappeared as an explicit subject of attention.[6] It has been replaced instead by 'perception', 'awareness' or 'cognition' – mirroring

---

[5] German more usefully spreads these meanings over two words: *Erfahrung* – derived from *Fahrt*, 'journey' – conveys experience as accumulation, whilst *Erlebnis* – derived from *Leben*, 'life' – describes the present 'living through' of 'an experience'. In Japanese, the two characters *kei ken* mean passing through (gaining experience), whilst *tai ken* stand for body/trial (meaning 'individual happenings').

[6] My search wasn't exhaustive, but it did include more than twenty classic texts of the last twenty years, ranging over music psychology, neuroscience of music, musicology, music education and music therapy.

how the concept 'person' has been replaced by mind, brain or consciousness. Interestingly, however, the word 'experience' is still used informally, as part of everyday language, by nearly all the writers (but not referenced as a theoretical term). Its logical connection to perception and cognition is, however, never tackled (or, indeed, it seems that no reason to tackle this is recognised). I've come to think of musical experience as a 'phantom referent' in recent thinking about music. By this I mean that, whilst it is *referred back to*, 'musical experience' as a phenomenon in itself remains ghostly: it is gone but not entirely forgotten. The objective vocabulary of perception, cognition and consciousness is retained, but with 'experience' as the (undefined) ultimate referent. The concept survives a little more in those fields that have explicitly explored people's everyday musical lives, such as ethnomusicology and sociology, but detailed treatment is still rare.

However, 'experience' has also been steadily creeping back as a term within interdisciplinary music studies via certain trends in the emerging neuroscience of music, as these theories have increasingly acknowledged the need for a first-person perspective to complement the objective data of brain scans – reporting on what music is *like* as it happens (Clarke and Clarke 2011). But still it seems that musical experience is more a phantom referent than an explored phenomenon. This trend suggests, however, that 'experience' retains some functional conceptual purpose when we are trying to understand the relationship between people and music. To put it another way, if we can't do without 'musical experience' then what conceptual work *does* it do? A tentative answer I'd give for now is that thinking about experience grounds the humanistic view of a whole person in relationship to their whole musical ecology. The alternatives (perception, cognition, neural processing) tend to reduce both people and music to parts and objects.

ॐ

One tradition that kept its faith with 'experience' is phenomenology. This has consistently attempted the most 'experience-near' account of how music and people relate. I came across Thomas Clifton's (1983) phenomenological study of music, *Music as Heard*, in Cambridge University Library when I was an undergraduate. The title caught my eye because it was different from the recommended reading, which mostly followed the structuralist-inspired notion that you discovered 'how music worked' by analysing its 'bone structure' in terms of internal relationships of melody, harmony and rhythm within a broad formal architecture. A problem was that you mostly didn't need to listen to the music to do this! You looked at the score instead and worked it out analytically. The other problem was that it left *people* out of music – only the notes remained. Clifton's work was a welcome corrective to this, starting off instead from the seemingly commonsense view that understanding music meant exploring musical experience. Later, when I was training as a music therapist, I came across Victor Zuckerkandl's monumental two-volume philosophy of music *Sound and Symbol* and *Man the Musician*, which expands a phenomenological perspective on music into a whole worldview.[7]

A phenomenon is something given to my experience.[8] As such, the logical starting point for understanding music is from a first person, '*me*-perspective'. As Thomas Clifton puts it, 'music is what I am when I experience it' (1983, p. 1). Understanding music phenomenologically means living through it, and trying to reflect upon and to describe how its properties, qualities and tendencies – the way it is in the world – appear to our experience. It tries to find out how music is *musical* by staying near to human experience. This is very different from how an acoustician, cognitive psychologist or music analyst would approach understanding music.

Through this introspective method, phenomenology usefully shows up a certain 'strangeness' in our experience of music that we often overlook in both everyday and more scientific accounts. But the phenomenologies of music have some key limitations that are related to their cultural origins and underlying assumptions. They are written by musicologists and philosophers who typically think of 'music' only as Classical, pre-composed works, rather than as the contextualised activity of musicking. Consequently they also focus largely on the main 'Classical' parameters of pitch, melody and harmony, whilst downplaying rhythm and timbre. Musical experience is boiled down to basic 'essences' that are portrayed as universal. This leads in turn to the sense that music has a power 'in itself', a quasi-metaphysical force that we rather passively receive. Lastly, these traditional phenomenologies of music are too solipsistic, trapping musical experience as only a private content of consciousness, without much consideration of how a social and cultural community both builds and sustains the possibility of shared musical experience.

໕

These tendencies towards passivity, solipsism and 'internalism' are shared by most of the other current approaches to understanding music, however different their theoretical starting points might be. Cognitive psychology models perception as a computer-like processing of information that produces an internal representation. Neuroscience sees consciousness as generated inside the brain. Musical analysis sees musical meaning as generated through structural patterns. All present a common picture of 'internal goings-on' as key to their explanations (Noë 2010, p. 169). The same has been true of most therapeutic theories up to now – that what's wrong and needs understanding is 'inside'. Such internalism is typically twinned with individualism, the view that we are essentially separated by the boundaries of our brains and our skins. But as we saw from the examples of Adam, Rachel and Mary at the beginning of this chapter, and as our own musical experiences

---

[7]   Some key works or commentaries on musical phenomenology broadly conceived are: Clifton 1983; Zuckerkandl 1956, 1973; Bowman 1998; Ferrara 1991; Scruton 1997, 2009.

[8]   Phenomenon – the order or logic (*logos*) of that which appears to us (*phainein* – 'show', 'shine', 'be seen').

surely confirm, this can't be the whole story. Just because experience is personal and subjective, it doesn't mean that it's also private and internal. The particular puzzles of musical experience perhaps show this up in a way that encourages us to pause and consider this standard assumption and to think more ecologically about experience.

The philosopher Alva Noë (2010, 2012) suggests an alternative view that is gaining credibility:

> If we are to understand consciousness – the fact that we think and feel and that a world shows up for us – we need to turn our back on the orthodox assumption that consciousness is something that happens inside us, like digestion. It is now clear, as it has not been before, that consciousness, like a work of improvisational music, is achieved by action, by us, thanks to our situation in and access to a world we know around us. We are in the world and of it. (Noë 2010, p. 186)

Coming out of our heads and into the world is not to lose the concept of experience, but to relocate and redirect it.[9] As Noë hints above, it could well be that attending to the experience of music might help us to understand the music of experience in different ways.

Thinking Ecologically about (Musical) Experience

There is a growing critique of 'internalism' in a variety of professional fields, including music. This aligns with the more ecological way of thinking about the relationship between people, music and situations that I outlined in Part I, Musical Worlds.

This alternative tradition of thinking about experience has roots in American pragmatism, particularly in John Dewey's philosophy. Whilst phenomenology introspects to see how phenomena arrive on our individual 'mental stage' and what we can know about them from this, pragmatism, true to its name,[10] is more interested in following what we *do* with things, and with defining their meanings more outwardly and practically. It sees experience as emerging primarily out of action rather than reflection, and acknowledges how it is always involved in the immediate social and cultural ecology. Dewey thought of our 'inside' and 'outside' as fluidly continuous, writing how 'we live as much in processes across and "through" skins as in processes "within" skins' (in Shusterman 2008, p. 214). Experience for him is the conscious registering of this transaction between our body–mind and the world: 'the result, the sign, and the reward of that interaction of

---

[9]   Noë makes no theoretical distinction between experience, consciousness, awareness and similar terms, writing, 'I think of experience, broadly, as encompassing thinking, feeling, and the fact that a world "shows up" for us in perception' 2010, p. 8.

[10]   From the Greek *pragma* – 'deed' or 'action'.

organism and environment which, when it is carried to its full, is a transformation of interaction into participation and communication' (Dewey 1934, p. 22).

More recently, the pragmatist sociologist Richard Sennett (2007, p. 289) has suggested that we need to think of experience in both inward- and outward-focused ways. We certainly need the *Erlebnis* type of experience that makes an emotional inner impression on us. But equally we need its complement – experience as *Erfahrung*, which turns *outwards* towards the world. Sennett suggests that this second form of experience is more like a craft, shaping raw sensory impressions alongside others, sharing experience as a journey. A pragmatist keeps an eye equally on how experience feels, and what it does.

Although the pragmatist position mostly concentrates on 'everyday' experience, Dewey also reflects on the distinctive or 'consummatory' type that he terms '*an* experience'. As usual, Dewey looks at the continuity between the more everyday and the more special: from a good meal or conversation to unique works of art. To varying extents these are all aesthetic experiences, which for him represent 'the clarified and intensified development of traits that belong to every normally complete experience' (in Johnson 2007, p. 212). Artistic processes and experiences are not separated out into a unique category, but rather represent a heightened instance of the normal transactive process. The particular quality that they have as *an* experience is a feeling of unity that 'is constituted by a single quality of the entire experience in spite of the variations of its constituent parts' (Dewey, in Johnson 2007, p. 74).

A summary of the pragmatist perspective would be that experience is always situated, embodied, holistic and interactive. It involves the whole person and is not limited to sensation, perception or cognition. Experience links the physical, mental, social and spiritual, with these domains seen as potentially continuous.

Certain key features characterise such active experience. Firstly, it is temporal and emergent: the process of experiencing is an ongoing and creative process in time. Experience is not a product, but the *process* of living through the transaction between self and situation. Secondly, it is qualitative: the 'how' of experience is as important as the 'what'. We experience qualities not 'in' things, but *between* ourselves and the ongoing flux of things, people and situations. Such qualities are 'picked up' according to what they offer us as affordances, and what the organism needs to appropriate for its purposes here and now. Lastly, experience is by nature transformative: it drives growth, development, and the ongoing process of understanding and responding to our environment. Such understanding is therefore not private but social and shared. It is deeply involved with the habits and culture of the lifeworld.

In contrast to the specific 'phenomenologies of music', pragmatist thinking has influenced music studies in a more indirect way through interdisciplinary approaches that study music as part of a wider view of human social and cultural experience – drawing on interactionist and 'everyday life' orientations.[11] What these different scholars show in common is a 'praxial' orientation that compensates for the rather passive 'internalism' of musical phenomenology.

৪৩

Recent 'post-phenomenological' perspectives are blending aspects of these previously distinct traditions. They typically respect the detailed attention that phenomenology gives to exploring the specificity of our ongoing experience, but also acknowledge the pragmatist demand for attending to action and situation. This strand of thinking is often related to philosophical or sociological studies of areas of applied practice – such as science and technology studies, embodied cognition, extended mind, or 'everyday life studies' (including those of musicking).[12] What's shared is the need to get away from a limiting and outdated vocabulary of subject/object, inner/outer, mind/body when exploring psychosocial life and its practices. As Bruno Latour writes, 'Object and subject might exist, but everything interesting happens upstream and downstream. Just follow the flow' (2005, p. 237). That is, we may find something more interesting by noticing the entangled flow of people and things within everyday actions and situations. This leads to a more pragmatic attention to 'things in action', exploring how things 'appear' to us sometimes only *through* action, and that what things 'are' is a direct relation to what they allow us to be and to do. What's interesting is precisely how things allow such being and doing.[13] This perspective gets us beyond the 'spectator sport' of phenomenology, whilst keeping its disciplined focus on the crafting of experience. For this, it needs to add the 'everyday life' and ecological focus of pragmatically based studies, which are concerned with how experience can be seen to be assembled within action.

We saw many of these features in the music studies of Tia DeNora and Eric Clarke (see Chapter 1). Their work has initiated a specifically ecological approach to thinking about music, and to seeing how musical experience (or musical consciousness) can be attended to without lapsing into internalism and individualism.

---

[11]   These include work by philosophers Mark Johnson (2007) and Richard Shusterman (2000); music educationalists David Elliott (1995), Christopher Small (1998) and Keith Sawyer (2003); music psychologist Eric Clarke (2005); and music sociologist Tia DeNora (2000, 2003).

[12]   Although it's Ihde (2009) who specifically uses the term 'postphenomenology', there is a distinctive postphenomenological flavour to the work of people from different intellectual camps: Johnson (2007), Sennett (2007), Latour (2005), DeNora (2011a).

[13]   To an extent, this way of thinking had its origins in later phenomenologists such as Heidegger. See Ihde 2009 and Ahmed 2006.

Experience as 'Skilful Access'

A useful perspective in this broad postphenomenological tradition that brings together some of the key aspects of the ecological model with the concerns of how music helps is Alva Noë's (2010, 2012) 'actionist' theory of experience.[14]

Noë rejects the 'old and tired idea' that experience is simply what happens inside us as a result of sensory information impacting on our eyes or ears, which we then passively process as if digesting food, ending up with a duplicate representation in the brain. Rather, he suggests that:

> we should think of what is experienced as what is *available* to a person, as what is available to a person *from a place*. The seeing does not happen in the head. Rather the experience is achieved or enacted by the person. We do it *in the world*. The scope of experience is a matter of what is available to us. And what is available to us depends on not only what there is, but also, crucially, on what we can do … What is available is that to which we can have access …. (2012, p. 114)

Noë's alternative metaphor to experience as digestion is experience as touching or handling (or, later, dancing). We experience the world and what it offers because we have bodies with sense organs that actively search out, move around and pick up what's there. Things show up for us, become present, have a quality and a meaning exactly as we contact them and begin to assemble them in practice, opening up their possibilities for further action (rather like Gibson's account of affordances). When we adjust our physical stance in relation to things, they change too, showing another aspect, or another path of possibility. In this way, Noë suggests that, instead of thinking of perceptual experience as going 'in' and 'out' of our heads, we think of it as going from 'here' to 'there', as the path of our action out in the world.

Experience is in this way an *active process of skilful access*. But such access is inevitably based on who, where and in what state we are – and as such, experience is fragile. What Noë usefully adds is the thought that we must think of capacity in relation to access. If experience is enabled by skilful sensori-motor ability and understanding then there will also be situations where access is more or less disabled – and consequently so are people disabled. Experiential worlds will close down instead of opening up if the social and cultural ecology is not supportive. But equally, access can be enabled in a variety of simple ways: by moving, for example, musical material (physically or symbolically) within reach, or by mediating appropriation, to return to Tia DeNora's formulation, such that musical affordances are more habitable and shareable.

---

[14] Noë (2012) variously calls his perspective 'actionist', 'sensorimotor', 'enactive' and 'direct realism'. He also relates it (2010) to theories of extended or distributed mind. Behind this and similar work is an eclectic blend of scholars such as Heidegger, Merleau-Ponty, Ihde, Bateson and Deleuze.

I think here of Mary playing her bell. She heroically reaches out to play, and her ears and mind reach out also to gain skilful access to what the musicking situation affords her. But she also needs help to gain full access to this situation, which is why she reaches out in a different way, co-opting *my* musical experience in order to extend her own.

ℰℜ

In this chapter, we've arrived at a way of thinking about musical experience as skilful practice. To *do* musical experience is to catalyse music's active presence within the self, and to explore the range of its qualities, properties and affordances. To *give* or *share* musical experience is then to move outwards with this musical presence, towards others and what is possible together.

Alva Noë writes, 'Experience is not something that happens in us. It is something we do. Experience itself as a kind of dance – a dynamic involvement and engagement with the world around us. To study the experience, we must study the dance' (2012, p. 130). He intentionally moves to an artistic metaphor as he suggests that experience itself is an aesthetic stance, and that 'aesthetic experience [is] the very paradigm of a perceptual experience' (p. 129).

For this book and its focus on how music helps, the 'dance' begins with the person in music, who is in action and interaction both with music and with other people. To begin studying this 'dance' is to come back to the phenomenology of situated action – to attend precisely to the steps of the musicking person who draws on the phenomenological specificities of music, and who acts musically with and through them with others.

Chapter 4
Aspects of Musical Experience

Music 'exists' at the intersection of organised sounds with our sensorimotor apparatus, our bodies, our brains, our cultural values and practices, our music-historical conventions, our prior experiences, and a host of other social and cultural factors.

Mark Johnson[1]

Musical Experience in Action and Situation

Phenomenology's favourite trick was to show us how strange music becomes when we try to pin down how we experience it. The newer perspectives we explored in the last chapter have reframed this problem by suggesting that musical experience is something achieved rather than received, as something between us and the world, and not just inside our heads. Music, that is, shows up as experience when we're part of the action. This is to take a *musicking* perspective on musical experience, emphasising how we make or enact musical experience through our skilled access to the ever-varying aspects of music's forms, properties, processes, qualities and affordances.

However, I also want to keep some of phenomenology's careful insights into how music can move in mysterious ways, to see in particular how our experiences of musical 'time', 'space' and 'motion' relate to the more everyday realities of 'occasion', 'place', and 'action'. Overall, then, what's needed is a *situated phenomenology* that adds an ecological dimension to a phenomenology of musical experience. In this chapter, I experimentally sketch such a hybrid *eco-phenomenology of musicking* – though this is not one I'd claim as comprehensive or definitive. Rather, I outline a series of key aspects as initial sketches that could perhaps signal a route for further thinking in this direction.

This close focus on aspects of musical experience does not aim to characterise the whole musical ecology, but rather concentrates on the area of *tone–people relationships* that comprises the experiential 'inner core' of a musical ecology (see Fig. 1.1, p. 29), and that forms a foundation for other levels of personal, communal and transcendent musical relationships.

---

[1] Johnson 2007, p. 255.

Towards an Eco-phenomenology of Musicking

We are experiencing music when…

- …through our situated body and its skilful sensori-motor actions we can…
- …recognise and respond to sounds as musical…
- …as located both in actual and virtual spaces…caused by human gesture…
- …emerging in specifically *musical time*…projecting in *musical space*… flowing in *musical motion*…
- …as *musical events* happening within a charged field of dynamic *musical activity*…
- …conveying vitality, affect and other dynamic qualities that put us in touch with other musical people who can share our present musical experience.

Such statements perhaps sound unduly abstract. But I hope to show how these core phenomenological 'aspects' often mirror how people informally describe their musical experiences or the musical behaviour of others. The aspects can also be seen as the 'enabling conditions' through which musicking can go on to afford benefits for us on particular occasions and in particular places. What an eco-phenomenology adds to a traditional phenomenology of music is to go beyond the boiled-down, abstract 'essences' of musical time, space and motion. Instead, it suggests the more active musicking equivalents, where *tone relationships* are juxtaposed with *situation relationships* and *people relationships*, as the musicking model suggests. An eco-phenomenology of musicking therefore explores:

- musical time-in-action (and interaction), as timing and occasioning
- musical space-in-action (and interaction), as placing and relating
- musical motion-in-action (and interaction), as dynamic happening and developing.

That is, people and their situations are returned to the musical scene, but without losing how the specific qualities of *musical* time, space and motion interact with these. An eco-phenomenology of musicking therefore aims to show how the phenomenological specificity of music as a medium and process underpins the personal and social affordances of musicking.

The following sections profile the key five aspects of musical experience that I suggest underpin the material I'll elaborate further in Parts III–VI of this book.

Aspect 1: Musical Bodies

> **Mercédès:** A friend and I decided to hit a club in Pretoria. I hadn't been to one for ages, it was midnight by the time we got there, and prior to this I'd been lying at home on the carpet listening to Brahms in preparation! [*laughs*] So

we entered this club and the noise was incredible… I remember going up this escalator, and thinking this is a rite of passage into another world, my senses assaulted by all these dancing people, this music, this space… I'm not sure I can separate these three things. So we piled onto the dance floor and at first I hated it, I saw all these young people and felt alienated. Then they played a more melodious music that I recognised, and I started to get into dancing, becoming aware of this whole event. The more we danced, the more I lost sense of myself, and started to become aware of the event as a whole. After a while, I had a strong sense of the difference between dancing and not-dancing in a place like this. But equally the experience of dancing was deeply affected by what music was being played. This is the visceral aspect of music. If my body didn't like the music, I found it difficult to move. It's linked to how intimate music is for me. If the music doesn't feel quite right my body won't go there. It's a bit like a lover with whom you can't move when you make love…. It's not just rhythm, the melodic element's also really important for dancing. That's the phrasing, whereas the rhythm's all driving and repetition. It's also a cognitive thing, I suppose – the different levels of perception. Your body shifts from the driving beat to something else, which has a contour, which enables the body to flow more, which moves you horizontally… which is the thing about melody. When I was out of the music, I started to feel claustrophobic in this place. So the whole scene only worked for me as a musical experience.

Mercédès articulates here a fundamental aspect of musical experience: that it's our bodies that first make 'visceral sense' of the whole situation we find ourselves in. The body responds immediately both to the scene as a whole, and by interacting with the specific affordances that emerge and show up within our ongoing experience, as features of the situation.

We experience music only because we have a body – and we experience music as an embodied phenomenon that is closely related to features and processes of our bodily life. Music has energy, movement in space and time, pulse and tone, force and attraction, tension and release, intention and direction – just like our bodies. This regularly came up with the 'locals' I interviewed, who often started by talking about their bodily relationship with music. They moved, danced and engaged with it not as 'something over there', but as something directly impacting and directing the body with its energy and dynamic contours. This also applied to music that was only imagined, hallucinated or dreamed. Within this 'internal' music, people still experienced the ebbing and flowing of musical sounds and energy as a quasi-bodily movement.

Against the traditional assumption that we first make sense of the world through our mind (with the body merely its servant), contemporary interdisciplinary theory has increasingly argued how it is through our thoroughly *embodied self* that we make and undergo experiences and construct knowledge (Shusterman 2008; Stern 2010). Thomas Clifton's phenomenological account of musical experience takes this view, that it's our body that initiates our understanding of music:

> [music is] the actualization of the possibility of any sound whatever to present to some being a meaning which he experiences with his body – that is to say, with his mind, his feelings, his senses, his will, and his metabolism. (1983, p. 1)

So when we describe music as 'coursing through me', 'moving', 'ebbing and flowing' and so on, this *is* what music is for us then. It's not just a descriptive metaphor but an accurate depiction of what music is within our embodied experience. The body gives the music its situated meanings, as we see in Mercédès's example above, because of how the body understands the immediate affordances for helpful action and interaction within a situation. One of these helpful affordances is to transcend the limits of the body through music, and to flow into the situation as a whole. Mercédès and Adam (earlier) described how they experience the boundary of the self loosening within musicking. This happens as part of a reciprocal attraction and transaction between the musicalised body and the embodied music of the overall scene. The point comes when they are not sure where they end and where music begins.

There is a long history in esoteric traditions of characterising the body itself as a musical instrument that 'resonates' with music sounded in the external, or even cosmic, world. The music therapist Paul Nordoff often began his explanations of his work by remarking that we are rhythmic and tonal beings. Musical elements and processes characterise our internal physiology and our external actions such as talking and moving. It is because of this core embodied musical sense that we can respond to a musical 'call' coming to us from outside. Scholarship in interdisciplinary music studies is increasingly taking musical embodiment seriously, exploring aspects such as movement, gesture, proprioception, and the chronobiology of rhythm in relation to questions of how we access music, how it 'works', and how it can help (Osborne 2009; Clarke and Clarke 2011; MacDonald, Kreutz and Mitchell 2012).

Aspect 2: Musical Sounds

Nigel: I remember as a young kid watching and listening to this woman playing the piano in a pub... and realising that when she pressed certain keys down it made things happen... I remember being fascinated watching her hands and seeing the formation of pushing the notes down and how she made these sounds happen... which I heard as music!

ꙮ

Rachel: I always relate my understanding of the physical–spiritual nature of music back to the moment when I was very young, when I suddenly realised that you don't get sound without movement! I almost wept when I realised that! I was lying in my bed at night... I was about six... and I was listening... they were quite new sounds, because we'd just moved into this country vicarage. I was listening to the mice scuttling around in the attic, and they scared me! So I was thinking of the sound of them, knowing what they were... it was in the dark... and I don't know how I came to this, but I started thinking about sound, trying to think about it, as I could hear the mice moving around. 'Can you get a sound without something moving?' I was thinking to myself. And I thought of all the sounds I could think of... and I thought 'No, you can't!' Sound is dependent on something moving. And I suddenly realised that those two truths were the same, or at least dependent upon one another. So this was a realisation in my child's brain, this is the way the world works! It was a revelation... like a great intake of breath. And from that moment onwards I started knowing about music too. It was as if this experience and this revelation woke up my inner perception of music. I started improvising on the piano at this point, I think....

Linking sound with movement forms the foundation for beginning to recognise and imagine sounds *as* music, as something that is neither entirely out there in the world, nor inside our mind. Thomas Clifton suggests that 'a group of sounds becomes constituted as music partly due to the quality and amount of care which one exhibits towards these sounds' (1983, p. 277). Music shows up for us in a particular situation according to how we turn to it, relate ourselves to it, and make sense of it.

There's been a tendency in traditional musical aesthetics to draw a rather sharp distinction between worldly sounds and music. The philosopher Roger Scruton writes, for example, that 'understanding music involves the active creation of an intentional world, in which sounds are transfigured into tones – into metaphorical movements in a metaphorical space' (1997, p. 364). Sounds in the everyday world are typically still tied to their physical causes, as for example when you hear a crash and look out of the window to see the cars that caused it. Scruton argues that what's different in musical experience is that sounds become separated from their causal physical event (in a way you can't separate the car-like shape from its being a car). He calls our ability to hear sounds *as* music the *acousmatic* experience of sounds. This lets us listen to musical sounds as events relating with each other within their own virtual musical world. Sounds are transmuted into *tones*.[2]

Ecological psychologists of music such as Eric Clarke (2011) have argued back that we often experience sounds *both* as 'everyday' and as purely musical at the same time. We hear music as both embodied and disembodied; 'here' and 'there'; real and virtual; specifying its physical causes, but also peeling away from these into music's virtual world. Another way to put this is that music continues to interfuse with and mirror our everyday experiences of life – our bodily and mental

---

[2]   Although the word 'tone' usually suggests 'pitch', the overall logic of 'hearing sounds as music' should apply to any form of transmuting sounds into musical events – e.g. a beat, rhythmic pattern, timbre or texture, etc. Pitches, however, do have a particular phenomenology, particularly in Western art and popular music because of the dominant place of the tonal system in musical construction and meaning.

transactions with things and people in time, space and motion – as well as creating a further, specifically musical way of experiencing and understanding this reality.

We see Nigel and Rachel doing just this in the quotations above. Their early experiences of music involve developing an understanding of 'how music works' by linking its particular form of life to their developing exploration of how the everyday world works, whilst at the same time moving beyond this.

What a person can understand through this metaphorical process of mapping music and life will depend on both their situated needs and their capacities to actively explore the world musically and to discover the musicality of the world. But what is there to be explored and discovered is how music provides experiences that are not only continuities but also extensions of our core human experiences of time, space, motion, event, relationship and causality. To put it another way, *tones* come to have properties that everyday sounds cannot (direction, energy, relationship); and, from these possibilities, musicking affords experiences that can extend our living within, and our understanding of, time, space and motion. These experiences open up for us what the musical phenomenologist Victor Zuckerkandl thought of as a musical conception of the external world.

Aspect 3: Musical Space, Time and Motion

I am lying in a cabin on the edge of a semi-tropical forest on Magnetic Island in Australia. Surrounding me is a cacophony of birdcalls. Listening to it as one soundscape, it seems to organise into various spatial planes: near and far (related to loud and soft); sounds approaching and backing off. Temporally, all the events fall together in a constant present. Just as I'm getting weary of this ongoing randomness (it's becoming noise for me, and stopping me sleeping), a flute starts playing in the distance. My ear instantly identifies this as 'different from birds' and attunes to it (even though it's soft and distant). My ear follows the flute's melody – which now has a 'backdrop' of bird sound. The flute's sound begins to create its own and different order of space and time. I listen to the melody's intentional journey through musical space, which my ear somehow orientates to – both within, but also separate from, the natural space in which it drifts towards me in the gathering dusk. Time changes and gathers as I become absorbed in the music's own unfolding time, which both takes and gives time. I am moved by this music.

ಬಿ

Living as an embodied person means being in time, space and motion. But are musical time, space and motion the same as we experience ordinarily through our everyday bodily life? Phenomenological theories of music give an ambivalent yes/ no answer to this question, and then try to map the distinctive features of musical space, time and motion that are taken to form music's distinctive experiential world. Thomas Clifton's (1983) and Victor Zuckerkandl's (1956) treatments of this perspective are too complex to describe in detail in this chapter, but I hope the following summary of their perspective shows its overall logic. The key message of these musical phenomenologies is to encourage us to attend to how music radically inflects our experiences of time, space and motion. This comes, it must be said, with the important caveat that it is not that music transcends these basic experiential categories, but rather that it affords an alternative and sometimes compensatory experience of them for a while – as *music's* time, space and motion. An eco-phenomenological angle to this material then asks what these specifically musical experiences afford musicking people in everyday action and situation.

Music's Space

Music's space is where we find ourselves when musicking. We take up temporary residence there, experiencing musical action and movement within this space. We find music's space not an 'empty space' but one that is alive and active, even a space that itself seems in motion. Zuckerkandl calls this 'the placeless, flowing space of tones' – a space in which, 'when tones sound, we enter a different order in the whence of encounter and the where of relation' (1956, p. 330). If we attend more closely to the features of 'music's space', they can seem unusual in comparison to 'everyday space'. The 'space' of tones or the space of chords, for example, points to a paradoxical and multi-levelled 'space without places'.

However, as we noted earlier, there's also the possibility of hearing such purely musical space overlapping and interpenetrating with the everyday space of people moving their bodies to play instruments, and to gesture their emotional and relational intentions. An eco-phenomenology would therefore see musical space as necessarily multi-dimensional, according to how we attend to musical sounds, and in relation to what we need to do with them. We shall explore how the phenomenology of musical space influences musical relationship and community in Part IV and Part V.

Music's Time

Music's time is often experienced as radically different from the 'clock time' (*chronos*) that music externally 'takes' – where each segment has a discrete duration, where the past decays, and where the future is unknown. Instead, writes Zuckerkandl, 'the moment the tone sounds it draws us into time, opening time to us as perceiving beings' (1956, p. 253). Time in this sense is not something that we pour music into or measure it by, but is rather a quality of timing and timeliness created *within* musicking.

Clifton (1983) describes how music simultaneously stores up the past through 'retention', anticipates the future through 'protention', and focuses the present through 'attention'. The dynamic overlapping of these temporal horizons in music presents us with 'a future anticipated, not just awaited; a past retained, not just remembered; a present lived, not just encountered. Musical time is time opened out onto and richly resonant with lived human experience' (Bowman 1998, p. 273, paraphrasing Clifton).[3]

When we are musicking 'within' music's time, we can experience time as *kairos* – an alternative quality of time that is charged with meaning and occasion, and that navigates the precious 'timeliness' of the present moment. We shall explore how this phenomenology of musical time influences musical transcendence in Part VI.

Music's Motion

'When we hear music,' writes Zuckerkandl, 'what we hear is above all motions' (1956, p. 76). Hearing sounds as music is to be moved by them, both physically and emotionally – to become part of music's motion for a while. But the puzzle is that physically nothing moves in music – or at least not in the way that we understand movement in our everyday experience. We are apt to think that a melody moves in the way that, if I throw a ball through the air to you, there's a successive change in its spatial position over a predictable slice of time, but with the ball remaining the same object. But no tone shifts its position in this way in musical space, despite this being phenomenally what we hear. Rather, the movement and motion somehow travels *through* the tones. This is perhaps explained again by the kind of 'double hearing' that we noted above concerning musical space. We transfer the sense we have of things moving past us, or our moving with them, to the imaginary space of music, where tones move. We experience the qualities of musical motion and relationship in motion with which our bodies acquaint us. Music is a good example of how easily we pass between 'real' and metaphorical dimensions of body-based experience.

ಐ

Our musical experience is therefore grounded in our real embodied experience of time, space and motion. In this way, as Roger Scruton comments, in music 'we have to hear up and down, towards and away, soaring, plunging, coincidence, distance, density, proximity, mirroring, inversion, forwards, backwards, same direction' (2009, p. 46). But paradoxically it's often possible to experience all of these everyday forms of life just within music's world for a while. Mostly, perhaps, we have an ear in each world. This is why music often seems such a strange phenomenon yet is so useful precisely because of this double life.

---

[3]   Zuckerkandl also makes the same point about music and time: 'Every melody declares to us that the past can be there without being remembered, the future without being foreknown – that the past is not stored in memory but in time, and that it is not our consciousness which anticipates time, but that time anticipates itself. The possibility of music and of every temporal gestalt rests entirely on the premise of a time so constituted, of a time that stores itself and anticipates itself' (1956, p. 235).

Aspect 4: Musical Activity

Susanna: I think of a piece of music I love, like a bit of a favourite Mozart Piano Concerto... how you anticipate a melody coming... if you know the piece... and then physically you make a gesture as if you want to join in... then often I actually start singing it at that moment, and then I get a profound sense of satisfaction that it's happened – although I know that it's going to happen! And yet it never loses its breathtakingness – which it normally does when something's known to you. That's what's so peculiar about it – it's expected, you know what's coming, and yet every time there's a physical tension and release. Then when it's gone, there's no disappointment.

The first three Aspects outlined so far pave the way for our being drawn into music's own activity. When Susanna listens to the Mozart she finds herself joining in, but not literally by pretending that she's playing the piano that causes the musical sounds. Instead, she participates, both in mind and body, in the more subtle musical activity of sounds becoming tones and then developing in musical time, space and motion. She moves and is moved by this seemingly abstract process.

When we musick, we pick up on the activity of sounds becoming 'charged' by their dynamic and logical relationship to all of the tones around them, and through this creating a musical force field that choreographs their ongoing activity and potential meaning. As Zuckerkandl writes, 'Musical tones are conveyors of forces. Hearing music means hearing an action of forces ... to hear dynamic qualities is to hear what tones say' (1956, p. 37). He also suggests that we think of this conversion process as from tones into *symbols* – similarly to how the Christian cross is 'charged' by taking its place within a hugely complex system of relationships within a culturally located belief system.

In most musical systems, we hear this dynamic activity both sequentially (as melody) and vertically (as harmony).[4] Zuckerkandl suggests that this process of sounds becoming *music* begins from the gesture of a single charged tone, and elaborates itself into complex aural patterns of activity. As usual, this activity both mirrors everyday human intention and action, and passes beyond this, seemingly into an abstract patterning of its own.

Most phenomenologies of music explore this charged activity in reference to the Western diatonic system,[5] in which tones become active events through their

---

[4]   The same 'charging' happens with rhythmic phenomena, if in a different way. What's common across all musical phenomena is that a sound occurrence becomes a musical event, and is experienced in dynamic relation to the whole, and in relation to the intentions and interpretations of those jointly involved.

[5]   A similar phenomenon of the 'musical force field' could be explored in other musics, as the logic is that this is dependent on the relationship between both natural and cultural determinants.

positioning and movement within the musical space of the diatonic scale.[6] Try, for example, singing or hearing the tones of this scale in your head – moving upwards tone by tone. Notice how each step is not a neutral action, but rather how each tone becomes 'charged', both with a force that motivates it and a direction that orientates it towards the next. The scale pattern in the Western diatonic system establishes this dynamic 'force field' in which each tone operates, moving either 'away from' or 'towards' where it 'wants' to go. These forces in a scale have a strange 'cyclic' quality. If **1** is the 'home' or 'key' note, then the first move, **1→2** has a dynamic 'away-from' quality, as does **2→3** and **3→4**, until a partial 'half-way resting place is found' at the arrival at **5** (the 'dominant'); then **5→6** and **6→7** are further moves 'away from', until unexpectedly the move from **7→8** is experienced as a 'towards' or even 'arrival at'.[7]

'Real' melodies in all their individuality play themselves out within this natural dynamic field of the scale. Zuckerkandl writes that the scale sets the stage for the drama of tonal motion to happen. Experiencing music as musical activity is then to hear how each tone becomes active, and how the force within it is conveyed to the next tone (or one simultaneously sounding), creating meaningful motion in and through tones. We hear instantly, that is, what tones have to say – albeit mostly within the cultural 'language' of music with which we are familiar.

In the same way in which the quasi-spatial 'field' of tones operates, we can think of musical time and motion within experience. Beats have their own dynamic activity when organised into metrical patterns and when rhythms play across the metre. Our bodies dance to the repeated 1–2–3 metre of a waltz, whilst the musical quality of the waltz is to do with how the more individual rhythmic patterns play across this metre (in combination with the dynamic melodic patterns). Think, for example, how you experience *The Blue Danube* as more than just its '1–2–3/1–2–3' metre. Whilst this metre organises your steps, the interpenetrating dynamic fields of melody and rhythm give your dancing a lovely feeling of direction and flow.[8]

Experiencing music – whether of a piece we know, or an improvisation that's unfolding before our ears – means being within and amongst music's activity, and experiencing how it is simultaneously our eventful activity too.

Aspect 5: Musical Vitality

Eric stands up slowly and tentatively whilst the piano plays the introduction to 'You'll Never Walk Alone'. He hides his head behind his word sheet and is tentative coming in on the first note. His first phrase is breathy and quavery as he

---

[6]   The following is based on Zuckerkandl's account in *Sound and Symbol* (1956).

[7]   See Zuckerkandl 1956: chapter III, 'The System of Tones' (pp. 32–40), and chapter VIII, 'The True Motion of Tones' (pp. 88–116).

[8]   Such 'musical activity' is not necessarily physically enacted. A person who could not move could still potentially experience music's phenomenal movement and direction.

tries to master his nerves. But halfway through the first verse he begins to find his confidence, and his voice steadies and surges in tone and volume. Unfortunately, this means that he also rushes the tempo and the accompanist has not only to skilfully follow him a little so that they keep together, but also to emphasise the steady pulse so that Eric stabilises his timing. By the second verse he's found his nerve, and he looks out more confidently to the audience as he sings in a broad and generous sound, perfectly in shared timing with the pianist. As people clap, he breaks out into a smile and waves his arms from side to side.

৪১

Eric's musical experience, and ours if we were there listening to him, includes not just what happens musically, but also *how* it happens. This is the qualitative and dynamic side of musical activity and musical experience. *How* is a tone sounded? Confidently, or tentatively? *What* is the grain of the voice? Is it rich or breathy? *How* is the timing kept? *How* does a melodic phrase emerge? Strongly, tenderly and slowly – or with growing force, energy and speed?

To ask about this *how* dimension is to focus on how the music's performed, both in a technical and in a personal sense. In traditional music, the 'dynamics' of music are the expressive devices a musician uses in their performance of a piece of music to 'bring it to life' or to 'add feeling', as a music teacher might say. These devices include how to change intensity over time (*piano/forte, crescendo/ decrescendo*, etc.); how to stress and accent certain tones or rhythms (the 'weight' and 'force' of music as performed); how to make changes in tempo and pace (*accelerando, ritenuto*); and how to inflect the texture and timbre of the music through how you play.

All of these dimensions can be related to core experiences we have of what Daniel Stern calls the 'forms of vitality' of our own body and others' bodies. Ultimately, Stern writes, 'the dynamic aspects of experience are what 'aliveness' is about' (2010, p. 35). Our musical experiences naturally orient towards this *how* dimension. We discern this aspect because of the double listening we give to music – to what it is and to who is playing it, and perhaps even why. Within an ecological perspective, this 'musical *how*' is a vital dimension that encodes and communicates the human body and its qualities of aliveness and emotion, indicating the intentions of others and the possibilities for our own actions within a musicking event.[9]

৪১

As we saw in Part I, music only becomes real and active for us within musical worlds in which the community of minds and bodies that form our culture

---

[9] This aspect overlaps with human 'communicative musicality', which we'll explore further in Part III.

continually makes and remakes its musical forms, media, conventions and values. The specificity of the musical affordances that come from how our bodies and minds pick up and work within the eco-phenomenology of music (Aspects 1–5 above) can to an extent only be appropriated in relation to the overall cultural world in which we participate in specific acts of musicking. Ethnomusicology has warned us of the risks of formulating abstract musical universals from a Western perspective, given the enormous diversity of musical systems around the world. But surely there are nevertheless some limited musical universals that derive from how all humans share experiences of the functioning and moving body and its relationship to musicking? As the anthropologist John Blacking wrote, 'Many, if not all, of music's essential processes may be found in the constitution of the human body and in patterns of interaction of human bodies in society' (1973, p. x). This is to characterise an ecological perspective where the various nested systems – physical, social and cultural – work together to generate meaning and potential benefit for us within a particular situation.

The Flesh, Blood and Bone of Musical Experience

Imagine that, in continuing to read this book, you are relieved to come back from a dull meeting. You free your mind as you cycle through a wood, along a well-worn path to your goal – home. There you go immediately up into your study, in which you feel calm and contained; you force yourself to concentrate on an article (feeling the pressure to get to the end by tomorrow); focus on the page; and are soon weighing up the ideas, some of which attract you, if a few repel! But then you recall the friend who's slipped your mind, and feel the burden of guilt, lose track of the author's point, go over it again, and finally give in to the temptation of a glass of wine in order to unwind the tensions of the day and to lift your mood.

   Notice in this short sketch how closely the physical, cognitive and emotional dimensions are interfused, as you experience up/down, back/front, through and over, into/out of, beginning/end, path–goal, force/pressure, weight/burden, tension/relaxation, attraction/repulsion, freedom/containment, each of which is often carried across the different domains of everyday experience. This shows the fundamental continuity between all levels of our functioning: perceiving, thinking, feeling and acting. The philosopher Mark Johnson and linguist George Lakoff (Lakoff and Johnson 1980, 1999) have suggested possible mechanisms for this continuity in their study of 'embodied meaning' (also called 'metaphor/ schema theory'). This theory fuses phenomenological and pragmatic/ecological perspectives, and Mark Johnson (2007) has specifically applied it to the puzzle of musical experience. Unfortunately, like many of our previous theorists, Johnson talks only of listening to pre-composed music, not the full range of musicking. Despite this, the theory usefully points from an embodied perspective on musical experience towards its potential for a more ecological music-in-action perspective.

Mark Johnson writes, 'Thinking about how music moves us is … an excellent place to begin to understand how all meaning emerges in the flesh, blood, and bone of our embodied experience' (2007, p. 255). Schema theory suggests that our experience of music is based on a core metaphoric process.[10] In fact, as we've discussed earlier, any experience *is* just this continual interactive psychophysical coupling with the world around us, and the ongoing 'carrying over' between 'bodying', thinking and feeling through what are called 'image schemas'.

Look back again at the first paragraph of this section and see how both the physical actions and their 'carried-over' mental aspects are based on very simple body-based aspects of everyday human experience: UP–DOWN,[11] BACK–FRONT, SOURCE–PATH–GOAL, CONTAINER, PASSAGE, PRESSURE, ATTRACTION, FOCUS, BALANCE, TENSION. Johnson describes these 'image schema' as 'a dynamic, recurring pattern of organism-environment interaction … as basic structures of sensori-motor experience by which we encounter a world that we can understand and act within' (2007, p. 136). Image schemas organise our everyday experience seamlessly across physical, emotional and cognitive domains.

Johnson considers the arts, and music in particular, as exemplary of his thesis that our most fundamental meaning making is grounded in body-based experience, and that meaning does not have to be language based. As he writes in his chapter 'Music and the Flow of Meaning',

> music is meaningful because it can present the flow of human experience, feeling, and thinking in concrete, embodied forms – and this is meaning in its deepest sense. A fundamental fact about music is that it appeals to our felt sense of life … Our very experience of musical meaning is fundamentally shaped by conceptual metaphors that are grounded in our bodily experience. (Johnson 2007, p. 236)

These 'conceptual metaphors' are not just imaginative projections 'onto' the music: 'such image schemas actually constitute the structure and define the quality of our musical experience. They are in and of the music as experience; they *are* the structure of the music' (Johnson 2007, p. 258).

Johnson suggests that three metaphor schemas underpin our experience of music:[12]

- **MOVING MUSIC** – based on MOVING TIMES
- **MUSICAL LANDSCAPE** – based on MOVING OBSERVER

---

[10]   Metaphor, from meta = across, pherein = to carry over.

[11]   Capitalising these 'schemas' is a convention Johnson uses.

[12]   They are not the only ones, of course – just the foundational ones (which also relate most clearly to the phenomenological categories we've examined in this chapter – musical time, space and motion). For a more complex account of music and schema/metaphor theory, see Johnson 2007 and its many references to other studies, and Aigen 2005.

- **MUSIC AS MOVING FORCE** – based on LOCATION EVENT–STRUCTURE

As we've seen previously, there's typically a fusion of time and space when we think and talk about music, and these 'schemas' explain why. We experience music in and as motion because of how the 'source domains' (as Johnson calls them) for such experience originate from our bodily experiences of witnessing movement, and of moving and being moved as a body in time.

In the first metaphor (MOVING MUSIC), music is in motion relative to us. We watch musical events moving towards and past us (as Susanna, above, lives through a Mozart piece she knows, anticipating a favourite phrase 'coming', then 'passing'). Technically (according to schema theory), the 'source domain' is therefore our sensori-motor experience of physical objects in spatial motion and our perception of these; the 'target domain' is musical events in motion and our lived experience of this process. The link between the two is theoretically metaphorical, but 'real' in terms of our perceptual–cognitive experience. As with real objects moving past us, we also talk about music proceeding in steps and leaps, and we experience it flowing, racing, suspended, exploding, and so on.

The second metaphor (MUSICAL LANDSCAPE) adds the complementary experience of our moving along *with* the musical motion, and this derives from our basic bodily experience of moving our bodies through a physical terrain. Our experience of music in terms of this schema is therefore of being in and among musical events in motion, at a particular point according to where the music 'is', then moving along with it. We participate in the music's unfolding in time, move in motion with it, are 'transported' by it. We *are* the music whilst the music lasts.

A third metaphor is needed to complete this picture: a 'cause' for musical motion. MUSIC AS MOVING FORCE derives from a complex schema relating to our fundamental bodily understanding that motion is shaped by physical forces that include attraction, inertia, blockage, and so on. We move ourselves, and are moved by other forces. Music itself is experienced as a motivating, dynamic force, as causing its own motion. This is perhaps why we talked about 'being moved' by music, of being 'blown away'. The dynamic motion of music moves the hearer or player from one place (= state) to another. Though Johnson does not make this connection, the obvious parallel is to Zuckerkandl's concept of music existing within its own dynamic field of tonal and metrical forces that operate on 'tone events' and give us the experience of living within their 'play of forces', of 'going away from' and 'towards'.

Schema theory leads to the same kinds of awkward questions that we met with Zuckerkandl's and Scruton's ideas about music: *Is musical motion/force real?* The response is similar: that a core metaphor is 'real' in terms of our experience and describes 'what' we experience phenomenologically when we experience music. It is a 'phenomenal' reality in the sense of its taking place between different domains of our being – from the core 'mapping' within our physical experience to its 'carrying over' through the metaphor schemas into our imaginative, social and cultural activity.

ಬ

Johnson's theory aligns well with the various ecological perspectives on music we have explored in Parts I and II. His approach also places music within and amongst our everyday embodied and embedded experience of the world. Just how we experience music – and what help it can give us – will depend on what kind of body we have; what kind of enculturation and personal history we have; and, lastly, the immediate context in which the possible meanings of music are accessible, and can take shape for us. In summarising the 'meaning of the body' in relation to cultural material and activities like music, Johnson writes:

> Meaning is a matter of relations and connections grounded in bodily organism–
> environment coupling, or interaction. The meaning of something is its relations,
> actual or potential, to other qualities, things, events, and experiences ... Aspects
> of our experience take on meaning insofar as they activate for us their relations
> to other actual or possible aspects of our experience. (2007, p. 265)

Our specifically musical experiences surely match this statement. They are not only highly individual and special to us, but also a shared part of the social fabric; they both retain their musical specificity and hold at least the potential to carry over beyond music to our lives as a whole.

Chapter 5

Helpful Musical Experiences

Experience is enacted by conscious beings with the help of the world.

Alva Noë[1]

... music provides us with a domain in which to explore and experience 'what it is like to be human' in terms that are on the one hand familiar, and on the other transformative.

Eric Clarke[2]

How do these perspectives on musical experience relate to situations where music is called upon to help? They suggest, perhaps, that music's help is potentially there for the taking, but that we need to attend more closely to how skilled access through musical experience can be achieved by ourselves or facilitated for others.

Music therapy theorist Ken Aigen (2005, 2009) has suggested how two of the theories introduced in the last two chapters are relevant to music therapy. Aigen offers the image of Zuckerkandl and Johnson approaching the territory of musical experience from opposite directions and nearly touching in a shared area. Whilst Johnson's schema theory pictures our general embodied human experience reaching towards musical experience, Zuckerkandl's detailed characterisation of the phenomenology of the purely musical world reaches towards universal human experience. Reconciling these theories is probably neither possible nor desirable, but what can perhaps be gained from their juxtaposition is a better orientation towards how musical experiences can be helpful.

Aigen suggests that, if schemas show the basic bodily templates underlying our musical experience, one way of looking at music therapy experiences is to consider the nature of the schemata underlying them. A music therapist might begin, for example, by assessing how aspects of a client's lifeworld have been restricted by illness, disability or deprivation in terms of core schema. For example, for a person with a congenital physical disability who has always used a wheelchair, the UP–DOWN schema will probably be restricted for them. For someone with a stroke and a weak side, both LEFT–RIGHT and BALANCE will normally be affected. Someone with a congenital sensory impairment (blindness or deafness) will have differently developing SOURCE–PATH–GOAL and FORCE schemas, and their consequent experiences. For someone with a temporary sensory

---

[1]   Noë 2010, p. 47.

[2]   Clarke 2011, p. 209.

impairment, ORIENTATION will perhaps be an issue (physiologically, but also cognitively, emotionally and socially). For many people with a mental illness, the CONTAINER schema may be distorted by perceptual, emotional or relational factors. These examples may seem rather material and physical at first sight. But we must keep in mind the central insight of schema theory: that our bodily sensori-motor experience is the foundation for all other complex forms of subsequent experience: cognitive, affective, relational, social, aesthetic. As Johnson states, 'experience comes whole and continuous' (2007, p. 145).

Aigen's suggestion is that certain musical experiences – particularly those that are professionally mediated by a music therapist and that happen within the security of a music therapy relationship – can be thought of in relation to such core schemas being activated to function in a compensatory or enhancing fashion for people. In all of the scenarios in the previous paragraph, music (as musicking) can provide what Aigen calls an 'alternative experiential domain' (2005, p. 201). This relates to the eco-phenomenology we explored in the previous chapter – with its demonstration of the specifically musical aspects of activity, direction, orientation, balance and containment. The value and meaning of a given musical experience for a client relates to how it carries over to other dimensions of their embodied experience, and to the varying needs for compensation or enhancement there. This goes back to the fundamental question of how the musical and the para-musical can become helpfully linked.

Many clients in music therapy are not able to speak to us about the quality or usefulness of their music/music therapy experiences. However, as Aigen writes, 'the understanding of music evidenced in the person's engagement with it is the clinical rationale' (2005, p. 176). Therapists are usually, that is, able to directly hear and see how a musical experience is helping.

But there are also people who can reflect on and talk eloquently about their helpful musical experiences. In the next section, we shall revisit two such people we first met in the Introduction: Christina, who discovers her own form of musical help, and Louis, who can reflect in detail about his music therapy experiences. Both experience a particular kind of reorientation that comes from an active seeking and finding of the helpful affordances of musical space, time and motion.

Christina's Musical Reorientation

> 'Two days after the operation I needed music,' says Christina. 'I'd only brought two CDs with me to the hospital, both with music stemming from the Orthodox faith – Arvo Pärt and John Tavener ... I saw them as good-for-me music.'

Christina's brain surgery had involved damaging the auditory nerve to the left ear and Christina finds herself disorientated by the trauma at every level in the following months: physically, cognitively and emotionally. Music has always been an important part of her life and she instinctively turns to it for help at this time. Her rich and detailed account of this self-administered music therapy brings out many of the aspects of helpful musical experience that we've been exploring.

Importantly, music has always been intimate and embodied for Christina, ever since as a child she used music as a 'carpet' to dance on. This 'participatory' relationship with music and her propensity to moving with music increases during her rehabilitation:

> Since my operation I've had the experience of the movement of music reinforced. I've been extremely sensitive to everything in my environment – especially sound and music. When I heard music I liked there was an involuntary movement. Feet would start trembling and wobbling, and then their movement would become rhythmic. At first I was embarrassed, then I thought, 'Oh just let it happen!'

We could say that the MUSICAL LANDSCAPE schema is still active with Christina. She still finds herself travelling along with music's journey. But Christina is more strategic with music now, not simply enjoying its flow. She has an instinctive feel for how music can help with the spatial disorientation she experiences after surgery, but the way she expresses this is interesting in its active stance: 'So I appropriated music to orient me in space'. Whilst she doesn't use the word 'affordance', it's clear that her use of music is based either consciously or instinctively on an understanding of potential musical affordances, and how to mobilise these.

At one level, the account might seem to depict a rather mechanical and physical solution to a problem that had been caused by a 'mechanical fault'. The severing of the auditory nerve resulted in deafness in one ear, and in associated problems of physical balance and orientation (also perhaps associated with the tumour, pre-surgery). This is quite natural, as the physiology of the ear supports the overlapping functions of regulating hearing, balance, orientation and movement. The various mechanisms of the inner ear not only regulate the orientation of the head (up–down), but also orientate us to things, and to movements in relation to us in our immediate surroundings. However, it is still relatively unclear how the physical mechanisms translate through brain processes into conscious qualitative experiences of orientation.

To an extent, Christina's appropriation of music as an orientating device therefore seems entirely logical. She's not able to find her 'own' internal orientation, so she looks for a way of locating this 'externally', in the music. But this is far from a simple mechanical procedure of the music's orientating her. Rather, Christina's precise account tells us rather how the music's help comes from a subtle blend of what its phenomenology affords and what she is able to pick up and 'action' for strategic use at this time.

Her account distinguishes various dimensions of music (she's precise as a musician). First, there's the character of the music as a whole and its key features:

> I chose these particular pieces – *Tabula Rasa* and *Fratres* – because there are big blocks of sound with simple descending gestures, all quite simple, nothing too dramatic, or with too big an emotional charge, or too thick a texture, which I'd have found confusing.

Her particular problem at this time is a temporary loss of orientation to up–down, right–left, front–back:

> I felt at that time like a thing without gravity or direction, which was contained only by the faster spinning in space of the music [...] It was if the music was like a gyroscope,[3] turning and moving, turning in an orbit with 360° movements, but at the same time having a direction, which I absorbed at a time when I had no sense of what was upright, what was floor level. It was the musical path that gave me equilibrium. The spatial property of music seems all the more bizarre given that my hearing is now monophonic. But despite this flatness now of my equipment... just the one ear, music implied depth – in both senses of the word. Perhaps the relative movement in music implies a three-dimensional world: up–down, side-to-side, back-and-forward....

This takes us away from the purely physical and mechanical level into the more complex area of music's phenomenology. For there is something 'bizarre' (as Christina remarks) in how she experiences the direction, motion and spaces of the music as actively useful. As we've previously noted, it's not clear that music actually possesses any of these features in a 'real' way that matches everyday bodily orientation, direction and spatial order. But what the musical space *can* do, as Zuckerkandl suggested, is to make space alive for us, even if it has different properties to 'external' physical space. From the modest electronically produced sounds coming from a small portable CD player, Christina manages to make spaces that stabilise her world, and that she appropriates as what she calls 'musical hand-rails'.

Seen from a schema theory perspective, Christina's musical experience activates core schemas that are directly compensatory for what she lacks. The orientational schemas UP–DOWN, SOURCE–PATH–GOAL and CONTAINER work in dynamic relation with the musical movement schemas MUSICAL OBSERVER and MUSICAL LANDSCAPE. The properties of music's 'virtual' space, time and motion afford Christina experiences as if they are normal sounds in the everyday environment, specifying useful information for orientation and stabilisation.

I want to emphasise that it's important to resist the temptation to see this help in too mechanistic a way. Christina chooses the Tavener and Pärt pieces for what they afford as a whole. As she listens, the music takes her beyond just the 'physical' world, reorientating and reconnecting her with other dimensions of her lifeworld.

---

[3]   A gyroscope uses a spinning ball in motion to give equilibrium to the thing it's fixed within.

As well as a pleasurable sound, she describes the music as 'another world than the one immediately around me':

> ... beyond the properties of the music itself – though I'm not sure you can distinguish this – there's the place where the music was recorded, which I've always felt very sensitive to. You can feel the space where it originated. And I felt the spaces of this music were nice spaces, large... they didn't make me feel small or hemmed in. They were expansive and allowed me to grow, like in a cathedral or a big Victorian railway station. I knew this was religious music... and it was this that helped me feel something about people as wonderful and enabled.

Here, the continuity of a musical ecology meets Christina's need for social, spiritual and existential reorientation too after her trauma, the necessary sense in the early stages of rehabilitation that the world is still habitable and meaningful. As the philosopher Sarah Ahmed (2006) comments, orientation is not just a matter of aligning, but also of comfortably inhabiting our body and our world. For people like Christina, the challenge is to feel 'at home' again in their lifeworld as a whole, including its social and aesthetic dimensions. The two CDs help Christina also to orientate and inhabit something of the physical and emotional space in which the music was recorded, and even the spiritual attitude of the composers. Together, these qualities afford support and sustenance in a way that is accessible in the most direct manner through the simplest of means.

Christina tells me that, when she played this same music later in her recovery, it didn't have the same effect. This is a telling remark that underlines the key aspect of this example. In the original, acute situation, Christina 'gave herself' to this particular music, with its particular features and qualities that matched her then-current needs. She appropriated its seamlessly connected web of physical, psychological and spiritual affordances. But the music did not itself orientate Christina. She actively created and enacted these helpful musical experiences through which she could begin to orientate herself.

Louis's Musical Reorientation

We also met Louis briefly in the Introduction, when I described how his longstanding enjoyment of music is disturbed by a severe episode of mental illness. Voices in his head invade any music he plays or listens to. By the time Louis comes to music therapy with me, this phase of his illness has passed yet has left him both apprehensive about music and suffering from a debilitating long-term depression. He describes how his low mood leaves him stranded in an unpleasant and anxious present, where he typically sits doing nothing.

As with Christina, Louis's account of how music comes to help him again gives us an invaluable insight into his musical experience.[4] For Louis, the character of his illness means that he's not able to mobilise his musical resources to help him at this time, which is why he comes to music therapy. Louis's story is also valuable as an account of how musicking in this context affords him a way of reflecting on his life and illness 'through' his musical experiences, using powerful words and images. Louis starts talking about this with a theme that keeps surfacing in the sessions: music, 'good time', and 'bad time':

Louis: *I don't feel this is just therapy, but this is my participation in music: it gives me a sense of fulfilment, and of actively doing something useful and good. When I came to these sessions I could be a bit depressed at the beginning... but usually during the therapy the mood lifts up and it also helps me concentrate on other things. Because when one is making music one really needs to concentrate: you need to listen to the other person; what they are making; what the sounds are. You have to put two heads together to make music together....*

I think basically music gives a person some insight into the past, the present and the future. My way of putting it is that you need time to make music, but music is not time; and time is not music. And if you just sit there, doing nothing... time goes by, you just hear the clock tick. And usually nothing happens – you can sit there for hours. And I think that by the end of such hours, if you just sit there, you become very anxious about time passing by. But if you make music, or listen to music as the time goes by, you feel that the time that's gone is being utilised in a very useful way.... And so I think in a sense music is like a brush with some paint – it paints a picture in time....

Gary: What does it paint a picture of?

L: *Well, it can paint a picture of anything! It could be a picture of oneself, or a picture of music making, of the musicians... or a picture of the future.... It's very interesting... when I'm playing music, the brain just goes completely blank... except there is music! And I seem to have forgotten everything... everything else goes to the back of the brain – and I become focused, and I'm thinking only about music.... Because if someone keeps thinking about things all the time, and he or she will be thinking too much. And thinking too much will lead to a consequence of having too many thoughts on the brain. And having too many thoughts on the brain will lead to a consequence of anxiety... and also the person who thinks a lot would not be able to concentrate to do something....*

---

[4]   This material comes from a research interview with Louis that took place after ten sessions of individual music therapy. Louis generously agreed to it being used to help any further attempts to understand the music therapy process.

G: So the music helps you to focus down on one thing at a time?

L: *Well, not only that, but the music itself.... The thing is that as I'm either with the drum or the cymbal or the metalophone, I need to think ahead... of what the next note's going to be. So it gives me a sense of planning... immediate planning... what to do next. Because in the past, when I was very ill... I could not think about what to do next. I was so occupied by the present and the past.... But by playing music – particularly in this environment – gives me a chance to quiet down... and then concentrate on planning the next note....*

G: So there's a kind of musical future for you? How does that make you feel, if this is possible for you? What's the effect on your mood-state?

L: *I think it lifts the mood... and it sort of gives me a sense of a little light at the end of the tunnel. So planning what the next note's going to be would in a sense lead me to think about planning the next step in my life... because there was a time when I thought there would not be a future... there was a time when I was so ill I thought, 'That's it... that's the end....' But I think basically I experience here the music painting a picture of the present and the future to me. And that picture basically is some light at the end of the tunnel!*

છ૦

The musical experiences Louis has within music therapy afford him a variety of different things that help to compensate for some of the more troubling aspects of his illness. The music therapy situation and music itself function as a CONTAINER schema, helping him safely participate, concentrate, and become absorbed in something that he finds satisfying and productive. This allows him to create a musical relationship with the therapist and to feel safe about sharing intimate experiences with another person.

What stands out most in his narrative is how Louis uses music and the music therapy situation to 'work on time', his main anxiety related to his illness. Features of his musical experience provide a template for reflecting *about* time in his life from a more benevolent and reassuring perspective.

As he learns to improvise in his sessions, Louis changes the way he experiences himself in music. From being a rather anxious 'outsider' who's fearful of how he might react to music, he relaxes into its emerging creative flow. That is, the MUSICAL LANDSCAPE schema becomes activated again for him. Through this engagement, he accesses the particular phenomenology of music's time that we characterised in the previous chapter. In contrast to his usual anxiety about the 'empty' clock time of *chronos*, improvising music affords a compensatory experience of time as *kairos*, where there's an active and 'filled' interpenetration between past–present–future. When Louis talks of 'planning what the next note's going to be', he is describing this contrast between the 'empty time' he fears and the more active and hopeful time that he discovers in music.

This comment also suggests that the core SOURCE–PATH–GOAL schema comes into play, carrying across the qualities of purposeful musical direction into their everyday bodily and psychological experiences. We also saw earlier how Zuckerkandl explained how the experience of musical motion and direction comes from the ongoing dynamic field in which tones 'want' or 'need' to travel from somewhere, towards or away from somewhere. This evokes the MUSIC AS MOVING FORCE schema. Musicking provides Louis with a template (based on 'planning what the next note's going to be') for profiling broader patterns of motivation, action and thinking.

At this complex level, Louis 'carries over' his embodied musical experience into his ongoing reflections on how music, time and his illness are woven together in his lifeworld. Increasingly, Louis is able to mobilise in a practical sense, and to conceptualise, a different attitude towards time. Like many people suffering from chronic depression, time has lost its complexity and richness and become just 'bad' for him. Louis finds in music therapy, however, a compensatory experience of 'good musical time' that helps him model a more habitable image of time for his wider life. In short, Louis's musicalised version of time is a hopeful one for him – it gives him a way of reflecting on an existential dimension through a very concrete and embodied experience. Music has again become a way that Louis cares for himself.

The Foundations of Musical Experience

Musical experience shows up in the active relationship between musical things, people and situations. We've seen how musical experience is better seen as something done and enacted – a case of skilful access – rather than as something that only happens within or to us. It certainly doesn't just happen in our heads, but rather *between* us and the musical world that we become involved with, and live within. What is musically present and available has the potential to help. Music's specific features, properties, qualities and processes form the foundation of music's help in the four key areas of the broader musical ecology that we'll explore in the remainder of this book: the creation and maintenance of musical personhood, relationship, community, and transcendence.

PART III
Musical Personhood

Are we human beings because we are musical?

John Blacking

Man is a musical animal, that is, a being predisposed to music and in need of music … In this sense, musicality is not something one may or may not have, but something that is constitutive of man.

Victor Zuckerkandl

Music doesn't just happen, it is what we make it, and what we make of it. People think through music, decide who they are through it, express themselves through it.

Nicholas Cook

Personhood is a relational condition, and I am a person insofar as I can enter into personal relations with others like me.

Roger Scruton

Music is about the self alive, about the time and tensions of moving. Its experience is free of the named facts of memory, it can think or feel in new ways about the future – about who the person alive in the music is, what kind of person 'I am and will be', with what hopes and anxieties, and about the people who are 'my friends'.

Colwyn Trevarthen

Chapter 6
Musical Recognition

To be is to be perceived … Perception brings into being and maintains the being of whatever is perceived.

James Hillman[1]

'Piano Man'

In the summer of 2005, a mystery briefly attracts the international media. On the Isle of Sheppey, a distressed man is found walking along the beach in wet clothes, as if he's come out of the sea. Mute and confused, he's taken to a local psychiatric facility. A BBC television news presenter shows a picture of a young, blond man and asks, 'Does anyone know who he is?' Nothing helps identify him; even his clothes have had their labels removed. Captioned 'The Mystery Man', his story is avidly followed by people around the world.

Because he can't or won't speak, his identity can't be established; and neither does any family member or friend 'claim' or name him. Interpreters of various languages are recruited, and a doctor diagnoses 'retrograde amnesia'.

When he draws a grand piano on a piece of paper, staff take him to the hospital chapel. He sits and plays the piano there, to the staff's surprise. 'I cannot get within a yard of him without him becoming very anxious,' says his social worker, 'yet at the piano he comes alive. I can stand close to him and he is oblivious. It is extraordinary.' His new media identity is born – 'Piano Man'.

Comment on the story spreads and 'Piano Man' turns into a contemporary parable. BBC Radio 4's 'Thought for the Day' meditates on how he exemplifies the modern dilemma of identity – how we are only someone through being known and missed by others. 'He seems to have fallen out of life,' says the commentator. 'He's a nobody.'

The Guardian newspaper headline in May 2005 reads (with suitable pun), 'Music therapy could hold key to identity of mystery "piano man"'. His social worker says, 'The only way is if we get expert people working with him who are able to use his music and get his identity'. He is described as 'a brilliant concert pianist, an autistic savant, or an asylum seeker'. But whilst one report describes 'a four-hour concert-standard performance' playing themes from Tchaikovsky for other patients, another states he only plays one note continuously.

---

[1]   Hillman 1996, p. 127.

By August 2005, the story collapses and the *Evening Standard* reports, 'Piano Man saga ends on a discordant note'. After four months he suddenly tells staff that he's from Bavaria, is gay, and has two sisters. The German Embassy contacts his parents, who confirm his identity, and he is released and repatriated. The press ask whether he faked his symptoms of mental illness and the hospital announces that they discharged him after a marked improvement in his condition. The Missing Persons Helpline issue a statement: 'He was with us as an unidentified person, but we believe he has now been identified so he is no longer with us.'

જી

Hoax or not, this strange case serves as a good introduction to the key concern of Part III: how maintaining personhood and establishing and developing identity are two interconnected basic human needs that are crucial to our ongoing health and wellbeing. Music can often help with both.

Piano Man is fortunate in how people strive to maintain his personhood. As soon as he's found on the beach, he's consistently acknowledged and treated as an intact person despite his identity being unknown. By 'identity', I mean not only his individuality and character, but also those distinguishing categories such as 'German', 'middle class', 'teacher' that help to stabilise our social identity. Piano Man catches the media's attention because of how unusual his situation is in contemporary society. Even as a stranger somewhere we can usually identify ourselves to others, such that normal social interaction can follow. Because this man couldn't or wouldn't do this for himself, others try to do it for him in order to stabilise 'who he is'. They suggest possibilities based on his nationality, status (asylum seeker) or pathology (autistic savant, mental health patient). 'Mystery Man' serves as a provisional identity for him.

When he draws and subsequently plays a piano, there's relief that a more stable identity is possible – as 'Piano Man'. Music gives both him and others a resource to help navigate this unusual situation in a variety of ways. A musical identity is a way of his being *someone* for others ('a musician'), able to be identified through his action and skill. This musical identity then helps him build a social identity through performing for other patients. Finally, music gives him an expressive medium in which to characterise himself – not only *as* 'musical', but also through how others perceive him playing in a particular way, performing himself musically. The *dénouement* of the case is ironically prosaic, showing how everyday categories of identity – gay, Bavarian, two sisters – quickly reinstate him as normal and no longer interesting to professionals or to the media.

Many people around the world identified with Piano Man as some kind of everyman who exemplifies issues of identity, value and belonging in modern society. That this story turns into a parable perhaps highlights a more general anxiety about personhood and identity today. Do people ever really know us? How easily can we lose our identity and personhood? Are we just the abstract social categories of our identity? Who *are* we if nobody knows us, nobody claims us? How do we show people who we are, especially if we can't use words? Without a stable identity, do we become a non-person, an object? How will people treat us then?

These questions have been particularly linked to the problems of people living with autism, dementia and mental illness. These conditions can disrupt the very basis of personhood – being acknowledged by others as a whole person. This is turn influences how these people think and feel about themselves in relation to others – their subjective identity. These are at once practical, philosophical and ethical issues.

The original Latin word *persona*[2] suggests that we are 'sounded beings' first and foremost, whatever roles we take. A baby immediately characterises herself through sound, and the mother responds, giving the child her first, aural mirror. Our subsequent development as people is likewise partly bound up with how we sound, and how we are heard. This is all possible because of what I'll call our 'core musicality', a faculty that is common to every human being.

Part III explores how this shared 'core musicality' underwrites 'musical personhood' – the acknowledgement of the full humanity of others that comes through sensing them musically. Core musicality is also at the root of how we can explore, define and develop who we are, and with whom we belong, through our musical identities. Fortunately, it seems that core musicality is remarkably resilient in the face of illness, disability, trauma or deprivation. When these conditions threaten or undermine who we feel we are, and how others see us, music can help ensure our continuing personhood, whilst our ongoing musical identities can provide resources for coping and recovering.

Recognising People Musically

Paul Nordoff admired Elgar's characterisations of his friends in the *Enigma Variations*, and one of Nordoff's party pieces was to sit at the piano and improvise witty musical portraits of people, then to see whether they recognised themselves and how they responded. However, in 1959, when Nordoff was first exploring music therapy, he found himself in a situation where this skill of musical characterisation was put to more serious use. He and Robbins were visiting a school for children with special needs run according to the principles of Rudolf Steiner. The head teacher suggested that Nordoff and Robbins begin by working with a recently admitted five-year-old boy. When Nordoff said he wasn't sure how to start, he was told: 'Just go and play music with him, and tell us what you find.' The boy, Johnny, was an extremely withdrawn child with no speech, and was heavily medicated to calm his disturbed behaviour. He was brought to the room where Nordoff had a piano, and left there. As Johnny moved around the room, Nordoff began improvising

[2] *Persona* first meant an actor's mask in Greek times, through which a character sounded. It gradually shifted to its modern meaning of 'an individual' who is recognised and treated as human and who looks and sounds unique.

music to the slow pace of his steps. Then, on an intuition, he improvised on a Chinese pentatonic scale, and Johnny's mood and pacing seemed to respond to the easy, open character of the music, his steps getting lighter. Experimentally, Nordoff changed the idiom – shifting to an 'altered pentatonic' that had slightly more dissonance. Johnny cried. Nordoff changed back to the open pentatonic and his crying stopped. A few repeats of this process confirmed an understanding that subsequently became a principle of Nordoff–Robbins music therapy: that not only can specifically tailored, improvised music often make contact with children like Johnny, but it also gives a way of recognising and exploring *who they are in music*. That is, we can recognise who a person *is*, and call *to* them, through making music *with* them. As with Piano Man, music elicited something crucial about this boy that was not available in other ways.

During his subsequent months of music therapy, Johnny continued to listen acutely to Nordoff's music, but didn't go on to actively play himself. So it was his varying receptive responses to specific musical elements that gave an indication of his sensitivities and preferences. However, other children joined in quickly with Nordoff's music, using drums and other percussion instruments. Just *how* they played, Nordoff and Robbins realised, quickly built a detailed 'musical portrait' of how they were – physically, emotionally and relationally. This showed up in the way they played rhythms or sang melodically, how they formed phrases, and how they could vary pace or intensity. In responding to these musical specifics, and also to the general mood of 'their' music, they revealed something of who they were.

Aspects of these children's disabilities and abilities were also shown in ways that had often not been apparent outside of music. Nordoff and Robbins talked of a 'musical signature' that a child makes through their playing, and of how the therapists were able to chart the unfolding 'musical geography' of a child as they continued in therapy and began emerging as 'musical persons' in distinct and vibrant ways.

ఞ

In an early film of Nordoff and Robbins's work in a special school in Denmark, you see a child come into the music room fearful and uncertain. The music Nordoff improvises to greet him is warm and reassuring, and he's gradually coaxed into playing on a drum to the clear beat of a tonal march. Another child comes in sluggish and unfocused, and is met by music that has intermittent sharp and arousing sounds in a less predictable rhythm. This music gets her attention and wakes up her musical response. For each child shown in this film, Nordoff's musical characterisation meets the child exactly where they are and then calls them further into musicking. How they respond or not gives a fuller picture of their character, their current limitations and their future possibilities. In their ways of playing with him, Nordoff suggests that these children are implicitly stating: 'Here I am; this is me; I can do *this*!'

This work in the 1960s contributed to an important shift in thinking about how music could help disabled children. Previously, music teachers had mostly just sung pre-composed songs to the children, expecting them to fit in. Instead of this, Nordoff created improvised music that he shaped precisely for each child. He made their music from their immediate qualities and character. His music not only adapted to their limitations, but also drew out their musical character and potential, allowing the children to sound out in the world as musical persons. Paul Nordoff talked about this personal and improvisational process as giving a child the message,

> 'I accept you. I understand you. I want you. Here is music for you. Here I am, there you are. And eventually we can create something together.' And then comes the child breaking out in an expression of himself through music which can always be structured at any moment.[3]

The principle is the same whether in Elgar's *Enigma Variations* or in Nordoff's party trick, or in the profound work with these children: that a person can be perceived musically, and then called to through a musical characterisation. This involves recognition, acceptance and understanding – three vital human responses to another person. This simple yet profound principle has guided much music therapy since, when working with many different types of clients.[4] The question each time is, *How can music be used to recognise and encourage the development of a person, when their personhood or identity is threatened?*

So, when music calls to people and asks them musical questions, how do they answer?

ɞ

A woman I worked with on a locked psychiatric ward was giving no answers, I was told. As her parents had taken her to the hospital, she was 'someone' in a factual sense – she at least had a name, Jay, and a social identity, 'daughter'. But her continued muteness and strange stillness made it seemingly impossible for the staff to find out anything more about her and what was troubling her. 'We can't get a grasp on who she is,' a nurse said to me. She seemed, as her psychiatrist put it, to be on 'psychic retreat'. I'm asked to see what I can do. I visit her room.

Jay hardly moves. She gives nothing away of who she is or of how she feels. Her body language is also still, quiet, frozen. She searches my eyes slightly, but makes no other movements or response to questions or invitations. I try to perceive Jay musically, listening to the precise quality of her silence and stillness, attending closely to the small gestures she makes – to any energy and direction they have.

---

[3] From the film Irvin *Can Beat the Drum* (1972) made by Norwegian Stage Broadcasting about Nordoff and Robbins's work. See Robbins 2005, p. 204.

[4] For more on Nordoff–Robbins's music therapy in relation to 'musical portraits', see Nordoff and Robbins 1971/2004, 1977/2007; Robbins 2005.

This is who she is 'musically' at the moment. Can I make contact with her at this level? Could this help me understand her?

I try communicating within a purely musical channel, giving her a small hand-drum and a stick, turning away from eye contact. I play a few beats on my drum, a musical question or invitation to her. To my surprise, she gives a few fleeting, tentative beats in answer. Then she stops and retreats again into stillness. A few visits later, there's a breakthrough between us. As part of my playing to her, I offer the cliché rhythm *da da-da daa daa...* – and Jay completes it, **DA, DA!**, with a flourish of sudden energy and a small smile that nobody has yet seen on her. With this musical moment of contact, something happens to Jay – she emerges a step from her psychic 'hiding place' and is partly knowable and contactable by another person. Her 'musical character' emerges first, perhaps because music is safer than words – which we later find have betrayed her so badly. She is willing to be 'known musically' for the time being, and something of herself comes back into the open. She becomes a social being again, able to share something musically with another.

ဆ

Music used in this specialist way helps restore basic contact between people.[5] Jay later told me that she experienced how in music therapy I was really listening to her despite her unusual state. It gave her a sense of someone else recognising her at a time when she felt her self slipping away and nobody able to help her catch it.

ဆ

When I started working in a rural hospital in Germany, my music therapist colleague Dagmar Gustorff asked me whether I wanted to see some new work she was doing. She'd been giving sessions to a man on the neurology ward who'd suddenly fallen into a coma and had been taken to the intensive care unit. Having had such an intimate relationship with him in music before this, she felt that she couldn't abandon him, so she continued with the therapy even though the man was now unconscious. This decision was unusual for the time, as music therapists seldom worked with patients in non-conscious states.

Suitably attired in protective clothing and mask, I watched Dagmar work with this man. Ironically, although the patients in this unit were passive and silent, the machinery that kept them alive was surprisingly loud, with mechanical pumping sounds, beeps and clicks. It felt an unnerving and impersonal soundscape, into which Dagmar added music in a very particular way. She began by standing close to the patient, holding his hand, and observing and listening for a while to the few remaining signs left of who this person was, of 'where' he currently was. She tried, she said, to listen to this man in exactly the same way that she'd done when he was fully conscious and playing music with her in the music therapy room downstairs.

---

[5]   This case is discussed in more detail within a chapter focusing on theories of musical communication within music therapy in Ansdell and Pavlicevic 2005.

For the music of this person *was* still discernable. The quality and tempo of his breathing was visible by the movement of his chest, and his heart rate was indicated by monitors above the bed. These music-like features of his bodily functioning were currently the only remaining signs of his identity. When Dagmar sang to him, her voice was quiet but intensely focused, in an improvised single-line melody that entrained with his breathing tempo. She also reflected in her singing what she perceived of his emotional state in that moment, or of any micro-level responses he gave by seemingly delaying his breath just a fraction in order to match Dagmar's phrasing. The qualities of melody seemed very important to this encounter. Melody somehow counteracted the physical and mechanical qualities of rhythm in this setting, and lifted the patient's body music into the more purposeful future of tones reaching forwards. After ten minutes of music, his breathing had calmed and his agitation lessened. But something else was happening through this unusual musical relationship that was far from a medical outcome. When conscious much later, this man reported that he'd been aware of music in a dream. It had called him back to life.[6]

I found this work incredibly powerful. The patients in this setting seemed so isolated and lost, surrounded mainly by the noise of the machines keeping them alive. But here too was a single concentrated human presence in Dagmar's music – not just observing and treating them, but recognising and acknowledging their personhood and calling to their precarious identity. Some patients were able to give responses to the music that they couldn't manage to any other stimulus, and through this gave important evidence of responsiveness and potential.

Dagmar said that her attitude to these patients was simply to accept them just as they were – not to think of them as lacking anything, but as still available to make musical contact. It was simply two people making music together despite the extreme situation.

Attributing and Evoking Musical Personhood

Fraser: I'm thinking of a woman I work with who has very severe dementia, and is also an opera lover. She has no speech left at all, but her appreciation of music seems totally intact. It's very difficult for her to make any intentional movements, she can't play any instrument. What she can do is to hold a beater and wave it in time to the music. She also has an enormous range of facial expressions. And what I'll often do is to take an operatic aria as a starting point. When I start playing it, her face lights up, and I'm observing all the movement she's making in response to it: the movement of the beater, but also the tappings of her foot and the kind of eye contact she gives me. She's somebody who gets very drowsy, and easily falls asleep. It's interesting for me to go back

---

[6]   See the story of Herr G, told to me by Dagmar Gustorff and reported in Ansdell 1995, p. 59.

and look at the videos I make of these sessions and see the moment that her
eyes close! It's something to do with my getting a balance between the music
she knows, but also the need to explore something new. When I get that bang
on, she's absolutely right there with me, and there's this electricity between
us. I can tell by her gestures, it's very much to do with that... it's not just about
attuning to her, it's each of us attuning to each other....

Being with people seemingly so lost within states of dementia, autism or psychosis
can sometimes lead to doubting whether a person *is* still there. Whilst this doubt
can prompt philosophical and ethical conundrums about what a person really is,
the crucial practical consequence is for how people are seen and treated. There are
occasional scandals involving intentional cruelty, but mostly poor-quality medical
and social care comes from staff who stop seeing those in their care who are in
extreme or vulnerable states *as* persons.

The psychologist Tom Kitwood championed the idea of *personhood* as key
to his vision of an improved 'person-centred care' for people with dementia
(Kitwood 1997; Baldwin and Capstick 2007). Kitwood suggests simply that how
we think about what a person is determines how we treat them, and how we see the
ongoing possibilities for their life. The danger is to treat people as 'human objects'
or non-persons, even if objectively the care given is 'good enough' at a physical
level. The increasing application of business models to health and care systems
often unwittingly promotes depersonalising attitudes and behaviours at all levels
of treatment and care.

Religious and political beliefs have traditionally helped people decide what
a person is and how they should be treated. But in the modern, scientific West,
we tend now to approach the question, 'What is a person?', by asking what they
have or can do. *Are they conscious? Are they rational? Can they speak?* Kitwood
suggests that this approach is too individualistic, functional, and 'diagnostic'. We
can't define personhood by what a person possesses or does; rather, personhood
must simply be *attributed* to any human, in any state, in any situation. Personhood
has to be bestowed, not diagnosed. On this logic, in a chapter entitled 'On Being
a Person', Kitwood defines personhood as 'a standing or status that is bestowed
upon one human being, by others, in the context of relationship and social being.
It implies recognition, respect and trust' (in Baldwin and Capstick 2007, p. 246).
Personhood is more than personality, status, or any of the individual attributes we
may have. Personhood is based on the moral commitment: *that* I am precedes *what*
I am.[7] As Kitwood comments,

> In an ethical sense, personhood is attributed even to the new-born infant. In an
> empirical sense, personhood emerges in a social context. This personhood is
> not, at first, a property of the individual; rather it is provided, or guaranteed, by

---

[7]   For more on personhood, 'first-person being' and self-identity, see Tallis 2011, in the
section 'Finding the Self'.

the presence of others. Putting it another way, relationship comes first, and with it intersubjectivity; the subjectivity of the individual is like a distillate that is collected later. (Kitwood, in Baldwin and Capstick 2007, p. 246)

This is the second important strand to personhood: that it is a relational and ecological phenomenon. A person emerges and flourishes in relation to who they are with, and where they are. This differs from the credo of our modernist and individualist culture that tends to think of people as separate first, and then added together socially. A theory of personhood gives a more sophisticated picture of our social being, as made up from three interdependent dimensions. Firstly, our *individuality* is our being someone unique, and this is accompanied, secondly, by our *subjectivity*, the ongoing sense of being uniquely ourselves in our lifeworld and the subject of a unique history. But importantly, these two dimensions of individuality and subjectivity are only guaranteed by a third, *relatedness* – our basic reliance on others to recognise us, communicate with us, and try to understand our situation and how we feel about it. To truly bestow personhood on another is therefore not simply to acknowledge them, but to take responsibility for how they can only retain individuality and subjectivity through our relatedness with them. *I am 'through' you; you are 'through' me*.[8]

When these three principles slide into the background (through ignorance, neglect or abuse), people shrink to objects, and their personhood diminishes or disappears. This becomes a vicious circle, as the less personhood is evoked, the less it is recognised. Of course, it's a challenge to continue attributing and helping maintain someone's personhood when their condition is actively destroying the usual ways of relating person to person. The *de-menting* of dementia involves a loss of the integrity of the self that we usually take for granted, and with this a threat to 'social being'. Individuality, subjectivity and relatedness are threatened not only by the illness, but also by how sufferers are seen and cared for. Kitwood argued that dementia care needs to offset or compensate for the ongoing fragmentation of self and experience that sufferers experience. They need to be 'recalled to the world of persons, where a place is no longer guaranteed' (2007, p. 246). Such care needs to be primarily relational and social – what Kitwood called *person work*. All involved need to acknowledge that independence needs to yield to greater *interdependence* between people:

> It is as if faculties which were, for a long time, the property of an individual, are now to be made over again to the interpersonal milieu from which they originated … The other is needed to hold the fragments together. As subjectivity breaks apart, so intersubjectivity must take over if personhood is to be maintained. (Kitwood, in Baldwin and Capstick 2007, p. 144)

---

[8] Kitwood notes that the most comprehensive exploration of this relational understanding of personhood is found in the dialogical philosophy of Martin Buber – which we shall explore further in Part IV.

ॐ

In the vignette at the beginning of this section, Fraser's skill as a musician and music therapist shows exactly this kind of 'person work' in action, enabling this woman's personhood to be recognised and engaged with at a time when it is severely under threat from her dementia. Fraser works from a music therapist's faith that everyone is musical, and he also acknowledges this woman's particular relationship to music built up through her life. The success of this work, however, lies in how he uses his precise craft as a musician and music therapist to fine-tune the ongoing relatedness between him and the woman. He attends to her precisely through his listening, he calls musically and engages with all her responses as *musical* ones, attuning and adjusting his playing to keep their musical contact and dialogue going. All of this Fraser described as 'precarious… like building a tower out of playing cards!' Nevertheless, it works while the music lasts: this 'musical person work' sustains and to an extent restores personhood to this woman. It's key that Fraser finishes by saying, 'It's not just about attuning to her, *it's each of us attuning to each other*'. Personhood is always mutual.

We saw a very similar process happening with 'Piano Man', the autistic boy, the man in a coma, and the woman in psychosis. All were threatened with a loss of personhood because of the difficulties others had in recognising and engaging with 'who they were as people' through the normal channels of communication and contact. In each case, music helped by laying a ground for contact and response on which further relatedness and recognition could be built. Being able to have a 'musical view' of a person meant having a stronger sense of the person 'still there' under the layers of pathology.

We might say that the 'musical person work' in these examples recognises, evokes and elicits the *musical personhood* of these people. I suggest we think of 'musical personhood' as a dimension of general personhood that emerges and is cultivated specifically through musicking. As such, it's only possible to perceive and work with this *in relationship* and *in situation* (it is not, that is, an abstract or ideal 'label'). Musical personhood is fully realised when people find themselves at home together in music.

Like personhood in general, 'musical personhood' is not primarily an individual possession or an ability that needs proving, but rather an active recognition and acknowledgement of someone *being a musical person*. John Blacking asked the question, 'Are we human beings because we are musical?' (1987, p. 4). Music therapists daily experience situations where the answer to this question is a clear, 'Yes.'

Chapter 7
Core Musicality

This remarkable, beautiful faculty of being able to grasp the meaning of music; to follow it, to be moved by it, to understand it.

Paul Nordoff[1]

Musicality's nature of engaging one with an other, or many with many, intersubjectively, is intrinsic to musicality's healing potential.

Stephen Malloch and Colwyn Trevarthen[2]

Homo Musicus

Recognising and acknowledging others as musical persons suggests a different way of thinking about musicality than is usual in our culture. Being musical is not a special gift of the few, but part of being human. Everyone has a musical core.

Of course, some people have a particular talent for music, and most cultures recognise 'musicians' as a specialist group. But such specialism has usually stood happily alongside the belief that everyone's musicality should be recognised and cultivated within a community. The anthropologist John Blacking (1985) reports seeing an infant being given a tin bowl and spoon to join in the collective musicking of her Venda tribe. Her musicality was taken as given, something from which the form of her participation could be gradually cultivated and refined, just like any other routine social activity in her community.

A similar attitude towards musicality is now belatedly developing in the modern West. Victor Zuckerkandl made an early commitment to this in his book *Man the Musician*, arguing that musicality is a basic human endowment, an attribute of our species.[3] A more contemporary expression is to think of musicality as a human faculty like speech or reason, something that not only defines us as human beings, but also promotes our development, and flowers into a variety of culturally directed musical behaviours. The music psychologist Donald Hodges summarises the latest consensus drawn from a range of research perspectives:

---

[1]   Paul Nordoff, in Aigen 1996, p. 13.

[2]   Malloch and Trevarthen 2009, p. 6.

[3]   Zuckerkandl traces the notion of *Homo Musicus* to Plato's dialogue *Phaedo*, in which Socrates on the eve of his death talks of the dream he had (and acted upon) to 'make music and work at it' (1973, p. 1).

> It is becoming increasingly apparent that all human beings are biologically equipped to be musical and that this genetic predisposition for musicality has important consequences for us not only artistically, but emotionally and socially as well. (Hodges 2006, p. 51)

A problem with this kind of statement from an ecological perspective, however, is that it's too 'internalist' – a tendency that we explored earlier in Part I as being typical of recent theories about people and music. Musicality in this view is seen primarily as something within us – as biological, 'hardwired', 'genetic'. What's lost here is the sense of how musicality as a faculty is as much 'outside' our heads as inside them. We need to see how musicality as a personal capacity (which doubtless has biological origins) is nevertheless crucially activated, supported and extended within and by the surrounding sociocultural ecology.

To illustrate this perspective, Mercédès Pavlicevic and I have suggested a more ecological and holistic model of musical personhood (Pavlicevic and Ansdell 2009), where:

- **MUSICALITY** is a core human *capacity* that enables a musical engagement with the human world. It is our 'natural' relationship with music, though sometimes it needs to be awakened and mobilised with the help of other people and situations. Our core musicality motivates the gradual development of...
- **MUSICIANSHIP** as a *facility* that is cultivated by our musicality in action within the socio-cultural world. Developing our relationship to music requires an increasingly skilled and knowledgeable engagement with our musical community and its history. The 'mechanisms' of musicianship include learning about and working with a range of musical affordances (musical 'aspects', instruments, texts, traditions, etc.) through...
- **MUSICKING**, the engaged, social *activity* of musicianship in action, which is grounded in specific musical occasions and performances.

These three dimensions are necessarily dynamically interdependent. They are also cumulative, as we develop as musical people across our lives. But in any one situation of musicking (whatever age or condition we're in), the three levels will always be simultaneously interacting to some extent, as Fig. 7.1 shows through the arrows running up and down the sides of the inverted triangle. The demands of musicking draw on our musicianship and evoke our musicality. But equally, without the foundations of musicality and musicianship, no musicking is possible. This model shows that, when musicality is not seen as a purely individual and internal phenomenon, any individual limits or limiting conditions of a person can then be compensated for by others, and by the shared resources of the culture. A musical ecosystem is one where interdependence rules. Core musicality is the only basic need, and this is guaranteed for all humans.

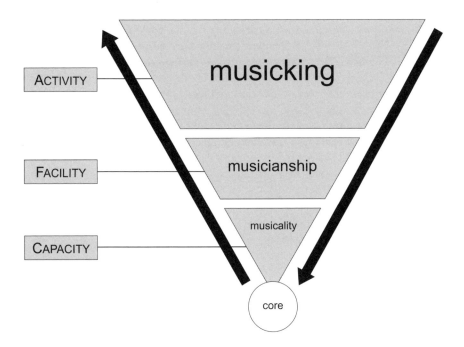

Figure 7.1   An ecological model of musical personhood

The Developing Musician

William is just one year old and lives with his British parents in Malaysia. His mother's a musician and there's often music in the house.

I'm playing their electric piano and William turns his head to the source of this sound, and when I change from 'piano' to 'vibraphone' he registers the change in timbre. His mother puts William on my lap and he immediately reaches out with both hands and plays three metrical clusters of notes on the piano. He looks up at me and squeals with excitement, showing me his pleasure and gauging my reaction. I copy him immediately with three almost identical clusters, matching as closely as I can the type of sound he makes, and its phrasing. He answers me quite carefully, and soon we have a little conversation going, accompanied by shrieks of enthusiasm. He looks to his mother as if to say, 'See me doing this!'

At just one, William's other skills for communicating and doing things with others are still fairly limited. He has no verbal language yet; and whilst he uses facial expressions communicatively, I notice that these are mostly in reaction to others engaging with him. In our brief musical conversation, on the contrary, William initiates and sustains a more subtle and intentional dialogue. At his current stage of development, music is a helpful way for William to perform and rehearse his 'I-ness' with another person.

William could be called a 'musical boy' in the sense people normally use this term. His musicality is apparent through how he responds to music, and how he is beginning to do things with it and through it with other people. His developing perceptual and cognitive abilities lay the ground for his musicianship to be further cultivated, such that he can increasingly musick successfully with others. There is a welcome and increasingly common view in music psychology and music education that every developing child is also a developing musician. A variety of interdisciplinary research and theory is coming to a consensus that musicality is a faculty rather than a gift, and that musical development can rightly be compared to the other crucial dimensions of our development as persons (McPherson 2006; McPherson, Davidson and Faulkner 2012). Whilst there is no single overarching theory of musical development (as indeed there's not one of general development), the following key aspects sum up the current consensus on the developing musician.

Readiness for Music

Our brains prepare us to process and produce meaningful sounds from the first stages of development (Hodges 2006, p. 51). The 'musical brain' is complex at an early stage and follows the same path of development as other core faculties, remaining plastic and adaptable during childhood. It increasingly seems that all humans have the capacity, through the structure of both brain and body, to find particular patterns of sound especially meaningful, and to make such sounds themselves in the service of social interaction and pleasure, both of which could arguably promote survival.

Music Before and After Birth

Studies from 'prenatal music psychology' (Parncutt 2006) give evidence for what mothers have long suspected: that the foetus listens in the womb to patterns of the mother's sound and movement. The foetus' auditory system is prematurely advanced at sixteen to twenty weeks, with the auditory environment a privileged stimulus for it to attend to. The foetus probably listens in order to 'tune in' to its mother's physical and emotional state, as a preparation for post-natal bonding. Good listening before birth is in the service of making a good relationship with the mother after birth.

A mother instinctively calls out the musicality of her new-born child in order to communicate with her and help to regulate arousal and mood (Malloch and Trevarthen 2009a). Likewise, a newly born baby instantly mobilises her musicality to characterise and communicate herself and her basic needs and enthusiasms, engaging her mother in their first musical conversations – a system called *communicative musicality* by theorists of early interaction.[4]

---

[4] We shall explore communicative musicality in more detail in Part IV: Musical Relationship.

Infant Connoisseurs

A mother or carer continues to 'mentor' a baby's musicality and developing musicianship by inducting him into musical culture and socialisation with largely improvised songs and musical games. But recent studies have also emphasised the reciprocal efforts and surprising abilities of so-called infant 'musical connoisseurs'. Careful studies show that an infant possesses much more sophisticated perceptual and expressive musical skills and facilities than had previously been thought – able to detect fine degrees of variation in pitch, pitch contour and rhythm. Infants are motivated and attracted by music, remember it well, and are open minded to sounds. At this stage of development, Sandra Trehub (2006) suggests, most children are 'musical prodigies'. We probably lose some of this sensitivity, and our fascination with sounds, as we become enculturated into one type of music.

The Ecology of the Developing Musician

It's tempting to continue this account of the 'developing musician' in fixed stages that unfold internally as perceptual or cognitive 'processing' skills, and that neatly link with other areas of child development. But recent theory has suggested that this is too individualistic,[5] and that a more flexible and ecological perspective is needed that sees a child developing musically only through musical participation with others. This comes firstly with the primary carer, then with peers, within which we could call (after Vygotsky) *musical zones of proximal development*,[6] where a child performs at a higher level musically than they could on their own. Through such social engagement, the developing musician gradually builds competence for what music is *for*: giving us access to close relationships with others; sharing thoughts and feelings non-verbally with others; making musical actions that influence and shape others' actions; becoming increasingly creative and equal members of our cultural community.

In all of these aspects, we can see the constant dynamic interdependence of the three dimensions of Fig. 7.1: musical *capacity*, *facility* and *activity*. A developing musician is always someone, somewhere, doing something musical – usually for a social purpose.

---

[5]   For a critique of traditional cognitive 'stage' models of musical development and an outline of a more socio-cultural/ecological perspective, see Bamberger 2006; North and Hargreaves 2008.

[6]   Vygotsky's (1978) famous zone of proximal development (ZPD) captures his socio-cultural theory of development, which suggests that children often find themselves performing 'above' the level of their age-related individual skill, because of the 'guided participation' of more developed others within a particular social situation. Learning and development is always situated, social and collaborative. The term musical zone of proximal development is my own coinage, though this is near to Margaret Barrett's similar 'community of musical practice' (2005, see pp. 261–280).

ဢ

Jamie is four and autistic, and in contrast to William he seems to have little sense of 'I-ness' or of himself as separate from his mother. He sits besides her, expressionless and moving only minimally, but taking small cues from her to do things. In his early music therapy sessions (without his mother), he is equally silent and still. The music I make for him attempts to draw him into responding, but only slight flickers across his face show any recognition of me, or of the music. Typically, he sits with his back to me. Many weeks later, occasional movements of his body seem to respond to the musical gestures I offer – small signs of vitality and musical connection between us. Over the period of a year, Jamie gradually moves from the periphery of the room to its centre, where the piano is, and where the music comes from. Gradually his occasional gestures on a small drum begin to connect with the music I improvise for him. Finally, he sits by me, and when I point to myself during a 'Hello song' he shocks me by suddenly singing my name and then acknowledging my reference to him when I sing his name. We are becoming musical companions.

ဢ

As a music therapist, I'm careful not to take normative models of human or musical development too literally. Musical persons develop differently, in relation to a host of factors. At first, Jamie's autism masks his musical responsiveness, though I always attributed both musical personhood and musicality to him from the outset. So it would be a mistake to say that William is musical and Jamie not. The current consensus on musical development that I sketched above suggests that seeing a person as musical should be judged less on surface assessments of skill, and more on how musicality pervades them as a whole – whether they can express it or not, or need help from other people and particular situations in order to bring it out. Musicality, just like other faculties, emerges according to a variety of ecological conditions. When Jamie's musicality emerges and works for him, it accomplishes the same thing as for William – helping to find a sense of himself in active and reciprocal relationship to another person.

Working with people who are 'differently developing' often highlights the complexities and anomalies of normative perspectives, as often people's musical receptivity and responsiveness is out of step with other areas of their development – or, alternatively, with their decline at the other end of life. Music therapists regularly work with people whose musicality and musicianship seems exceptional in some way. As some of the cases in Oliver Sacks's (2007) book *Musicophilia* show, musical sensitivity and ability can be affected by a variety of impairments, although sometimes for the better – such as with Williams Syndrome, where musicality seems to be enhanced (p. 317). But we also need to bear in mind that musical ability and development are adversely affected by physical, cognitive and social limitations as well. For example, what is the effect of an impairment that restricts movement on the development of rhythmic perception, and the ability to produce it? What is the effect of a learning disability and its usual cognitive problems on the development of musical processing, memory, and intentional musical actions? How do emotional problems or social deprivation affect the normal flow of 'communicative musicality'?

However, the more common situation that music therapists witness is where a person's innate musicality is noticeably *unaffected*, but the cultivation of their musicianship and the available opportunities for musicking are strongly impacted by their illness or disability. An ecological perspective would consider what relational and enabling conditions might help with these individual limitations, and reciprocally, what the 'differently abled' might offer back to our musical culture.

The Musical Lifecourse

Throughout our lives, core musicality motivates our musicianship to develop and our musicking to flourish. But again, we should be wary of taking a too individualistic or biological view of this progress, such as the fixed stages of the 'life-cycle' model. A more ecological perspective is given by the idea of a *lifecourse* (Hunt 2005; Lievegoed 1979/2003), which pictures how the uniquely personal course of our lives is organised in shifting individual *phases* that relate to biological shifts and ageing without being totally determined by them. Instead, these very personal phases of our biography take shape in relation to the physical, social, cultural and spiritual environments within which we are nested, and as a result of what happens to us (for good or ill). There is a certain 'melodic' sense to a lifecourse: in how our personal 'theme' emerges, develops and resolves across phases – counterpointed with the lives of others, and weaving into the broader story of our times.

For many people, their relationship with music plays a key role in their lifecourse. It accompanies, characterises, shapes, reflects and helps them navigate its phases. We might perhaps think of a *musicourse*[7] that runs in counterpoint to a lifecourse, our unique musical story that helps compose the broader narrative of the lifecourse. But whilst there is increasing scholarly study of particular uses of music in people's everyday lives, only very recently is scholarly attention being directed to how music accompanies the flow of the lifecourse as a whole in this way (McPherson, Davidson and Faulkner 2012; Pitts 2012).

Again, a music therapist's eye and ear need to be sensitive to the inevitable disruptions, discontinuities and re-routings of a person's lifecourse, through illness or the impact of sudden unwelcome change. I've often worked with people who have experienced 'normal' development in all areas, but whose lifecourse is suddenly thrown off course by the onset of an illness or acquired disability. Amongst many changes, these events also affect the expression of people's musicianship and their participation in musicking. In a later section, we shall look

---

[7] This is my (admittedly inelegant) neologism. I'm trying to encourage people to give it more attention.

at such 'biographical disruptions' and how people often 'cling creatively to music' at these times because of how it affords both immediate help and often also a way of reflecting on or changing their identity, and re-orientating their life.

Musicality as Vitality

Musicality may be core to us, but this core still remains something of a mystery. Why is this faculty of musicality so early to emerge in us, and so late to eclipse? Why does it motivate us so much? Why does its help remain when other faculties are defeated? In short, *Why do we need to become and remain musical persons?* A theoretical perspective from the developmental psychologist and psychoanalyst Daniel Stern (2010) helps to probe a little more deeply into the roots and fruits of musicality.[8]

When we meet a strange person, how do we know 'what they are like'? Firstly, we look, but we also listen – to their movements and gestures. We instinctively 'read' and experience people in terms of the form and quality of their aliveness – which, Stern suggests, is expressed through a complex *gestalt* of the tempo, tonal/expressive qualities, and coherence of their actions. Initially, we are often more interested in *how* someone is doing something, rather than exactly what they are doing. This instinctive receptivity to how people appear can be seen as a competence based on our core musicality. As Stern writes,

> 'Musicality' is composed of pulses that are formed by timing, in the rhythmic sense, and its temporal contouring, and the deployment of force in time. This is the backbone of vitality dynamics …. (Stern 2010, p. 53)

Our musicality attunes us, that is, to human forms of vitality. We routinely characterise people and their actions through adverbs: *exploding, surging, seeping, dragging, slipping away, bouncing, jagged, smooth*, and so on. Our musical sensitivity to these qualities tells us something basic about other people's mood, intentions, health, and the likely threat or opportunities that they present to us.

Movement, Stern suggests, has 'four daughters': force, time, space, and direction/intention:

> Vitality forms … unite the elements that put flesh on experience so that it is felt and seen as coming from a living person existing in our real daily world – someone who moves in time and space, and with force and direction. (2010, p. 30)

---

[8] Stern's main work has involved the close study of mother–infant interactions, how such 'basic intersubjective communication' is achieved, and what it means psychologically for infant and mother. Here, I focus only on the more individual aspect of the theory, as the dyadic will come later, in Part IV.

Without movement, we are possibly dead, certainly ill in some way, at the very least difficult to know. All of our meaningful movements are based on how our gestures take a qualitative and dynamic form in relation to the 'four daughters'. Our innate musicality is the source of this readiness and capacity to attune to, and intuitively read, the relational and social meanings of:

- **tempo of movement** and its character/spirit – e.g. *andante* as 'walking tempo';
- **rhythm of movement**, which groups actions and gives them intention and character;
- **changing intensity over time** – the expressive dynamics of music, represented as *piano/forte, crescendo/decrescendo* in musical notation;
- **stress and accent** – the 'articulation', emphasis and weighting of sounds;
- **flow and shape** – the phrasing and flow-shape of the ongoing stream of sounds.[9]

Stern describes these parameters as composing 'the backbone of vitality dynamics' (2010, p. 53). Together they produce a *protomusic* that reflects the basic musicality of human and animal life. Dynamic forms of vitality emerge within us, and between us in communication, signalling our mutual aliveness, arousal and vitality. They can be seen as musically formed and expressed, and musically received and responded to.

This protomusic can also be elaborated within cultural forms and processes through the cultivated dimensions of musicianship and musicking. Vitality forms infuse composed and improvised songs and dances. But they also emerge through just *how* the performers enliven the pieces – the distinctly personal life that they couple to the music's life.

The core of musicality is therefore about the qualities of moving and being moved; it's about motion and emotion, along with the forms of music and the styles of its performance. Musicality's source is vitality, and these phenomenologically specific music-like forms of vitality underpin our musical experience of both people and things. Like other faculties, it has both receptive and expressive capabilities. The receptive 'inner readiness' to musical forms of vitality is complemented by an expressive competence to characterise and perform ourselves musically through the 'signature' of our dynamic forms of vitality. This is how other people 'read' and recognise us as persons, and are able and motivated to interact and play with us.

---

9   Stern's section on music proper (2010, pp. 82–84) gives a longer account of these 'codes that music uses to mark dynamic forms and thus create vitality forms'. But we need to keep in mind that Stern usually has a traditional idea of composing–performing, rather than the more spontaneous musicking with which we're often concerned in this book.

The Resilience of Musicality

> **Cleo:** *People think that mental illness somehow affects your intelligence.... It doesn't! It may affect your ability to remember things, or to function... but your innate musical intelligence never goes away... and your innate music doesn't go either. So once it's been triggered... it's a life-enhancing thing, overtaking the illness. It's the stronger force in me... it's the wellness in me. My voice comes from the core of my being... and that can never become ill. So should I become ill again... I can hold onto that in consciousness, and know that this part of me is alive and well, no matter how ill I become [...] I remember my experience as that the voice will still come through... even if you see the illness as well... but in the midst of that... if you have ears to hear it... the voice will still come through.*

Cleo's words echo a key concept that Nordoff and Robbins developed in the early years of their music therapy work. They experienced many times how profoundly disabled children still responded to music when almost nothing else would reach them, and one day in a public talk suddenly the idea of the *music child* emerged to characterise what it is in a person that responds to and engages with music, despite the barriers of pathology or circumstance. Nordoff and Robbins came to see the 'music child' as subsequently motivating and guiding the unfolding of the healthy personality and the desire to make music with others.[10] This is not to say that it always spontaneously emerges. A music therapist's skill is often needed to stimulate and motivate the music child, such that the faculty of musicality can work for them. This belief in a core area of musicality that Nordoff and Robbins demonstrated so convincingly has inspired many who followed them. In this chapter, I've relabelled the music child concept as 'core musicality' in order to give it a broader currency.

Cleo identifies for herself exactly this region of 'core musicality', which she links to an innate 'musical intelligence' that is a motivating and health-promoting force capable of standing up to and overtaking the ill parts of herself. She identifies her musical 'voice' finally coming through as the evidence that she is alive and well, just as Clive Robbins reports of one of the early cases with which he and Nordoff worked:

> We're reaching [this child's] musical intelligence and this will be a wonderful thing for him to use, because he can use so little intelligence in life. But musical intelligence he's got and can find satisfaction in, and this can change his whole state of alertness .... (Robbins, in Aigen 1996, p. 13)

---

[10]   For more on the 'music child' concept, see Nordoff and Robbins 1977/2007, Part 1: 'Meeting the Music Child'; Robbins 2005, 'Enter the Music Child' (pp. 24–27); Verney and Ansdell 2010, *Conversations 1 and 2*.

Our core musicality is naturally resilient. This can partly be explained in physiological terms, given that the brain structures that support musical receptivity and expressivity are widely distributed and usually avoid the damage that other capacities such as speech often sustain through localised trauma. But this is not the whole story. Core musicality as we've been exploring in this chapter is more than a brain area or a cognitive function. It stands as the sign and proof of an enduring existential wholeness and aliveness in us that is relational, social and ecological – not just individual. As such, musicality is the core of musical personhood, allowing us to recognise people in their wholeness and aliveness through how we hear and engage with them musically, natural musician to natural musician.

Homo Musicus – 'Man the Musician' – as Zuckerkandl describes us – is a picture of our species as not only made to musick, but as beings standing in need of music, and beings sometimes redeemed by music. For many of us, our musicality is the key both to finding and to keeping ourselves, and each other, as persons.

Chapter 8
Musical Identities

We become ourselves through others.

Lev Vygotsky[1]

The sense of 'self' is locatable in music. Musical materials provide terms and templates for elaborating self-identity – for identity's identification. Looking more closely at this process highlights the ways in which musical materials are active ingredients in identity work, how respondents 'find themselves' in music.

Tia DeNora[2]

'Project Me' and its Challenges

In a *New Yorker* cartoon, a kid is listening to a busker playing the saxophone. His mother drags him away, saying, 'Come on honey, that's not *real* music – he's just making it up!'

Likewise, we may feel uncomfortable with the thought of 'making ourselves up' as we go along, rather than following some grander script of destiny. But probably most of us in the modern West feel that we're indeed improvising our identity in relation to who we need to be with others, or for others, or for a context. We're all busy working on what the philosopher Mel Thompson (2009) calls 'Project Me'.

Asking the question, 'Who am I?' (and then worrying about it), is a telling feature of modern times. In traditional societies, identity is more of a given. One's place, role, status and probable future are mostly fixed through birth, kinship and gender. Stable social structures tell you who you are and who you will become as your life unfolds relatively predictably. In contrast, within contemporary societies, people move around a lot, and have become more individual. Consumerism assures people that they are both masters of their destiny and authors of their identity. The sociologist Zygmunt Bauman (2004, p. 68) talks about the 'liquid' state of late modernity, where our biography often feels like a defective jigsaw puzzle. In his colourful metaphor, this 'identity jigsaw' often has bits missing, or – more worryingly still – there's sometimes no picture on the front of the box! Who guides us, then, when putting ourselves together? The liquid modern world

---

[1]   Vygotsky 1989, p. 56

[2]   DeNora 2000, p. 68.

gives us freedom to be many things, but in doing so it has turned identity into a challenge for many people.

The parallel musical metaphor would be that we are improvising our identity because the 'score' of society is missing, or that it tells us less than before about who we need to be, what we need to do, and where we need to go towards. So both our identity and our biography become more of an anxious improvisation that we find ourselves performing. The Latin *improvisare* means 'unforeseen'. The shape of our life, and who we will be, is literally unforeseen when we think forwards.

Seen more positively, identity has become a creative project, something we have to work at, plan and chart, using what social and cultural materials we find to hand as help. This gives possibilities for experimentation, but also for increased risks, threats and uncertainties.

❧

At an exhibition called *Identity*, I stand in front of a special mirror that electronically manipulates the reflection it gives back. As I look into the mirror, I see myself as usual – that is, in parameters of space and time that match the sensory feedback my body gives me internally. But the mirror is also taking a film of me, which it then plays back just slightly time lapsed. So then when I move, I see 'me' firstly stay still, then move independently of my experiencing 'I'. 'Is that *really* "me"?' I think. It's very uncanny – very soon the usual easy fit between 'I' and 'me' is drifting apart – uncoupling my experience and my world. Existential questions quickly force themselves up in the cracks of this situation: *Is that me I see? Who am I, then? Who's 'he' in the mirror?* A friend walks up to me and says, 'Are you done looking at yourself, Gary?' I'm relieved – I'm evidently still myself!

❧

This scenario shows just how quickly self-identity comes into question. Since the work of the pioneer social psychologist G.H. Mead (1934), the 'I'/'me' distinction has been used to help think about the 'mechanics' of identity. There are two aspects to this, shown in the vignette. Firstly, there's how 'I' as an experiencing subject look out from my eyes for evidence of 'me' as an acting body in the world.[3] When 'I' and 'me' don't exactly match up, a crack opens up between what I experience I am, and what I perceive and believe myself to be. I quickly get worried. Secondly, there's how 'I' get instant recognition and reassurance about 'me' when my friend recognises me and speaks to me. As Christopher Bollas (1995) points out, both socially and linguistically 'me' often goes through 'you' first. We ask, 'What do *you* think of *me*?' How you see and react to me helps me to establish, remember and restore my self-identity.

---

[3]   I say 'eyes' here in reference to the vignette, but the same could apply to any of our outer senses, or the 'inner' kinaesthetic/proprioceptive sense that helps us to maintain the usual coupling of self and world.

These 'mechanisms' of identity consist of at least three mutually supporting dimensions: the outer and inner evidence of the acting body; the inner processes of the psyche (including memory and imagination); and the ongoing public and social affirmation and witness of others and the wider community. All three dimensions need to align adequately for our identity to keep running smoothly. This all shows how identity is fundamentally a personal and social *reflexive* process – how it literally involves a 'bending back' of attention, perception or imagination in order to process and stabilise who and what we are. Some kind of mirror (both literal and symbolic) is needed to give 'feedback' on our selves. Such moment-to-moment feedback then motivates or continues an inner process of reflection and internal dialogue between me and myself, through which I can further elaborate the 'story' of myself – or just keep it going.

Mel Thompson suggests that this healthy play between 'I' and 'me' in relation to 'you' and 'the world' helps us build a personal 'map' that we use to make sense of ourselves over time, find our way around, and relate to the people we share our lives with. When all is well, this self-map provides a secure feeling of personal integrity: the sense that we *are*, and that we are *someone, somewhere* who endures over time despite many internal and external fluctuations. Seen this way, identity is not some abstract philosophical question but the everyday, ongoing work we do on 'Project Me'.

Music's 'Magic Mirror'

The musical metaphor of 'improvising identity' can also be understood in a more concrete way when we explore how music helps specifically with 'Project Me'. Increasingly, music is being appreciated as perhaps the central socio-cultural material being used for 'identity work' in modern times (MacDonald, Hargreaves and Miell 2002). We've seen in a previous chapter how music interfuses people's experience, giving them an embodied but non-verbal sense of themselves. For some people, such strong musical experiences also afford self-reflective work on their identity. Tia DeNora's (2000, 2003) work in particular has explored the musical elaboration of identity, and what this suggests about selfhood and the importance of people's access to cultural resources:

> Music is a 'mirror' that allows one to 'see one's self'. It is also, however, a 'magic mirror' in so far as its specific material properties also come to configure (for example, transfigure, disfigure) the image reflected in and through its (perceived) structures. Like a cultural performance ... music too may serve as a repository of value, or self-perception. (DeNora 2000, p. 70)

The important point that DeNora stresses in her theory is that identity work happens fully in the sociocultural world, and not just as a psychological process inside people's heads. It is the affordances of the encompassing musical worlds that we explored in Part I that allow people to accomplish their ongoing improvisation of self. 'Musical materials', writes DeNora, 'are active ingredients in identity work, how respondents "find themselves" in music' (2000, p. 68).

Identity as an active and ongoing project is particularly highlighted when under construction during childhood and adolescence, when in transition over the lifecourse, or when it is challenged or breaks down for some reason. In the following sections, we shall look at examples of some of these situations in relation to the particular help that music can give.

Identities in Transition: Three Teenage Music Needers

Three of the 'locals' told me elaborate stories about the importance of music during their teenage years. This was no surprise – an extensive literature has charted how involved this age group is with music (a fact the music business is only too happy to capitalise on), and how it often helps them in the psychological and social adjustments they need to make during adolescence (MacDonald, Hargreaves and Miell 2002; McFerran 2010). In more traditional societies, communal 'initiation rites' help youths through this transitional or 'liminal' state and over the threshold into adult roles and identities. It is often a more individual and sometimes troubled path for adolescents in Western late modern society, only partially compensated for by the profusion of cultural resources in the form of music, dance and clothes that help them navigate gender, ethnic, sexual and class identity alongside their peers.

Psychological theory has traditionally portrayed adolescence as a period of 'identity crisis' that usually resolves naturally. The psychoanalyst and developmental theorist Erikson's lifestage model describes the particular conflict of adolescence as being between identity and 'identity diffusion' (Simanowitz and Pearce 2003). An adolescent needs to actively 'find' a new identity, social role and sense of belonging as part of maturing sexuality and social independence from family. But this often involves a temporary identity diffusion, where the self comes uncomfortably into question. As a compensation, adolescents then often make strong external identifications to shore up their shaky sense of self: attaching to role models or to a peer group identity by modelling themselves on templates of taste through choices of clothes and music. Critiques of this psychological model, however, say that it's too individual, and that the 'crisis' depends more on social context given that the key aspect of adolescence is the transition of social identity.

Looking at the particular help that music seems to offer adolescents perhaps shows how it's not useful to choose between psychological or social factors, but rather to consider their world more ecologically, where there's a dynamic flow between things, people and situations. Music can be appropriated both for the more 'inner' focus of identity work, but also as part of the outward-going process of creating group affiliations and social relationships. Each feeds the other.

Most adolescents weather this 'identity crisis' relatively easily. Our focus in this book is, however, where more challenging life phases have been navigated, and the help that music has afforded – as with the stories of Adam, Richard and Simon.

'Brahms ... he was writing for me!'

Adam had a challenging adolescence in some ways. He had the emerging sense of being gay, he was introverted as a person, and other people found him difficult to get to know:

> **Adam:** I had two goals when I was a teenager. One was to play music, the other was to explore my sexuality. These two things were about the same thing: two ways of finding out who I was. I needed things to resonate with; I needed to see men who wanted to be with men... and I needed music.
>
> Music was a friend, something that's held my hand throughout my life. Emotionally I had something that understood me, as much as I understood it... that I could spend time with it, in a solitary way – just me and music. I think that music at this time in my life was a journey inwards. For me, music wasn't this, 'Let's get together with the guys and jam', but rather about me going into myself....
>
> Music helped me know that what I had inside was OK, that my emotional life was accepted. How do you get to know what's inside? How do other people get to know what's inside you? For me, this is what music let me do: get to know me, in an indirect way. Here I was, wondering, 'Who am I?', and not seeing me outside in other people around me, and thinking, 'If I'm not that, then how can I be something else?' Having to think about these kinds of things as a young person, that's a lot to think about! So the music I needed emotionally needed to be mature music, because it had to be equal to this inner struggle I was having, this confused passion for things....

Adam talked about playing his parents' classical records on their Hi-Fi, selecting out the Romantic repertoire:

> I played them over and over, a thousand times: Tchaikovsky's *Romeo & Juliet*... and then when I discovered Brahms I thought, 'This is pretty much me...'.
>
> It was almost as if Brahms wrote music the way I wanted to play it! He was writing for me! That's pretty much the way it felt. I also felt like I knew him – and that he knew something about me! The stuff I played on the piano then... I had this feeling of digging in, of really getting my hands dirty. I think, personality wise, that's what I was striving for, to not shy away from the gutsy stuff in life. Brahms, some Beethoven, Die Meistersinger... I played that endlessly... the way it gets so bold. Because I wasn't bold then, in terms of relating to people. But I knew I was bold inside....

The next step for Adam was to go 'outwards' with music. He started playing piano for school musicals, and when his schoolmates wrote in his yearbook at the end of school, they said, 'It was great to get to know you when you played the piano for the show.' Adam says that this was an important recognition and validation for him, a sign that he'd managed to get through this phase of his life: 'It was validation that people were getting to know me through music.' Music helped Adam with two of the key issues of adolescence: coming to know oneself, and allowing others to know you as part of this solidifying of a maturing identity.

ဢ

'This is for *me* [...] *This* is how I feel'

Richard looks at his extensive CD collection as if it's the most important thing in the world to him. He's just finished restoring it to alphabetical order again after his children have messed it up.

Richard also talks of his adolescence being a difficult time – coming to terms with himself, finding life socially difficult at school. What made the difference for him was music: going to pop gigs and building a music collection. Richard tells me that, when he felt alone with his teenage problems, music always seemed to be there to help:

> **Richard:** It's the sense of listening to some singer on disc, and feeling that it's being done for my benefit, for *me*! Often certain lyrics will really come home, which are actually about *your* life, about something you're feeling at the time... that's when music's probably at its most powerful. Despite the fact that millions of people may have bought that record, to actually think, 'This is for *me*', that's an incredible feeling!
>
> If you look at lots of gig videos, say of people going to see The Jam in the 1970s, you'll see people not only going to the gigs, but they'll wear the suit and the shoes, they're trying to be Paul Weller. It's about the person you want to be, and music can really help convince you that's actually within touching distance. You may really think, 'I could never be Paul Weller', but when you listen to the music it actually takes you halfway there! Because you can listen to it and it can give you a shot in the arm. It puts something in touching distance that can seem unreachable. But you get swept along with it – the music gives you a connecting point with these people. When you're younger, you're angry, you've got lots of issues in your head you want resolving... you want to kick out at your parents but you don't know why, or how to... and then you see someone like Elvis Costello on Top of the Pops, staring at the camera, snarling and shouting and having his say... all those lyrics about self-empowerment. When you're young, that sort of thing is massively influential. Because you might have all

these feelings lurking in there, but when you see him you think, 'This is how I feel...'. You can't articulate it, but he's actually telling you what you feel then.

'Wagner... *this* was my Bob Dylan!'

Simon: As a teenager, I found in music a kind of sublimation of everything I was going through personally, but not being able to share with friends or siblings. So I'd say that the role music's played in my life since grew from this... and why it's always been how I find comfort or inspiration... and also how it's helped me find a direction through my life.

I know that many kids use pop for this... but I think there's no difference between pop and classical music here: just like some people feel it with Bob Dylan, I felt it with Wagner's Ring! The first time I experienced this piece, aged sixteen, was probably the single profoundest musical experience of my adolescence. An inspirational teacher said to me, 'Between now and next week, I want you to go and listen to the Ring... you can get the records out of the library... and we'll talk about it.' And I said, 'Isn't it kind of long?' But I did it, I shut myself into my room for a week with Solti's Ring... and it was the single most transformative musical experience of my life. I just had no idea that such fantastic music existed. Not only was this music incredibly sensual and emotional, but also there's the whole story being about these archetypal human emotions that you're beginning to clutch at as a sixteen year old... and this is why I made the comparison to Bob Dylan! You read about the story of Siegmund and Sieglinde, or Wotan the troubled father who can't quite deal with the difficult daughter... these are archetypal situations. The music completely tells you about the characters and what they're going through.

So as a late teenager, this was my Bob Dylan! It spoke to me as no other music I'd heard in my life up to that time. It helped me understand where I was in my life; it helped teach me about my emotions; about moral dilemmas... which Wagner's good at! It helped me to begin to confront some of those big things in life, that only become realities later in your life... but which you're just beginning to grasp as a late teenager. So for me it was a learning experience both about things I was feeling then, but also about things I'd feel in the future....

At the end of Simon's interview, he comes back to this theme, with an even clearer account of how music provides a template for his finding out about himself, and charting a pathway through life:

Throughout my life, I've had a soundtrack, but rather than having an original score it consists of pre-existing music. So I've woven together this tapestry-like soundtrack of my life – which includes everything from The Beach Boys to Tallis. And it's both illuminated the way forward *and* shown me where I've already been. Actually, it's been both at the same time. It's helped me find the way forward but also reflected what I was at any particular moment. Partly it's a narrative of hopes, of what you think might happen in the future... and sometimes that future becomes the present... then the past.... Hard to put into words! But definitely a soundtrack, and very much located in places and times... different songs, pop music especially... even single days of my life!

I know what it does for the present – it helps illuminate the present, and narrate the present. The past is clear – it's a repository for your memories, an aide-memoire which helps locate and set memories, like spraying fixer on a painting. But the future... this is difficult... it's in the sense of finding my way, helping me to think forward... but this is so elusive....

Most of my best thinking about the issues of my life is done through music. Most of my best thinking about what my life means... what I'm doing and where I'm going... depends on music. Even mundane things like cooking in the kitchen with Brazilian music on... being on my own but not on my own... or sitting in a concert hall listening to Schumann... or sitting in a darkened room listening to Bach... all very different kinds of musical experience, but all of which facilitate the germination of thoughts and ideas, and the crystallisation of emotions and self-revelation. Music throughout my life has been an incredible aide to self-knowledge.

୨୦

Adam, Richard and Simon show how the process of maturing self-identity appropriates different types of musical material and musicking situations as 'magic mirrors', in Tia DeNora's phrase (2000, p. 70). They each locate in music aspects of the selfhood they are in the process of finding, recognising or shaping for themselves. They then identify and communicate with these musical people and musical things they find, and take them back into their own world. As we explored in earlier chapters, our musical worlds are a continuous flux of musical people, musical things and musical contexts that we live through, and through which we can sometimes meet our core psychological and social needs. We see in the three teenager's stories their identifications with other people's characters and energies (Brahms, Paul Weller, Wagner) and how this involves moving and re-positioning their current selves within both time and space. Adam is playing with Brahms across time; Richard is 'halfway there' across space towards Paul Weller; Simon discovers timeless character archetypes to guide him forwards. The inner reflective process that accompanies or follows these experiences then helps their continuing improvisation of self and self-identity at this transitional time of their lives. Their experiences at this phase also establish for each a habit of using music to support the ongoing elaboration of self and self-direction through later phases of their lives.

But can we say anything more precise about how this process happens? Daniel Stern suggests that what happens particularly clearly during adolescence highlights how identifications are at work for all of us much of the time. We identify with others as part of the work of keeping going 'Project Me'. But the more complex question is, as Stern asks,

> What is it about another that we identify with? Is it what they do, or why they do it, or how they do it? It is all three … We are perhaps taking a step toward understanding better 'taking in', ie the general process behind identification, empathy and internalization. (Stern 2010, pp. 141 and 146)

Stern links such identification with his theory of 'forms of vitality' that we explored in the previous chapter. Vitality forms are more than emotions, rather the music-like dynamic properties that give people that individual 'signature' that conveys *how* they are. Healthy identification, Stern suggests, is the psycho-social process of learning to empathise with others and to internalise aspects of them in the service of our own emerging self-identity. A musical identification latches onto the unique vitality forms of a composer, piece or genre in order to use these as a template or organising structure for self-reflection and construction. It is quite literally the 'taking on the life of' someone else whom we instinctively locate as being able to help us understand and shape ourselves 'through' them. Through understanding who, how and why they are as they are, we can in turn better understand who, how and why *we* are. But importantly, says Stern, it is not 'them' (or parts of them) that we internalise but rather the whole relational experience of being with their vitality forms, and recognising how they make us feel, sensing their match with who we feel *we* are, or are becoming.

For Adam, Richard and Simon, it was a reassurance to find that others had been and felt just like them before. The work of identity is to find a comfortable style, and a coherent story for ourselves.

Challenged Identities

An elderly woman with advanced lung cancer asks in her music therapy session whether I can help her sing a Viennese waltz like the ones she remembers from family gatherings eighty years ago. Amazingly, she finds the breath to sing with grace and charm. She tells me that she'd felt that she was fading away, but that now, after the music, she feels 'gathered together' again.

ഃ

A man who's been on a psychiatric ward for three months refuses to improvise a note of music, but willingly sits by me at the piano as we sing through large chunks of Mozart's *Magic Flute*. He tells me how he'd been taken as a child by his father to see this opera in Prague, and that this music has remained a talisman of health and continuity for him when his illness seriously disrupts his sense of who he is.

ଓ

A well-known German conceptual artist is dying of AIDS at a tragically young age. We improvise on two pianos together – long complex, atonal landscapes of splintering sounds. He tells me of his composition lessons with a pupil of Xenakis. His identity remains that of a bold, creative artist to the end of his life. He says that his musical personality can't be touched by AIDS; it's as strong as it ever was.

ଓ

A second area in people's lives where a crisis of identity shows up clearly is when their selfhood comes under threat – from illness, disability, or disruptive social circumstance. The sociologist Zygmunt Bauman suggests that at these times identity shifts from being a creative to an anxious and defensive project, where 'you are cast outside the social space in which identities are sought, chosen, constructed, evaluated, confirmed or refuted' (2004, p. 39).

In the 'liquid modern world', there are a variety of reasons why people find themselves outside the space where identity comes easily. Increasingly people are displaced or relocated, losing social support and the sense of belonging, and instead being given an 'underclass identity' as an immigrant or migrant. Then those who are born physically disabled, or who suffer from long-term physical or mental illness, can have a 'spoilt identity' imposed on them by others through stigmatisation or stereotyping. Finally, many people experience a severe challenge to their identity when a seemingly normal lifecourse is disrupted by an acquired illness, disability or trauma.

Though the cause may be different, people in each of these groups are likely to experience a similar threat to their personhood and selfhood. No longer recognised or respected as the person they've been used to being, they can find it increasingly difficult to believe or maintain the story and style of their identity. The easy creative dialogue between 'I' and 'me' falters when the 'reflecting material' around them – in the surrounding culture, or in people's responses and attitudes – serves only to distort or disfigure.The term 'biographical disruption' has been suggested for people who have become seriously ill or disabled within a 'normal' stretch of the lifecourse (Hunt 2005). All the 'taken-for-granted' aspects of life become disrupted at physical, social and existential levels. And if the 'story of your life' has not turned out as expected, this may lead you to rewrite the past too, given that previous hopes and ambitions are put into a new light from the perspective of an acquired illness or disability. When a biography is disrupted, so too is the relational ecology in which it is embedded. People treat you differently, and think of themselves differently in relation to you.

The three teenagers that we heard from earlier were in a more natural phase of identity transition, and could independently draw in cultural materials for their short-term identity work. In contrast, many people with disrupted biographies are more dependent on others to make the 'magic mirrors' for self-reflection both accessible and useable. The woman with dementia who Fraser worked with, for example, remains a person, a character, an individual and an experiencing self. But her extreme memory loss has disrupted the ongoing story of her life that she can recall for herself, and tell to others. Instead she's left passive and reactive because she can't improvise her identity fluently without help now. As Tom Kitwood suggested in the case of dementia, 'As subjectivity breaks apart, so intersubjectivity must take over if personhood is to be maintained' (in Baldwin and Capstick 2007, p. 144). Identity work, that is, must become relational and communal.

A welcome positive perspective on identity transition comes from the neurologist and writer Oliver Sacks, whose famous case studies often show people creatively working with their severely disrupted biographies and identities. But, as Sacks admits, it's often tricky to understand what exactly people are doing in this process of identity repair:

> In earlier books I wrote of the 'preservation' of self, and (more rarely) of the 'loss' of self, in neurological disorders. I have come to think these terms too simple – and that there is neither loss nor preservation of identity in such situations, but, rather, its adaptation, even its transmutation, given a radically altered brain and 'reality'. The study of disease, for the physician, demands the study of identity, the inner worlds that patients, under the spur of illness, create. (Sacks 1995, p. xiv)

People seem in particular to cling creatively to music at these times, as many of Sacks's classic cases illustrate (Sacks 2007). Indeed, music often seems like another character in many of his stories – a personified help. It's a thought I've had about some of my own cases at times.

Clarissa's Search for the Perfect Trill

After her death, a friend of Clarissa's leaves an envelope addressed to me at the hospital. The note says that Clarissa had valued her music therapy sessions and missed them when she was suddenly moved. She'd regretted not being able to say goodbye to me. There's also a small photocopied picture of a striking *grand dame*, imperious but with a twinkle – a woman of presence and a certain style. Stapled underneath the photo is a crudely typed poem by Clarissa that the friend says she wants me to have – adding that she thinks it had been written many years earlier.

On Hearing a Symphony by Samuel Wesley
It is morning;
After the sulphurous dreams of night
I wake in a mood of delight.
Turning on the wireless,

I hear a symphony by Samuel Wesley,
Driving, urgent, sharp;
It focuses my morning,
So I settle down to work.
But my glance alights on the green grapes
Round and inviting
Vivid in a bowl,
So I decide to laze for longer.
It occurs to me, that when
A high note is reached
There is a sense of achievement:
Notes wending up and down,
Intersheaved with horns,
Violins suddenly cascading,
Echoes of Haydn; now
More melancholy still,
With one note piercing through
The other – then back to root stem,
Musical growth being pruned,
A rectilinear growth
Broken only by sweet horns.
Holding another pen, a softer
Blue one, with an easy sliding action,
I realize the symphony is too hard.
My morning today
Needs softer notes,
To go with my new clean clothes
And my fresh sense of prettiness.

Clarissa furiously guards her privacy and her past. She complies neither with medical assessments nor any attempts to help her. She sits in her increasingly chaotic hospital room, smoking (illegally) and playing Classic FM on the radio. Few fellow patients or staff would guess that she writes poetry and is something of a musical connoisseur. They know her only as an awkward patient who spent years on the streets and is often threatening and frightening. Asked to see Clarissa, I gingerly approach her room.

'I was wondering whether you'd like to do some music therapy with me, Clarissa.'

'Later!' she booms and shuts the door in my face.

And later, she indeed agrees. As we walk along the corridor, Clarissa nurses her distended abdomen (her twenty-seven-year phantom pregnancy puzzlingly coupled with the further long-term delusion that she's twenty-eight years old). She asks me whether I've been to any good opera recently.

'I went to *The Dialogue of the Carmelites* last week actually, at ENO....'

'Oh yes,' says Clarissa, 'that's the one where all the nuns get murdered at the end, isn't it? Super!'

In the music therapy room, she goes straight to the drum and cymbal, I play on the piano, and we launch into a spirited improvisation. Clarissa's playing is precise and purposeful, with experiments in dynamics and tone. There's a sensitivity in the dialogue between us that takes an unusual turn when Clarissa starts musically testing me, changing tempo, pausing slightly to see if I'm with her. I'm a bit taken aback. In an assessment session in music therapy, it's supposed to be *me* 'testing' *her*, if anything. She finishes the first improvisation – which has become a Viennese waltz – with a flourish.

'I played the drums in Austria once... I was hoping we could play something of Stravinsky today – *Oedipus Rex* especially. I used to do my housework to *Oedipus Rex* – I just love it! Do you know the French recording? The one where Jean Cocteau narrates... **SPECTATEURS!!!**' The last word is declaimed at great volume, and I wonder what people will think we're doing.

Clarissa tells me she learned piano as a young woman and I invite her to play a piano duet with me. Hampered by very long and dirty fingernails, Clarissa launches into the melody of Bach's *Two-part Invention in D Minor*. I provide a bass line to go with this, but too late, and Clarissa's off into another remembered fragment, with me following rather lamely. After a while of this rather frenetic chase, I suggest we improvise something slower. I introduce a slow melody, which Clarissa instantly picks up, embellishing it in a way that becomes characteristic of her music – Baroque turns and lavish trills.

'Fun, isn't it!' says Clarissa. 'We could go on the stage with that – comedy team with piano! But I'm still searching for the perfect trill... not there yet!'

The playful quality to her playing, and the overwhelmingly communicative and companionable nature of our playing together is quite at odds with the medical picture I've been given of Clarissa by colleagues – of a hostile, isolated and deluded woman. Music seems another world for her, where I feel she experiences herself differently, and where I can also perceive her, and be with her, differently.

ॐ

Something uncanny happens in the next session. Clarissa is playing a set of tuned wooden blocks and I'm playing the piano. As usual, there's a sensitive musical rapport, and then I hear a voice in the musical texture. I look up, expecting to see Clarissa singing. But she's not! The singing, however, was palpably in the room. I realise it not to be Clarissa physically singing, but somehow a 'singing' coming from her and her playing.

'Do you sing, Clarissa?' I intuitively ask.

'A bit... but my voice has gone now – a nurse poured some acid down my throat....'

'Your voice is still there Clarissa, I can hear it... sing with me now....'

And she does – in loud, raucous tone – but with such character. She begins with scales, but is soon into a wayward melody that I have some difficulty accompanying.

'Terrible, terrible,' she says. 'Oh dear, oh dear... but such fun!'

She tells me that she'd like piano lessons from me. I explain that I'm a music therapist and don't do piano lessons as such. Clarissa is unimpressed.

'But I don't think of it as *therapy*, Gary,' she says. 'I just think of it as enjoying myself... I've forgotten all my piano... if someone asked me to play a perfect trill, I'd be quite hopeless....'

But somehow, in this and future sessions, we nevertheless manage to continue the search for the perfect trill. These turn up in most of our improvisations, defining something indefinable about style, manner and technique that comprises the curious essence of Clarissa.

∞

We work together for about six weeks, then she tells me: 'They're sending me to some ghastly nursing home in Southampton, Gary. With all those old people – and I'm only twenty-eight or thirty....'

Perhaps cued by this thought, Clarissa launches into the hymn 'O hear us when we cry to Thee / For those in peril on the sea'.

I go up to the ward to collect Clarissa the next week, but her messy room's been cleaned out. She and a friend appeal against the move, but Clarissa dies before any decision is made.

I look around for shreds of consolation in this rather desolate end. When I receive the poem, these lines stand out: '*It occurs to me, that when / A high note is reached / There is a sense of achievement*'.

Clarissa did go out on a high note, courageously her own person to the end.

∞

The commonest thing people said about Clarissa was that she was 'a character', meaning by this that she was unique, memorable, and difficult. The psychoanalyst Christopher Bollas writes of the musical sensing of what he calls a patient's *idiom*, which is 'the dense particularity of personality' (1995, p. 44). For Bollas, a person's idiom is an aesthetic, even erotic, force that is elaborated and differentiated through a unique life, and that is responded to and answered by others. A person's idiom, writes Bollas is 'a music of one's character, a song line in the aesthetic of one's being' (1993, p. 151). How we respond and engage with another person's character is then perhaps rather like the way we do with a composer's voice, or a style of music.

Despite all her struggles, Clarissa was still elaborating the music of her character to the end – in both a literal and metaphorical way. Whilst at one level the story of her life had become tragically fixed and almost a self-parody, in music therapy she found the materials to go on singing the real songline of her character.

Here there was still room for creativity and relationship, a space temporarily free from the pressure to be who others required.

Bollas asks, 'Exactly who do we become as we express our idiom in play?' His answer makes me think of Clarissa the 'character':

> To be a character, to release one's idiom into lived experience, requires a certain risk, as the subject will not know his outcome; indeed, to be a character is to be released into being, not as a knowable entity *per se*, but as an idiom of expression explicating human form. Even in these moments of self-expression the individual will not know his own meaning, his reflections will always lag behind himself, more often than not puzzled by his itness, yet relieved by the *jouissance* of its choosings. (1993, p. 54)

This musical improvisation of identity, however, does not happen by itself. It needs a further process, a social and outward vehicle that is again both a musical and a personal process: the performance of self.

Chapter 9

Musical Performances

If Man is a sapient animal, a tool-making animal, a self-making animal, a symbol-using animal, he is no less a performing animal, *Homo Performans* … His performances are reflexive – in performing he reveals himself to himself.

Victor Turner[1]

Tony: For me, music's like another world… It's more like… how shall I describe it? It's like me being *me*. I can be *me* – I can show my true self. I can show my true happy, or not happy… It feels that I'm completely someone else, playing to a whole audience.…

It's like when I was in the St Thomas Centre with you, and we had that concert for the patients and the staff. That was really marvellous to me. Because I was actually in front of me. We had some rehearsal, I went home and had my tea, came back and done the whole thing. And I really enjoyed doing that in front of the complete audience. I played 'Amazing Grace', and I even composed a bit of it myself! People clapped at the end, and everyone came up to me, and I was talking to them… there was no difficulties.…

But when I came down to earth, and reality, people see me and they think, 'Oh you look miserable'. I don't know whether I am a miserable person or a happy person.… Sometimes when I've not been doing anything, or just looking after my mother again, it's just a matter of doing the shopping, or someone might talk to me, and I've known what they've said, but I've been a complete statue. See, I'm like two different people, though I'm actually one people.…

Tony has been blind from birth and has had a tough and disadvantaged path through life. I wrote about his music therapy sessions in my book *Music for Life* (Ansdell 1995), where I gave a fairly conventional account of our work in a traditional private therapeutic setting.[2] At the end of the case, I briefly mention the event Tony remembers, which I then thought showed a successful outcome of the individual music therapy process. Fifteen years later, when I talk to Tony for this book, I'm surprised that it's a key memory for him, and that he reverses the priorities of my story. For him, the performance comes first!

The strange phrase he uses – 'I was actually in front of me' – links with his earlier statement, 'It feels that I'm completely someone else'. I think he means by

---

[1] Turner 1987, p. 81.

[2] Tony's case is told there under the pseudonym 'David' (chapter 12). For the current book, Tony wants to be known by his real name.

this the different experience he gets of himself when performing, which contrasts with his more usual feeling of being trapped within himself, socially and culturally excluded. But this leads to a seeming paradox as Tony continues to talk about how music helps him and says that, in music, 'It's like me being *me*. I can be *me* – I can show my true self.' That is, Tony feels more himself when this self is more public.

I say 'seeming paradox' because of how this idea goes against one of the key assumptions of most traditional therapy: that it's a private and confidential process, where the need to put on a social performance for others is temporarily suspended, giving the client the space to express and develop a more authentic self. Given this belief, many therapists from the psychotherapeutic tradition would question Tony's report that performance helps, and rather suspect it of further distorting his identity. Music therapists have tended to follow this line and believe that musical performance is a musical affordance best avoided in therapy. But these views are based on the kind of individualist and 'internalist' theory that we've been questioning in this book. When we instead see how personhood and selfhood need to be socially and culturally midwifed and maintained, there is no reason why public performance can't in some circumstances be helpful and therapeutic for people.[3]

However, to support this, we need to look at an alternative and more nuanced understanding of performance that's been developed both in music studies and recent sociocultural approaches to therapy. This goes beyond the outdated cliché that to perform is to lose oneself. On the contrary, it may sometimes be the only way to find who we are, and could be.

'Being who you aren't, doing what you can't…'

Tony's story illustrates what I've called the 'paradoxes of performance' (Ansdell 2010d), the sense of how performance can sometimes allow us to be ourselves through 'being someone else'; can enable us to do what we 'can't do'; can allow us to reflect on the real through the unreal; can be personal yet public; can be shared yet different for everyone.

A long history of social theory has explored this idea of self and identity as a performance rather than an essence. Erving Goffman's famous book *The Presentation of Self in Everyday Life* (1959) showed how social life requires us to strike a balance between making an expression of ourselves whilst managing a favourable impression on others. This balancing is often a precarious social and cultural performance. Our 'social skills' and knowledge help most of us keep the performance going for most of the time. But stressful circumstances or illness can quickly undermine this competence, and show up the whole game. At the least, it seriously questions what it could mean to 'just be yourself'.

---

[3]   For more on music therapy's ambivalent relationship to performance, see Ansdell 2005a, 2010d; Stige and Aarø 2012; and sections of Part V of this book.

However, there's another angle to the theme of self-performance, as illustrated by Tony's story. A 'heightened performance' on a real or metaphorical stage can sometimes be the making of us. It can represent a breakthrough into broader social competence, and towards a fuller reflexive sense of the self. Whilst not a solution to his problems, Tony's various musical performances have since helped him experience and think about himself as a person in different ways. Performance has provided Tony with an accessible and usually enhancing 'magic mirror'.

Recent theory from both music studies and therapeutic theory has been moving towards similar conclusions. A 'turn to performance' promoted by Christopher Small (1998), Nicholas Cook (1998, 2003) and others is rebalancing the almost-exclusive attention to abstract musical texts with a new interest in performance processes. Cook (2003) summarises this as a move from a concept of 'music *and* performance' to 'music *as* performance'. In an analysis of this shift, Stan Godlovitch (1998) outlines a stance he calls *personalism*. Why do we attend musical performances? Godlovitch suggests it's not just to hear the structure of musical works being reproduced, but to hear real people performing them live. We witness something at stake for these performers, something humanly vital happening:

> Personalism reminds us that performance is a way of communicating, not especially a work or a composer's notions, but a person, the performer, through the music. Personalism intimates that a proper understanding of performance must … appreciate ritual forms of communication, action and its significance, human benefit and reciprocity, and a good many other concerns belonging naturally to social conduct. (Godlovitch 1998, p. 145)

Another useful suggestion comes from the anthropologist Victor Turner (1982), who was particularly interested in the connections between ritual and performance. He suggests that our assumption that the word and concept 'performance' means projecting a work 'through the form' is only one possible etymological interpretation. Instead,

> *Performance* … is derived from the Middle English *parfourmen*, which is itself from the Old French, *parfournir* – *par* ('thoroughly'), + *fournir* ('to furnish') – hence performance does not necessarily have the structuralist implications of manifesting form, but rather the processual sense of 'bringing to completion', or 'accomplishing'. To perform is thus to complete a more or less involved process rather than to do a single deed or act. (Turner 1982, p. 91)

This sense of performance as completion of a process assumes then that something *needs* completing, both in the cultural form that is the performance vehicle, and in personal and social life. It suggests that in the creative 'carrying out' of performance something is transformed, personally and socially. In this sense, performance events are closer to ritual events in being both heightened social events and potentially reflexive ones – showing back to people something about themselves and the society they belong to. Turner became especially interested in the rehearsal or preparation process for performance. He commented on how an actor moves from taking up a role (= 'not me') to assimilating this in performance as 'not not me'. The aim, says Turner, is '*poiesis*, rather than *mimesis*: making, not faking'. He sums up his concept of performance: 'A performance, then, is the proper finale of an experience' (1982, p. 13).

There's a tendency today to think of performance as 'showing off' to an audience. But we might also usefully think of other performance-based activities and contexts, such as when a sportsman's performance is a case of 'bringing it off' rather than 'showing off'. This accomplishment might only be possible when witnessed and spurred on by an audience. Thinking of the self as performed in this way reinforces the understanding we've been building up in Part III: that, as an ongoing psychosocial process, identity needs appropriate props, a stage and an audience. As Goffman famously said, 'All the world is not, of course, a stage, but the crucial ways in which it isn't are not easy to specify' (1959/1990, p. 78).

୫

Thinking about performance this way helps us to think about how Tony experiences an important transition between 'me', 'not me' and 'not not me' through musicking. His public performances give him a platform to accomplish or complete something that is witnessed, supported and appreciated by others. As a result of this, he becomes more visible and more appreciated within the social fabric as a whole – both to others and, through their recognition, to himself. Tony becomes more himself through others.

Given these positive affordances of performance, it is perhaps no surprise that therapeutic theory is now belatedly acknowledging this truth. A good example of this is the work of the radical 'social therapist' Fred Newman, who makes the wonderful definition of performance as 'being who you aren't, doing what you can't' (1999, p. 100). He maintains that human development is an 'unnatural act'; that we become who we 'are' by continuously 'being who we are not'. Newman's critique of traditional therapy is inspired by Vygotsky, the pioneering Russian developmental psychologist. Vygotsky (1978, p. 102) suggested how a child can find herself 'a head taller' in ability and confidence when inducted into what he calls a cultural 'zone of proximal development' based on talking and doing things with more developed others. In this zone, adults literally perform above the child's current developmental level, but whilst in that cultural performance space the child then finds herself performing 'beyond herself' – raised a level. A similar process could happen to any of us.

This idea links in turn with Victor Turner's (1987) definition of performance as something 'completed' along with others. Newman's work takes a performative stance on therapy itself – where he encourages people to learn to perform themselves differently in ensemble with others. The aim is to transform the whole 'zone' of relational experience such that people experience themselves differently together. Newman writes that people in his therapy group 'were learning to perform beyond themselves … they were breaking out of the habit of simply being themselves to discovering not who they were but who they were not' (1999, p. 129).

Seen this way, Tony's music therapy was clearly a form of 'social therapy'. His performance of 'who he was not' was simultaneously what David Aldridge (2004) has called a 'health performance'. When Tony performs, he moves towards a healthier relationship with the social ecology on which he is dependent for his long-term wellbeing.

In the light of this understanding of the connections between performing and wellbeing, one of the possible roles for a music therapist is sometimes (in ways that I didn't fully understand when I worked with Tony twenty years ago) to help mount appropriate 'stages' such that the 'performance of the self' can continue and flourish.

Musicianhood

I started off the earlier chapter on core musicality by saying that we need to get away from the outdated view that this is a special gift visited only on the few. I hope that you are indeed now more convinced that everyone is musical. But it's also true that certain people have a particularly strong relationship with music that becomes formative of their personal and professional identity across the lifecourse. *Being a musician* is a role that is performed and elaborated across all aspects of the self – with both positive and negative aspects. It concerns both how 'musicians' experience themselves, and how they experience others' perceptions of their talent and accomplishments, and their social role.[4] This kind of identity is best described by Jane:

> **Jane:** Music *defines* me. It keeps me from being lonely; it makes me feel special in front of other people, as a performer; and it helps me share, communicate and participate with other people. Music's made me what I am. I couldn't hide the fact that I was a singer when I was at school, and I could have given up when the kids made fun of me, but my attitude was 'sod you!' – so somewhere I beat myself into doing it. A lot of it's about my personality really... but I chose to do it with music – that's the interesting thing. I think I saw my identity much more as a singer somehow, because the voice... my voice vibrates and makes these particular sounds, the quality of me.

For people like Jane, music helps define the membrane of her self, and through this opens up a space for innerness, as well as giving a model for characterising the

---

[4]   MacDonald, Hargreaves and Miell in *Musical Identities* (2002) suggest the category 'identities in music' to describe the ways of being, becoming and remaining a musician that are based on social categories and cultural musical practices. But I think Jane's narrative (and that of several other 'locals' I interviewed) suggests a more complicated picture than this.

complex relationship between 'internal' and 'external' aspects of self and identity as a musical flow of engagement with the world:

> Music keeps me in *me*! In my world, my *in-world*.... It's like I could sit in a chair for twenty minutes and someone could ask me what I've been doing... and my head's just been full of this bloody stuff, this music! It's defining in some way the 'inner me'. *Outer* me is Jane the performer, Jane the dancer, Jane the talker... but this *inner music* is much more to do with where I am, where my thought processes are. It might be low-level synaesthesia, I suppose!
>
> Talking about all this is showing me that I have lots of different relationships with music, but it's all music in me. There's inner me, all this musical stuff in my head, then practice me, which disciplines aspects of myself, then performer me, which emerges in how I present myself... and then there's the me that flies, above and beyond....

Stan Godlovitch (1998) suggests the term *musicianhood* to characterise this type of all-encompassing musical identity. There are similarities with the more general category of personhood that we discussed previously. Like personhood, musicianhood is partly a status *attributed* to someone by others. But it isn't merely the social category 'professional musician', nor is it just about talent or the quality of performance. Musicianhood, rather, comes when there is a particular match between how a person experiences themselves in relationship to music, and how this comes to be recognised and acknowledged by others. As such, musicianhood is typically long lasting, but it can also be a transitory yet key happening in a person's experience (it does not need to be a prolonged state to be significant – as many examples from music therapy could attest). But the value of this state of musicianhood accounts for both its ecstasies and its occasional agonies. There are, that is, times when this particular identity is a burden for people, or it invokes conflicts within the psychological or social ecology of lives (when, for example, illness or disability interferes with the natural functioning of musicianhood). Musicianhood is a strong and mostly helpful identity, but – like any strong identity – also a potentially vulnerable one.

Sounding the Ecological Self

An independent and autonomous individual is a modernist, Western invention – and often a problem. Whilst a normal everyday life might sometimes give us the illusion of our self being private, fixed and stable, it only takes illness or almost any social disruption or displacement to remind us quickly of our *inter*dependence and vulnerability, and of the frailty of identity and personhood.

Our exploration of the musical self in action in Part III has suggested a more ecological conception of personhood and identity, as existing within a fluid and creative continuum between private and communal reality. As an 'ecological self', we are both semi-autonomous and boundaried (as self-directing and unique persons), but also 'porous' and socially embedded. We emerge fully only in and through relationship with others, and are recognised, nurtured and sustained in our personhood and identity by ongoing communications within a supportive community.

Within our social ecology, we can use musical materials to project and impress on others who we are now, and who we are in the process of becoming, or wish to become. Music can help furnish a sense of 'me' through the ongoing process of self-identifying, self-crafting and self-performing – all of which are processes that are mobilised individually but can only complete themselves within the social and cultural theatre of everyday life.

Many recent studies and texts expand on how music helps to create, stabilise and preserve the broader dimensions of familial, cultural and national identity, class and sub-cultural affiliations, ethnic and sexual identities (MacDonald, Hargreaves and Miell 2002; Clayton, Herbert and Trevor 2003; Hesmondhalgh 2013; Pavlicevic and Ansdell 2004). Some of these areas naturally came out in my interviews with the 'locals'. Susanna and Christina, for example, talked about the relationship between their evolving musical identity and their family culture and identity. For one of them, this was a revered classical music culture invoked by memories of sitting underneath the piano hearing her father playing Bach; for the other, it was the sometimes comic tension between parental Italian catholic and English protestant culture being played out through music. For Oksana, the cultural resonances are even stronger, living as she does as a Ukrainian in exile. For her, there's a powerful immediacy in the music of her cultural heritage, which she describes as giving instant reconnection to place, event and collective energy.

ॐ

The ecological self is a musical performance. We hear its vitality, its tone, style and inflection as the unique soundings of a body, mind and spirit. A core musicality motivates the need to connect and identify with the musicality of others, and to use such relationships to perform what it can be and can do within social life. It is helped in this creative self-elaboration by its immersion in culture and in the immediate improvised scenes it is required to perform, finding its part and place within the social polyphony.

PART IV
Musical Relationship

When someone is singing and cannot lift their voice, and another comes and sings with them, another who can lift their voice, the first will be able to lift their voice too. That is the secret of the bond between spirits.

Martin Buber

Musicking is about the creation and performance of relationships ... It is the relationships that it brings into existence in which the meaning of a musical performance lies.

Christopher Small

Because music is an outward sign of human communication ... the function of music is to enhance in some way the quality of individual experience and human relationships; its structures are reflections of patterns of human relations ....

John Blacking

Communication is a process of sharing experience till it becomes a common possession.

John Dewey

Music tells us the one thing we really want to hear. We are not alone.

Bryan Appleyard

Chapter 10
Musical Connection

All music calls to an ear that is not the musician's own ....

Martin Buber[1]

The Variety of Musical Relationships

Musicking is connecting: tone with tone; tone with person; person with person; place with tone with person... and so on, in a spiralling web of relationships. This is Christopher Small's (1998) ecological vision of what music really offers us – a model of ideal relationship that can be incarnated and performed as an everyday activity. Music is always calling, and always being responded to.

We saw in the Introduction how people often talk of their relationship to music as if it were to another person. Music is intimate, inspiring, supportive and sustaining; it changes, develops, survives rifts and celebrates reconciliations. We also saw in previous chapters how music can forge relationships with others that transcend the usual norms. Adam felt close to Brahms, and David talked of how, when he goes to a concert at the Wigmore Hall, he sometimes feels as though a singer is performing directly for him, even though he knows that many other members of the audience are having a similar feeling. Other 'locals' reflected that music was a key ingredient of their relationship with a family member:

> **Oliver:** I'd never had a relationship with my father that was close in the traditional sense. Yet I do think that through music we had a language that we understood together, that my mother didn't. So this was something that we shared, it was my father who took me to different kinds of concerts, and this strange eclectic musical language that we began to share was something we could communicate in. And it was convenient that this was something about which you didn't have to give away too many facts about yourself.

Whilst familial relationships are givens that need nurturing, friendships and erotic connections need discovering and elaborating. Music can help this process of getting to know and getting close to another person. Alan puts this most blatantly: 'This girl I fancied in high school was a cellist, so I studied cello so we could both be in the orchestra together! That was an early example of so many of my musical experiences being based around relationships'. Alan also introduces another

---

[1] Buber 1947/2002, p. 30.

dimension of musical relationship that will emerge many times during this part of the book:

> **Alan:** I've had some very powerful relationships with people in music… and even though I might not know a lot *about* them, I *know* them… or I feel that we know each other. There's a certain mutual trust here that I don't think I could get just talking to them. I'm thinking of when I play with David… we often play two pianos… and these are some of the most powerful times for me! I just want it never to stop… it's so *joyous*… and that's about jazz, because that's how he and I relate musically. One of the most beautiful and exciting things about music is connecting… finding out parts of myself that resonate with another person…. Maybe I discover things about myself that I didn't know… and also finding out about that other person… in a relationship that feels new and exciting. But it's more than a relationship… it's like we're *building* something….

How musicking can afford this depth and complexity of relationship without recourse to words is especially important for people who for a variety of reasons have significant problems connecting and communicating with others. Examples from music therapy often highlight the key aspects of the phenomenon of musical relationship by showing it happening *in extremis*. Matthew, for example, tells me about a client he worked with in a neurological rehabilitation unit:

> **Matthew:** Music's basically about connection, connectedness… people become really cut off and isolated when they have brain injury. So it's about *making* connections in music therapy… welcoming people back, almost… and music is particularly good at this!
>
> I worked with a young woman who had no controlled movement of any kind. No voice, no means of communication. Music making happened through her blinking… and she couldn't even control her blinking enough to do a yes/no… but she could control it enough for brief periods to do rhythm. I'd play familiar songs to her… 'Yes Sir, that's My Baby' was the best one! Occasionally she'd get the rhythm before me…. It's extraordinary how you get these situations of extreme human tragedy and these strange songs come out! But it worked… and it was the only way she could actively communicate with somebody in real time. By 'communicate' I don't necessarily mean 'transmit information', though there is information being sent and received… like yes, I understand you or yes, I know there's a person inside there. But what I mean is the sense you get of a presence communicated within the music making. Suddenly I'd be in a situation that had all the qualities of full relating, of being with another person when you're having the most intense interaction… as if with someone with all their faculties intact….

Rachel remembers first realising music's potential to afford this kind of connection when she heard an early music therapy presentation in the 1970s by Paul Nordoff and Clive Robbins. They were playing a tape of a session in which a child was screaming and Nordoff playing the piano:

Rachel: Paul was hearing this screaming as music... and he sang and played quite forcefully with it... and then there was this extraordinary moment when the child's voice began to change from screaming into singing! So instead of being sound, it becomes *music*. You could say exactly *when*, there's an actual point.... What I heard that afternoon was the *turning* of that person... it's something to do with *that* child at *that* moment: something reached out... something in the child... and... that hackneyed word... *connected*. You heard the turning of that person, from 'being screamed' to *I am singing*.... Then they became music together....

The Ecology of Musical Relationships

Becoming music together is the prime, if perhaps most mysterious, way in which music helps. In a variety of ways, music affords connection, companionship, and occasionally a depth of relatedness that is both shocking and healing. But how?

In Small's (1998) ecological model, music simply *is* relationship, or rather a dense network of relationships that connect together all the various dimensions of our lifeworlds. But for this part of the book, I shall keep mainly to one level of this ecology. Although a network has no 'core' as such, it does have nearer and more distant relationships (as do individuals within a 'Russian dolls'-style nested system – beginning with intimate familial ties). The following chapters will concentrate on music's intimate 'near relations': those between tone and tone,[2] between tone and person, and between person and person in music. Parts V and VI will then explore the broadening relationships that musicking also affords, as community and transcendence.

Tone relationships are the intimate connectors of a musical ecology. In Chapter 4, we explored the key aspect of a musical eco-phenomenology – how sounds transmute into tones when we hear them musically. They then begin to operate in a musical world, and we step into this world too as we attend musically to their ongoing patterns of relationship (and, of course, our own participation in this patterning). 'No musical tone is sufficient unto itself,' writes Zuckerkandl; 'the smallest particle of music is not properly the tone but the connection of tone with tone, the interval' (1956, p. 93). Pitch connections are either of the 'horizontal' sort when tones reach out or point towards each other in melody, or alternatively within the 'vertical' plane where tones cohere together to form chords.. 'Non-pitched tones' relate in rhythmic, textural and timbral ways to form further patterns which connect. All of this adds up to a bewildering complexity, even in a

---

[2]   Remember that, by 'tone' in this book, I mean any musicalised sound – a rhythm, pitch, or any other foundational element that makes musical connections.

simple nursery rhyme. But as we've seen previously, our lived understanding of this comes naturally, and doesn't have to be an intellectual experience.

Musical relationships can show up unfamiliar aspects of the phenomenology of relational space and time that are subtly different to those of the everyday world. Zuckerkandl suggests, for example, that music reveals an enlarged, dynamic concept of space as a medium of encounter:

> Space… is not only that whence something encounters me; space is also that in which what encounters me is mutually related; space is the whence of the encounter and the where of the relation. […]
>
> [Music] is the space which, instead of consolidating the boundaries between within and without, obliterates them; space which does not stand over against me but with which I can be one; which permits encounter to be experienced as communication, not as distance …. (Zuckerkandl 1956, p. 302)

In the light of this understanding, we need now to explore how aspects of an eco-phenomenology of musicking afford something qualitatively different for person-to-person encounter, relatedness and co-action.

℘

Matthew makes an important distinction when he says that, by 'communication' through music, he doesn't just mean 'transmit information' (though it can do this too sometimes). Instead, he talks of experiencing in musicking the quality of 'being with' his client, of communication as a sense of presence, recognition of personhood, and of mutual connection and sharing of musical experience.

This is essentially the difference between mechanical and ecological communication. In a mechanical model of communication, a precomposed message is sent and received, successfully or not. This is a linear, predictable, and mostly uncreative process. In contrast, living systems, however simple or complex they are, communicate in a more messy, non-linear and creative way. They do so by ongoing and mutual *inter*action with each other in a process called 'structural coupling'. As each organism responds, the structure of each changes (however slightly) and something new emerges *between* them. Communication here is a process of coordinating behaviour rather than just transmitting information. The biologist Humberto Maturana (in Capra 1997, p. 279) gives the nice example of the mating ritual of African parrots who perform what seems like a shared song, but on closer inspection is the common result of a duet where each contributes and extends the other's response. The process is the product. They are responding, not just reacting.

Here, as in many examples that we'll see in Part IV, communicating is a dynamic, relational activity that is embodied and performed. Meaning and action emerge from interaction, but are not necessarily defined before (or indeed, after). Instead, we can say that communication has taken place such that something is now known, understood, done, or found possible between people – but without necessarily being able to state exactly *what*. Communication is in the broader service of forging meaningful ongoing relationship. Musical communication is exemplary of this kind.

∞

I sometimes describe my work as a music therapist as initiating musical conversations, and then developing these with clients in ways helpful to their individual needs and situations. Music therapy has increasingly defined itself within such a relational, psycho-social understanding – not trying directly to fix or to treat people. Rather, the therapy *is* the ongoing process of communication, dialogue and relationship, understood within as broad an ecology as possible. The primary therapeutic aim is to help people find or re-find connection, companionship and community through mostly musical means (Ansdell and Pavlicevic 2005).

Chapter 11
Musical Companionship

Our musicality serves our need for companionship just as language serves our need for the sharing of facts and practical actions with things.

Stephen Malloch and Colwyn Trevarthen[1]

As he projected himself into a new intensity of human relationship, the boy experienced musical companionship.

Paul Nordoff and Clive Robbins[2]

The Discovery of Communicative Musicality

Since the 1970s the developmental psychologist Colwyn Trevarthen has been part of a pioneering international network of researchers who have capitalised on emerging video technology with slow-frame analysis capability to study early communication between carers and infants,.By concentrating on the micro-detail of these 'early duets' for the first time, this research has revealed how an infant's communication is both intelligent and creative (rather than passive and reactive, as previously taught). It suggests that babies are usually fine communicators almost from birth, instigating non-verbal 'conversations' with their mothers or carers. What these researchers hadn't quite managed was to encapsulate their findings in a satisfying unifying concept to convey what such communication is 'made from'.

Stephen Malloch was a young postdoctoral student of Trevarthen's who, one day in 1996, was sitting in a windowless office in the psychology department of Edinburgh University, listening to some old tapes Colwyn had made of mothers and children. Hearing baby Laura and her mother 'talking' led to a small epiphany:

> As I listened, intrigued by the fluid give and take of the communication, and the lilting speech of the mother as she chatted with her baby, I began to tap my foot. I am, by training, a musician, so I was very used to automatically feeling the beat as I listened to musical sounds. There was no doubt in my mind that the melodious speech of the mother had a certain musical quality to it. It suddenly dawned on me that I was tapping my foot to human speech – not something that I had ever done before, or even thought possible. I replayed the tape, and again,

---

[1]   Malloch and Trevarthen 2009b, p. 6.

[2]   Nordoff and Robbins 1971, caption to photo on p. 67.

> I could sense a distinct rhythmicity and melodious give and take to the gentle promptings of Laura's mother and the pitched vocal replies from Laura … A few weeks later, as I walked down the stairs to Colwyn's main lab, the words 'communicative musicality' came into my mind as a way of describing what I had heard. (Malloch, in Malloch and Trevarthen 2009b, p. 4)

Stephen listened *musically* and found music in these mother–infant duets. As with many good theories, all of the pieces were lying around, but nobody had quite completed the picture. Previous research had indeed noticed the proto-musical features of early interaction (Deliège and Sloboda 1996), but what Malloch, Trevarthen and others subsequently did was to use the unifying concept 'communicative musicality' to focus and elaborate a broader range of inquiry. A seminal book, *Communicative Musicality*, was published in 2009, containing wide-ranging interdisciplinary research and theory inspired by this concept. Altogether this varied work suggests that musicality is an evolved psychobiological capacity that supports infants' immediate needs for human companionship, and that its influence continues throughout our lives in supporting intersubjective contact with others.

Malloch used his knowledge as a musician and expert in acoustic analysis to define in more precise and objective ways the musical parameters of these infant–carer 'musical conversations'. The key point is that a genuine duet happens during these interactions. Both partners show an equal natural skill in receiving the other's part, for producing their own in response, and for mutually creating something new between them. What it's palpably *not* is a mechanical message 'sent' by the infant and 'received' by the mother (the old-style 'telegraph model' of communication). Rather, there is the 'co-production' of meaningful communication that emerges spontaneously and improvisationally, and is 'about' the here and now of the immediate relationship in the making between parent and infant.

Colwyn Trevarthen defines communicative musicality as 'the dynamic sympathetic state of a human person that allows co-ordinated companionship to arise' (2002, p. 21). Malloch and Trevarthen further explain:

> To capture the essence of movement and its values we use the metaphor of 'musicality'. To recognise that our experience in movement is shared by a compelling sympathy we call this activity 'communication'. (Malloch and Trevarthen 2009b, p. 9)

This emphasis on movement represents a key feature of the theory. Communication happens not just with sounds but through an integrated flux of sounds, movements and gestures that compose and vitalise an interaction. Communication is naturally cross-modal, allowing sounds and gestures to be understood as 'one thing'. A sound can, for example, be matched and mirrored by a movement, which is then playfully elaborated by the duet partners as they attune vocalisations, bodies and minds. Malloch and Trevarthen (2009b) propose three basic parameters of communicative musicality: *pulse, quality, narrative*:

- *PULSE* describes the regular temporal succession of sounds or movements – allowing partners to 'time', anticipate and coordinate their responses, and to share musical events together.
- *QUALITY* describes the ever-changing expressive contours that give the 'feel' of a vocal sound or movement. Dynamic changes in force, timbre, pitch, volume or shape can come from both sounds and gestures (often with 'cross-modal' mirroring and matching).
- *NARRATIVE* describes the evolving form of the non-verbal 'short story' that partners spontaneously shape as their interaction moves through small 'phrases' or even longer sequences.

We can see how these 'proto-musical' parameters link with the more conventional musical descriptors of rhythm, melody/dynamics/timbre, and form – as applied to both composed and improvised music. But the key point is that an infant already has an innate sensitivity to these 'foundations' of pulse, dynamic quality, and narrative. This allows 'a music-like composition, an improvised song or dance of companionship with someone we trust' (Trevarthen 2002, p. 35).

Music therapy often highlights this basic need and potential for musical companionship. The particular craft of a music therapist is to mobilise and support communicative musicality in a client in the service of finding a connection and developing a relationship with them.

Improvising Companionship

Felicity is working as a music therapist with an infant called Julia, who has significant developmental problems. The child is crying loudly, arching away and averting her gaze from Felicity, who cradles her and sings strongly back.

Felicity doesn't try to calm the child down, but rocks her and sings 'Ju-li-a' in a short downwards phrase (C'–A–G), matching the short bursts of the crying and synchronising with the rocking. There's a 'messy' pulse and an up-and-down dynamic contour of their singing/crying – and as the pitch of Julia's crying rises, so does Felicity's response, picking out both the shape of her phrases and some precise tones. Sometimes Felicity sings *with* the child, matching the length of the bouts of crying; other times she fits in her 'Ju-li-a' call as the child breathes between phrases.

Suddenly I hear it as a musical duet, something shared rather than a struggle. The two singers begin sharing the same pitch areas, and the same lengths of small phrases. Julia's eyes and movements seem to take in Felicity and what she's doing, as if to say, 'I know what we're doing now!' They seem to experiment with their duet for a while, with matching swoops up and down, and I find myself questioning who's leading and following now – there's rather a mutual interplay, a shared duet. Suddenly both pause. Julia stops crying, turns her head and looks Felicity straight in the eye... *Connection!*

୫

Richard is working as a music therapist with a woman with advanced dementia. She has no language left, just a series of empty gestures that seem cruelly to parody the kind of social communications she once made adeptly. Within the care home, she's often isolated and distressed.

She sits in a wheelchair, with Richard facing her. He calls to her with a rising melodic phrase (C–D–F–A... G–F...) sung with open vowels (*oh... aye... ee...*). She sits up, moves her upper body towards him, and smiles broadly. Richard mirrors her movement by leaning towards her as he repeats the phrase. There's more musical tension this time, and you notice how this extends the duration of their relatedness. She seems to match her breathing to Richard's during this phrase, tracks his actions by listening and looking at him, synchronising her movements with the up and down of the tones. Every musical and physical gesture in the next two minutes is exquisitely choreographed spontaneously between them – a micro *pas de deux*! At the level of timing and phrasing, and within the melodic contour and intensity of the music, there's a precise synchrony between sound and movement. Richard matches the timing of his sung phrases to the pace she can manage, and she seems physically suspended on the ongoing string of tones, her upper torso and head raised up energetically. Her mouth is open as she wordlessly mirrors Richard's voice, her eyes shining. At the apex of the harmonic tension of this phrase, she reaches forward, clasps Richard's hand, and utters a single, placed 'Ah!' with a bowing gesture... *Connection!*

୫

We are clearly dealing with a very similar phenomenon here with these two very different people. What's in common is how in each case the music therapist hears the person musically, and through this helps to mobilise communicative musicality. Felicity and Richard listen and watch carefully as they make music, picking up the precise musical dimensions of the sounds and gestures of their client. They treat everything their client does as having a potential for musical communication, but without losing their own musical voice. Their own contributions invite and respond, helping to extend the musical conversations that begin to emerge. In order for this to work, they must attend closely to the dimensions of pulse, dynamic quality, and narrative shaping of the interaction, as the theory of communicative musicality suggests. The relationship that ensues is both musical and personal at the same time, as each pair finds the music shared between them. Julia and the elderly lady both step out of their isolation as they come into musical companionship with Felicity and Richard.

Another useful perspective on these vignettes comes from the psychologist Daniel Stern (2010), also a pioneer in early interaction. We looked previously at Stern's theory of *forms of vitality*, his version of the music-like qualities of human character, and how we instinctively 'read' these clues about others' inner states and intentions, and sometimes identify with these. Stern also suggests that vitality forms lie behind musical communication and relationship. Here forms of vitality are being actively *shared*:

> these forms of vitality are really the stuff that music creates and plays with, and it's what we, in communicating with one another, create and play with ... One of the beauties of forms of vitality is that they are communicable, sharable, can be contagious ... [so] singing a song achieves the job in part of making everybody feel like they have been somewhere within the other person's skin, or mind, or body. (Stern 2010a, pp. 92 and 93)

Stern suggests that sharing vitality forms through musicking needs a level of sensitivity and competence in three key musical/relational processes:

- *Attuning* – perceiving the vitality forms of another person and responding sympathetically with your own actions. This calls not for a slavish mirroring, but rather incorporating someone's timing, intensity and shaping in a response that presents your own vital signature too.
- *Dialoguing* – creating and developing forms of reciprocal action, ranging from simple turn taking to more complex forms that interleave actions. This involves some degree of shared understanding of the meaning and direction of the communication. Co-action generates something *between* the partners, moving the relationship forward through the mutual contributions.
- *Regulating* – making micro-judgements that 'titrate' *how* the dialogue moves forward, and the level of arousal it evokes. This needs a mutual sensitivity to how much, or how quickly, change can happen, such that surprise is balanced with tolerance. This mutual shaping and regulating of an interaction ensures that the relationship stays on track.

These three processes are complementary to the three parameters of communicative musicality: pulse, dynamic expression and narrative. Together these features and processes show just how precise and precarious this musical composition of communication is.

ঙ

Human communication in general (as well as some human–animal communication) rests on the mostly non-conscious working of these 'mechanisms' described by communicative musicality and vitality forms. But music therapists often make more conscious and strategic use of them when working with their clients. If communication is in some sense a 'musical problem', as it is for Julia and the elderly lady, then music therapy can offer a musical solution. As Daniel Stern puts it, in non-verbal therapies like music therapy, 'what is being sculpted is the nature of relatedness between patient and therapist – the therapy itself' (2010, p. 138).

Felicity and Richard achieve an unexpected quality of musical communication and interpersonal intimacy with their two clients in situations where isolation and non-communication are sadly the norm. This therapeutic benefit comes not through luck or magic, but because of how these two therapists use their professional judgement and musical–personal skills to reach their clients' core musicality and to link this with the potentials of communicative musicality (that is, using their relationship *to* music to promote relationship *through* music). In the musicking within each example, we hear an unexpected sharing of experience via sequences of sounds travelling on pathways through time. Through precise musical means come key human outcomes. Julia knows that Felicity knows her; Richard knows that the elderly woman knows that he knows her... if only for precious seconds.

追

This type of music therapeutic work follows on directly from the discoveries that Paul Nordoff and Clive Robbins made, which not only were very practical but also illuminated a whole philosophy of human relationship through music. A key perception was of how the isolated and challenging children with whom they were working seemed often to make a relationship first with music itself, and how a music therapist could then invite the child gradually into a more inter*personal* contact through the musicking. They write of one boy, 'as he projected himself into a new intensity of human relationship, the boy experienced musical companionship' (1971, p. 67). 'Companionship' is perhaps the best way of describing what follows musical contact and connection, where a journeying together in music can begin. The etymological origin of 'companionship' – breaking bread together – conveys the qualities of mutuality and solidarity through something being shared. For musicians, there's also the related sense of *accompanying*, the supportive travelling together through the music that one musician offers another.

A Musical Bridge to Cultural Belonging

From the 1990s onwards, many music therapists enthusiastically adopted the explanatory possibilities of communicative musicality for their work. But after a while, some critical questions emerged about this. Firstly, is this really *music*? How does the *proto*-music of early interactions relate to 'proper music', to the developed skills and activities of a musical culture? Secondly, how do the early relationships depicted by communicative musicality theory compare with those happening in mature musicking between people? Behind these questions was the suspicion that musicking was being reduced to 'only' preverbal infant–carer interaction. Music therapists were, after all, also working in therapy with adults where there were often sophisticated musical and interpersonal relationships. Was communicative musicality really a sufficient explanatory basis for this work too?

Responses to these critical questions have come both from within developments of communicative musicality theory, and from music therapy itself. In his outline of a more culture-oriented understanding of music therapy, Brynjulf Stige suggested that 'no person moves directly from protomusicality to musicking.

Musicking, based on human protomusicality involves appropriation of music as culture' (2003/2012, p. 173). This relates to the view of musicality I suggested with the 'inverted pyramid' model in Chapter 7, showing the need for a dynamic movement between the three interdependent levels of musicality, musicianship and musicking. No single level is sufficient in itself. Seen this way, communicative musicality helps to explain the foundational level of musical capacity, but it also needs to link to those above it – to how the cultural and social aspects of musicking are necessary to any complete picture of musical relationship.

To be fair, communicative musicality theory always did address these aspects to some extent, even if music therapists did not always notice this. Colwyn Trevarthen (1999) described how the 'sympathetic human company' developed through communicative musicality helps to induct an infant into cultural learning. A more recent cross-cultural study by Maya Gratier and Gisèle Apter-Danon (2009) explores sixty mother–infant dialogues. All these showed the expected core features of shared pulse, expressive dynamics and narrative. But each cultural group could also be recognised from how the proto-conversations reflected the broader communicational styles of each cultural community. Indian mothers and infants spent more time vocalising simultaneously than French or American, whilst pauses between conversational 'turns' were related to the norms of each language. The wider point for us is to see just how soon, and how strongly, 'natural' musicality and socio-cultural learning intertwine. As Gratier suggests, 'the feeling of belonging is acquired through musical engagement and attunement, and opens up new spaces for an intimate communication supporting culturally based personal styles of "being together in time"' (in Gratier and Apter-Danon 2009, p. 303). Carers soon introduce infants to improvised and ritualised songs and games (*peek-a-boo*, *pat-a-handies*, etc.) that model for the child how play and interaction happen within that particular culture.[3] Musicking is a bridge both to being someone and to belonging somewhere.

What happens, however, when this education doesn't unfold so naturally? The musical bridge to belonging can be compromised either when early development is impaired or interrupted, or later in life if illness or disability interferes. What is lost is not just the easy fitting in with others, but also the chance to experiment with personal styles of expression and communication, and to enjoy sharing experiences with others.

✲

Oliver is an energetic yet frustrated and often isolated teenager. His learning disability means that he can neither speak nor understand most of what people say – or, presumably, guess what they think, feel or intend. Not being able to enter into play and symbolic interaction means that the cultural materials ready to hand for other people are remote from him. So, too, are the chances to share

---

[3]   For the relationship between communicative musicality and improvised songs and games with infants, see Malloch and Trevarthen 2009b, p. 7.

experiences and belong together that other teenagers enjoy. It's no surprise that his response to others has become increasingly defensive and aggressive.

His music therapist, Richard, is one of the few people Oliver tolerates in close proximity. Music is perhaps the only medium in which Oliver can readily participate and begin to share successfully and satisfyingly with another.

I watch a video of a short musical encounter between them, with Richard and Oliver facing each other:

- Oliver's head is down as Richard sings *aye-yaa* to him on a downward 2-note motif [G–E], playing a Spanish-style chord on the guitar to match the energy of his voice...
- ... to which Oliver responds with a small *i-i*... and immediately there's a little to-and-fro dialogue between O and R for a few turns, with O adding a raised finger that points his sounds out in the air...
- ...then O raises his head, addresses R with *aye-ya*, more emphatically, and within the tonal world of the guitar. It's not just an echo, as O inflects the two-note motif his own way, as if to say, 'Like *this* now, *my* way'...
- ... to which R responds with a different energy, momentum and texture in his voice and guitar (they're still on the two-note motif, playing with it between them)...
- ...then O suddenly pulls up his body... puts his arms up parallel and horizontal... and there's a charged pause, like in a Flamenco dance before another bout of action, and we feel, *What's going to happen NOW?* until...
- ...O and R pull out an *aye-yaa*... **together**... with an increase in volume and intensity...
- ... which resolves into a jointly discovered new episode of music that has a dramatic ongoing pulse, seemingly cued by how O now moves his body to the music – or is this movement *creating* the music? The rhythmic movements start at the bottom of O's body and pulse up through it and through his arms, working up to his head in waves of energy that form a curious Flamenco-like gesture through forwards-and-backwards shifts, in a dance of pulse and vitality. The musical energy literally shakes up through O's body as he slaps his thighs rhythmically and looks ecstatically at R.

On a platform of communicative musicality, Richard and Oliver compose a unique musical interaction that involves all the parameters we've explored above: pulse, dynamic expression, narrative, and the skilled relational processes of attuning to forms of vitality, dialoguing and regulating. Through their spontaneous and responsive musical actions, Oliver and Richard develop an emerging understanding of what each other is doing, thinking, feeling and intending. Both continually shape and re-calibrate their relationship in and through the musicking. For Oliver, such an immediate, companionable and enjoyable dialogue is unfortunately an unusual experience in his life.

However, when you listen to this event, it's clearly more than just a proto-musical interaction. Oliver and Richard are also sharing and elaborating cultural resources that move them into a broader web of human meaning and belonging.

It might be assumed that it's Richard who adds this level, with his musicianship and cultural competence in playing guitar flamenco style. But whilst Oliver can't produce these elements unaided, he shows an uncanny sensibility towards them. And to a certain extent, it's the vitality forms of Oliver's gestures and responses that lead Richard spontaneously to play flamenco in the first place. Through the interaction, Oliver can in turn appropriate these cultural resources and, in the words of Tia DeNora, be 'drawn into the fold of a socio-musical frame' (2000, p. 143) that affords increased possibilities for his social and cultural belonging.[4]

The question, 'Is proto-music *real* music?', is therefore too simple. What we see in the various examples in this chapter is how the capacity of communicative musicality prepares, supports and leads into more sophisticated forms of musicking that progressively induct us into a particular musical culture. So there is rather a *continuum* between *proto*-music (which is mostly non-conscious and spontaneous) and what could perhaps be called *meta*-music (which is self-aware and other-directed). These two aspects are not always shared symmetrically within a given musical interaction, either between infants and carers, or between music therapists and their clients. But what matters overall is the consequent musicking *between* these people. This is based on an amalgam of the mutual human responses and available cultural resources that each person brings to a unique situated event of musicking.

Being in Concert through Musical Co-/inter-subjectivity

There are a variety of ways of being together with others in music. David's account of being in an audience in the Wigmore Hall illustrates one type, where he experiences a special relationship between himself and the singer on stage but says that his pleasure is enhanced by knowing other members of the audience are simultaneously experiencing this too. This mode of sharing experience has been termed *co-subjectivity*.[5] This is based on a kind of emotional contagion that happens when a group of people feel something together when responding to something outside of themselves (such as a musical performance). They experience the event individually yet in concert with each other. Whilst they may imagine a feeling of togetherness, their actual social communication with each other is usually minimal. And unless they already know their concert neighbour, this momentary relationship is unlikely to be enhanced much by a co-subjective experience. This perhaps helps to explain how recorded music can evoke strong sympathetic emotions even when we don't know the performers, or could not possibly contact them directly (McGuiness and Overy 2011).

---

[4]   It's interesting to see how DeNora views a music therapy case from a music sociology perspective (2000, p. 142ff).

[5]   DeNora (2000, pp. 149–50) characterises co-subjectivity as 'a new and "postmodern" form of communitas', which she contrasts with intersubjectivity.

Co-subjectivity is sometimes contrasted with the more well-known concept of *intersubjectivity*, which describes what can happen when more active and direct communication between people leads to a reflexive awareness of the *I-know-that-you-know-that-I-know* type. The psychologist Ben Bradley describes intersubjectivity as 'our capacity for interleaving our mental operations' (2005, p. 61). This could sometimes start off with a more co-subjective situation, doing something alongside someone else. But often a point comes when we experience (however vaguely) something of *their* first-person perspective too. For this, we must have a sense of the other person as both different from us – in terms of their intentions, thoughts and feelings – and as responding from some awareness of *our* intentionality, thoughts and feelings. This interleaving of experience possibly happens when the music-like *vitality forms* that Stern described as communicable, sharable and contagious get coupled within a live interaction. Seeing exactly how someone moves, talks or sings in relation to us helps us get under their skin, and they under ours. A growing neurological theory based on so-called *mirror neurons* is exploring the brain's role in this process, but as ever we need to be cautious of reductionist and 'internalist' perspectives.[6]

Communicative musicality demonstrates how infants have an 'innate intersubjectivity' that is, in Ben Bradley's (2005) nice phrase, a 'psychical pass-key' to relationship and belonging. Much psychological and social theory has now incorporated an intersubjective or 'second-person' perspective on psycho-social life. As the sociologist Anthony Giddens remarks, 'intersubjectivity does not derive from subjectivity, but the other way round' (1991, p. 51). Instead of thinking, that is, that we are fundamentally isolated individuals who struggle to connect with others, it's probably more accurate to think of the opposite of this: of an interdependent 'ecological self' that is born into and thrives within what Stern (2010) calls the 'intersubjective field'. We are primarily relational and social beings from the start, and our subsequent development is to find a healthy balance between joining with and separating from others.

However, this 'natural' intersubjective capacity is also vulnerable, and can falter in hostile environments or when conditions such as autism, psychosis or dementia short-circuit it. This is when music therapy and other non-verbal approaches can be helpful. By returning people to the level of communicative musicality, such approaches can help to open up, enhance or 'repair' the intersubjective field again, giving them the sense that they can still be contacted, known and understood 'from the inside'. Music is a particularly good vehicle for this 'catching' of another's first-person perspective, perhaps for the simple reason that, as we've seen, intersubjectivity seems itself to be a 'musical' phenomenon.

---

[6]	The discovery of 'mirror neurons' in the brain has become an increasingly popular way of conceptualising interpersonal communication. But whilst they may be a necessary, they are certainly not a sufficient explanation of the kinds of musical relationships we explore in this part of the book. For contrasting arguments on this topic, see McGuiness and Overy 2011, Stern 2010 and Tallis 2011.

But are these two types of musical togetherness – co-subjectivity and inter-subjectivity – really distinct? It would perhaps be better, as usual, to think of them along a continuum. Our capacity to share a co-subjective response to music is often preparatory to being able to share an intersubjective relatedness with others in and through musicking. This is certainly the case in music therapy, as we've seen in Nordoff and Robbins's work with isolated children. There's also an ever-shifting temporal and qualitative element to what intersubjectivity feels like within music. To put it simply, it's not a case of its being simply there or not there, like a light's being on or off. The qualitative sense of being with another intersubjectively will fluctuate continually within an interaction. It can wax and wane according to the situation and the immediate state and action of the partners. This is especially so when we are talking about people who have impairments that influence their tolerance of intimate relationship. So rather than the digital on/off, there's rather the sense of a more 'analogue' continuum in levels of intersubjectivity: from flickers of contact – an 'intermittent intersubjectivity' – to a fuller mutuality. This perhaps links with the parallel shifting levels of intentional awareness and response that are found with people with conditions that impair consciousness.

Lastly, whilst the principle of intersubjectivity models a mutual and symmetrical relational process, this balance is seldom attainable in real-life situations. We shall discuss this more later; suffice to say now that 'mutual but asymmetrical' need not be a contradictory description of a successful musical or therapeutic encounter.

ಬಿ

The psychoanalyst and paediatrician Donald Winnicott suggested that 'the sign of health in the mind is the ability of one individual to enter imaginatively and accurately into the thoughts and feelings and hope and fear of another person' (in Phillips 1988, p. 12). The remainder of Part IV explores further how musicking promotes and develops this key human and therapeutic accomplishment of benign 'mind reading' that is intersubjectivity. But successful music-therapeutic relationships stand on more than just the processes of communication that communicative musicality helps to explain (necessary though these are). We also need to think about the basic attitudes and commitments we have towards intimate relationship in the first place – drawing on broader ethical, existential and aesthetic concerns. This takes us into an exploration of dialogue, and its help in keeping a person in human company and community.

Chapter 12

Musical Dialogue

The basic movement of the life of dialogue is the turning toward the other ....

Martin Buber[1]

To be means to communicate. Absolute death (non-being) is the state of being unheard, unrecognized, unremembered.

Mikhail Bakhtin[2]

Call and Response

On the last day of my uncle's life, I maintain a vigil at his bedside, and every so often I sing to him. But not just *to* him, since I also sing *for* him, and even to an extent *with* him. The song that comes to me is 'Swing Low, Sweet Chariot' – cued, I think, by how the line 'Coming for to carry me home' feels right for this task of accompanying someone in their last hours of life. I can also attune the simple melody to my uncle's laboured breathing. From occasional micro-adjustments he makes in his breathing and head movements, I know that somewhere he hears me, and turns to me. I hope he feels less alone.

ဆ

Nigel: Working with people who are dying has taught me that the core of the music therapy relationship is simply about you and me and something happening. For me, this way of being with somebody musically is probably the most uncomplicated form of love – that's the only way I can define it. Love as being attentive to someone, being tended to, being listened to.... In the hospice here, they talk about that form of love within their whole philosophy. What's always surprising is getting into that experience, even when you've been working for it. When it happens, it's always surprising, never, 'Oh, here we go again', because it's being there differently with a different person. So the surprise is that, even though there's a meeting of these two people, somehow at the same time the two people aren't important – it's the *meeting* that's important! I always have a stronger sense of who I am as an individual in those moments – and I think this is symmetrical, that the other person's feeling this

---

[1]   Buber 1947, in 'Dialogue', p. 22.

[2]   Bakhtin, quoted in Frank 2004, p. 12.

too. People have said things that make me sure of this. So it's this sense of a person feeling, 'I'm more what I am because of this quality of relationship with another person.' My image of it is that there's this centre, and suddenly something comes together [*makes gesture with two hands folding together*], and the two people who are involved in this actually go away from each other.... But it's so complicated to describe in words!

ಬಿ

The example with my uncle may seem an odd way to begin a chapter exploring dialogue. We usually think of this as fluent and mutual, whereas my uncle is only fleetingly conscious and no longer capable of overt response. And Nigel's privileging of the event of meeting above the actual people involved is also perhaps counter-intuitive. But both of these examples serve to introduce a perspective on musical–personal relationship that goes beyond the mechanics and processes to the underlying ethical imperative: *How can we hear the call of others? How can we respond?*

Does music help us find answers to these questions?

Dialogue with the dying provides an exemplary 'limit case' to what matters and what's possible. One of the key philosophers of dialogue, Emmanuel Levinas, argues counter-intuitively that the primary reality of intersubjective relationship is not being *with* another, but the more fundamental and asymmetrical obligation of being *for* another.[3] He calls this the 'ethical relationship'. The person we encounter is someone we are responsible for, who tests our 'response-ability'. Levinas uses the poetic metaphor of the face to convey this situation. We face another and meet *their* face – not just its features, but that person in their wholeness facing us. We meet a total otherness or alterity, looking from their perspective at us – but also calling *to* us, demanding we respond to them. The face of another is vulnerable and exposed for Levinas, both an epiphany of that person, but also quite naturally evoking their most extreme need. Levinas writes of 'hearing … a voice that commands; an order addressed to me, not to remain indifferent to that death, not to let the other die alone' (2006, p. 146). This face in death is a symbolic touchstone for all other face-to-face relationships for Levinas. The call of the other must be responded to without any expectation of response or mutuality, but simply with presence and care. As Levinas wrote, 'The tie with the Other is knotted only as responsibility; to say "Here I am"' (in Gordon 1999, p. 50).

---

[3]   For a collection of Levinas's work, see Levinas 2006; for insightful discussions of Levinas's thought in relation to therapy, see Gordon 1999; for an account of Levinas's ideas in relation to healthcare, see Frank 2004.

A Dialogical Stance

Pushing the idea of dialogue[4] to its existential limit like this emerges from a long tradition in European philosophical and social thought that has campaigned against materialist individualism.[5] As theory, the 'dialogical principle' is simply that human being is innately relational; that a minimum of two is required to successfully maintain identity, meaning and wellbeing. This stands against the pervasive modern Western belief that *one* is enough. Dialogical thinkers believe on the contrary that a second-person *I–You* stance is key, and that what is most important emerges between us. While our individual voice and view is important, it is necessarily partial and unfinalised. Our speech and thought is always addressed to another, and called forth by another. Dialogue prefers *we* over *me*.

Practising this principle requires us to take a dialogical stance towards others, being prepared to experience our relationship with them as an invitation, call or demand. While a monologue dominates by directing our voice *to* or *at* another person, dialogue means allowing another's voice to count as much as our own. It involves reaching over and allowing ourselves to be reached, and to risk being changed by the encounter. Dialogue happens on the precarious boundary *between* us, where the life of a unique communication hovers and sparks in the improvised here and now. We can't control what will happen there, where the dialogue will lead, and when it will end. We allow others to shape our voice as we shape theirs. But this can only happen where both sides of a dialogue maintain their separate voice, not merging into each another. Genuine dialogue is *with* whilst *apart*. Alterity, or 'otherness', preserves the dialogical space.

The philosopher Hans-Georg Gadamer considered 'ideal dialogue' to have the 'logical structures of openness'. By this he meant both the openness of dialogue partners to each other, and how dialogue can bring things out into the open through its spirit of free play and receptiveness. Gadamer writes, 'Anyone who listens is fundamentally open' (in Gordon 1999, p. 73). We might add to this, *anyone who acts on their listening to another* is in dialogue.

Dialogue in this sense is clearly an ethical practice. It enacts key values about human relationships: not just respect, but also our responsibility for keeping each other 'in conversation' (in the widest sense of this); for co-creating and re-creating each others' experience and reality. In a dialogical relationship, who *I* am depends on who *you* are for me at any moment, and *vice versa*. Our relationship is contingent, mutable and fragile. Being dialogical means never finalising a person, a relationship or a situation, but trying to keep things in play between us.

The dialogical principle is an exacting one, and it perhaps becomes clearest when it is hardest to put in practice. We tend to think of dialogue in its ideal form,

---

[4] From the Greek *dia* = through/across + *logos* = speech/meaning.

[5] A roll call of such 'philosophers of dialogue' would include James, Mead, Dilthey, Buber, Wittgenstein, Heidegger, Merleau-Ponty, Levinas, Gadamer, Adorno, Bakhtin, Bohm, Kristeva, and a host of others.

as a fluent and mutually enriching exchange. But often the situation or outcome is far from the ideal. Think of many of the case stories in this book already, where musical dialogue is heroically pursued even when it is a struggle, or barely reciprocated. Equally, dialogue may not always be so visible or explicit: we can be solitary and yet in dialogue with others through imagination, memory and culture.

It Takes Two to Musick

> **Henry:** *When you picked up that thumb-piano today and I picked up this guitar... we just played together... I had to quieten down in order to hear you... and then we played gently together, not one over the other, but going together, a nice balance... which is kind of difficult to get in life, isn't it?*

ತಿ

Inspired by the philosophers of dialogue (Hans-Georg Gadamer in particular), Bruce Benson's book *The Improvisation of Musical Dialogue* (2003) suggests rather provocatively that we consider all musicking as exemplifying the dialogical principle. The conventional categories of composer, performer and listener are taken out of their separate boxes and imagined as participating in a generous and continuous network of 'open' dialogical improvisations with each other. This includes not only the real-time dialogues between people playing music together, but also the more virtual dialogues we often have with pieces, composers and performers across time and space. Benson suggests we think of 'being musical with the Other' as both the core obligation and potential of musicking:

> The 'ideal' composer, performer, or listener is one who is really ready to encounter an other who (as Gadamer puts it) 'breaks into my ego-centredness and gives me something to understand'. To treat the other as other requires that I recognize the other as having a kind of claim on me. (Benson 2003, p. 167)

Benson's model of musicking reinforces this ethical stance: that any musician (which means anyone involved in any way in music) is entrusted with a gift, and is consequently both free and constrained to improvise a dialogue with 'it' and with all those equally involved in the musicking. In Benson's nice phrase, 'All performance is resuscitation' (2003, p. 179). We are all equally responsible for bringing music to life, and through this for bringing each other into the life-enhancing dialogue of musicking. As such, musicking always involves a precarious balance that is probably never quite successful – 'that of allowing the voice of the other to speak, without it swallowing up one's own voice' (2003, p. 189). But as we saw previously, music's phenomenology itself provides the model for this difficult aim: without the distance between tones (an interval), there can be no melody; without simultaneous sounding of tones that do not merge, there is no harmony or complex musical texture.

As in music, then, so in life: the dialogical dilemma is to be together whilst staying apart; to improvise shared meaning without being able to see through to a predictable end. Instead of just playing *to* others, we need always to invite them into the dialogue, with all its risks and possibilities. As Benson concludes, 'Since music making is something that we inevitably do with others (whether they are present or not), musical dialogue is *fundamentally* ethical in nature' (2003, p. 164).

⁎

If, however, the dialogical principle's slogan is that *it always takes two*, where does this leave the many solo performances of music, or the 'silent' private music that often accompanies us in our heads, or that we turn to for 'musical asylum'? (DeNora, 2013) I think the answer to this conundrum lies in Martin Buber's statement that '[a]ll music calls to an ear that is not the musician's own' (1947/2002, p. 30). That is, the single player's or composer's musicking is still always addressed to another – even when this is not immediately obvious. The single listener is still always being addressed and responding.

Another philosopher of dialogue, Mikhail Bakhtin, helps to explain this seeming paradox – though his work as a literary theorist is primarily concerned with verbal communication.[6] Bakhtin famously said that any word we speak is always already half someone else's. What he meant by this was that our every utterance is both addressed *to* another and created *with* another. It is simultaneously a unique product of the here-and-now interaction between us, and drawn from the history and culture of the language we use:

> *word is a two-sided act*. It is determined equally by *whose* word it is and *for whom* it is meant. As word, it is precisely *the product of the reciprocal relationship between speaker and listener, addresser and addressee* … A word is a bridge thrown between myself and another. If one end of the bridge depends on me, then the other depends on my addressee. A word is territory shared by both addressees, by the speaker and the interlocutor. (Bakhtin, in Gordon 1999, p. 69, italics in original)

A musical utterance is likewise both the bridge and the territory of communication. It always takes two to musick – even if one is (seemingly) silent. The reciprocal sounding and listening of a musical dialogue is made both *for* and *with* another. There is also the same additional dimension as in verbal language: our immediate musical communication involves a vicarious dialogue (as Benson argues) with

---

6   For discussions of Bakhtin's version of the dialogical principle, see: Frank 2004; Shotter 1999. For an exploration of how these apply particularly to music and musicking, see Love 2003, pp. 71–72.

a multitude of historical and cultural others who have musicked before us, and who have helped to make possible the musical conversation that we now have in this moment. There is an important intersection of the personal and the cultural woven within the fabric of any dialogue. Our music is both always, and never, our own. Rather, there's always this sense of a collective building and interweaving of meaning that's not only improvised for our unique purpose, but that also necessarily transcends this.

Bakhtin suggested that two 'dimensions' of language are operating in any utterance we make, forming two 'forces' pulling in opposite ways: the *centripetal* that ensures convention and unification, and the *centrifugal*[7] that drives personal expression within a particular situation. A musical utterance could likewise have these two dimensions:[8]

- *What?* [*centripetal*]: the store of musical 'readymades' that a culture provides through its styles, idioms, and previously composed or improvised material. Bits of these form the 'raw material' to be selected and used in...
- *How-for-whom?* [*centrifugal*]: the expressive 'forms of vitality' that characterise how this material is addressed within the present utterance to *this* person, *this* interaction, within *this* situation. We use pace, expressive rhythm, changing intensity, stress and accent to shape, personalise and particularise the musical utterance.

Every concrete dialogue serves as a focus for the tension between these two opposing forces. Partners in musical dialogue play within this charged, creative space.

৪১

A 'musical utterance' is any musical communication addressed to another, and a musical dialogue is any communication that expects an answering response. This can range from infant–carer interactions to sophisticated musical partnerships. In common is the dialogical principle that 'one is not enough', and the ecological principle that relationships are always somewhere, and that context matters because we live on the narrow boundary between ourselves and others, and alongside those things like words and music that help bring and hold us together.

Dialogue as 'Generous Care'

'The art therapist told me I shouldn't have done this,' says Spiros, showing me a *papier-mâché* 'fallen angel' clad in black leather. This figure had emerged not only from his rather unconventional imagination, but also from his resistance to

---

[7] 'Centripetal' means seeking the centre, 'centrifugal' fleeing it.

[8] I have adapted this aspect of the significance of Bakhtin's work for musical improvisation from Love 2003.

what he feels is 'being treated' by an art therapist who has prescribed a technical exercise for him using modelling clay. So Spiros stops going to art therapy and comes to music therapy instead. It's 1993, in a hospital where treatment for people with advanced AIDS, like Spiros, is largely palliative, as the lifesaving drugs have yet to become available. Spiros is an internationally successful avant garde artist who's also studied musical composition with a pupil of Xenakis. He has a very developed personal aesthetic and a strong confidence in his artistic identity. For him, art is life! But he tells me that he's not played much music for ten years.

In the music therapy room, Spiros improvises dramatic monologues using Greek words and an assembly of percussion. Throughout these 'performances', I remain on the periphery, although I try to respond and contribute to the music in the way I'm trained to do as a music therapist. But Spiros doesn't seem to want or need this. Indeed, he seems hardly to notice me, and at best tolerates my contributions. It's odd for me to feel an accessory to the situation rather than my usual experience of trying to encourage a patient to play. At the same time, I find myself sharing pleasure in the aesthetic of this wild improvised music, and the creative energy that's in the room. I relax from my professional role of needing to 'make contact', and in a few moments I experience a few fleeting signs of Spiros listening to what I'm doing within this organised chaos...

I'm surprised when he says at the beginning of the next session, 'I have the impression you hear everything I do', and that this matters to him. He's distressed today – his partner is also very ill, and he says he needs to escape from the hell he's in. He walks over to the second piano in the room and begins playing wild and fast splinters of atonal sounds that resemble his main musical influences, Xenakis and Ligeti. But the music also represents something about him and this situation. I look out of the picture window to a forest landscape of wildly flurrying snow. The music, the snow, his emotional state... each mirrors the other, a pattern which connects. I join him on another piano and for twenty minutes we play an intense improvisation of swirling notes, ebbing and flowing louder and softer, relaxing and then tightening – a dynamic flux that sounds chaotic on the surface, but is anchored in a controlled overall form that both of us help regulate. Now the music feels like a close collaboration. We listen and respond to each other within this flow, such that we are both caught up in how the sound flurries merge with the snow flurries we both watch outside the window, and with the rush of energy between us in the music.

There's a long pause after the end of this improvisation and Spiros weeps silently. He says, 'I felt I was again just going with the flow of life then... a dynamic chaos... I felt free again.'

We look at each other, and there's an understanding – literally a standing *with* the other, freed (if only a bit) from the grip of our separate lives, and their separate fates. This encounter touched me then, and remains with me nearly twenty years later.

ॐ

This is a story of monologue and dialogue. It begins with an art therapist who 'prescribes' for a problem rather than a person. This doesn't take into account Spiros' individuality as an artist, and as a man whose main need at this crisis point in his life is simply to be acknowledged and responded to as a whole person, not as an 'AIDS patient'. He needs his therapy to be a conversation about his experiences and talents, his culture and aesthetic preferences, as well as his immediate problems or symptoms. He still wants his voice to shape another's through artistic and human dialogue. He wants to be worked *with*, not *on*.

However, in music therapy it's Spiros who at first creates the monologue, retreating within his own musical and personal world. I wait and contribute what I can, and eventually contact happens between us when he hears my listening to him, and my willingness to begin on his ground and reach over to his. For what Spiros really craves at this time is simply companionship with someone who can bear to be with him and his mixture of pain, energy and anger – actively, strongly and humanly. But perhaps the truest moment of dialogue is silent and beyond the music, in that flash of mutual understanding and recognition afterwards, when we were both changed.

୨୦

Spiros challenged people's attitudes towards him as a patient and as a person. His story stands for a larger and still ongoing challenge to some Western cultures of care. My experience, however, is that, whilst some individual practitioners do not want to risk genuine relationship with those they care for, most do. But they are frustrated by medical and managerial models that stress systems and efficiency above relationships of care. Where problems are seen only as needing to be treated and fixed, separable from the person who has them, monologue will dominate.

The sociologist Arthur Frank (2004) describes a current 'demoralisation of care' that needs re-imagining through what he calls a model of 'generous care' based on dialogical principles. Frank re-imagines such a 'practice of generosity' by replacing the demoralising labels of 'provider' and 'consumer' with *hosts* ('those temporarily in a position to offer care') and *guests* ('those needing care'). This is not to deny medical expertise and resources, but to acknowledge that the guest has these too. The overarching metaphor of generous care is *hospitality* rather than delivery:

> Generosity begins in *welcome*: a hospitality that offers whatever the host has that would meet the needs of the guest. The welcome of opening the doors of one's home signifies the opening the self to others, including guests who may disrupt and demand. To guests who suffer, the host's welcome is an initial promise of consolation. (Frank 2004, p. 2)

Guests who are suffering need not just treatment but consolation, understanding, and sometimes appropriate challenge. They need to feel less isolated and stigmatised through someone daring to meet their distress directly, if only for a moment. A 'relationship of care' is a dialogue guided by the virtues and values of hospitality, courtesy and mutual obligation: to speak with someone, not about them; to face their suffering, hope and demands; to address them and to invite them into dialogue by attending, listening and giving time. Of course, when such a dialogue opens up it may not be easy to close it, and it may disrupt or change both partners. To enter into dialogue is to 'entertain' each other, and while the host cannot take on the sufferings of the guest, there is an acknowledgement that 'we are all in this together'. It is these particular dialogical attitudes that transform ungenerous into generous care within a 'health ecology'.

Therapeutic Dialogues

Katya: *My psychosis takes me out of relationship into an imaginary world where I don't have to face the here-and-now world of relationships. But music therapy helps me stay here. When you've got the music, it helps you to take your mind off the scariness of being with another person, because the music kind of keeps you there... music's a thing! Then you suddenly hear the other person... and you can tell them that you can hear them, because you play music back to let them know you're listening, don't you? By the way you're playing you let them know that you can hear them....*

₭

Matthew: Some of my most formative experiences of making musical relationship with people was when I worked at the Medical Foundation for Victims of Torture. With some of the clients I saw there... there was this enormous distance travelled from absolutely *no* contact with each other... despite us making sounds together... to extremely close contact. And also this kind of freeing from the world when we really got into making music together... away from the physical world, away from our own selves....

Traditionally, the therapies have been ambassadors of 'generous care', often drawing inspiration from the dialogical philosophers.[9] The psychotherapist Paul Gordon (1999, 2009), for example, defines therapy simply as an 'ethical space' that affords encounter and dialogue, guided by the values of invitation, hospitality and responsibility. What develops within this space is a relationship about relationships – a *meta*-relationship – of the kind Katya describes above. This, at least, is the ideal. But there's always the temptation for any therapy, however well intentioned, to become sucked into the values and habits of a managerial care context, or a fixed theoretical model. This can mean compromising 'generous care', or adopting other

---

[9] For a good survey of the influence of dialogical philosophy on (psycho)therapy, see Friedman 1992.

healthcare professionals' images of what 'therapy' or a 'therapeutic relationship' is, or should be. At this point, genuine dialogue usually withers.

How the idea of relationship has developed within music therapy gives a good example of this. The overall tendency has been to borrow a model of '*the* therapeutic relationship' from psychotherapeutic and medical traditions, turning it into a rather fixed 'thing' that can often seem to take on a life of its own. Of course, music therapists need to maintain the ethical stance of any professional relationship. But within this, it's surely helpful to think of how the specifically *musical* relationship between client and therapist offers something different or unique. Music therapist Rachel Verney has suggested we should look more closely at this:

> [Music] therapists always talk about '*the* relationship' as if it's a thing. But actually what we're working on are *qualities of relatedness* – which is something quite different from 'a relationship'. In fact I'd like to throw out the concept 'therapeutic relationship' for a while and see what comes instead of it ….
>
> By 'relatedness' I mean the moment-to-moment qualities of distance and intimacy between two people. And music allows these exquisite subtleties of relatedness – such as if you sing in *that* way, I can accompany you in *this* way … and we are put suddenly into completely different quality of relatedness to each other. Or, say I sing in unison with you at the same pitch, then at the next phrase I sing in unison with you an octave higher. Then you've got that amazing quality of being together that's only possible in music: you're both the same as someone, but also separate from them. So that's what I mean – those qualities of relatedness. That's *relatedness*, not '*a* relationship'. (Verney, in Verney and Ansdell 2010, p. 82)

A distinctive factor in music therapy and other arts therapies is that the relationship between therapist and client often also interfaces with the personal and aesthetic relationship that each person has with the artform itself. In music therapy, *music* is like a third person in the relationship. We saw earlier how Nordoff and Robbins's work capitalised on this in how they allowed a child's relationship to music itself to pave the way to achieving a more interpersonal 'working relationship' with the therapists through music. The ongoing therapeutic process was therefore simultaneously a musical and a personal one. We also see in Katya's and Matthew's remarks above that a 'sideways' relationship with music is therapeutically useful at times in deflecting or modulating the directness of the face-to-face relationship. Concentrating on music rather than words as a way of making relationship in music therapy also helps create a situation that is 'intimate but not personal', in the useful formulation suggested by Rachel Verney and Nigel Hartley.

The art therapist Cathy Moon (2002) has also helpfully explored this overlap between artistic and therapeutic relationships. She writes of cultivating a 'relational aesthetic' in her work, thinking of the therapeutic dialogue as between two artists working together within a therapeutic context. Shared perceptions of the qualities, beauty and value of art are central to the work of therapy for her. The relationship that happens in music therapy is even more co-creative and co-productive than is usual with art making in art therapy, given that musical improvisation usually involves both client and therapist playing at the same time. But Moon's overall approach holds true for music-centred approaches to music therapy, which also think primarily of musicians working together, whatever the professional context. As such, aesthetic judgements about what's 'good musicking' are necessarily also 'ethical' judgements about the ongoing quality of connection and relationship within the creative process. This also evokes what Bakhtin says about utterances: that our words are always half someone else's. In a 'relational aesthetic' within a music therapeutic context, each partner sounds both themselves and the musical voices of others that come from real and virtual musical relationships outside the therapy space.

For Cathy Moon, this understanding of therapeutic dialogue is a reaction to inappropriate power relationships in therapy and care that silence other voices, one of which is the aesthetic. 'Our art-based practice', she writes, 'is inclusive rather than elitist, based in an ethic of care, encompassing of a generous concept of beauty, and grounded in a concern for quality in relationships' (2002, p. 154). Successful examples of musical dialogue within music therapy have also been helpful in exemplifying the idea of therapeutic dialogue as generous care.

Present Musical Moments

Attempts to define the 'therapeutic relationship' tend to get caught up with competing professional models. Perhaps a better way is to ask *when* or *how* relationship emerges. In *The Present Moment in Psychotherapy & Everyday Life*, Daniel Stern suggests that the key experiences in therapy that allow change to happen are often unspoken, relational and momentary. 'The present moment,' he writes, '[is] our microscope for viewing how change comes about' (2004, p. xix).

కు

Pam describes to me how she has used music as her personal therapy for most of her adult life, as a form of emotional management. 'It always does the trick,' she says. Pam has been in and out of hospital during the last few years and we've built up an ongoing, trusting relationship through playing music together in individual and group music therapy sessions. Pam finds coping with her psychotic illness extremely difficult at times – in particular, the dramatic and unpredictable shifts in her mood states. Music, and music therapy in particular, seems especially helpful with this aspect of her illness.

Today, Pam is playing a xylophone in her individual music therapy session. Before the session, she has felt very unstable, but so far the session has been unremarkable. Suddenly, there is an unexpected crisis. Pam hits the xylophone hard with the beaters and throws them towards the piano, which they hit, causing the piano strings to vibrate. She shouts, 'This fucking life!', and becomes very upset. (I later find out that the outburst was cued by Pam's seeing the letter names on the xylophone spell out abusive messages to her from an internal voice.) Immediately after the 'blow-up', I encourage Pam to come to the piano to sit beside me, and I draw her back into musical engagement again. She begins playing a few notes on the top of the piano, which leads into a short piano duet and then into shared singing with me. Pam takes over the singing herself after a short time (accompanied by me on the piano), becoming involved and expressive. The music seems to take her somewhere else. After the music cadences Pam sighs and says, 'That's better!' She has gone from 'This fucking life!' to 'That's better!' in just four minutes.

A week later, there's another key episode in Pam's therapy – this time it lasts just two minutes and forty seconds. Pam is 'high' and tells me how uncomfortable and irritable she feels. A sung duet between us sounds like a speeded-up cabaret item, including a rapid to-and-fro sung dialogue with Blues singing and yodelling. Within this dialogue, I nevertheless manage to 'sculpt' the musical interaction such that we both go 'up' together, and also that we somehow 'land safely'. In the last phrase, Pam's voice softens and relaxes as she cadences. Somehow, music and person have been modulated together.

৪৩

When members of the hospital team hear these excerpts in a case conference, they generously tell me that few other interventions could help with such a volatile state in a way that is also humanly satisfying. But how was Pam able to change her state so quickly and effectively with music therapy's help? What do episodes like this tell us about how and when therapy happens, and what role the therapeutic relationship plays?

Interestingly, recent interdisciplinary theory about verbally based therapeutic work with people with mental health problems like Pam has itself increasingly used musical metaphors to describe how a patient's affective state can be positively regulated through the intersubjective relationship between therapist and client.[10] Daniel Stern applied his micro-level focus on how key 'present moments' in therapy and everyday life become 'our microscope for viewing how change comes about' (2004, p. xix). Stern's research found that these 'present moments' are music-like phrases of two to eight seconds that define the process unit of our here-and-now lived conscious experience.[11] These phrases are, he suggests, the

---

[10] Apart from Stern's (2004, 2010) work, communicative musicality theory and the attachment theory perspective of the neuro-psychoanalyst Allan Schore (2003) has been influential in shaping this understanding.

[11] A more comprehensive definition of 'present moment' is given by Stern: '[a present moment] is the span of time in which psychological processes group together very small units of perception into the smallest global unit (a gestalt) that has a sense or meaning

building blocks of relational experience, and hence the smallest identifiable span in which therapeutic change can happen. Present moments also stack up to form a typical sequence of action he found happening in ongoing therapy relationships, where:

- client and therapist are 'moving along' nicely (without event)...
- ...until they reach some kind of crisis, a 'now moment', which...
- ...finds resolution in a *moment of meeting* between the pair.

Stern calls these overall episodes *shared feeling voyages*. They have a micro-plot and involve the sharing of the 'forms of vitality' we've explored before. The voyage usually enhances the intersubjective relationship, and this often in turn positively shifts something within the client's state of feeling or thought. All this happens within a present moment.

Stern is describing verbal therapy, but is this process also true for a non-verbal therapy that is actually rather than just metaphorically musical? I took part in an interdisciplinary research project that explored this emerging theory about therapeutic relationship and change in the light of experiences of music therapy with people like Pam (Ansdell et al. 2010). The research group comprised a psychiatrist, a music psychologist and three music therapists. We explored the phenomenon of 'affect modulation' within music therapy using Stern's 'microscopic' method, studying in detail the two examples from the work with Pam described above.

The group made a detailed micro-analysis of the first episode where Pam became distressed at the xylophone yet within only four minutes had re-established her emotional equilibrium through the musicking. At first, we found that there's some ambiguity in whether therapist and client are attuning to each other again, but then an increasingly shared musical journey takes off between them. This pursues a mutual trajectory and ends with Pam's finding both vocal freedom and the sense of having 'gone somewhere else' emotionally and musically. We summarised this musical–relational process more abstractly as having both temporal and spatial dimensions. Firstly, this relational event happens in and through *musical time*, the various shared micro-relational phrases ranging from eight to thirty-five seconds (with a median of thirteen and a half). These matched what Stern calls 'extended present moments'. Perhaps '*musical* present moments' are exactly this: extended or stacked experiential events.[12] Secondly, the relational event happens in and through *musical space*: the sense of how the musical, relational and emotional

---

in the context of a relationship. Objectively, present moments last from 1 to 10 seconds with an average around 3 to 4 seconds. Subjectively, they are what we experience as an uninterrupted *now*' (2004, p. 245).

[12]   This time phrase also relates convincingly to what Malloch (1999) calls the 'stanzas of musical activity' that undergird the non-verbal communication of mothers and infants, showing an average of thirty-second sequences.

voyage takes the dialogue partners *from somewhere to somewhere else*. We described this whole music-therapeutic process as *being in time together towards somewhere*. The help that Pam took from music therapy seemed to centre in this spatial–temporal affordance of the 'musical present moment' that in turn creates a particular quality of the music-therapeutic relationship.

We then looked in even more detail through the 'microscope' at the second episode from Pam's therapy – where in just two and a half minutes this time there is an emotional and therapeutic shift from mania to some calm. This excerpt represented the 'moment of meeting' in the session where a therapeutic shift seemed to happen. We looked here in a high level of detail at what Stern calls the 'relational moves' within this present moment that prepares the meeting. According to Stern, 'relational moves are overt behaviours (including speech or silences) that are the smallest units for which an intention to alter or adjust the relationship can be attributed by an interactive partner or observer' (2004, p. 245).

The first phrase of the excerpt, for example, represents a 'musical present moment' of fifteen seconds – consisting of four 'musical/relational moves' between therapist and client (see Fig. 12.1):

1. In *MOVE 1*, the therapist initiates the 'offer' of a little musical turn (*dee-dee-da-da*), as if to say, 'How about this?', to which Pam 'replies' musically, *da-da-da-daa* – as if to say, 'OK, I hear you... what about this?', returning the musical gesture like a tennis player. Technically this move is a form of mirror antiphony, a leading/following pattern, possible through an implicitly shared pulse, and a rough analogy between pitch patterns at different registers [the therapist's C–B–C–C → Pam's A–G–A–A].

2. In *MOVE 2*, the therapist repeats the simple pattern, implicitly telling Pam, 'I hear you hearing me...', to which she counter-responds again as if to say, '...and I hear you hearing me hearing you!' This confirms the mirror antiphony of the first phrase. It also confirms Stern's test of genuine intersubjectivity: not just that the therapist 'mind reads' the client, but that the client mind reads the therapist's mind reading! But who is leading *who* now? The fast-emerging musical–relational pattern is shaped both in musical time and musical space.

3. In *MOVE 3*, the therapist repeats the pattern for the third time – and this time the mirror exchange is taken up by Pam and elaborated/extended into a half-cadence at the phrase end (... *da daa*), as if she is saying, '...which leads up to this.' This point cues the end of a ten-second 'present moment'. A micro-narrative has (almost) been completed as a 'lived story'.

4. Finally, with *MOVE 4*, there's a five-second add-on. This perhaps functions to further rehearse or embed the relational pattern that has been established in the first ten seconds – or perhaps to test its further possibilities. At this point, Pam actually breaks this pattern, leading into the next phase of the improvisation.

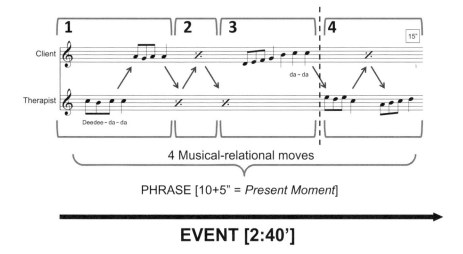

Figure 12.1   Four relational moves in a 'musical present moment'

There's an almost 'holographic' sense in which what we see in the micro-detail of these musical–relational moves here characterises something important about what is happening relationally in the whole event between Pam and the therapist. The musical meeting is a 'lived story' in a grain of sand, to use Stern's metaphor. 'Musical present moments' can be windows for relational and therapeutic change. But they demand great care and attention by both partners in dialogue.

The process of both everyday and therapeutic relationships is being seen increasingly as a 'musical' one. It seems, though, that when music is itself the overt medium for the relationship, as in music therapy, something further happens. Musicking together can allow both an intensifying of the intersubjective contact and an expansion of the 'present moment'. Musical time, that is, can expand relational space. This is perhaps how a music-therapeutic relationship seems to be able to help a person like Pam from a bad place to somewhere better in a remarkably short time.

ର

George: *Why do I come back to these sessions? Well, it's because I enjoy your company, musically.... And you forget about your personality, when you're playing with someone else. You just think of the music... and to be synchronising with the other person. I really don't think of myself... I think it's good to work with someone else, you can develop a kind of rapport. It's almost as if I'd known you for years. With someone you've known for years you can be instantly relaxed, that's what it's like when you're playing here....*

Chapter 13
Musical Meeting

All real living is meeting. Everything is changed in real meeting.

Martin Buber[1]

Max sits beside a ninety-three-year-old woman with advanced dementia. She's sleepy and hardly notices him, but he stays and improvises a quiet, simple melody on his violin, making a gentle call to her attention, but also matching the music to her low energy level. He moves to a more regular pulse and increases the energy when he notices her foot tap to his playing. She looks up at him, seeming surprised. Then she falls asleep. A week later, he tries again with the same woman. She's livelier now, but shows no sign of recognising him or wanting to take part. This time, Max has little sense of contact with her in the music he plays during the first ten minutes. Then suddenly something in his music catches her, and she makes five quiet claps, which both Max and the woman carefully time together, including a final clap that marks the mutually agreed end of the phrase. She looks up at Max and says, 'You're the young man who made music for me last week!' Then she falls asleep again.

ఠఠ

Here's a woman who forgets people from minute to minute, but recognises Max a week later. This surprising moment of recognition arises from a 'present musical moment' that culminates in what I've previously called a *musical meeting* (Ansdell 1995). These can surprise and even shock when they happen in situations where intimate relationship is not expected. Musical meetings stand out then as unexpected and often joyful breaches of isolation. But they are about more than just enhanced communication – though they are certainly prepared for by this. Such meetings are rather a consummation of the whole phenomenon of musical relationship that we've explored through Part IV. They show, that is, how relatedness through music can lead towards an existential or spiritual quality of encounter between people that Martin Buber (1999b) has called 'healing through meeting'. This rests on the experience (sometimes against all odds) of what's at the heart of the dialogical principle: two selves in their wholeness sharing a common world, and through their mutual recognition and companionship restoring full humanity to each other.

---

[1]   Buber 1999a, p. 245.

Musical Meetings in the 'Musical Between'

I experienced a few such musical meetings early in my own work as a music therapist, and I remember being disturbed and disconcerted by them. I was in my mid-twenties then, a rather closed and defended person outside of music, though I found a relational freedom within it – just like many of my clients. I'd also prejudged the kinds of contact that I could make with the profoundly autistic children and adults with learning disabilities I was working with then. They seemed so different from me, and the truth is that I expected little of them – at best, perhaps, that we'd essentially remain strangers to each other even if we managed to make music together. I was proved quite wrong in this when the musical meetings started to happen – rarely, but surely. Luckily, I had two forms of help to understand and cope with these experiences: a wise supervisor who reassured me that they were a natural and important aspect of this music therapeutic work, and Martin Buber's philosophy of dialogue.

Buber's formulation of the concept of 'meeting' also began with a disturbing personal experience that Buber tells in his autobiographical fragment *Meetings*. This decisive event in his life came when Buber has a visit from a troubled young man and, preoccupied with other things, Buber gives his time but not his whole presence. The man leaves without an answer to his burning question, and Buber later finds out that the man has probably killed himself. Reflecting on this, Buber sees that his responsibility to this man was 'surely a presence by means of which we are told that nevertheless there is meaning' (1967/2002, p. 54). He'd failed to respond to the call for dialogue, and the possibility of a crucial human meeting was missed.

'Presence' and 'meeting' take us to the heart of Buber's philosophy of dialogue, which he explained further through his famous pair of 'relational words': *I–It* and *I–You*.[2] Our relation to objects is usually *I–It*: as things to use. Another person, however, we can only truly address as *You*. But Buber pointed out the double stance we often take towards each other in modern society; treating people also as quasi-objects, and only rarely meeting them fully person to person. Of course, we need both I–It and I–You stances to live effectively in the world, and we naturally see-saw between them as situations demand. So think of these stances perhaps not as an either/or dualism but rather as poles on a continuum, each preparing for the other – a natural alternation of relating and distancing. Nobody can (or would want to) live continuously in the heat of the I–You stance. But Buber's point is that it's crucial to our interpersonal and spiritual lives that we can tolerate, trust and value the reality of I–You. As we've seen many times in this book already, this is difficult for many people, for many reasons. But only when we address and

---

2   There's a language problem here. In the original German, Buber's book is entitled *Ich und Du*, using the German informal pronoun 'du' that conveys closeness and intimacy – to people, things, God. Unfortunately, English translations rendered this into 'I–Thou', which gives almost the opposite impression, suggesting an archaic, formal and removed relationship. For this reason, I'll use the form I–You (as many Buber scholars do today).

are addressed fully as *You* is personhood and relationship nourished.[3] In Buber's story, his relational stance to the young man was closer to I–It, where it needed to be I–You, helping to open up a second-person space for dialogue between them.[4]

Buber's philosophy is a poetic one, and he never intended it to form a practical system. But his writings are nevertheless a sure guide to understanding and practising what he called the 'life of dialogue'. Let's go back to the example of Max and the elderly woman, and use this as a way of exploring Buber's perspective through the 'phases' that led towards that particular musical meeting. It's important not to treat this special moment as just a lucky occurrence, but to explore what factors made it possible. From Max's side, he has his skills as a musician and his training as a music therapist, both of which help prepare the ground for musical meetings. But this situation is relational: the woman also offers herself to the event. Buber's view of dialogue presents a sequence of factors that help move towards meeting.[5]

Turning Towards

Max turns towards the woman not just physically, but also with his full attention and presence as a person and musician. He addresses her with an *I–You* stance – not as a patient or as an old woman with dementia, but as a whole person. He looks and listens to how she is here and now, searching for any potential point of contact between them. Buber used the German word *Umkehr*[6] to convey this quality of opening and orienting yourself wholeheartedly to the presence of another. 'The basic movement of the life of dialogue is *turning* towards the other,' writes Buber. This is both a turning *from* separation and self-preoccupation, and a turning *towards* the other and their current reality. It involves the 'making *present*' of the other person in our consciousness, even when it seems that they are distant and that there is little hope of mutuality. When Max turns musically to the old woman, he orients himself through his playing towards her in a particular way, both calling to her with his own musical character and practising what Buber called 'obedient listening' as he takes in *her* reality through his skilled listening-in-playing. He has faith in her ability to respond as a musical person.

---

[3]   For an insightful commentary on this 'second person stance', see Scruton 2012, chapter 2.

[4]   It's perhaps worth mentioning that the kind of dialogue that Buber suggests is not necessarily verbalised, gestured or sounded; it can be silent too, as can its 'questions' and 'answers'.

[5]   The following description is my own, but it is based on Buber's writings and his basic terms.

[6]   *Umkehr* is Buber's German translation of the Hebrew *teshuvah*, meaning an *act of turning*, and not just 'return'.

Including

Max's playing on the violin is directed not only to her, but it also arises partly *from* her, as he allows his improvised playing to be shaped by the small signs he perceives of her character and the forms of her vitality. This involves taking in aspects of her pace, mood, and any small non-intentional and intentional gestures that convey a sense that she is turning towards the music, and to him. Buber talked of the practice of *inclusion* in dialogue, meaning not just some general empathy but how a quality of generous response shows another person that they are present to us. Buber's original German word here was *Umfassung*, meaning a process of grasping or binding, but also the more human responses of embracing or encompassing. Such inclusion is a process that both takes and needs time. In *musical* time we hear Max attuning to, and then adjusting and enriching, the precarious thread of emerging musical contact with the woman. Inclusion preserves the autonomy of each partner whilst actively preparing something that could be shared.

Cultivating the 'Musical Between'

Often something quickens when a person hears themselves being heard – and when they sense that they are being included in something outside themselves. Max suddenly notices the woman's foot tap to a few of his beats, and he carefully attunes his playing to this, matching the timing and quality. She looks up at him in some surprise, 'turning' towards him, musically and personally, in Buber's existential sense. From within the fog of her dementia, she is suddenly present both to herself and to Max. There's then a symmetry of response within their musicking as they include each other in these seconds and moments of musical time and space. The mutuality of I–You has flowered into '*We*'.

A week later, five hand claps and a violin's tones attune to each other, and again open up something experienced *between* them within musical time and space. This pulls their attention and presence towards each other. The moment has both an objective and a subjective quality. We can observe the sudden synchronisation of their actions, but more important is the sudden collapse of the subjective relational distance between them. They step into an intersubjective, shared space of present action and experience (even if this lasts only seconds of musical time, and covers only a few steps of musical space).

Buber called this mutual relational space the sphere of the *Between*. Not only is this prepared for by turning to and including the other, but it is also an elusive and precious state that happens spontaneously only when the conditions are right, and it can neither be guaranteed nor controlled.[7] In his book of 1947, *Between Man and Man*, Buber writes that 'the Between is not an auxiliary construction, but the real place and bearer of what happens' (1947/2002, p. 202). Buber thought

---

[7]   For more on Buber's notion of 'Between', see Friedman 2003; Kramer 2003.

that any form of art is a special case of the Between – both a product of the I–You relationship and a help in its further creation.[8]

A '*musical Between*' is perhaps one of the most powerful sites for genuine dialogue, for all the reasons we've explored before. The phenomenology of music affords particular forms and qualities of relatedness through musical spacing and timing, helping to breach the boundaries that usually keep us separate. A tone (like a word, as Bakhtin suggested) is always half someone else's, calling to another ear. Max plays tones that are half the woman's within their dialogue, and these two people perhaps also share a cultural recognition that's evoked by particular melodic shapes or rhythms. The 'musical Between' always needs careful cultivation, but once established it becomes a space that people turn towards and step into, 'companying with the other', in Buber's beautiful phrase.

Meeting

Max and the woman precisely time the five beats between them, mutually agreeing the final one just then and there at the end of the phrase. In this present moment, they meet in the music. Whilst the whole episode has gradually brought them together, the musical meeting has a precise time and place in music (which is not necessarily aligned with time and place as we know them *outside* music). This musical meeting simultaneously allows a profoundly human meeting to take place, an epiphany of the Between. As Kenneth Paul Kramer comments,

> By 'meeting' (*Begegnung*) Buber means the event that actually takes place when one steps into a mutual 'relationship' (*Beziehung*) and reciprocally meets 'Thou' [You] in the present moment, whole person to whole person. Indeed, the living actuality of meeting always takes place in the present moment. That is, meeting *Thou* happens, and only after *Thou* becomes *It* do we speak of meeting in other verb tenses, as 'having happened' or 'had happened'. (Kramer 2003, p. 43)

The recognition of such meetings is often signalled by a smile or a puzzled look. 'Moments of meeting' can variously be joyous, transcendent, shocking or disturbing for people.[9] For Max and the woman, the meeting results in a literal recognition and remembrance when she says, 'You're the young man who made music for me last week!' Their mutual relationship is confirmed.

Buber (1937/1958) summed up his dialogical philosophy with the famous motto 'All living is meeting', to which Buber scholar Maurice Friedman importantly

---

[8] Buber wrote that 'art is the Between become form'. By this, he meant that the dialogical process of addressing and responding (to people, things, God…) becomes structured into artworks, which subsequently provide the material that mediates further dialogue, as people engage with them, or perform them within shared physical and mental space.

[9] In Buber's term for meeting – *Begegnung* – there is also the stronger sense of 'encounter' or challenge, which can define the quality of some meetings, particularly in therapy.

adds that such meeting is 'not in space and time but space and time in meeting' (1955/2002, p. 39). These encounters, that is, take us outside the quantities of clock time and physical space, and reveal to us instead the qualitative and existential timing and spacing of genuine relationship – a timeless present that can flare in the placeless space between us. Perhaps nowhere is this phenomenon better shown than in musical meetings.

୫ଠ

Having presented this sequence, we need to acknowledge also that the opposite is true: musical meetings can spontaneously happen, with little preparation. Our understanding of this phenomenon requires an acknowledgement of paradox and mystery. Sometimes the sequence is reversed when there's an unexpected 'meeting' that jolts us into the possibility of the Between and an I–You relationship. Equally, the aspects described above are not necessarily causal or predictable. Buber cautioned that, when we leave the objectivity of the I–It stance, so too the objective qualities of causality, fate, time and space become qualitatively different. This leads to something of a paradox, since the preparation for meeting requires many factors of the objective world. We need to coordinate objective time and space to physically bring people together. Communicational skills such that we see in mother–infant or therapist–client dialogue need cultivating and applying. Buber's point, however, is that these objective 'mechanics' of relationship are necessary but not sufficient – they don't automatically lead to meeting. More mysterious factors are in play, too – where timing is waiting, and where spacing is an art. According to Friedman, Buber was asked once whether the demands of the 'way of dialogue' as he described them were not too difficult, or indeed impossible, for others. He said, 'It's not difficult at all, it's a grace' (in Czubaroff and Friedman 2000, p. 253).

Healing through Meeting

Buber suggested that the consequence of an I–You relationship is to accept, affirm and confirm another. As with Max's work, the encounter can seem small and fleeting, but serves to illuminate the potential for a completely different quality of relationship in situations where intimacy based on acceptance, affirmation and confirmation may be rare. The particular approach to musical relatedness that Max takes with the woman illuminates the potential of musicking within a therapeutic or caring relationship to prepare for true 'meeting'. The quality of relationship that this creates can be experienced as 'healing' in its broadest sense (for client and therapist alike).

Buber's dialogical philosophy became popular within therapy circles from the 1950s onwards, as part of the campaign to shift understanding of the therapeutic relationship away from the style of doctor and patient roles typical of the medical model. Carl Rogers used Buber's I–You concept within his 'person-centred' theory to characterise the ideal therapeutic relationship. It was ironic, then, that in a famous public dialogue Buber told Rogers that this was not accurate! Buber argued instead that a therapeutic relationship, like a teacher–pupil relationship, was not mutual and symmetrical, and was effective precisely because of this[10]. What's more, Buber also argued that, whilst a therapist needed to 'confirm' the whole being of the client, this did not need to involve 'unconditional positive regard' (Rogers's key concept) as the therapist may need to actively 'wrestle' with the client against their self-limiting factors: to challenge them and focus on what they *could* be rather than what they are. However, Buber clearly thought some more about this after this encounter, as he added an important postscript to his book *I and Thou* in 1958, in which he acknowledged that the therapeutic relationship indeed had aspects of a limited form of the *I–You* relationship, but that there were certain 'normative limitations of mutuality' (p. 165). Like a teacher–pupil or a priest–parishioner relationship, there is a degree of necessary one-sidedness, and should the roles collapse the professional function will normally be impaired too. As we saw earlier, this was also Levinas's critique of dialogical approaches (including Buber's): that they over-emphasised the necessary mutuality of the relationship over the responsibility that each has to simply be *for* the other, whether there is reciprocation or not. Levinas thought that Buber sentimentalised dialogue.

From our perspective, looking at examples from music therapy, it is clear that there are indeed professional limitations on full mutuality and symmetry. But equally, those moments where a musical meeting happens in the 'musical Between' do indeed seem to be exemplary of the full mutuality of an I–You relationship and are often healing for clients precisely because of this. This paradoxical aspect in such relationships deserves attention.

Instead of simply asking whether a therapeutic relationship is mutual or not, we could perhaps see a 'complex mutuality' where several requirements are kept simultaneously. The basic context determines that a client comes to a therapist for help, and not *vice versa*. Culturally accepted boundaries of the relationship and context reinforce the duty of care one side has to the other, as maintained in most other professional relationships. So rather than say that a therapeutic relationship is or is not mutual, we might better ask, '*When* is it mutual?' That is, we need to add a temporal dimension to such relationships, not assume that the roles or the dynamic remains static. What therapists often report – especially those therapists working within music – are 'wormholes' of unexpected mutuality and 'musical meeting', where genuine mutual dialogue flares up for a second or moment. Even when these do not last, they can be transformative of the therapeutic relationship. Something has been shown, known and sometimes transformed in these moments of graceful meeting. But they do not have to adversely affect the professional frame of the enterprise as a whole; nor do musical meetings take away from the autonomy or responsibility of either partner.

---

[10] For the famous live dialogue between Buber and Rogers, see Anderson and Cissna 1997.

Despite Levinas's critique, it seems to me that Buber's later comments on the I–You relationship are clear that, within a dialogical relationship, the respect for the autonomy of the other and the potential for both to become 'We' are not in conflict. The existential I–You relationship and the professional role-based relationship will sometimes configure in unexpected but helpful ways. As music therapist Rachel Verney questions,

> I'm left wondering… *Do* we have a 'therapeutic relationship' with our clients? Maybe we don't! I'm left thinking that my aim as a music therapist is not to cultivate or work on 'the relationship' – because that happens anyway, you can't help it…. It's something different. My aim is to guide a certain musical/personal process that is constantly ebbing and flowing, and the goal of this process is to be in a state of 'meeting'. In music you *do…* or rather you *can…* stay in a constant *state of meetingness*. But this state is often too much on the cutting-edge – it's too much in the *now* to be 'a relationship' as such. It's almost as if a relationship is something from the past. If you're in the *now* you don't have '*a* relationship'… *you **are** meeting*…. (Verney, in Verney and Ansdell 2010, p. 82)

Another reason for Buber's reticence in seeing a therapeutic relationship as exemplary of I–You was his suspicion that therapists who worked from a particular theory were therefore necessarily taking an I–It stance towards their 'patient'. But again he seemed later to change his mind, commenting, 'I have had the impression of a certain change in psychotherapeutic practice in which more and more therapists are not so confident that this or that theory is right, and have a more "musical" floating relationship to their patient' (Buber, in Agassi 1999, p. 236). Within such a relationship, Buber saw the connection between his understanding of the Between, meeting, and the core of how therapy works. In a later public dialogue with a group of American psychiatrists, Buber responded to a question by the psychoanalyst Leslie Farber:

> *Farber*: Does your theory imply that healing takes place through meeting rather than through insight and analysis?

> *Buber*: A certain very important kind of healing – existential healing – takes place thus, healing not just of a certain part of the patient, but of the very roots of the patient's being … The existential element means bringing the patient to self-healing … *Everything is changed in real meeting*…. (in Agassi 1999, p. 242)

Buber also wrote a short essay called 'Healing through Meeting' (in Agassi 1999) as an appreciation of the work of his friend, the psychotherapist Hans Trüb, who had followed through the exacting implications of Buber's dialogical philosophy for the therapeutic situation. The therapeutic relationship, writes Buber, is 'the elementary situation between one who calls and one who is called', involving the 'necessity of genuine personal meetings in the abyss of human existence between the one in need of help and the helper' (pp. 18–19). In this understanding of therapy, the quality of the human meeting *is* the therapy, not just a vehicle for it. Buber made a poetic statement of this understanding in one of his Hasidic stories:

> When someone is singing and cannot lift their voice, and another comes and sings with them, another who can lift their voice, the first will be able to lift their voice too. That is the secret of the bond between spirits. (Buber 1947/2002, p. 63)

Buber's biographer Maurice Friedman comments that 'the title that Martin Buber gave this Hasidic story was not "the healer" or "the helper", but "When Two Sing"… it might have been called "Healing through Meeting"' (1983, p. 121). Friedman adds that, for him, 'healing through meeting occurs when the meeting between therapist and client is the central, as opposed to the ancillary, aspect of the therapy' (p. 39).

A musical relationship is indeed perhaps the best analogy for how Buber linked his understanding of human relationship with the challenge of therapy: to find a quality of dialogue that responds to the call of another, but is mindful of the limitations of the traditional 'helping relationship' – finding instead something more mutual, creative and musical – as when two people sing together.

ജ

A man with advanced dementia makes raw, grating, seemingly habitual vocalisations that sound like an animal in distress. And they are indeed distressing to everyone around him in the nursing home. A music therapist comes alongside him, playing her cello in response to his call. She plays small melodic motifs that seem almost to pierce the raw sounds of his voice, to come near them, and then to weave around them, picking up the forms of his vitality through musical tone, rhythm and texture. Then suddenly there's a lifting of the man's voice and a thinning of the rawness as the two voices come into relatedness, going roughly up and down in parallel for a while in similar arcs of melody. Then there's a pause from both, and the cello reiterates the short motif and the man answers it. Against all expectations, these two people meet in the music, and you hear that this man has been welcomed back into the world of relation – if only for a precious moment.

ജ

I try to improvise with Hettie, but I feel no contact between us. She is floridly psychotic, fuelled by exuberant fantasies and wild bursts of random energy. We play music in the same physical space, but not together. Then quite unexpectedly we suddenly meet in the music, and land together at a shared cadence. We look at each other with some surprise, and Hettie seems to land into reality. In that split second (outside the music this time), something is mutually known, and something accepted, affirmed and confirmed – both about each other, and about something beyond each other.

'Is it a comedy or a tragedy, Gary? ... I think it's a comedy!' says Hettie.

৪৩

Such healing encounters are equally challenging for therapist and client. A client once described to me his experience of meeting in music as 'the *shock* of contact!' Therapists too can feel such shocks when there is a sudden authentic human meeting between you and someone seemingly lost in the fog of psychosis, autism or dementia. Sometimes just a small gesture indicates something unexpectedly shared. Other times, it is more dramatic – a sudden, mutually experienced wormhole through which we reach something real and precious.

As musicking with people can afford these sometimes unexpected experiences of intimacy, it needs careful ethical attention within a therapeutic context. The shared play of tones and the gestures of invitation and acceptance can sometimes be experienced or interpreted as varieties of Eros. There are often glances, smiles of acknowledgement, recognition and pleasure at the experience of the musical Between, and their occasional consummation in moments of meeting. This particular 'musical Eros' needs to be kept carefully within the music if it's to be safe for both client and therapist. Music therapists are trained to be skilled in maintaining both the musical intimacy and clear personal boundaries. But whilst this can be a precarious tightrope to tread, it is also an important dimension of musical relationship for many people whose life and illness have often precluded any kind of intimacy or Eros. When professionally and humanly negotiated and contained, such 'safe Eros' can be a liberating and healing experience for both client and therapist. There's a certain freedom when a client doesn't need to tell their personal story in words, or indeed doesn't need to establish a conventionally personal relationship with the therapist at all. Musical intimacy can just happen, in the twinkling of an ear, and can be conducted in an emotional idiom that can be helpful to a client through its paradoxical stance of closeness and distance. This is perhaps more like the other forms of love that Greek philosophy and Christian theology has so carefully discriminated between: *Phileo*, a bond more akin to companionship, existing between people sharing pleasure within a common activity, and *Agape*, a caring that comes unconditionally from one to another. Nigel talks in his interview about his experience of this as a music therapist:

> **Nigel:** For me, the way of being with somebody in music is probably the most uncomplicated form of love, really – that's the only way I can define it. Love as being attentive to someone, being tended to, being listened to....

In his 1929 essay *Dialogue*, Buber writes that, whilst we should not directly equate dialogue with love, equally there is no love without dialogue, without reaching out to the other, without 'companying with the other'. Music and love will always accompany each other at some level.

৪৩

Examples of 'healing through meeting' show both what is required in the moment and what may be needed beyond it. We've seen how a modern therapeutic relationship still echoes its Greek ancestor, the *therapeutes*, who offered the service of companionship to people through difficult stretches of their life. In music therapy, such companionship has a satisfying double significance. There is the sense of the therapist as a musical accompanist who supports and sometimes challenges the client musically both in and through musical time and space – understanding them as musical persons, and helping to prepare the 'musical Between' and the possibilities of 'musical meetings'. But there's also the important further sense of maintaining and developing such musical companionship over longer stretches of time, the staying with a person and their particular predicament and suffering. Within a sustained therapeutic alliance and therapeutic process, there's also the shared search by therapist and client for the possibility of change and development, for new and more hopeful musical and personal pathways.

Why Does a Man who Wants to Die also Want to Sing?

Craig says that he wants to die. But he also wants to sing. Why does a man who wants to die also want to sing?

Though still in his twenties, Craig has been ill for the last ten years. A neurological disorder distorts his body image so that he arches himself backwards in a bow shape when standing or walking. A parallel psychiatric disorder also distorts Craig's personal identity at times. He has believed himself to be the late Michael Jackson and other celebrities. The worst of his symptoms have been controlled by medication, but he's been on a psychiatric ward for nearly a year now, waiting for a suitable placement in the community. Craig has withdrawn almost completely from staff or fellow patients and is very isolated. His psychiatrist describes his withdrawal as a 'blanket protest' of the kind political prisoners sometimes make. But Craig's protest is against life itself – he has enough insight to know that his life seems in ruins, and nobody seems able to help.

'I want to die – it's hopeless', is a mantra-like statement Craig often repeats again and again, not particularly as a communication, just a loop. And indeed, sometimes he does look like the living dead, withdrawing into the isolation of his room, often incontinent, lying in a pool of his own urine. 'I've got problems,' he repeats over and over.

℘

I'm asked whether I can see Craig, and I find him lying face down in the corridor outside the nurse's office, people stepping over him. He ignores me when I talk to him, so I go back downstairs to fetch two hand-held drums and two drumsticks. I put one of these close to his hand along with a stick, sing his name and play two sharp beats on the drum. Craig reaches out, takes the stick, hits the drum twice, and throws away the stick. When I tell him there are more instruments to play in the music therapy room downstairs, Craig unexpectedly gets up and we go together down the corridor in a curious crab-like motion, him leaning heavily on my shoulder. We look like two drunks and get strange looks.

In the music therapy room, Craig picks up a drumstick and plays a side drum and cymbal with great force, creating a defensive wall of sound. I rush to the piano and play as loud as I can to match the force of his playing. I see my hands moving, but I can't hear myself. After five minutes of this he stops, leaves the room, and staggers back up to the ward.

The contrast between this frenetic activity and his usual passivity is striking. I begin to see Craig twice weekly and during the following sessions the same thing happens: an assault of frantic sound that prevents any dialogue between us. His playing is a strange blend of participation and resistance – but at least he's doing something with another person. The staff are curious about why Craig wants to make music at all.

In subsequent sessions, Craig gradually relaxes and begins listening. By the fifth session, I get the first hint of mutuality – of us playing music *together*, rather than just making sound in the same space. Craig plays a tambourine and I play the piano and sing. We listen to each other in order to coordinate the beat of the music. Craig unexpectedly says, 'Shall I do some singing?', and when he can't think what to sing I say, 'Let's make something up', and start by singing an improvised musical phrase to him that's like a question, to which he responds with an answering phrase. It's a breakthrough. Whilst Craig keeps everything else in his life safe, repetitive and private, this improvised singing is spontaneous, shared and daring.

∾

During the following months, we continue working together twice each week, music therapy being the only activity Craig will tolerate – though sometimes he refuses this too. The ups and downs of Craig's general state are mirrored in his music. As well as improvising, we build up a repertoire of songs, and Craig often initiates his 'theme song' 'Let It Be'. How he performs this is the barometer of his vitality, and this can suddenly change in a session, from a low-energy, faltering performance to a sudden burst of exuberance. But at the same time, Craig will often still keep his verbal mantra going: 'I've got problems, I want to die...'. I find myself thinking over why a man who wants to die also wants to sing, and I ask my supervisor this question. 'Thanatos redeemed by Eros,' he says. There's still life energy and desire in Craig that singing seems to tap into. Craig's singing also helps to create an increasingly intimate and refined human relationship between us.

∾

Six months later, Craig is still coming to sessions and there's recognisable progress in our work. But outside them, he's become withdrawn and depressed again. He comes into the next session muttering, 'I'm a bit scared', but I know that anything I say is unlikely to reassure him. I start singing instead, an improvised 'Good

Morning Craig' in a Blues idiom, which he answers with a stylistically inflected 'Good Morning' on an upward motif. I carry on improvising:

'*Woke up one morning... Singing the Blues,*' I sing back to Craig.

'What's "Blues"?' he asks, but then copies my phrase and sings back, '*Singing the Blues... You've got me singing the Blues...*'. His singing is idiomatic – he knows the style, perhaps instinctively identifies with it. In Blues style, I sing back to him some of his hopeless-sounding 'mantra phrases' I'd heard him saying just that morning: 'He don't know what to do...,' I sing, which Craig copies, and then I answer, 'That's why...', which Craig completes, 'he's singing the Blues...'.

This feels right: Craig as 'Blues man' now – a voice and identity he can borrow and inflect to match his existential situation. It's a personal 'subject position', but his Blues voice also puts Craig back into a cultural dialogue with the outside world in a small way.

'Is that fifteen minutes yet?' Craig asks. Recently, for reasons best known to himself, he's had a self-imposed limit of fifteen-minute sessions with me. 'I don't know,' I reply somewhat disingenuously, and Craig checks on the device I'm using to record the session how many minutes have elapsed. This leads to me singing humorously to him, '*He does fifteen minutes – and that is that*', which Craig picks up and riffs on with equal humour. The session has ranged over the entire gamut of musical and personal expression, and it's wonderful to finish with humour, that most natural (but in Craig's circumstances most rare) of humanly shared emotions.

ॐ

There are advances and setbacks in our work together over the next phase, as in general for Craig. He is continually promised that he'll leave the hospital, and this hope is continually knocked back. Equally, I find myself getting stuck in these sessions, perhaps also losing hope that music therapy makes any difference. Then chance helps this *impasse*. A student nurse has befriended Craig and he tells her about music therapy. She joins one of the sessions and Craig performs his repertoire of songs to her, and somehow this revitalises the session. Possibly Eros has something to do with this, but I also see how Craig needs a broader platform for his musicking to be witnessed by others.

Just before Christmas, a choir of patients and staff launch the unit's party. Craig sits in a chair very close to me at the piano, with his own word sheet, and sings heartily. It's almost the only time I've ever seen him part of something bigger, in any way in community with people, rather than warily skirting around them. Later, to my amazement, I see him disco dancing!

After Christmas, we turn the occasional choir into a regular singing group, and Craig unexpectedly tags along with the others coming down from the ward. This is a surprise – he's never joined in any communal activity before. People pick songs from a collection of 'favourites' and usually start off by singing solo. When it comes to Craig's turn, I ask him, 'Which song for you then, Craig?', and he surprises us by saying assertively 'Let It Be' and launches into the song in the strong gravelly voice of a young man, with occasional uncontrolled cracks. His fellow patients seem amazed by the transformation of this man before their eyes. He beams with a touching smile at the end as they clap. 'Was that OK?' he asks.

ᘘ

I suspect that the last session before my summer holiday might be our last, as Craig has finally been offered a suitable placement. We sing through our repertoire of songs in a low-key way. Our musicking together has become easy and companionable. As ever, some of the songs we sing seem to have lines that speak poignantly for Craig and his situation: 'Hey, Jude, don't be afraid / Take a sad song and make it better...'.

I think, what a brave man! It is a sad song – like his life, seen one way. But he finds the courage and spirit to make the sad song better. Here we are, finally, two musical companions, singing it like it is.

After my holiday, Craig is indeed no longer in the unit. Jimmy, the ward cleaner, asks me about Craig every time I go up there. He says he associates me and Craig and music together. Have I heard how Craig is doing?

The last I heard was that he was doing well. His new social worker locates me and passes on a message from Craig: have I written up his case yet, and if not could I please get on with it!

Musical Answerability

Craig's case usefully brings us back to the key questions of Part IV: What does the prefix *musical* bring to the possibilities and qualities of human relatedness? What *is* a 'musical relationship'? We've seen through the four chapters on this area how relating in and through music is both similar and often very different to its more conventional verbal equivalent. Music offers possibilities and qualities to relationships that are especially helpful in some circumstances. Where communication is physically or psychologically disrupted, where words are not available, or distrusted, or too personal, music can help make initial contact, and can then nurture connection in a way that is not threatening, and is even potentially enjoyable. When sparks of relatedness are quickened into a developing dialogue, musicking with another person can afford particular qualities of intimacy, companionship and support, generosity and love. Musical meetings can be life changing.

As such, musical relationship necessarily has intertwined aesthetic, ethical and spiritual dimensions. Being musical with the other is to be responsible, to be answerable to their voice. This *answerability* to the musical voice[11] is possible because of what music specifically affords human relatedness: intimacy with

---

[11]   The music therapist Karette Stensæth writes about 'musical answerability' in her (2007) discussion of Bakhtin's dialogical philosophy in relation to music therapy.

distance; a fluid boundary between self and other that nevertheless retains the autonomy of self; the hearing of oneself within the voice of the other; the simultaneous sounding of two complementary voices, and so on. These are the properties, processes, values and virtues of musical relationship.

For the people and situations we've been discussing in these chapters, these are all key to offering 'generous care' within a 'health ecology'. Such care depends on practising the dialogical principle in a way that musicking both exemplifies and affords – contacting, connecting and, through dialogue, helping bind a person back into the network of relationships they may have fallen out of through their condition or situation. Perhaps people are often so moved by music therapy cases because these show how it's simply the quality of human relationship that matters. Caring has many facets, but its prime responsibility is not to leave another person alone.

As Craig's case showed, intimate musical relationships often point towards their outward-bound connections to the broader musical and social ecology – to musical groups, cultures and communities. Each musical relationship echoes and mirrors something of the whole pattern. Musical relationships help because they both model and perform the ecology of relationships that we all need to flourish.

PART V
Musical Community

Community is where community happens.

Martin Buber

[U]sing the verb musicking emphasizes that not only is music an activity, but also it's a form of human encounter in which everyone who is present is taking part, and for whose success or failure as an event everybody who is present has some responsibility. It is not just a matter of active performers doing something for, or to, passive listeners. Whatever it is that is being done, we are all doing it together.

Christopher Small

The need for community is the same thing as the need for dialogue. Community is the meeting place of different voices talking together, exchanging and debating experience and knowledge. Music is one of the instruments of this process, a means of social experience ….

Michael Chanan

We like music because it represents, in crystallized form, the essence of human social life.

Keith Sawyer

Chapter 14
Musical Togetherness

Together is a crucial term, for a sense of community takes hold, and these patients who seem incorrigibly isolated by their disease and dementia are able, at least for a while, to recognise and bond with others.

Oliver Sacks[1]

[T]he question of the social emerges when the ties in which one is entangled begin to unravel; the social is further detected through the surprising movements from one association to the next ....

Bruno Latour[2]

'Tea for Two', Togetherness for Many

The sitting room of this residential care home is decorated in a homely, somewhat genteel way. Eight residents with moderate to severe dementia sit around the edges of the room, occupying the same physical space yet isolated socially from each other.

Richard, the music therapist, starts playing the verse of the 1930s song 'Tea for Two' on the piano. Almost instantly there's some recognition, and a few residents walk over to Richard and gather around the piano. It looks like a domestic soirée now – a scene that many of the residents (who are mostly in their eighties) perhaps remember from an earlier stage of their lives, when many social occasions would have happened like this.

Almost everyone in the room responds to the music in some way. At one end of the spectrum, there's the lady who stands next to Richard, ready to sing, comporting herself with a slight tilt of her upper body in a dance-like gesture that matches the music's style. Then there's a man who I'm told for the rest of the week sits silently and inactively, but who now taps his hand on a small flat drum on his lap – in time and phrase with the music. Looks and small gestures signal that other residents are also coming out of themselves into something more shared. Their recognition of the music seems linked to their recognition of each other, and perhaps of the social meaning of the event that is gathering momentum. As the chorus of the song arrives, the signs of participation increase,

---

[1] Sacks 2007, p. 345.
[2] Latour 2005, p. 247.

with more physical orientation towards Richard and the piano as the source of the live music, as well as attention to the song's structure. People try to sing the words, some a bit behind and vague at first, but then 'catching' a phrase and its melody together with someone else, who perhaps for the first time in many hours or days is sharing time and space with another. This event feels more than just 'music' or 'singing' in a simple sense. There's a sense of occasion that somehow scoops these people up into social life again.

A care worker looks into the room, sees something nice is happening, comes in – and she too is drawn into the event by the lady by the piano, who seizes the chance for a dance partner. They take a few stylish turns around the room, and Richard responds to this developing situation by improvising out of the song to better support the dance. At this point, another man, who's been very passive up to now (and is evidently often aggressive, refusing any kind of participation with others) looks up towards the dancers, tries to get up, and seems to offer his hand to another seated woman resident. Unfortunately she doesn't notice this, and his invitation goes unrequited. But this shows that somehow the occasion has a clear and perhaps irresistible pull towards participation. It's now a 'tea dance' – something that will have specific social meaning to many of these people.

Time and space have become active and interactive again, creating togetherness and belonging amongst residents and staff alike.

℞

How does musicking achieve this unexpected social transformation?

It's tempting to answer, 'The music did it' – that it stimulated the senses, or the brain, or the memory, or the emotions of the residents. But one reason why this explanation is too simple will be recognised by anyone who's been in a similar situation where just a CD is playing, or the television is constantly left on. The residents will seldom even notice these, and will usually remain passive and isolated. In contrast, the social event described above happened because of the unique and timely alignment between the music, the people and the whole situation. Richard's skill as a musician and music therapist helped the collective event to emerge and to find shape, but it also needed the residents' purposeful responses, and the care worker's sensitive participation. As Christopher Small remarks about any musicking, 'It is not just a matter of active performers doing something for, or to, passive listeners. Whatever it is that's being done, we are all doing it together' (2010, p. 6).

Dementia has unravelled much of the residents' social experience, often leading to a profound isolation that is also distressing for those who witness it. Against this, the musical occasion above seems almost miraculously to generate the social virtues of recognition, cooperation, hospitality and conviviality. It both enacts and symbolises a form of social hope.

There has been an explosion of interest recently in how music offers such social help. When I say that I'm a music therapist, people's first association is often now the high-profile, large-scale musical–social projects: Daniel Barenboim's West-Eastern Divan Orchestra or the Venezuelan Simón Bolivar Youth Orchestra. But on a more modest level, community musicians have for decades now been working musically in an outward-focused way with disenfranchised and at-risk groups and communities, emphasising the values of cultural democracy and social justice (Higgins 2012). As we saw in the sketch of professional practice I made in the Introduction, music therapists have in contrast often been too exclusively inward-focused, and consequently ambivalent about the social and cultural possibilities of their work. This attitude has gradually changed in the last decade with the development of the Community Music Therapy movement and its advocacy of broader musical work with vulnerable groups (Pavlicevic and Ansdell 2004; Stige, Ansdell, Elefant and Pavlicevic 2010; Stige and Aarø 2012). These various professional currents are possibly now converging to form a more integrated 'musical–social work'.[3] The shared belief is that music can do more than help individuals – it can also respond to social problems through fostering musical community, which can in turn improve personal wellbeing. A simple equation is increasingly being both empirically and politically recognised: decrease isolation and you increase wellbeing. Music is seen as a good way of tackling key social issues of our time.

The sociologist Richard Sennett (2012) comments that 'social problems' have typically been approached from two angles: either 'top–down' or 'bottom–up'. The former tends to impose political solutions through new initiatives and restructuring, whilst the latter usually starts from a more grassroots level, simply trying to open up communication, get people doing things together, and nudge a challenging situation towards something better. That is, 'bottom–up' strategies tend to be dialogic in the sense we explored in Part IV. Where social life needs building up (or re-building), a dialogic approach tries to foster new associations in whichever way suits the context. But you need to keep your ear to the ground to hear the resulting incremental changes.

Part V will suggest that musical community happens when musical relationship is free to proliferate within a wider context. And just as with musical relationship, musical community is not a thing. It is not some kind of stuff that can be applied as a 'social solution' for social problems. Instead, we need to think of musicking as a dynamic social process in which musical togetherness is assembled link by link in often modest yet transformational ways.

This more down-to-earth perspective on music–social work also cautions against the growing tendency to draw music's potential for bringing social hope into a utopian rhetoric. The danger is that the real achievements of musical-social projects become distorted by the symbolic work they are then forced to do for broader political agendas. Partly this trend stems from the continued influence of one of the foundational myths of music therapy, Plato's *harmonia*. This theory

---

[3] I use this term pragmatically as there's currently no common agreement about terminology.

portrayed how the cosmic harmony of the spheres influences the social harmony of the civic world below. Contemporary versions of this quasi-metaphysical theory still tend to see social harmony as something rather grandly 'given' by the spiritual and therapeutic powers of music. The problem is that this still-abiding metaphor is too idealised and too top–down. It can lead us to look in the wrong place when trying to understand music's social powers. Perhaps not up in the stars any more, but often away from the mundane and ongoing local work of forging musical community link by link.

Music's social power needs to be understood more as an ecological and cultural phenomenon than a quasi-natural one such as Plato's *harmonia*. A more earthbound 'harmony' will not be some static ideal, but rather an achieved result of people relating within *communities of practice*. This will also involve recognising, living and working through periods of discrepancy, disunity and dissonance (each of these being locally and culturally defined). In music, many different people can be together simultaneously in a meaningful and creative way. But we need a more complex and local understanding of how voices can successfully sound together yet retain their identity. We need to know what are the potentials and limits of such musical togetherness.

The focus of the chapters in Part V is therefore on the detailed local processes of creating and sustaining musical community. As a social help, musicking affords the basic needs of being included, participating and belonging. It promotes the basic social values and virtues of respect and hospitality. It supports ritual, and sparks enjoyment, celebration and conviviality. At best, there are also moments of 'realistic utopia' where the hope for a better future is realised here and now in the present.

Why do Three Tones Form a Triad rather than a Triangle?

This odd question, posed by Zuckerkandl (1956, p. 297), takes us into the strange world of musical togetherness. As we've seen before, the phenomenology of music rests on how tones and other musical elements continually relate, point towards and combine with each other in an ongoing flux. How we hear musical space is crucially different to how we see visual space, as Zuckerkandl's question suggests. Put three things in physical, visual space together and they merge or at least block each other, which is why we think first of three-ness in terms of a triangle. But a musical *triad* is precisely three separate sonic things in the *same* musical space and time that combine creatively whilst retaining their individual identity.[4] Put this in

---

[4] Although the triad represents a foundational relationship between tones within the Western tonal system, the same phenomenon could happen within any system of simultaneous sounding of tones – though not noises, which will tend to separate out into a conventional spatial order rather than work together dynamically to form something musically new, as tones do.

terms of an eco-phenomenology (that is, putting people and musical action into the picture) and you can see the significance of the triangle/triad comparison. Three people can't occupy the same physical space, and three people talking together obscure each other's voice. But three people *can* very comfortably and very creatively occupy the same space in music – even when singing words together. Musical space becomes productively 'filled' when people sing or play instruments together, each retaining a voice or part whilst coming together (in whatever way) in the ongoing whole of the music. Zuckerkandl's explanation of this is that tones are dynamic *states* and *events* in motion, and not 'things'. Therefore, their musical space is not so much 'occupied' as 'potentised' – ready for relationship and transformation. Whatever the explanation, there is clearly a specific and unique phenomenological reality that governs musical *ensemble*.[5]

In the West-Eastern Divan Orchestra, two players from opposite political sides often share a music desk in the orchestra. Daniel Barenboim comments on what musical space affords within a situation where the human and social stakes are especially high:[6]

> Music makes it possible for all the Israeli members of the orchestra to support an Egyptian oboist's solo, and for all the Arab members to support an Israeli flautist's solo ... Music teaches us ... no element is entirely independent because the relationship is by definition interdependent.[7]

Zuckerkandl himself gives the example of a classic operatic ensemble, the quartet from Act II of Verdi's *Otello*, where the four melodic lines of the characters are woven into a unified musical texture in musical space. Not only do these voices blend together whilst maintaining their individual identity, but they also *develop* together through the musical process. Consequently, writes Zuckerkandl, 'from the simultaneous voicing of four meanings arises, not the destruction of meaning, but a super-meaning, the meaning of a whole' (1956, p. 322).

Zuckerkandl has a further useful insight into what happens when people sing together. He notices how 'speaking man' and 'singing man' relate differently because of the natural direction they face. In speech, we face towards the other because we are directly communicating something; whereas when we sing (either solo, or in chorus), we face *outwards*, away from the self, away from the other. But importantly, this facing out is part of what Zuckerkandl calls the 'authentic togetherness' of the musicking ensemble:

---

[5]   From the Latin *in* + *simul*, 'at the same time'.

[6]   I shall discuss later the political implications of Barenboim's so-called 'metaphysics of music' in relation to the Divan. For now, this is just to illustrate Zuckerkandl's point.

[7]   Reported in *Observer* newspaper, UK, 29 July 2007.

Singing is the natural and appropriate expression of the group ... [expressing] the individual in so far as his relation to the others is not one of 'facing them' but of togetherness. [...]

[T]he singer encounters himself coming from the outside ... in the one tone that comes from all, I encounter the group as well as myself. The dividing line between myself and the others loses its sharpness ... The very existence of tones is evidence of a stratum of reality in which unity shines through diversity. (Zuckerkandl 1973, pp. 28 and 42)

Another pioneer in the understanding of musical togetherness was the sociologist Alfred Schütz (1964), who thought that musical ensemble crystallised something of the essence of social life. He takes Mozart's famous operatic ensembles as the best examples of what he calls 'group intersubjectivity'. Up to six people are singing together whilst retaining their individual characters, motives and relationships to each other – including that one pair of characters is sometimes in conflict with another pair. They keep their own personal stance on the situation, but also, as Schütz comments, 'they act together, feel together, will together as a community, as a We' (1976, p. 199). In this way, Schütz saw the musicalising of social relationships as somehow distilling and thereby highlighting an ideal for everyday social life: that people can be together in ways that balance individuality and togetherness. Interestingly, Schütz remarks that it makes no difference whether the voices are cooperative or antagonistic amongst themselves – they are still bound in a 'We' relationship whilst the music lasts.

In his famous essay 'Making Music Together' (1964), Schütz looks further into this phenomenon of group intersubjectivity, emphasising how musical time and timing affords such togetherness. When people make music together, Schütz suggests, there's a uniquely musical form of 'tuning-in relationship' between them. This happens through musical time, which is not the 'clock-time' that the music 'takes' to happen, but the subjective time created within the mutual movement from one tone to another as the music unfolds.[8] This allows 'this sharing of the other's flux of experiences in inner time, this living through a vivid present in common, growing older together while the musical process lasts' (1964, p. 173). There's also a lesser though necessary spatial dimension to this 'tuning-in', in which players share both musical and physical space together, and co-ordinate their musical inner time through seeing and sensing each other's movements, facial expressions, posture and overt gestures. Although this could perhaps be

---

[8]   Schütz refers to musical time as polythetic, which must proceed step by step in its own 'inner time' in order to yield the meaning of something like a piece of music, or a poem to us. Polythetic time can't be reversed or paraphrased, and it has only a secondary relation to measured clock time. By contrast, monothetic understanding can come from a single glance, in which a meaning 'outside' of ongoing time is grasped as a whole and can be separated out from the process of the vehicle that has transported it.

measured in some way, its essence is a relational 'inner space' that corresponds to 'inner time'. Schütz ventures that this overall experience of sharing time and space within musicking constitutes the 'vivid present' of an intersubjectivity that is foundational to social relationships. What Mozart manages in his musical–social scenarios, Schütz suggests, is no less than to establish a 'community of intersubjectivity', a social situation where people are attempting to understand each other and themselves in their mutual and ever-changing relations: 'And this is precisely the condition in which each of us finds himself [*sic*] in everyday life. I am always involved in a situation' (1976, p. 17).

Musical Grouping

Alan: You know Noah and Frank? The three of us have been playing music together for twenty years. Sometimes we get into this state when we're improvising, but we're also telling each other these really funny jokes. We're not actually saying a word, but it's like when we're improvising on a song... and then we bring in *another* song that's related in some way to the first song... and how it's related is often very funny! There are times when we go into a certain state of consciousness and I'm not thinking, 'Hi Frank, I'm talking to you' or whatever... we're just all in the *music*... and we get into this state... we could play for five hours like this... improvising off songs we know, then someone else brings in another song, and then another related to this. I don't know how to describe it, but it feels like an altered state of consciousness... that we're in a kind of ecstasy of release and laughter. There's also a cleverness, a bit of competition between us... not in a mean way, but a funny way... like, 'What are you going to do with *that*?' And all this feels like it's based on the trust of knowing each other, knowing we've done this so many times before... and knowing a body of music together. It might be jazz songs, but it could be anything... like a fragment of a tune we heard in an Indian restaurant... some obscure folksong, a TV theme... anything! So it's about knowing each other's relationships to music too... like, 'I know that's funny because *you* know...'. But because it's *music*, there's something very creative going on... discovery and uncovering... there's a certain expressive satisfaction too, because it's sustained and flowing. Certainly the very physical element is important... the actually *doing* something together... so there's so many layers... like, *Who's going to do this part as we all play at the same time?* But it does also feel that we *go* somewhere together... I don't know how to explain it... we're still in the room, but it's suddenly *different*....

ɞ

Susanna: When I'm playing viola in a quartet, it's the harmony of the people together, the rightness of the relationship *between* us that's so satisfying. If you're a listener to music, there's a kind of communication with the music, which you feel is of some ultimate value to you, but which at the same time you believe also has an objective value, not just to you. But then when you play or sing with other people in a way you have *both* of these things, because of the communal experience. I think I find it more when I'm playing than singing... which is strange! Maybe it's because one's voice is so loud in one's head! Or perhaps it's because where my real musical heart lies is in the string repertoire. Certainly doing quartets – however crashingly badly one's going through them – it's extraordinary the effect it can have. I'm always amazed that I seem to be able to ignore that it's all out of tune and out of time! Because somehow it's playing in my head at the same time as it really should be. But also there's the fun of things going wrong – as well as occasionally right! Then there's that kind of communication with people trying to prevent it from falling apart. I suppose that's why people often think of a string quartet as an analogy of well-working social relationships – that even if you're playing badly, you're still trying to get a perfect balance between all the voices, making intimate musical and social adjustments to keep it all going....

These two vignettes present 'communities of intersubjectivity', in Schütz's phrase – where music is helping people to act together, but also through their joint musical action to think and feel together. They illustrate well the various perspectives on musical togetherness suggested by Small, Sennett, Zuckerkandl, Barenboim and Schütz. Many of the key features of social life are going on during those two situations: contacting, relating, thinking, feeling, cooperating, competing, joking, creating, breaking down and repairing, and so on. The key factor that music seems to bring is to focus and enhance social communication. We also see in the two situations how competition and breakdown-and-repair are not always negative in musicking. They can become part of the ongoing creative play.

In short, we are led to thinking of the social in music as a fully dynamic process, not a thing. This matches Bruno Latour's (2005) plea not to think of the social as some strange stuff that we evoke to stick people together or to solve their problems. When we think of *a* community or a group, it's already become something too settled and static – *asocial* – and the danger then is that we stop attending to how anything social needs continual making and remaking, is 'a movement in need of continuation' (Latour 2005, p. 37). So understanding the musical–social process in the examples above would be a matter of tracing the ongoing musical associations as they assemble, disassemble and recombine. Rather than asking what a 'musical group' is, we need instead to notice and explore the patterns and possibilities of dynamic musical *grouping*.

We come here to a familiar notion from earlier chapters on musical identity and relationship: that musical community is not something that 'is' but rather something needing to be *performed* – by real people, in real situations, for a specific purpose. Because of this, the *work* of ensembles and communities is to keep their performance going. And this is done only by further 'social work' –

repeating, refining, securing and sometimes defending particular associations. This is necessarily hard and repetitious work. As Latour states, no work, no group! – or, as he more poetically puts it, 'if a dancer stops dancing, the dance is finished' (2005, p. 37). We should never take the social for granted, but always consider it a continual and often surprising achievement.

The material for this work of assembling groups can be anything that people can or need to do together – family life, food, sport, politics and the arts. But none of these areas is innately social. The social only emerges from the creative 'assembly work' that these forms of life and their materials differently afford. Whilst music is indeed one of the most potentially effective of these forms of life, it is not a social material until it comes into action through musicking. Then, as we saw earlier in *Musical Worlds*, musical people, musical things and musical occasions become drawn into active and fruitful association. Just *how* the musical assembling happens is both similar and distinct if we consider the tea dance, the jamming buddies and the string quartet. Physical situations, personal histories and relationships, social and cultural styles, repertoire, and a host of other factors influence how musical grouping happens. But despite all the difference, all three vignettes demonstrate how musical grouping so successfully meshes musical action with social interaction. All three depend on the ongoing work of building musical associations and following where they lead, balancing ideas and voices, individual and shared history and culture within current in-the-moment happenstance. They show the processes of communicating and adjusting to keep the sometimes precarious yet precious togetherness from falling apart again. The outcome for those involved in each case is a quality of collective consciousness, a state of flow experienced together in the real-time improvisational process. Each person contributes to this whole, but it's the whole that generates the satisfying experience for them.

Collaborative Musicking

A new generation of scholars is investigating in much more detail the processes of musical grouping, in ways that follow the principle that time-based artforms assemble the social in helpful ways. Keith Sawyer's (2003, 2005) research is particularly interesting in its comparison of improvisation groups in both jazz and theatre. He explores their very similar process of group creativity that he calls 'collaborative emergence'. This, he suggests, consists of an interlinked series of key communicative activities and outcomes:[9]

- *Improvising* is how a group assembles itself in process here and now, not exactly knowing what it's doing or where it's going. What happens is

---

[9] The following account is my summary of Sawyer 2003, 2005.

delicately situational, reliant on those people in that time and place, on who does what and when. Nobody is instructed, but there's some common sense of what's right to do and where's right to go. This is based partly on shared cultural conventions – of how a melody goes, or of how you respond to a musical offering. But brand-new combinations of material also 'just happen' as people follow the flow.

- *Orientating* describes how group members 'tune into' and orient towards each other's gestures and actions, and to the shared unfolding musical material. They not only physically and metaphorically 'point towards' ('index' in the semiotic sense[10]) each other's musical utterances, but also draw what they know from past situations into this current moment, interleaving their personal contribution within the unfolding musical–social whole through turn taking or simultaneous sounding.

- *Collaborating* describes the *working* together to create the musical event. The social effect does not consist of a mechanical process of adding individuals into some external structure. Instead, the 'groupness' of the group is a result of collective timing and pacing. This results in group intersubjectivity (sharing intention and meaning), interactional synchrony (sharing the internal timing of gestures), and entrainment (performing gestures and movements in alignment).

- *Emerging* describes how the sense of groupness or community is not the sum of its parts; rather, the whole *creates* the meaning of the parts. The group only 'works' when there's a 'group flow'. This can't be forced, but suddenly 'takes off' when the conditions are right. The result is that something social as well as something musical emerges.

These key features of musical grouping all require far more than *being* together. Grouping needs continual musical–social *working*. The benefits of any group experience rely on ongoing cultivation and careful management. Usually, group members can manage this maintenance and repair work themselves through communication and negotiation – as with Alan's and Susanna's groups. But there is also the not-uncommon phenomenon of dis-banding bands and explosive groups. Because musical groups are powerful ways of people being together, they are also vulnerable to breakdown. Where musical groups find particular difficulties in keeping together, but also important benefits from being together musically, skilled facilitators and music therapists can often help to keep this music–social work going.

---

[10]   We use our 'index finger' to point out people and things. In a semiotic theory of communication, an 'index' is a sign that associates one thing with another (e.g. smoke indexes fire). So, in music, an indexical communication is something that refers, points or links to a musical utterance or gesture that someone else has or is currently performing – and this group process serves to gradually assemble the joint music. For more on this, see Turino 2008, pp. 8–10.

Mercédès Pavlicevic and I (Pavlicevic and Ansdell 2009) came independently of Keith Sawyer to a very similar understanding of musical grouping from our perspective as music therapists studying musical–social events within Community Music Therapy projects in the UK and South Africa. Our theoretical starting point was 'communicative musicality', as outlined in Part IV. This, as we saw in an earlier chapter, came to a detailed understanding of infant–carer relationships by putting them under the microscope of slowed-down film and seeing how they were 'musically' assembled. Communicative musicality portrayed a carer and infant performing an expressive *pas de deux*. But what happens, we asked, when the duet expands to an ensemble? How many of the features of communicative musicality are retained in musical groups? Does anything else happen? What is the role of culture, learning and convention in musical groups and how they achieve togetherness? It seemed to us that, whilst communicative musicality formed a necessary platform, it was also important to account for what is built further on this in order to address these questions, and to suggest a model for the further coupling of musical and social development. We proposed the concept of *collaborative musicking* in order to characterise emerging musical groups and to give communicative musicality a further, more social dimension. The model we developed is designed to explore the coupling of music–social experience that seems as naturally motivated at a group and public level as is communicative musicality at a more private and intimate level.

This theory begins with the 'inverted triangle' model presented earlier in Part III (p. 89). This suggests a three-stage progression starting from *musicality* (as a psycho-biological capacity), which prepares the ground for cultural learning as the cultivated facility of *musicianship*, which in turn facilitates the social activity of *musicking* with and for others. Each level of the inverted pyramid is needed for attaining the subsequent level: capacity leading to facility to activity. But the traffic is also two way: musicking stretches musicianship, which stimulates musicality. A second stage in this theory (see Fig. 14.1(i)) then shows an ideal model of social experience and development as a continuum ranging between I/You (remember, there is no 'I' independent of relationship), moving to the 'We' of dialogue, and finally to the 'Us' of community. As presented so far, communicative musicality takes us to the mid-point, 'We', of social experience and development.

Figure 14.1(ii) then amalgamates these two dimensions, to show us how musical and social experience/development might dynamically interact.

This juxtaposition produces two related but separately identifiable functions that unfold along the sloping diagonal (M) axis of ideal development: *communication* and *collaboration*. Our core musicality (a) naturally becomes communicative (I/ You). Musical dialogue and companionship ('We') helps facilitate the social and cultural development of musicianship (b), which allows the increasingly elaborate forms of musicking – an essentially collaborative and communal ('Us') activity (c).

Communicative musicality forms the territory above the circle at the origin (a), linking a mobilising of musicality in the service of communication— at the incipient 'I/You' level. A further arc outwards from this would then express how –

Figure 14.1 (i)   An ideal model of social experience and development

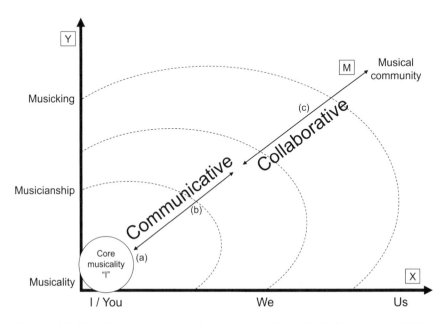

Figure 14.1 (ii)   Between communicative musicality and collaborative musicking

as the dyad takes in elements of musical culture (e.g., a mother's vocalisations and nursery songs) – communication begins to service the development of musicianship (the expression of musicality in and as culture). And thus, the successive arcs take us up the diagonal M-axis. When we reach 'We', a genuine musical partnership has been built on the platform of communicative musicality and the ongoing cultural induction of musicianship. At this point (b) moving towards (c), true musicking, becomes possible, if perhaps only in dyad relationship or small-scale contexts.

The theory suggests that a further function of the musical–social relationship then comes into being: not just communication, but collaboration. As a partner to communicative musicality, *collaborative musicking* is the outward and audible sign of musical community. Collaborative musicking builds community through making music together in a way that makes use of both natural musicality and cultivated musicianship. A few caveats here: this is not to say that communication and collaboration are simply discrete functions; rather, the communicative function transforms into a collaborative one in certain situations. Moreover, the traffic is not just from communicative to collaborative: in many circumstances

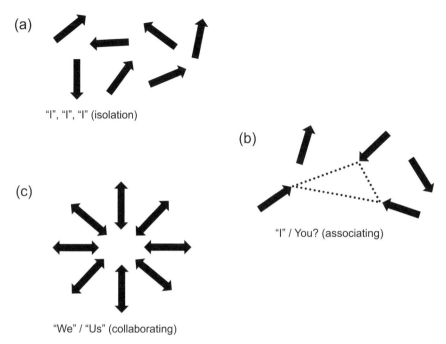

(a)

"I", "I", "I" (isolation)

(b)

"I" / You? (associating)

(c)

"We" / "Us" (collaborating)

Figure 14.2   Styles of togetherness

there may be an oscillation between these modes, as there is between the aspects of each of the axes: we live between I/You/We/Us, and similarly between musicality, musicianship and musicking.

℘

Let's think back now to the example at the nursing home at the start of this chapter in the light of these various ideas about musical togetherness (and using the diagrams in Fig. 14.2). Bruno Latour writes that 'the question of the social emerges when the ties in which one is entangled begin to unravel; the social is further detected through the surprising movements from one association to the next' (2005, p. 247). The residents' dementia pushes Latour's 'social question' into a 'social problem' because of the severity of how their illness unravels the social ties on which their continuing personhood and wellbeing depends. Their situation could be represented by the first diagram in Fig. 14.2(a), where each person is an isolated 'I', either unaware or unable to orientate to or to contact an other.

A 'musical solution' comes through how the social is reassembled through musical connections, leading to musical togetherness. Gradually, we see an orientating process by some of the residents – to the song structure and words and to Richard at the piano, but also as they 'tune in' to each other's actions and responses, recognising each other differently. The grouping moves to Fig. 14.2(b), a situation midway between individual responses and those that orient to each other.

Musical and personal associations begin to happen at the same time. At this point, it also becomes clear that it's not just Richard doing the work here: the residents' innate communicative musicality and their culturally learned musicianship are also coming into play with his help. People call on their memories – both in their heads and in their bodies. An intersubjective community is emerging in which the residents understand each other better within this situation because of what they are *doing* together. They also increasingly perform gestures of etiquette and hospitality to each other, and acknowledge shared pleasure. Here is the evidence that this event simultaneously has both musical and social value.

As the tea dance takes shape, there's a moment of social grace. Musical communication shifts into *collaborative musicking*, when all are (if for only a few moments) aligned into the living centre of the occasion. The effect of this sudden fitting together is an effortless musical flow where the whole is more than the sum of the parts. Fig. 14.2(c) shows this synthesis symbolically, the central star being created only through the alignment of the arrows that represent each person's contribution. That the arrows in this image point both inwards and outwards is important, recalling Zuckerkandl's insight that, whilst musical togetherness requires inner cohesion, it is essentially *outward* focusing. Collaborative musicking allows these people to come *out* of their isolation and to face outwards into a shared social world again for a while.

At this optimal moment, musical community happens. Somebody looking in the window at this tea dance happening would perhaps not realise the severity of the residents' individual problems or their severe challenges in managing to belong together in a meaningful way.

I would suggest that the only difference between the nursing home residents and the other examples in this chapter is that Alan, Susanna and their friends can assemble musical togetherness for themselves with relative ease, whilst the elderly people need Richard's specialist help to initiate, to sustain, and where necessary to repair the process. Everyone involved in these diverse situations of collaborative musicking experiences something of the core of how music helps create togetherness, and the welcoming of others into it. But we still need to remember the key message of this chapter: community is a social achievement, a performance. When the dancer stops, the dance disappears. As Martin Buber wrote, 'Community is where community happens' (1947/2002, p. 31). Musical togetherness is always in action, in situation, in time.

Chapter 15
Musical Hospitality

Generosity begins in *welcome*: a hospitality that offers whatever the host has that would meet the needs of the guest. The welcome of opening the doors to one's home signifies the opening the self to others, including guests who may disrupt and demand. To guests who suffer, the host's welcome is an initial promise of consolation.

Arthur Frank[1]

Musical Invitations

I described in an earlier chapter how pioneer music therapists Paul Nordoff and Clive Robbins found that many of the children they met who seemed isolated in a world of their own could be invited into music, and then into a musical relationship. When I work with individual clients, I welcome them into the room, and then invite them to start making music, to which I can respond. Other times, my music and I need to be there first – musically welcoming someone to a session, inviting them to join me 'inside music'. A child might need music to entice them to cross the threshold into the therapy room. It occurs to me that these are all variants on the etiquette of hospitality.

This same principle holds with groups: musical and social gestures are importantly linked. Music therapists and community musicians have discovered how a musical and a social invitation can helpfully be one and the same thing. Musicking can function as a form of hospitality, albeit sometimes a complex and paradoxical one. Musical hospitality involves the generosity of welcoming in, and then the challenge of entertaining – of coping creatively and respectfully with what can happen next.

৪৩

SMART is a hospitable place, and *Smart Music* takes place in the café, amid the bustle of people chatting, eating and drinking. The weekly music group has an ethic of unconditional welcome at its core – not only welcome to people, but also with the idea that music itself is welcoming. The event is a fusion between a music therapy group (open to anyone, with their music and their problems and struggles) and an 'open-mic' session (open to people's music and talent). Patients drop in from the next-door psychiatric hospital, members of the public drop in for a coffee, a postman occasionally stays to sing.

---

[1]   Frank 2004, p. 2.

Sarah, who co-runs the group and is also the music therapist in the hospital, brings along a woman today who has an hour's leave from the hospital ward. She's anxious and agoraphobic and only just makes it to the café. A regular member greets her warmly, sits next to her, and gets her a cup of tea, saying, 'You can sing a song later if you want, anyone can...', adding, 'If *I* can, *anyone* can! You should hear how bad I am, but it doesn't matter, anything's welcome...'. The music starts and the woman settles down, and fifteen minutes later she's beaming with pleasure and quietly singing. At the end of the group, she says to me, 'I really didn't think I could do anything like this, but I felt welcome here. I'm always afraid I'll burst into tears in Starbucks, but I felt the opposite here.... It's taken me out of myself.'

℘

Both music therapy and community music cultivate and celebrate welcoming because it represents the core ethical stance and values from which their work flows: inclusion, participation, equality, generosity, answerability and unconditional acceptance. Traditional therapy (including traditional music therapy) has seldom described itself in terms of hospitality, for reasons we've explored previously: its tendency is to follow the style and rules of medical relationships and contexts, where a certain professional distance and social artificiality has been the norm. More ecological perspectives, however, such as Community Music Therapy, have moved towards the alternative view that for many clients today the qualities of musical hospitality and conviviality are necessary therapeutic compensations for their negative experiences of exclusion, displacement and social isolation. We saw earlier how the sociologist Arthur Frank appeals in this way for the return to a more 'generous care' as part of a broader perspective of 'health ecology'. For Frank, this generosity starts with an unconditional welcome: 'a hospitality that offers whatever the host has that would meet the need of the guest ... Medical hospitality invites the ill to feel less stigmatised and isolated' (2004, pp. 2 and 3).

This picture might suggest that, within the 'caring professions', the gestures of hospitality are chiefly those of the therapist/workshop leader acting as host. She invites, welcomes, attends to, engages with, entertains, and generally places the guests' needs before her own. At times, of course, this will also include the host's tougher responsibilities of tolerating and negotiating with more challenging guests. Within a musical context, all of this may also hold true. But musical hospitality is interesting in how it can quickly subvert this easy symmetrical framework of hosts and guests. Something else may happen when a music therapist or community musician takes an 'improvisational attitude' to the situation. To improvise is essentially to musick hospitably and dialogically; to invite and accept all offers; to welcome the unexpected as normal; and to follow where people and music lead. Indeed, it has been suggested that a characteristic of improvisers is to *over*-accept, inviting anyone and anything into the musical event. The community musician Lee Higgins talks of 'keeping the inventive pathways open, always already welcoming the unexpected ... the impossible moments' (2008, p. 395). Within such musicking, we meet the other face of hospitality – the possibility that the 'household' of the musical–social event may be subverted or disrupted. In the live situation, musical hosts can suddenly become guests, and guests hosts. However, these unexpected aspects of musical hospitality can give us opportunities to enter into each other's worlds, and to experience our respective roles and their human responsibilities differently and more flexibly. For a time within music, we can find ourselves in an equal space where we can welcome, support and respect each other in a variety of ways.

Radical Musical Hospitality

'Hospitality' has some unhelpful sentimental and commercial connotations today. But like 'community' and 'experience', the roots and rich history of the word shine useful light on some of the complexities and paradoxes that musical hospitality entails in practice.

Hospitality has a double life. *Hospitare* means 'to receive as a guest', 'to attend to', 'to care for' – hence 'hospital' and 'hospice'. But a variety of complex linguistic associations have also built interesting tensions into the concept (Newlands and Smith 2010). The giver of hospitality also has a certain social power over the guest, and the guest in turn can also be (or turn into) a hostile stranger who can disrupt and disturb the household. Guest, stranger, enemy and host are therefore tied together in complex ways. Interestingly, there is also a connection between ancient hospitality (the Greek *xenia*), which meant assisting a traveller, and a *therapeutes*, who accompanied someone in particular need. These roots characterise the still-present ambivalences and stresses that surround how hospitality involves not only welcoming others over the threshold, creating space for 'strangers', being open to the needs of others, giving gifts... but also being careful not to lose mastery of the house.

Contemporary philosophers, theologians and politicians have used this more subtle understanding of hospitality to explore the modern dilemmas of acceptance and belonging within a cosmopolitan society. Jacques Derrida, for example, writes of hospitality as an 'open quasi-community ... a community without unity' (in Caputo 1997, p. 107). For community music and Community Music Therapy, this rethinking of hospitality in relation to community has been useful conceptually. It has provided a way of reflecting on the processes and practices of musical community that resists either sentimentalising it or 'naturalising' it – that is, seeing it as something 'already there' rather than achieved, and often ambiguous and ambivalent. What I shall call 'radical musical hospitality' stands rather for a realistic, unsentimental yet powerful practice that prepares, cultivates and manages musical community. It invokes the joint spirits of improvisation and hospitality to join forces within a musical event, ensuring that the unexpected is always welcome – both person and music. The natural tensions of musical hospitality that will often emerge can be worked with in a way that ensures a musical togetherness that is safe, open, inclusive and porous, but also exciting and challenging. Musical events can emerge that are not necessarily limited by a need for unity and conformity, and that can tolerate dissent and disruption. These stand the best chance of helping people find a satisfying musical home for a while.

Participatory Practices

To musick is to take part – in *any* way. This is Christopher Small's (1998) simple and profound message. Musicking naturally draws on capacity and ability whilst addressing need and hope. As such, it is necessarily tied up with issues of inclusion and social justice, not just aesthetics and entertainment. This might sound a very worthy and idealistic picture. Surely most of the world's music is now intended as a product to be consumed rather than an activity in which to participate? A midway position would perhaps be the ecological perspective – that music affords different things within different situations. The music anthropologist Thomas Turino suggests in his book *Music as Social Action* (2008) that there are both 'presentational'[2] and 'participatory' possibilities with music, though he is clear that he considers the latter to be the more urgent now for society to cultivate. He usefully outlines the following clear commonalities underlying *participatory music*, at the level both of musical materials and of performance practices across many cultures and genres:

- There is no artist/audience distinction, only participants and potential participants. Everyone is welcome to join in or bow out, whatever their overt level of musical expertise.
- Everyone contributes to the sound and motion of the event through playing instruments, singing, dancing, clapping, and so on. All of these activities are considered necessary.
- The sound and body interactions of participants are 'framed' as interactive social occasions.
- The focus is on *doing* rather than preserving; on the process rather than the product.
- The primary focus is towards each other, on the actions and experiences of everyone taking part. This leads to a heightened social bonding and usually a diminished self-consciousness.

These key characteristics link particular values, aims and musical processes and techniques that can be seen to be fairly standard over the various participatory

---

[2] '*Presentational music* is a field involving one group of people (the artists) providing music for another (the audience) in which there is a pronounced artist–audience separation within face-to-face situations' (Turino 2008, p. 51).

traditions around the world – including jazz and popular music traditions that combine participatory and 'presentational' modes. Participatory musicking both symbolises and enacts cultural values of inclusion, hospitality and social generosity. Good musical occasions are judged by how many people participated and how good they felt about this, and not about how 'perfect' the music was objectively, or to an outsider. There's an ethos of cultural democracy and equal opportunity, but this is also often twinned with the expectation that people *do* participate as a social duty. More skilled and experienced musicians see it as their responsibility to facilitate the musicking in a way that will enhance the overall experience and not exclude anyone. These 'core players' have often evolved ways of playing their parts in a way that will both invite greater participation from others and keep the process interesting for themselves. Musicking practices have emerged that can reconcile different levels of participation such that there is an adequate balance between challenge and comfort. Musical goals are therefore simultaneously social ones.

What's particularly interesting is the link between this anthropological perspective that generalises over a range of everyday musical traditions and the more specialist participatory music traditions such as music therapy and community music, both of which more consciously exploit the confluence between music and social goals. In all of these traditions, moreover, there is a further parallel in how the values and principles are enacted and embodied through specific musical practices, processes and techniques that lend overall sound features to participatory musics. Turino suggests the following generic characteristics and qualities of participatory musicking:

- '*Open form*' maximises players joining and finding a place through short, cyclical musical structures that might have messy beginning and endings (Turino calls them 'feathered'), lulls, or extended transitions where new impetuses or new people negotiate what comes next.
- *Repetition and groove* is maintained by a predictable rhythm that allows people 'security in constancy' within the music, whilst repeated melodic formulas and 'hooks' aid picking up the music and finding a part shared with others.
- *Roles and responsibilities* change as people move in and out, or 'forward' and 'backward' within the overall texture of the music, finding their place or function within the ongoing blend of musical relationships. Traditionally, musical texture is described as *monophonic* (single line), *homophonic* (accompanied line) or *contrapuntal* (coexisting independent lines). Participatory music usually has instead a *heterophonic* musical texture – as people elaborate a single line or rhythm that is often slightly discrepant in timing or tuning in relation to the whole. There's often an 'all-together' mode alternating with space for solo turns.
- *Texture and timbre* is often loud, dense and messy as a result of both the timing/tuning 'discrepancies' and the overlapping heterophony of voices

and instruments. Turino suggests such textures provide a necessary social 'cloaking function' that reassures and inspires further musical participation.

These features overall are in the service of a larger synchrony that Turino suggests is 'a crucial underpinning of feelings of social comfort, belonging, and identity. In participatory performance, these aspects of being human come to the fore' (2008, p. 42).

ℬ

Inclusion and participation are often presented as therapeutic aims that are also social aims. This makes sense given that the human needs of belonging and identity are often significantly undermined by illness, disability or deprivation. But a problem with this rationale is that participation is often defined as either happening or not, giving too simplified a picture of how musicking can offer genuine creative freedom. Music therapist Brynjulf Stige (2010) gives a more nuanced view of participation that came from studying an unusual cultural festival in Norway for adults with learning disabilities. Stige concentrated on just *how* people took part in a music therapy group at this event, suggesting that we should not think of musical participation simply as 'joining in' or 'not joining in' to a preset structure, but rather how people's different styles of participating was part of the inclusive drama of that particular situation, with its mix of conventions, expectations and sudden possibilities. In the music therapy group, Stige observed a continuum of styles of how the group members presented themselves at a musical–social level. This ranged from the 'silent participation' of one member, who is there but not overtly joining in, to the 'adventurous participation' of another member who suddenly but creatively goes his own way musically, such that he stands out in the group, but without completely subverting the ongoing musical activity. Within the drama of the situation, each of the members is making a personal elaboration of their style of participation. Overall, this all helps the mutual co-creation of the event as a whole – which, although it is formally facilitated by two music therapists, is also clearly steered and shaped by the varying actions and styles of participation of the five members. Stige suggests from this that participation is better thought about as a creative social/musical process that involves mutual negotiation between individuals in relation to the emerging group process. As such, it has many of the characteristics of a *ritual process* (something we'll look at in more detail in a later chapter).

This example again makes the point that I've emphasised many times in this book: that what music affords (in this case, social participation) only makes sense in relation to how people appropriate, or can be helped to appropriate, these possibilities. This caveat highlights the importance of access, freedom and choice – as well as the option and necessity sometimes for a measure of creative resistance and disturbance.

Musical Ethics as Performing Respect

The music afternoon at *SMART* café is hosting a visit from a music group in the East End of London called Musical Minds. For the first half of the afternoon, each group has performed a 'set', with the other group as the audience. After the tea break, we revisit some songs from the first half of the afternoon, with both groups singing together this time. We then ask if anyone has special requests.

Hester asks to sing a favourite jazz standard, 'If You Asked Me I Could Write A Book', and as the song is being announced, Luke pops up, enthusiastically says, 'I love this song', and is up at the front asking whether he can sing it with Hester. She seems fine with this, but because they are dramatically different heights there's some fuss for a few minutes arranging the height of the microphone they need to share!

So there's some pre-negotiation and accommodation before starting the song, and then increasingly more negotiation is necessary as the song goes on. It's clear that, although they both know the song well, there's a basic difference in how they usually sing it. Luke has a 'laidback' delivery – strongly behind the beat – whilst Hester 'swings' it yet is basically *with* the beat. The first verse is somewhat awkward for both, as they realise what's happening, but they find it hard to change their style and preference and accommodate to the other to produce a single performance. Luke looks at Hester with puzzled sideways glances, drops out periodically for a phrase, then joins her again, catching up by pinpointing a particular phrase that they can more easily 'get together'.

I'm accompanying this on the piano as a kind of 'musical host', attempting to arbitrate the increasingly obvious performance-style differences between the two singers. In order to help this situation, I change my accompaniment to a 'rhythmicised' delivery for verse two – which is a conscious move to subvert both of their habitual renderings of the song and get them to listen a bit more to each other (via listening to 'what's new' in the piano). To an extent this works, as both singers jointly converge on a third way of singing the song, which then allows others in the audience to more comfortably join in. Hester and Luke end the song together, shake hands, and smile towards the audience.

ဢ

As the therapists, Sarah and I take overall responsibility for the afternoon going well, whilst not wanting to control it. Luke is also a member of the hosting group, but at the moment before the song starts Hester also becomes a host of sorts too. She's at the microphone first when Luke asks to duet, and she politely invites him to join her – though, of course, it would be socially difficult for her to say 'no' in these circumstances. During the song itself, there's a complex musical–social process of mutual attention, accommodation and response within the ongoing navigation and negotiation of the performance. None of us wants a 'breakdown' with its embarrassment for either host or guest, so we all try to keep the show on the road despite the emerging difficulties. Hester and Luke are helped in this on-the-spot musical repair work by the non-conscious, 'natural' process of 'collaborative musicking' that adjusts the intersubjective musical timing and spacing between them such that they (just) keep together. But there's also the more conscious musical strategy I employ to help this negotiation, using my music therapist's toolkit for keeping people within music.

This scenario highlights the ambiguities and complexities of musical hospitality that I outlined earlier. It shows how something personal or social is usually at stake within musicking, and how this automatically brings ethics and etiquette into play too. Occasions of musical hospitality such as performing with others often involve tricky 'moral moments' when there's a tension between inviting others into a shared space, being open to what they have to give, and not losing your own needs, wishes or integrity.

Explorations of these scenarios and dilemmas within jazz give a useful parallel to music therapy and community music situations. The jazz musician and philosopher Garry Hagberg writes that 'jazz underscores this fact of ethical life – the flux of our moral interactions with self and others' (2011, p. 282). The face-to-face spontaneous interactions of jazz players are backed up by a 'musical etiquette' that has evolved to guide successful playing together. This informal 'code' consists of an attention to the relational and social quality of the immediate and local situation:

> What, jazz improvisation asks, is happening in *this* moment, with *these* people, in *this* setting, under *these* conditions? Given that *this* musical gesture has been made in *this* circumstance, what is *possible* now? Jazz improvisation indeed shows within its practice how much attention we should give to the complexities of real moral questions, real moral moments, people, settings conditions, and circumstances. (Hagberg 2011, p. 282)

Hagberg suggests that musical groups inevitably evoke 'moral moments' as players strive to:

- listen, attend, notice, and acknowledge others and their gestures – both musical and paramusical;
- utter and answer (with responsiveness and responsibility) in order to help and support others, and to keep the performance going;
- demonstrate respect for another's difference and autonomy;
- attempt to understand others' immediate action: where they are 'coming from', are 'going to' (even when this conflicts with their own trajectory);
- remain authentic in gesture and response;
- attempt to balance self against others so that mutual respect is demonstrated in the balance and flow of the ensemble;
- tolerate and work with tension, conflict of direction, immediate confusion, and to trust in the emergence of mutual flow...

Together, this is a tall moral order for any player. But this list of musicking virtues also underwrites the social values and principles of most participatory musics – and it contrasts sharply with those 'presentational' styles that are more concerned with delivering a perfect product. This brings us to the interesting territory of how ethics and aesthetics relate within musicking. A participatory perspective is by nature more interested in 'good musicking' than in 'good music'. That is to say, the goodness of a musical event is defined in terms of the quality of the relational experiences of participants and the overall social enhancement achieved.

A further step in this direction of musical ethics is the question of what musical conduct might afford the practice of moral conduct itself (not just the fact that to an extent it mirrors it). Is it possible that musicking actively encourages certain ethical attitudes and practices?

The sociologist and jazz pianist Howard Becker suggests that etiquette is 'particularly important when people think that everyone involved in some situation *ought* to be equal but really isn't' (2000, p. 176). Richard Sennett, another sociologist and amateur musician, makes this issue the central concern of his book *Respect* (2004), which tackles the huge dilemma of how to reconcile inequality and respect. In our age of centrally organised welfare and treatment, people often feel disrespected. The way that they get the help they need becomes part of their problem. The etymology of 'respect' tells us that it's to do with being *seen* in the right way.[3] But we might also think of the crucial aspect of how someone feels they are being heard or, more accurately, *listened to*. Certainly someone can diminish you by looking away, but the way you are attentively listened to is surely central to feeling really respected.

The 'problem' of inequality is structured into most of our relationships, both personal and professional. But we've seen previously how in therapy or teaching such 'structural' asymmetries can be compensated by mutuality in face-to-face interactions. Sennett's point is that you cannot respect a person by just intending to do so; it's something that needs to happen in practice: 'Respect is an expressive performance … in social life as in art, mutuality requires expressive work. It must be enacted, performed' (2003, pp. 207 and 259). Here Sennett draws on his experience as a performing musician, playing cello over the years in many chamber music groups. He asks us to imagine the problems the players have preparing Brahms' Clarinet Quintet for performance. The piece involves the rapid sharing of musical material between players, which means that the players must solve the problem of balancing the parts and coordinating the flux of musical gestures that weave in and out of the musical texture. How is this all worked out, 'made good'? 'They do so', suggests Sennett, 'by inventing rituals for performing together' (2003, p. 213). These musical rituals start in rehearsal when each player gives attention to both the notes and the gestures conveyed by the others' eyes and bodies in order to assemble their musical togetherness and shared understanding of the piece. These rituals are then carried over into the more charged space and

---

[3] From *respicere* (Latin) – 'to look back at', 'to regard'.

time of the performance itself, where their respectful practice helps to ensure a 'good performance' for all.

This model of musical collaboration in action encourages us to think about the broader problem of helping whilst respecting, and how this might mutually be accomplished by *both* helper and helped if thought about differently than usual. Musicking is collaborative respect in action. The specifically musical phenomenology of respect involves the careful 're-*hearing*' of a person – in their wholeness and potential – and then the acting alongside them. It involves attending to all dimensions of a person, not just to first or surface impressions. This can allow a particular kind of freedom, for both helper and helped.

Giving Musical Presence

Pam stands up at the microphone and addresses the room: 'I'm going to sing 'Fly Me to the Moon'... and I'm singing it for Stan, who's poorly at the moment. He loves this song... I hope I can sing it well enough!' People nod in agreement with this nice dedication and listen especially closely to Pam. This performance feels special because it involves Stan too.

ॐ

Part of musical hospitality is the giving of musical gifts – a song, an accompaniment, or simply a person's musicality and appreciation of others. At the *Smart Music* sessions, we noticed how people not only 'gave a performance' at the mic, but how a variant of this giving was a *dedication*[4] to someone who was absent (and because of this particular setting, who was often suffering or in hospital). This practice seemed a natural extension of the performance gift, an extended or distributed hospitality.

We've seen in the various examples in this chapter how musical hospitality involves 'giving space' and 'giving time' to the musical voices of others, openly receiving their musical gestures and intentions, and doing your best to work with them. The theologian and musician Jeremy Begbie (2000) points out how the word *present* in English means two things: *presence* (here and now), and *gift* (given and received). He goes on to make the theological point that this complexity is behind the Christian form of love called *Agape*, or 'hospitable love' – the giving of one's time and whole self to others. My experience is certainly that 'musical gifts' can be incredibly touching and sometimes transformative for people. But again we need to be careful here to acknowledge all dimensions of the phenomenon. Lee Higgins (2008) characterises community music work as a practice of musical

---

[4]   The etymology of 'dedicate' shows a particularly religious connotation: the word is related to 'devote', 'vow' and 'consecrate'. This shows the seriousness and spirituality of the gesture.

generosity, but he also brings our attention to the fault-line that runs through the concept of 'gift'. As anthropologists have shown, the rituals of giving, receiving and reciprocating are always complex. The shadow side of gifts is their potential signalling of self-interest, obligation and debt. This is not to undermine generosity, but to alert us to its social complexity, and to how this might produce tensions in practice. When will a musical gift be taken 'as given'? When will it rather bind the receiver through obligation? What conditions facilitate a genuine musical generosity? What would undermine this? Given the potency of the 'musical gift', we need, Higgins suggests, to maintain a morally aware reflexive stance.

Musical Conviviality

> **Nigel:** I ask myself, 'Whose music is it?' Well, I think it's both *ours*, but it also belongs somehow to the spaces we live and work in. So I think really that the thing about being the music therapist in an institution is that you're also a music therapist *to* an institution... not only to individuals. I first realised this when I worked at Queen Mary's Hospital, and I had a choir there for the children, and I was told that this wasn't what music therapy was! Then at the London Lighthouse we often had those ad-hoc choirs, it's what people expected me to do! Here at Sobell House, if there's a memorial service we always have a choir, with patients, staff and relatives... it's the whole community. Last Friday, when a colleague retired who's been here twenty-five years, someone said, 'Let's have a sing-song!', and we did. It means that we're together, doing something we can *all* do together....

A final necessary topic of musical hospitality is the connection between musicking, eating and drinking. Whilst to an extent community music has preserved this tradition, music therapists have been strongly influenced by the prohibitions of the traditional 'therapeutic frame', which eliminated the normal social processes of hospitality and conviviality from its austere rituals for theoretical reasons. But newer traditions, such as Community Music Therapy, that see therapy from a more sociocultural position have explored a judicious 'return to the everyday' as far as possible, and as therapeutically warranted. As part of this, the natural links between musicking, hospitality and conviviality are being rediscovered (Stige, Ansdell, Elefant and Pavlicevic 2010; Procter 2013). Can these activities be reincorporated into the 'ritual' of therapy in ways that attend to people's social needs?

ॐ

Sarah and I decide that 'convivial' is the best way to describe the Thursday afternoon group that's developed in the café at *SMART*. Partly this is because these sessions are not just about music in a traditional sense; you'd have to say 'song and dance' to be accurate, as people often spontaneously get up for a short dance, cued by a song or a rhythm – inviting a partner, or performing solo. Then there's the importance of the mid-afternoon tea break, where today the cook has prepared freshly baked scones and cream especially, saying, '...because Thursday afternoons *need* a nice tea!' Eating and drinking is naturally part of the event, as is chatting to old friends, and daring to make new ones. But, as Sarah points out, 'it's still the *music* that creates the energy... we wouldn't have this buzz on any other day here'. And this is perfectly true. The successful mix of the afternoon is about a mix of musical hospitality and conviviality – combining music, food and socialising. Perhaps more simply, it's called *partying*.

ജ

Partying is, of course, one of the oldest social remedies. Barbara Ehrenreich's book *Dancing in the Streets: A History of Collective Joy* (2007) traces back what she calls the 'ecstatic tradition' to Dionysian rites in Greece, and through an almost unbroken international tradition of 'dancing in the streets' – unbroken, that is, until recently. Her thesis is that there's a clear but little acknowledged causal link between the development of the Western concept of the individualised self, the growth of depressive illness, and the decline in 'technologies of collective joy'. If we possess this capacity for collective joy, and it works therapeutically for the social ills that most afflict us, why are we not using this resource? Ehrenreich's answer is that it has been politically repressed, as festivity and conviviality are nearly always incompatible with hierarchical systems, proceduralism and authority. As we've seen in this chapter, the benefits of musical hospitality, conviviality and generosity also run the risk of occasionally disturbing and challenging the 'household'. Modern administered systems of care and treatment with their fixed roles and systems of medical and social authority can get nervous when people sing and dance. As Ehrenreich suggests,

> While hierarchy is about exclusion, festivity generates inclusiveness. The music invites everyone to the dance ... At the height of festivity, we step out of our assigned roles and statuses – of gender, ethnicity, tribe and rank – and into a brief utopia defined by egalitarianism, creativity, and mutual love. This is how danced rituals and festivities served to bind prehistoric human groups, and this is what still beckons us today. (2007, p. 253)

Festivity especially beckons to those who suffer, which is a sometimes unwelcome surprise to those who think that conviviality is only for the well. We'll see later how ecstasy always remains a possibility, and music often its best catalyst and host.

Chapter 16
Musical Belonging

Community is a set of practices that constitute belonging. Belonging today is participation in communication.

Gerard Delanty[1]

Belonging in Music

Tony's[2] visual impairment means that he only notices other people by hearing them, but he's easily overwhelmed by noisy environments with too many people. Because of his background and his ongoing problems, Tony easily becomes socially isolated and culturally excluded. This is a shame, because he has much to offer people through his music.

Since his mother was taken into a nursing home, he's found social refuge and asylum in a local church. The rituals comfort him, but he says he can't understand what they're talking about. He can't read the service sheets like others, so he often says the wrong things in the wrong places. But he also tells me about a recent Sunday when he'd played melodica in an ensemble at the church that included the curate on guitar and another person on flute. He was pleased that he'd managed to do this kind of thing again, and he felt good when people told him that they hadn't known he could play music so well. In music, he feels competent, included and respected. 'I belong in music, not in words,' Tony says to me.

⁃

Over the last twenty years, Tony has used both music therapy and other forms of social support such as the church to help him connect to others and become less isolated. As I wrote in Chapter 9, when Tony remembered his music therapy sessions with me from fifteen years before, he focused on events that I'd thought peripheral at that time – such as performing at a Christmas party. It was the social and convivial aspects that he'd most valued. I'd argue, however, that it was probably the careful work we'd done in the private sessions that had enabled Tony to develop his initial skill and confidence to communicate musically with others, and to tolerate collaborating in a public performance. But still, it was clearly the sense of belonging with others in music that was the key experience he needed then, and still needs.

---

[1] Delanty 2003, p. 187.
[2] Tony's story appears in more detail on pp. 129–30.

Tony's story is in keeping with the picture that we've been progressively building up through this book: of how identity, relationship and community are not only closely connected, but are supported by the platform of our core musicality. Communicative musicality helps us to practise dyadic relatedness from infancy onwards. But whilst such close relationships are vital to survival, so is fitting in with others in our social and cultural surroundings. I've suggested how a further innate function of *collaborative musicking* extends intimate musical communication into the broader capacity and skills for musical belonging.

The psychologists Maya Gratier and Gisèle Apter-Danon write that 'the feeling of belonging is acquired through musical engagement and attunement, and opens up new spaces for an intimate communication supporting culturally based personal styles of "being together in time"' (2009, p. 304). Gratier's case for why belonging is vital to wellbeing rests on her studies of the musical capacities of mothers who've been displaced through migration, and who then struggle with feeling at home and adjusting to the cultural 'timing' of how people relate and do things in their new context. Not surprisingly, this disruption seems to translate into their vocal interactions with their infants. They tend to lose the improvisational vitality of normal mother–infant dyads and their music becomes highly repetitive and predictable, in turn inhibiting the infant's free response. Gratier suggests, 'the difficulty mothers experience with their sense of belonging is closely related to their sense of time and narrative. Immigrant mothers who feel uprooted live temporarily in a disconnected world; they need time to reconnect to the time of the place they came from with that of the place they came to, and to spin new stories in which one cultural self falls into step with another' (in Gratier and Apter-Danon 2009, p. 322). Their musicking is quite literally an embodiment of their social and cultural problem. And because belonging is woven from immediate relationship, it's likely that their children will also have difficulty developing the communicative flexibility that allows them to belong to their new community.

We are in familiar territory here for a music therapist, seeing how a seemingly natural capacity is temporarily disturbed by contingent and contextual factors in the lives of individuals (or potentially through successive generations at worst). But the positive side to this picture is that musicking is often one of the most accessible and flexible ways of fostering belonging when it is impaired, frustrated or disrupted. It may just be that a different form of musical hospitality is necessary to help people make the necessary cultural transitions to new forms of community.

The Promise and Ambivalence of 'Community'

'Community', however, is an ambivalent notion today – 'loved *and* hated, attractive *and* repelling', as the sociologist Zygmunt Bauman suggests (2004, p. 62). On the one hand, it can evoke a reassuring, warm and cosy scene of people at ease together. Depending on upbringing and culture, your image of community may be a close-knit rural village, an urban street, or a group of people with shared identity and values. But equally you may suspect the whole concept, having heard right-wing politicians call defensively for a 'revival of community', or bureaucrats label money-saving services as 'community care'. The concept is also prone to sentimentality, and to euphemistic or manipulative use. The remainder of this chapter will keep an equal eye on this double life, as it explores how forms of community in action – as 'musical community' – can perhaps be a way of revisioning something of the original meaning and potential to this fundamental social idea and experience.

'Community' derives from the Latin *communis*, 'what's held in common', and the Greek *koinōmia*, 'communion' or 'participation'. We might think about the various characteristics of community as orbiting this core concept: communication, concert, collaboration and conviviality. They don't all have exactly the same etymology, but they often work together in the practice of social and musical community. Like 'hospitality', community is one of those complex words and ideas that somehow subverts or carries its opposite within itself. As Lee Higgins (2012, p. 128) points out, our modern sense of community relates equally to *communis* (*com+munis* – common + defence), but also *communes* (*com+munnus* – 'meaning having common duties or functions, emphasising the doing of one's duty, "with gifts and services"'). What's significant is how the ideal of unity or commonality links to both defensive *and* hospitable work, to obligations *and* to threats. The issues of boundaries and borders, of inside/outside distinctions, of giving and receiving are part of the ongoing process of negotiating what's better in common, and what's best kept private. The political philosopher Roberto Esposito characterises what we might think about as the continuing paradox and challenge of community with this question: 'How are we to break down the wall of the individual while at the same time saving the singular gift that the individual carries?' (2010, p. 19)

This complex idea of community accompanies the development of the modern disciplines of sociology, psychology and political science. Here is not the place for a detailed account of this; suffice for current purpose to emphasise that definitions and uses of the word and concept 'community' have perhaps always been political and ideological, and therefore often ambivalent, contested and paradoxical (Ansdell 2004; Esposito 2010). When people talk of community today, they can still mean a place where people are involved in everyday face-to-face relationships. But it also increasingly stands for a more abstract and dynamic process that's part of some social, cultural or political agenda. Communities today are seldom just gatherings of people, but rather, as the sociologist Gerard Delanty writes in his book *Community*, 'a set of practices that constitute belonging' (2003, p. 187). As such, community is yet another performative entity, needing to be constantly assembling and renewing itself through processes of communication and collaboration. Community does not 'just happen' – it needs work that people do together in the service of something bigger than themselves.

Modern community could be summarised in four main types:

- *Communities of place*, where people live closely together in a self-contained geographical area (such as in traditional and pre-industrial societies, or in urban religious/ethnic communities). Their bonds are locally defined and sustained.
- *Communities of identity*, where belonging is based on shared characteristics (ethnicity, sexuality, etc.), beliefs or interests. Technology has now made 'virtual communities' possible, linking people globally in relation to such shared identities.
- *Communities of practice*, where people build togetherness and belonging through shared activities and projects. These involve mutual learning, collaboration, and sometimes performance.
- *Communities of circumstance*, where people live together temporarily due to illness, imprisonment or emigration. 'Circumstantial communities' could also emerge from a single occasion (e.g. being trapped together in an emergency situation).

All four categories involve the potential for mutuality, identification with others' experience, working towards something together, or 'being in the same boat'. They also necessarily involve some place or space in which forms of interaction happen – even if this is a virtual one. Lastly, it's possible for an individual to experience more than one kind of community as defined above. What, for example, is the meaning and experience of community for an immigrant who finds himself in a psychiatric hospital and not able to access a place of worship for his own faith? All forms of community both afford and disallow, bringing benefits yet also obligations and limitations.

Against this relatively neat and logical systematisation of the logic of community, there's been a counter-attack from some academic and political circles. Derrida, for example, emphasises the implications of the defensive etymology of 'community':

> I don't much like the word community, I am not even sure I like the thing. If by community one implies, as is often the case, a harmonious group, consensus, and fundamental agreement beneath the phenomena of discord or war, then I don't believe in it very much and I sense in it as much threat as promise. (Derrida in Caputo 1997, p. 107)

Derrida suggests reverting instead to the concept of 'hospitality', as 'an open quasi-community ... a community without unity' (in Caputo 1997, p. 124). Such critique has been reassuring to those who think positively about the social potentials of music but who are disturbed by the uncritical rhetoric that evokes musicking as the perfect metaphor for community cohesion or even the perfect society. It's easy to sentimentalise 'musical community' and in doing so to cover up ideological and political agendas. Mark Mattern, for example, has studied the bonding power of music within Chilean, Cajun and American Indian groups (for both good and ill in his view) and states that we need 'a realistic appraisal of music as a competitive, contested and conflictual arena characterised by power and politics, which can result in both democratic and undemocratic outcomes' (1998, p. 23).

Despite all of this, I think we still need to preserve a space for people's own personal experiences of the usually positive local and immediate affordances of musicking for giving them a sense of belonging and community. It's perhaps simply a matter of being aware that musical community, like any form of community, involves both benefits and dilemmas. Music therapists and other musicians are increasingly using music strategically in reparative social and cultural projects. A good example is music therapist Oksana Zharinova-Sanderson's (2004) work in Berlin with groups of refugees who had experienced torture. Musicking helped these people to forge a halfway house with each other – a cultural 'between' that built on their shared communicative musicality, as well as allowing a generous space for what could not initially be understood by others due to cultural, language and experiential barriers. Musicking together could instead slowly establish a fresh form of local and immediate musical community, and with this the beginnings of a new sense of shared understanding and belonging.

Musical Minds: A Musical Community of Practice

For two years, I followed and studied a wonderful music group in the East End of London called Musical Minds – attending their rehearsals, talking to them about their musical passions, and following their occasional gigs at local venues.[3] The group consists of about ten people with long-term mental health difficulties who meet weekly 'for musical fellowship' (in the words of their mission statement). They not only sing for themselves, but also plan and rehearse for more public performances. Music therapist Sarah Wilson facilitates the group, though they define themselves as a musical and social group rather than a therapeutic one. I learn from Musical Minds, however, how much musicking, belonging and wellbeing are linked together, and how precarious all three of these things are for these people sometimes.

ɞ

The Musical Minds concert tonight has a varied programme of group items and solos. A song in the second half moves me in particular. Eric has always seemed quite isolated, finding it difficult to connect to others even in the music. Tonight he's selected 'You'll Never Walk Alone', and sings this hauntingly. The group join with him for the second verse, and the togetherness wobbles for a moment as singers come in at different speeds and with different ways of singing the song.

---

[3]   A more detailed account of my research with Musical Minds can be found in Ansdell 2010a and 2010c.

But the audience help by waving their arms in the way that some football crowds do with this 'anthem', and the song stabilises again. My spine tingles, not just at the symbolism of this song for this man, but at how this musicking actually enacts it here and now: he's *not* alone – we're all together with him.

Then it's the finale, with all of the members standing along the stage. The song they've chosen is an up-tempo energetic favourite with a strong groove – 'Daydream Believer'. Visually they don't look very together, as each is expressing different responses to the music (slight swaying/dancing, one still sitting whilst others stand, etc.). And frankly there's something of a similar effect aurally as their timing of the major phrases of the song is often discrepant both with each other and with Sarah's piano accompaniment, as individuals arrive just before or after the beat. Sarah is attempting to communicate a 'consensual beat' with her head (or, rather, preventing the discrepancy getting too much so the song breaks down) and the audience are helping by singing and swaying sideways with rhythmic side claps. Then there's a rather sudden final cadence – seemingly in the middle of a phrase!. But it's all just fine – everyone seems pleased, the audience claps, and the singers look happy and relieved.

&

Musical Minds show me in their rehearsals and performances how musical community for these people has many of the affordances and ambiguities we explored earlier. The singers are relatively isolated in their hostile inner-city surroundings, and their shared illness is not enough to bring them together. What does help is their longstanding and regular rehearsing and performing music together. They talk passionately about their identity as Musical Minds and how for some it is the only thing that gets them out of the house the whole week. But even so, music is certainly no instant social panacea. The ups and downs of the group I witnessed over two years show that musical community is a difficult and sometimes ambiguous achievement for them. The constant tension is between individuality and community. Members want to 'do their own thing' musically, but at the same time they want to put on musical events together. Emily, one of the members, tells me: 'We're all individuals, and that's what makes the group strong… but it's also to do with singing together'. I see Sarah, the group's facilitator, constantly working to balance individual and group needs:

Sarah: This whole emphasis I've been trying to promote… doing your own thing *and* listening to others doing their thing… it seems to mean that people actually enjoy the process more….

Gary: Why does this matter?

Sarah: Because then they *belong* – they're part of it: I think they have the experience of being part of something that feels good, that they are contributing towards… that's different if they're not there… and something that's fun as well. They get on well together at these times... and they're not people that necessarily get on well in other places....

Musical Minds illustrates what Gerard Delanty (2003) calls a *communication community*, which he suggests typifies the process of modern Western community. That is, community is not just defined by its locality or homogenous membership, but also, simply, by how it 'performs itself' in and through its particular communicative processes. Put negatively, we see how individuals or groups with 'communication problems' often fall out of community. There's no place to belong if there's no opportunity to perform *who* you are with others. But with Sarah's help, Musical Minds work hard each week on their musicking, and through this seem also to enhance their social and communicative competences. Being in the group is an obligation, and rehearsing requires good listening, communication, collaboration and negotiation to achieve the 'finale' of their occasional public performances and their accompanying feelings of achievement and belonging together.

In this sense, Musical Minds could also be thought of as a *community of practice*. This model comes from social learning theory and describes how social bonding and group learning mutually reinforce each other in the service of a shared project.[4] Communities of practice are more informal and creative than formal schemes of training, and they thrive through mutual engagement, joint enterprise and shared repertoire. It's fitting that, for musicians, 'practice' also has the special meaning of the private and collective work done to bring music to life. I observed Musical Minds become a *community of musical practice*[5] as they worked to learn and prepare their music for upcoming concerts.

Whilst practice is important, it's performance that's key to how music helps Musical Minds to create community and belonging – for reasons that we've explored throughout Part IV. Their concerts are not only the finale of the preparation, but also the moment when their fragile yet genuine social network shows up and becomes visible, to themselves and to others. Friends and supporters turn up to their concerts from different areas – mental health services, the church in which the events happen, a few people from the local pub where one of the members sings karaoke. The experience of community – which the members of the group find so hard and elusive – becomes possible and actual in and through their musical community of practice, and how this can then be performed to the wider community.

Musical Minds is certainly an achievement, but it is not an example of a sentimental 'apple-pie view' of community where all disharmony vanishes. The second key thing I learned from this group is that their achieved musical community is neither defined by nor dependent on perfect unity or unanimity (either music or social). Rather, it's a real ongoing challenge for everyone to give space to

---

[4] Etienne Wenger developed the idea of 'communities of practice'. See Wenger 1998; Wenger, McDermott and Snyder 2002.

[5] The term 'community of musical practice' is from Margaret Barrett (2005).

individual voices and to tolerate and even enjoy being together, even when there's seeming discrepancy. This tension was clear in the detail of the vignette above when Eric sings 'You'll Never Walk Alone'. His nerves make him rush ahead and forget bits of the song, leaving Sarah struggling to accompany him on the piano. Then the drummer enters in the second verse and again there's a rapid negotiation between the three performers who try to keep the song going. But then it stabilises, Eric's voice becomes confident, the other singers support him during the chorus, and it ends triumphantly, with everyone feeling great together.

One of the reasons Eric's performance feels compelling is that you participate in this human drama of the second-by-second negotiating of musical togetherness. Its fragility and unpredictability is part of its strength. The ethnomusicologist Charles Keil (1994) suggests why this might be so. His theory of *participatory discrepancies* describes how, in many popular and indigenous musics, it is the minute performative variances that are the very lifeblood of music. This relates to the practices and techniques of 'participatory music' that we explored in Chapter 15. In this style of musicking, we saw how people neither want nor are able to produce perfect musical products. Rather, as Keil suggests, 'music, to be personally and socially valuable, must be "out of tune" and "out of time"' (1994, p. 4). Though it varies between traditions, Keil suggested that good performances are often more about how people are constantly negotiating and renegotiating their togetherness in human intersubjective time (the 'groove' of the music), and in how they bend pitches and create different musical textures by being slightly out of phase. Playing with discrepancy during performance is the social process of defining the character of *this* particular version of the music, by *these* people, in *this* place, here and now.

With Musical Minds, there are admittedly some other factors creating musical discrepancy, such as singers ceasing to listen, or losing their confidence. Sometimes this tips what we might call 'artistic discrepancy' into something unwanted, where the ensemble risks breakdown and could feel bad about this. This is where Sarah's skills and understanding as a music therapist come in – helping the singers during the course of their performance to negotiate (and where necessary 'repair') the timing and the 'placing' of the music, so that the show keeps on the road.

This very practical musical issue of discrepancy within unity stands for a larger and more important issue, which Musical Minds illustrates so well. As we explored earlier, the most serious critique of community as an ideal is that it stresses and sometimes enforces unity and uniformity at the expense of difference and heterogeneity. But I think this critique unnecessarily simplifies and caricatures community, at least in its everyday manifestations. What Musical Minds shows us is rather a more modest, practical and realistic concept of community that is built through an ongoing community of musical practice and negotiated week by week (if not note by note!) by the members:

Sarah: Yes, I do think that we have a sense of community... but as in any community, it's a variety of individuals who feel differently about different

> things on different days, and have different needs, talents, likes and dislikes. But they *did* work well as a group this time. When they stand up to do their solos, they're saying, 'Here's my music, here's my history'.... But at the same time it's shared with other people... that's very nice.

One of the singers I talk to during a rehearsal session tells me about his struggle to reconcile his personal singing style with what happens when he performs with the group. 'They don't sing the song the same way as I do,' he says, 'then I get my breathing wrong'. I'd noticed this in a rehearsal, how this man sings his preferred jazz and bossa-nova songs 'swung', whilst the other singers who join him for the chorus sing it 'straight'. 'But,' this man adds, 'I know it's good to sing together – so I've got to keep trying!'

Musical practice helps us think more practically about community in this way. We perhaps need a new version of the old 'social harmony' metaphor because this gives too ideal an image. The collective processes of musicking can indeed help in thinking about togetherness, but the picture it gives is not always 'harmony' as different tones blending perfectly, nor 'polyphony' as different voices interleaving seamlessly. A third option is *heterophony*, which suggests a rougher 'going together' of a variety of voices that may also include and accommodate elements of discrepancy, variance and dissonance in relation to one another. Voices in a heterophonic texture interact and can be 'hospitable' to one without merging together (Benson 2011). This encapsulates not only the problems that some members of Musical Minds raise, but also their local musical solution to this dilemma of community. The singers show how individuality and identity need not be sacrificed as the price of community. I hear this graphically at the end of the concert, as the final notes of their last song sound out triumphantly different in their togetherness.

The Politics of Musical Belonging

'All musicking,' writes Christopher Small, 'is a political act' (1998, p. 213). Thinking from an ecological perspective about musicking would therefore suggest that any factors that limit people's musical participation, or exclude them completely, are issues of social justice, not just aesthetics. Community Music Therapy takes this equation seriously by giving far more attention than previous music therapy models have to the personal, local and structural politics of musical opportunity and resources – inside and outside the therapy room. Typically, its projects not only work with individualised problems as conceived by the medical model, but also try to address some of the everyday barriers people experience to fuller musical participation and belonging in the wider socio-cultural community (Procter 2004; Rolvsjord 2010; Stige and Aarø 2012). This is an agenda shared with community musicians and, increasingly, music educators (Green 2008).

It is not always easy, however, for practitioners to locate and define the appropriate level of political attention. The 'macro' level of cultural politics often seems out of reach, whilst the 'micro' level is too individualist. The ecological answer to this dilemma is to focus mainly on the *meso* level, the 'middle way', where people, things, organisations and socio-cultural structures 'show up' by being connected up and performed. This involves a practical politics that attends to the factors, events, connectors and forces that help link (however modestly) the levels of the local ecology, and through this mobilise access, resources, networks, pathways and capacities for people. As Brynjulf Stige puts it, 'the situational is political' (2010, p. 125). With Musical Minds, for example, the meso-level describes how this group's musicking makes and sustains links at several levels – firstly, at ground level between the singers themselves, and then between the singers and their local support structure. Their public concerts in turn help to forge links between the group and the surrounding area, its people and their potential support and resources. On yet a further level, the raised profile that the performances bring might function as a form of activism to help the group and their supporters link upwards to those who make decisions on the resources and policies that influence the singers' wellbeing on a more structural level.

Another way of conceptualising this political emphasis on resources and social justice has been explored by music therapist Simon Procter (2006, 2011, 2013) through his work in psychiatric contexts in the East End of London. His patients suffer from similar deprivations to many of the groups we've seen previously. On the hospital ward, everyday communication is often painfully low between patients in this circumstantial community due to the combined factors of their mental states, high levels of medication, differences in language and culture, and general apathy. But whilst isolation is an immediate problem, a further consequence of patients' long-term stay in this closed medical environment is that it often further diminishes their general social resources, networks and competences. For people for whom recovery is both possible and politically desirable now, their discharge back into 'the community' ironically risks yet further social exclusion and marginalisation, and further risk to their mental health.

Procter runs a music therapy group that produces unexpected participation and enhanced interaction between patients on the ward. He describes this therapeutic gain, however, in a different way than music therapists typically do – one that keeps in mind the outward-focused needs of these patients' recovery process. In their music making, Procter suggests that something more than music or individual self-expression is being made – *musical capital*. This term is inspired by an increasingly used theoretical perspective called 'social capital theory', which explicitly links cultural participation with personal and social wellbeing – or, to put it more simply, doing things together helps because our health and wellbeing is relational and social, not just biological and individual. Procter defines social capital as 'a way of conceptualising the resources *between us* on which we draw in our everyday lives, including our sense of community, shared values and trust', adding that 'social capital might be characterised as a multi-faceted ecological web of social support' (2011, p. 6).

In his music therapy group, Procter suggests that the 'musical capital' the patients are generating is a kind of proto-social capital. That is, the musical capital that is jointly produced *within* the musicking is used to generate social capital that can then be used by the members outside of the specialist and time-bound musical event. For example, two people who are notoriously suspicious of each other on the ward generate an unexpected contact, and from this flows new respect for and trust in each other after having played music together. This could help both to trust others more in the future. Procter's detailed study of the coming into being of musical contact and interaction between patients shows how simultaneously they accrue the classic qualities and virtues of social capital: contact, collaboration, respect, trust, mutuality.

Of course, in this challenging situation, this process doesn't necessarily happen naturally: the music therapist uses strategic techniques and resources for drawing out musical participation and interaction. But an important insight of social capital theory is that any generation of social capital is always a reciprocal attainment, not just an expert provision. Within the music therapy situation, clients also bring *their* resources (skills, songs, enthusiasms) as much as the therapist. A therapist's role is often to keep the resources available, and an invitation constantly renewed. Social capital theory has its critics, and I sympathise with those who are uncomfortable with its unapologetically capitalist metaphors.[6] But it usefully focuses many of the issues of the politics of musical belonging, as well as making more robust theoretical connections between social models of musicking and social models of health and wellbeing.

Musical Community is Where Musical Community Happens

I tend to say just one thing to music therapy groups by way of verbal instruction: '*Listen* as you play – to yourself, to the others playing with you… and think of the music coming not just from yourselves, but from some central source *between and amongst you* – perhaps from the middle of the ceiling! You may then find yourselves *played* rather than playing…'.

This represents not just my experience of what helps musical groups to play sensitively together, but also an ideal of community that has been simply and effectively described by Martin Buber – and which is the logical extension of his *I–You* relationship that we explored in Chapter 13. Here is an image of my understanding of his concept of community applied to the situation of a musicking community:

---

[6] For a critical treatment of social capital theory in relationship to Community Music Therapy practice, see Stige and Aarø 2012, pp. 101–106.

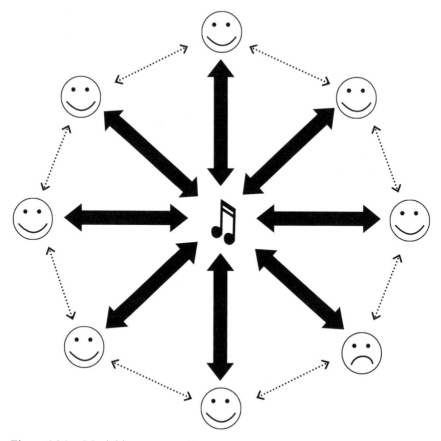

Figure 16.1   Musicking community

For Buber, you cannot plan abstractly for community. Rather, it emerges only when people manage to really listen and generously respond to one another in a particular way. In a famous passage in *Between Man & Man* (1947), Buber differentiates between the collective and the communal:

> Collectivity is not a binding but a bundling together: individuals packed together ... But community, growing community ... is the being no longer side by side but *with* one another of a multitude of persons. And this multitude, though it also moves towards one goal, yet experiences everywhere a turning to, a dynamic facing of the other, a flowing from *I* to *Thou*. Community is where community happens. (1947/2002, p. 37)

Buber's social philosophy is essentially an elaboration of the logic of his dialogical philosophy. We typically fall into multiple *I–It* relations to others – a collective of individuals in a given place and time. Genuine community, on the other hand, arises dynamically from multiple *I–You* relationships, where independent people experience a mutual and direct relationship to one another through a particular shared medium such as music. As in all *I–You* style encounters, the 'essential We' of community must be continually renewed through the accumulated interplay of genuine dialogues. How is this achieved? Through the *Between* – 'a relational space ever and again reconstituted in our meeting with others' (Buber 1947/2002, p. 241), generating community. When greater than the dyad, community comes not primarily from people's personal, subjective feelings towards each other, but through 'taking their stand in living mutual relation with a living Centre' (Buber 1937/1958), by means of which they also stand in living reciprocal relationship to one another. A community is built upon a living, reciprocal relationship, but the builder is the living, active centre. This 'generative centre' of community Buber describes as *Verbundenheit* – 'bonding' or 'binding together':

> This community is no union of the like-minded, but a genuine living together of
> people of similar or complementary natures but of different minds. Community
> is the overcoming of otherness in living unity. (Buber, in Kramer 2003, p. 95)

Musical community perhaps gives us the best glimpse of community that is released from the political euphemism and sentimentality that often haunts this concept. Because it happens in musical time and space, it also shows us something helpful: that musical community is (only) where musical community happens. Its achievement is by nature fragile and fleeting, and therefore precious.

Notice in the diagram above that the star in the middle is not perfect – at least one person is not quite in alignment. No (musical) community is perfect – that's why its music sounds interesting.

Chapter 17

Musical Ritual

Both ritual and the arts are gestural metaphors, in which the language of biological communication is elaborated into ways of exploring, affirming and celebrating our concepts of ideal relationships.

Christopher Small[1]

My education was sitting in an orchestra. And what a beautiful model for a society! Everyone together, listening to each other, with one goal. This is the best way I can think of to build a better world.

Gustavo Dudamel[2]

Performance Rituals, Ritual Performances

Mercédès: Church was my first case of musical ritual... those big Roman Catholic events... especially when I lived in Rome as a child. We went to St Peter's a lot, and I took part in splendid theatrical events there. I sang in a children's choir and took part in huge events steeped in the Latin Mass, and that is in my bones! I don't separate out the music from the ritual or the spectacle or the performance... it's all part of it.

ಬಂ

Stuart tells the audience gathered on a summer night in a church near London, 'Tonight's music is unique. You have not heard it anywhere before, and you will never hear it again. You may hear something extraordinary take place'. The Scrap Metal concert is the culmination of a unique Community Music Therapy project for a group of people with neurological problems, their friends and family. The audience both witness and participate in the event, which consists of prepared and spontaneous pieces improvised by an ensemble who play instruments made from things found in a scrapyard – including a car bonnet, typewriter, 'strung sink', bicycle wheel, and three buckets.[3] And indeed the performance *is* unique.

---

[1]   Small 1998, p. 106.

[2]   Quoted in a Guardian newspaper report (29 January 2011) on Dudamel's thirtieth birthday celebrations.

[3]   This event is described in full in Ansdell 2010b.

Instruments, music and people transform before my eyes and ears. Later I talk to Fraser, the organist in this group, who says: 'There was something really ritualistic about this performance as a whole.... It left me thinking how much performance itself is a form of ritual...'.

୫

These two vignettes show how closely related are rituals and performances. They often mirror each other, both ceremonies of belonging. There is a wealth of anthropological scholarship now to suggest that the arts as we know them today probably developed out of communal ritual practices. It's possible to see both of these key human activities as ways of 'making special', in Ellen Dissanayake's (2006) phrase. Rituals incorporate everyday things and behaviours and make them special by artifying and musicalising them through formalisation, repetition, exaggeration and elaboration. Reciprocally, on returning from a ritual, the everyday can seem special again, even sacred. Many people today would say the same of art. But because in the West now we tend to separate out the various artforms and concentrate on their unique features, we are apt to miss just how many aspects of ritual still remain in our ways of approaching and using the arts overall. It will be useful to bring these features back to the foreground as part of considering how musical performance can help individuals and groups. For the key aspect of any ritual is that it affords not just display or repetition, but also potentials for individual and communal transformation.

In his book *Musicking* (1988), Christopher Small sets out to highlight the ritual aspects of musical performance by explicitly choosing an event – a conventional symphony concert – whose very familiarity masks its ritual for many readers. Small nevertheless shows how, just like any other form of musicking around the world, a classical concert functions ritually 'as an act of affirmation of community ("This is who we are"), as an act of exploration (to try on identities to see who we think we are), and as an act of celebration (to rejoice in the knowledge of an identity not only possessed but also shared with others)' (1998, p. 95). But whilst ritual is the grand frame of musicking for Small, a specific musical ritual need not be grand itself. Rituals range from the relatively mundane and small scale through to the sacred and spectacular. Ritualisation can be as simple as the framing or re-framing of small gestures of everyday interaction, whilst in other situations its grand displays are designed to stoke utopian dreams. What all levels of ritual seem to share, however, is a way of gathering people together to catalyse and then to support *transitions* between roles, experiential states and situations – either individual or collective. This is perhaps why rituals and ceremonies become crucial at times of crisis, uncertainty, or where a new personal or communal identity is actively being searched for. Ritual helps us to come together, and then to move together towards something different.

The two opening vignettes of this chapter incorporate most of the key features that all rituals involve to a greater or lesser extent:

- a cross-sensory blend of action, music, symbolic speech, stylised movement, costumes, fragrance, lighting, staging – synthesising verbal and non-verbal forms of communication;
- participation and immersion in a shared scene and narrative structure that either derives from a collective history or is in the process of creating a new tradition;
- intense psychophysical states of anticipation, excitement, anxiety and ecstasy, bringing about transitions and transformations in feeling and thinking, both individual and collective;
- reconciling differences between individuals and sub-groups within the larger frame of the whole event.

The connections between these features and the stagecraft and emotional characteristics of the performance arts are obvious. A ritual relies on an infrastructure that organises and mobilises the staging, props and witnessing/participating audience that are necessary for its transformative purpose.

There's also a characteristic structure of most rituals that the first generation of anthropologists identified and codified from their comparative studies of many cultures. Most ritual processes have a simple three-part process: separation, liminality (or between-ness), and return to normality. At whatever level of complexity or importance, we are taken out of everyday life and its structures and rules, and out of quotidian time and its usual demands. We then experience a period where things are in flux and possibility, then we return again to 'real life' – but somehow transformed, either in social status or in a more individual and existential sense. This pattern could stand true for an adolescents' initiation ceremony in a traditional society, for a contemporary Western transition to marriage or to a new job, or for the experience of living through a concert or religious service.

ဆ

Smart Singers, one of the musical groups of the Chelsea Community Music Therapy Project, rehearse hard for six weeks before their scheduled performance at the next-door general hospital that has a lunchtime series of guest musical events every Thursday. Although Smart Singers' base is the nearby mental health organisation, the flier for the concert makes no mention of this. They are billed as an amateur singing group. They dress up smartly in black-and-white concert-style dress and stand in formation in the centre of the hospital atrium, a little back from the entrance hall. They perform a programme of solos and group items with enthusiasm and a confidence that belies the nerves and uncertainties that preceded the event. Their performance is particularly skilled at the human level, in how the performers engage the patients and members of the public and hospital staff who walk by the group or stop a while to listen before moving on. Some people stay to listen longer, including a woman in a mobile bed. The singers are applauded warmly at the end, and agree that it's been a success.

Individuals have performed well and there is a sense that their musicking has brought some spirit and focus to the usually chaotic aural environment of this hospital. For the public, what has defined Smart Singers is their skill and spirit in bringing off this performance event so successfully. But this event has also been a rite of passage for the singers. They have been witnessed, appreciated and acknowledged outside their usual context, both personally and as a group. Some members have gained confidence from this, and have made a small transition in their sense of themselves as people and musicians. The group together feels a sense of achievement and bonding as 'Smart Singers', their developing tradition of performing strengthened through this successful event. The performance has functioned as a ritual for them to explore, affirm and celebrate who they are and what they can be.

Musical Interaction Rituals

We are introduced to musical ritual early in our lives. In her study of caregiving in humans and animals, Ellen Dissanayake notes a parallel between the patterns of early interaction (such as we explored in Part III as 'communicative musicality') and ritual process. In particular she comments that the 'rhythmic and modal elements such as synchronising, turn-taking, imitating or matching, and sequentially patterned movements and vocalisations are the stuff of ceremonial ritual' (2000, p. 60). We begin our induction into ritual, that is, with its intimate side, which is improvised in everyday social life, whilst preparing us to understand and to participate in the more structured public forms of ritual action that we meet as our social life expands and develops. People with communication problems often highlight in their struggles how everyday social interaction is partly the challenge of participating in and creatively developing social performances and rituals (Goffmann 1959/1990). Music therapy often works on just this level – creating and cultivating small interactive rituals that can help transform people's personal and social experience.

ॐ

Weekly on Saturday mornings at a music therapy centre, a small group takes place for young children with communication difficulties and their parents. A surprising number of fathers attend, learning through the group to appreciate their children in a different way, and how to interact with them more 'musically'. The session has a reassuring ritual format, with everyone sitting in a circle on the floor, the forty minutes framed by 'Hello' and 'Goodbye' songs that are followed by a balance of predictable and spontaneous activities. Over the weeks, the repeated songs establish a tradition and become loved by all. The rest of the session involves both semi-structured and improvisational work, with the therapist setting up spontaneous musical interactions between children, parents and therapists. This usually takes the form of the therapist hearing or noticing some small vocal or bodily gesture that one of the children is making, picking this up and amplifying it musically. Through this response, he also orientates the other children or parents to this micro-musical event – which then becomes something collectively noticed and significant that can form the basis of a new interaction, answered by another person and jointly built into something bigger. Overall, it is a process of seeing and hearing where musical gestures, invitations and responses lead. Each child and parent has space to contribute directly, or to witness the small triumphs of personal and musical connection. There's also a sense of the group's functioning as a whole – repeating old things, initiating new things, and celebrating what emerges in the fun and achievements of the session.

A father later tells me how moved he was when his autistic son (who generally ignores other children socially) saw another boy in his group as he arrived in the lobby and spontaneously hugged him. This was a transformative moment, for both father and son. Other transformations regularly happen during the session – for children, parents, and for the group as a whole within these rituals of exploration, confirmation and affirmation.

ಬಿ

Brynjulf Stige (2010) has used anthropologist Randall Collins's theory of *interaction rituals* to study the process of a similar music therapy group, this time with adults with learning disabilities. Stige observed closely just how naturally the therapist and clients assembled together a small-scale everyday ritual situation within their group, picking up and elaborating everyday communicative interactions in a creative and musical way to build something that was more than the sum of its parts – and that had an overall transformative effect on the whole group.

An 'interaction rituals' perspective suggests that a performance situation of any type has its 'staging', repeated format, and 'props' that function to support and focus social interaction and meaning between people in ways that would not necessarily happen otherwise. The performance frame may be very modest, spontaneous and informal, but it will typically involve the following key features summarised by Stige (which I relate here to the children-and-parents group above):

- *Bodily co-presence* describes how the children, therapists and parents are physically orientated towards one another as much as possible, heightening their mutual focus. When physical gestures are 'musicalised', they become more noticed and significant to the group, pulling people further into face-to-face interactions.
- *Mutual focus of attention* describes how an individual's musical responses and interactions become increasingly 'circulated' and shared amongst children, parents, and the group as a whole. The music helps the group to find a mutual focus of attention and interest which can lead into joint action.

- *Shared mood*: the 'feel' of the songs and spontaneous interactions is both subjectively experienced by individuals and intersubjectively shared, with the highlights creating unexpected releases of musical and interpersonal emotion. Everyone experiences a similar progression through the charged time and 'musical shape' of the forty-minute session. Randall Collins suggests that the key to interaction rituals is that they are 'emotion transformers' for the group as a whole.

In many social and therapeutic contexts, these ritual features are repeated weekly, and they gradually shape and reinforce feelings of belonging and solidarity. Music therapy groups take time and careful repetition to bring out the potential for greater social interaction, and for the group members the regularity of the weekly session is often itself a helpful ritual. Although the Scrap Metal and Smart Singers events were one-off performances, their musical and social success was due to the weekly rehearsals in which many of the features of interaction rituals had been key. Brynjulf Stige suggests that what he calls 'ritual outcomes' can be viewed as therapeutic outcomes too. Social space is opened up and energised, and a sense of group mutuality and solidarity prepares for transformation – both individual and communal.

Musical Communitas

Ken: When you look at the transcendent moments in the Grateful Dead's music, what characterises them is the fact that it's not about the soloist and everyone else playing on behind... but it's communal improvisation, without explicit foreground and background. It was about a real equality of those six voices... not performing their traditional musical functions – solo, supporting bass – but coming together equally. So for me, this is to say that you *have* to have this equality and mutuality for the music to become liminal, otherwise you have a hierarchy.

When I play music, each person's contribution is always essential for me... but I think this is funny, because in pop music there's a structural hierarchy too: drums, bass, guitar on top... but in another sense you can't imagine the whole without the parts, so each is essential.

One of the key ideas I have is about music as a *liminal* experience. I've experienced this in my own musical experiences, and I've experienced it with clients in music therapy. The liminal state in music is a transition between fixed points. *Flow* is one of the prime characteristics of liminality; the intermediate stage which is the period between....

It's about music opening up experiential worlds we didn't know existed, and mediating between different states of being. I've had this experience listening to Paul Nordoff's music in therapy sessions when he's taking a child into a musical world that's freeing them from being fixed, taking them into a musical flow that's *between* them....

A common dilemma in modern life is the tension between structure and freedom; between hierarchy and mutuality; between individuality and belonging. We yearn not to be trapped in roles and structures that limit our freedom, or that make our social interactions with others formal or distant. Yet we realise there's no escaping structure altogether, and that it can provide safety and security. This situation is the same in a rock band, a symphony orchestra, a hospital or a therapy room. Hierarchical structures organise, direct and stabilise social and professional situations. They also fix, suffocate and disillusion people. When I set up a Christmas choir in a psychiatric hospital ward, I remember the doctors saying what a relief it was for them just to sing with the patients and to feel equal for once. They often saw their professional role and status as a burden to themselves, and as an obstacle to helping their patients.

The anthropologist Victor Turner (1969b, 1982, 1987) brings a useful perspective to this dilemma based on his comparative study of transformative rituals in traditional societies ('rites of passage') and of the artistic processes of rehearsal and performance in 1970s America. He was interested in the variety of different situations that brought out *liminal*[4] or in-between states and modes of relatedness for people. This could happen at 'in-between times' – for example, during adolescence, mourning, or within ceremonies that are designed to enact transitions of status and identity, such as marriage or graduation. Liminality also happens when people on the margins of society such as migrants, alcoholics or psychiatric patients find mutuality through their shared 'outsider' experience. A last group who consciously put themselves into transitional or in-between states are those participating in religious or artistic processes – where rituals, rehearsals or performance can create collective 'peak experiences'.

Turner suggested that the similarity in all of these situations is the move away from social structure towards a relative anti-structural dimension that he called *communitas*.[5] He used this term in order to get away from the everyday term 'community' and its tendency to always evoke a static place. *Communitas* is rather a dynamic experiential and existential state. Relieved of structural hierarchy, fixed roles, separation and control, people in communitas experience a 'between-ness' that has qualities of improvisation, spontaneity, mutuality and flow (and sometimes anxiety and confusion too). But whilst communitas is an antidote to structure and control, it still needs these features as its contrasting fixed points that allow the temporary freedom. The flow state of communitas can exist only because of the security of structure to which it can return. Turner therefore saw communitas as

---

[4] Liminality is being on the margin or threshold (from the Latin, *limen*), 'between-and-betwixt', 'neither here nor there'.

[5] Latin for 'belonging', but often connected with all the various aspects of 'community'.

a compensatory state, a necessary 'oxygenation' of social structure for when it becomes airless and dispiriting.

It will perhaps not surprise you that one of Turner's inspirations for this social state was Martin Buber's philosophy, which pictures the dynamic oscillation in human relationships between the structural and objective *I–It* and the mutual intersubjectivity of *I–You*. '*Communitas*', writes Turner, 'with its unstructured character, represents the 'quick' of human interrelatedness, what Buber called *das Zwischenmenschliche*'[6] (1969, p. 114). And like Buber's '*We* relationship', communitas is neither a fixed place or territorial or social structure, but is literally a 'happening' (Turner's term) in the *Between* – a phase, or even just a moment, that will then solidify back into something more structural when the moment is past (just as Buber reminds us that an *I–You* relation falls back naturally into *I–It*).

In his interview, Ken makes connections between a liminal state of communitas both in the music of the Grateful Dead and in Paul Nordoff's improvisational music therapy. Both experiences encapsulate something of the transcendent potential in rituals of communitas – where there's a sudden opening up of possibility, and where music mediates states of being by freeing up fixity and allowing flow and transition in the situation as a whole. These thoughts lead Ken to talk about a music therapy case he'd researched and written about that perfectly illustrates liminality and communitas.[7] An unusual musical–social process had evolved when Ken and fellow music therapist Alan Turry worked for six years weekly with Lloyd, an adolescent with a love of playing music together with others, and a real sensitivity to all kinds of popular music styles. Without his learning disability, Lloyd would naturally have formed a band with his mates. Instead Alan and Ken found themselves providing something of this experience during his music therapy sessions, as the three men experimented with forming their very own 'band of three'. To an extent, this meant that the traditional client–therapist–co-therapist role structure evolved into something different. In the musicking, they increasingly become equal musicians, experimenting with a range of popular idioms that offer varying types of relational and communal experience.

> **Gary:** Who *are* you three people when you're inside the music? I've noticed how you're all changing some of your habitual roles and identities... even perhaps of being 'therapists' and 'client'. Lloyd comes to you as therapists, but when you're all inside music, something else is happening, isn't it?

> **Ken:** Yeah, because it's the non-liminal distinctions disappearing inside the liminality of the musicking. So when you listen to some of the most liminal moments in that work that's where there's *mutuality*. It's not therapist and

---

[6]   *Das Zwischenmenschliche* is Buber's 'Between'.

[7]   Aigen 2002/2005. This publication also contains an extensive DVD that demonstrates the case wonderfully.

client, with control and fixing, it's about being in that musical *flow together*, getting into a place where you can live there without the usual distinctions.

⁎

At the end of his 1969 essay 'Communitas: Model and Process', Victor Turner links Bob Dylan's music to an Indian sect of musicians called the Bāuls, 'both liminars and communitas-bearers' (1969a, p. 153). Turner hints here that music is the best example of the phenomenon of communitas in action, attracting as it does both mutuality and a concern for 'humankindness' (p. 115). Music therapists have not surprisingly found *communitas* a useful concept to characterise some important aspects of their musical–social work.[8] I've previously (Ansdell 2004; Ansdell and Pavlicevic 2005) suggested a specifically *musical communitas* in relation to the affordances and potential outcomes of Community Music Therapy work. Think back to the varying examples in Part V: the elderly people in the spontaneous 'tea dance'; the public performances of Musical Minds; the Scrap Metal ensemble and Smart Singers; Tony at the Christmas concert; or Lloyd with Alan and Ken. All of these people and groups were, through illness or disadvantage, 'outsiders' to some extent, experiencing themselves (or being stigmatised by others) as 'weak' or 'other', or 'not belonging'. But through shared musicking we see them achieve a powerful state of *musical communitas* that mobilised individual capability and confidence and created group mutuality and solidarity – and with this forms of belonging and insider-ness. It also transforms the participants' habitual roles, identity and status, helping them to be seen and heard by others, and consequently by themselves, as something other than they usually are. Sometimes these existential transitions and transformation are the graced happening of a single moment only; sometimes they are path-building experiences towards a different future.

It could be fairly objected that the interventions needed from the therapist in each case still indicate role differentiation and structure. But this stage is often only a temporary and preparatory one that leads on to an experience of communitas shared on an equal level by clients and therapist alike. Musical communitas is equally the presiding spirit for Alan and his friends in their playful improvisational jams, and for Susanna and her fellow quartet players. These situations perhaps look different on the surface given that these people are not obviously 'outsiders' in the traditional sense. But they, like all of us, perhaps still need and hanker after what musical communitas sometimes uniquely affords: shared flow, ecstasy, joy, belonging, transcendence, possibility, hope, and maybe even a glimpse of a better world – where living is more like musicking.

---

[8] Even Ruud (1998, 2010) first suggested how the improvisational process of some music therapy group and communal work can be thought of as a ritual process that matches many of the features and outcomes of Turner's *communitas* concept.

> **Alan:** I *love* that feeling of communal music-making... people joke that when I'm doing this I'll often say, 'Why don't we just all *live* together!' But there's a part of me that would really like this feeling of intimacy in a communal way just to go on and on... I always feel that's *possible* when I'm doing music this way....

The Temptations of Musical Utopia

Siobhan rummages around in the large bag that contains all her precious things. She produces two crumpled articles from the *Guardian* newspaper, which she hands to me:

> I want you to read about these wonderful orchestras – one is the Simón Bolivar Orchestra from Venezuela, the other's Daniel Barenboim's West-Eastern Divan Orchestra. They're both such *hopeful* things for us in today's terrible world. Music's been so healing for me... and now – look! – thousands of young people are benefitting from music now.... Isn't that just wonderful?

Siobhan is one of many people who have cited these two 'poster projects' to me as evidence of how music offers unique social or humanitarian solutions. Perhaps more than any area we've explored in this book, 'musical community' has become increasingly recognised as a ubiquitous 'good thing' in the popular imagination. And of course the Divan and Sistema projects are considerable achievements that have given worldwide promotion to how music can help. But as we've also seen during Part V, there are often tensions and paradoxes running through any real-life practices of musical hospitality and community. It is perhaps useful to reflect on how some of these grand musical–social projects can cast shadow as well as light, tempted as they are towards a musical utopia that feeds on the 'hope trope' invested in them by broader (and less musical and benign) political agendas. This is not to diminish their achievements, but to relate them more realistically to the potentials and risks of musical community that we find in any musical–social endeavour – whether by cultural organisations, NGOs, community musicians or music therapists.[9] As we've noted previously, all musicking is to some extent a political act, with political consequences. *Musical communitas* does not live in glorious isolation from *societas*, the wider power structures in which any local social action is also nested (Stige 2003/2012, pp. 372ff).

Victor Turner (1969b) made a distinction between the spontaneous *existential communitas* that I outlined earlier and a further type that he called *utopian communitas*. By the latter, he meant how people try to preserve an inner experience

---

[9]   For accounts and studies of the broader practice of musical–social work, see Bergh and Sloboda 2010; Bergh 2010; Hesser and Heinemann 2010; Urbain 2010 – and the web-journal *Music and Arts in Action*.

of communitas by converting it into an outer structure. Whilst Turner does not state this directly, I read this as suggesting an abstract politicisation of communitas, where there's an attempt to duplicate the results beyond their original scope or meaning – or, more worryingly, to present idealised versions of projects. You can recognise such attempts from how their high-falutin' verbal discourse evokes universal values such as peace and harmony, justice, comradeship, brotherhood and equality. In a word, communitas becomes *utopian*.[10] Community talk often yearns towards utopia, and musical community seems to exacerbate this temptation.

℘

Whilst the Venezuelan Sistema project stretches back to 1975, it's probably only in the last five years or so that this and Barenboim's Divan venture have really captured the public and journalistic imagination as hopeful 'musical utopias'. There are now many angles of involvement in these projects: from those who directly participate, to those unconnected with them but who trade in these projects as image, metaphor or exemplar of social hope for their own purposes. Then there's a growing band of journalists and academics who relish in uncovering their less-than-utopian aspects that lurk behind the rhetoric. In this way, these 'poster projects' clearly stand for something more general about music, people, and the politics of current musical–social work.

Barenboim talks about the Divan project both as a purely musical one and as a 'realistic utopia' for the young players. He makes many of the same points we've explored previously about how musicking affords particular qualities of social relationship within an orchestra whose temporary membership embodies the fault-lines of Middle-Eastern conflict.[11] Barenboim and Divan co-founder and academic Edward Said write that 'once you have agreed on how to play one note together you can no longer look at each other in the same way again, because you then have shared the same experience' (2002, p. 10). It has been noted, however, how quickly Barenboim often moves from music to politics, even whilst claiming that the Divan is foremost 'a humanitarian idea ... We don't see ourselves as a political project' (quoted in Riiser 2010, p. 24). He playfully talks of 'the sovereign independent republic of the East-Western Divan, as I like to call it' (in Riiser 2010, p. 24), but the orchestra has not infrequently found itself involved in more serious political situations and symbolism. In August 2006, for

---

[10] Utopia means both 'no place' and 'good place' – the double-meaning coming because the differing Greek prefixes 'u' (no) and 'eu' (good, well) are homophonic in English and have become elided in the current meaning. The utopian concept has a long political and artistic heritage in the West that has entailed attempting to solve current problems by imagining some other place where things are ideal.

[11] For overall accounts of the *Divan* in relation to music and politics, see Barenboim 2008; Barenboim and Said 2002.

example, a Divan concert of Beethoven's Ninth Symphony in Seville coincided with fresh hostilities between Hezbollah and Israeli forces. The internal dilemmas and negotiations within the orchestra as to how to respond to this show that they are clearly concerned with more than simply making music. Sceptics of the project have also questioned the Divan's hopeful stories of music bridging ethnic divides amongst the players, suggesting that the best thing it does for Middle-Eastern musicians is prepare an exit route to the professional 'Divan Diaspora' in Europe.[12]

The now-famous Sistema project from Venezuela also explicitly links the musical and the social, but often in a lighter way than the Divan. The fun and conviviality of their concerts is infectious, and it's probably significant that their star conductor Gustavo Dudamel (unlike *maestro* Barenboim) rose through the ranks of this long-term project that started locally in 1975: 'My education was sitting in an orchestra' states Dudamel, 'What a beautiful model for a society! Everyone together listening to each other, with one goal. This is the best way I can think of to build a better world'. This non-hierarchical quality comes from the quasi-familial structure of the Sistema: 'we are a community,' says Dudamel, 'we *make* a community through music'.[13] Whilst the utopian rhetoric is still evident here, the politics are different. Sistema's founder José Antonio Abreu persuaded successive governments in Venezuela to bankroll his project, but this was politics in the service of the project infrastructure, not the stuff of international conflict. Abreu was clear from the beginning that Sistema was a social development programme that used music as its vehicle, rather than a cultural project.

Divan and the Sistema converge, however, in how they had captured the international public's imagination by the beginning of the twenty-first century, and are appropriated both at popular and political levels as part of a quasi-utopian 'hope trope'. In a *Guardian* newspaper article of 2009, Sistema is characterised as 'what may be the most important social institution in the world today', and 'music as social saviour'. Their project has been held up to copy directly, or to stand symbolically for more abstract social goods.

But is this critique fair? Barenboim is clear that an orchestra will not solve Middle East politics, no more than Sistema will solve deprivation in Venezuela. What it instructive is how both projects illustrate the abstract temptations of musical utopia and *utopian communitas*. For Barenboim also states that music 'is not an expression of what life is, but an expression of what life could be, or what it could become', and Dudamel talks of how the orchestra is 'a beautiful model for a society ... this is the best way I can think of to build a better world'.[14] The problem is that, under the weight of this rhetoric, the projects can cease to live only as

---

[12]   For academic and critical accounts of the complexities of the Divan project, see Beckles Willson 2009; Riiser 2010 – and on the Sistema, see Uy 2012.

[13]   As reported in Ed Vulliamy, 'Orchestral Manoeuvres', Sunday Observer, 29 July 2007.

[14]   Quotes from *The Guardian* newspaper report, 29 January 2011, on Dudamel's thirtieth birthday celebrations.

musical endeavours that might have either modest or profound impacts. Instead, they become projections of grander messages of social hope, cultural integration, conflict resolution, and so on. They become, that is, *utopian gestures* – and as such they get lifted out of the particular and the timely, and into the nowhere and no-time of utopia. There's the danger that a gap opens up between genuine effects and grander claims and expectations. Relieved of this utopian burden, however, more of the inevitable paradoxes and complexities of musical community could be acknowledged and understood. It would be helpful, for example, not to expect that any musical–social project will automatically travel well and be applicable to any context, or that music itself is a ubiquitous social solution. As ever, we need to pay careful attention to the ecology of local conditions and local politics – to the *where*, *when* and *how* of musical community. This applies equally to these grand projects as it does to any examples of musical social work by community musicians or music therapists.

Musical *Paratopia*?

In his book *Paths in Utopia* (1949), Martin Buber suggests that, whilst the search for community and the temptations of utopia are easily twinned, we should remain cautious about such links. Genuine community needs to be *made* as well as imagined, and is subject to local everyday contingencies and risks:

> Community should not be made into a principle; it should always satisfy a situation rather than an abstraction. The realization of community, like the realization of any idea, cannot occur once and for all time: always it must be the moment's answer to the moment's question, and nothing more. (Buber 1949, p. 134)

Is there a way of thinking about musical-social work that preserves the genuine hope-generating potential of musicking whilst avoiding these utopian inflations? Rather than utopia, perhaps we could think of the affordances of musical community in terms of a *para-topia*. By this, I mean a space alongside the immediate here and now, a parallel region that side-steps immediate problems and limitations yet stays with their particularity and locality. This is space and time 'beside' that opens up the potential for different personal, relational and communal experiences. A *musical paratopia* is perhaps one of the best ways we have for creating this kind of help.

Nevertheless, we need to remain cautious that the very real potentials of *musical communitas* that we've seen illustrated throughout Part V are a musical solution that may 'only' be, in Buber's wise phrase, 'the moment's answer to the moment's question, and nothing more'.

❀

A photograph shows a group of four people slightly angled towards one another. A man is standing just to the side of a piano, caught mid-song, projecting his voice beyond the heads of the other three towards an unseen audience beyond the picture. A seated guitarist looks up slightly towards the singer as he plays, whilst the pianist turns towards the singer. An elderly woman in a headscarf sits with a small cymbal on a stand placed in front of her, and the photo freezes her arm in an arc of movement that's just about to strike the cymbal with a steel 'brush'. She looks up at the others with utter glee, as if what's happening at just that moment is something very special....

⹃

From this 'still', we don't hear the sound of this ensemble, but it clearly shows how the players 'take in' and orientate towards each other physically and expressively as they play in concert – in this modest and local ceremony of musical community and belonging.

This frozen moment comes from the Smart Music project for people experiencing mental health challenges. One of the musicians in the picture says to me in my role of researching this project, 'I hope you're going to write about it warts and all, not just the best bits'.[15] I take this to mean that any honest and useful account of the development of the project is as much about its all-too-human struggles and limitations as it is about those rare but real moments of transformation when a 'musical paratopia' is touched, and sounded out for all.

---

[15]   This project is reported in full in the third volume of this triptych on music, health and wellbeing: Gary Ansdell and Tia DeNora (in preparation), *Musical Pathways for Mental Health*.

PART VI
Musical Transcendence

Because music exists, the tangible and visible cannot be the whole of the given world. The intangible and invisible is itself part of this world, something we encounter, something to which we respond. [...] Music still is, just as it has always been, the other power which, along with language, fully defines man as a spiritual being.

Victor Zuckerkandl

Music's nothing about what I can see. It's in itself intangible – and it speaks, for me, about all the intangibles of life.

Adam

To the extent that taking part in a musical performance puts humans in touch with the pattern which connects, in whatever form it might be imagined to exist, it is an activity that is always to some extent religious in nature.

Christopher Small

Chapter 18
Musical Epiphany

Realizing an epiphany is a paradigm case of what I called recovering contact with a moral source. The epiphany is our achieving contact with something, where this contact either fosters and/or constitutes a spiritually significant fulfilment or wholeness.

Charles Taylor[1]

Manifestations

Tragedy has come thick and fast for Rose. In just a month, her elderly father dies and her son is arrested for drug dealing. Rose's always precarious mental health falters and she comes back onto the ward. She asks to come to music therapy again, and we pick up the sessions from where we'd left off six months ago. 'I miss my father and my son…,' she whispers in a cracked voice as we walk to the room.

Although the small bell she plays first is equally quiet, I hear her listening to me as I play piano with her. Our previously established musical and personal dialogue is still there. Rose whispers, 'Can we do some singing?', but when she tries, nothing comes out. I sing for her for a while instead – a small two-note motif that we then begin to quietly exchange between us. There's a gradual expansion in both the range of the melody and the volume as she finds her voice. As ever with Rose, the music begins to free her and take her over.

৪৩

I accompany Rose on piano as she freely improvises a song about her sister, gradually adding in other members of her family, rhyming and half-rhyming as she goes along. I realise she's gathering together her current life in this song: her situation; the living and the dead; the regrets, hopes and fears she carries. It's the stuff of life in the raw – love, tragedy, reparation, hope – which Rose seems to be performing for a larger audience than just me in this small hospital room….

'And my dad's looking down and smiling at me…,' she sings. But this line then cues the story of his death, sung and sobbed out: '… and he died of pneumonia… living in that cold house by himself… I'm so sad…'. Rose weeps, and I keep a soft, gentle piano music beneath. 'It's good to let it all out,' she says.

The music comes to a natural pause, Rose looks up and smiles, and together we experience a shift in both mood and music. She selects wooden claves to play,

[1] Taylor 1989, p. 425.

their sharp sound cueing a lighter, almost humorous tone that flows into her next episode of singing in riffing phrases:

Can we dub it? Can we rub it? Can we scrub it?
Can we play it? Yes we can! ... with Mr Giri-Gary muuu-sic man!

I'm now the focus of Rose's incantation – and for the first time in the session, her voice really lifts in an improvised arc of melody:

He teach me muuu-sic... He teach me muuu-sic...

Her words fade as her improvisation on the instruments takes over again. The music is playful as we swap question-and-answer phrases. Then Rose pulls the tempo back, and again the music leads us into another place – darkening through a minor key. She sings again, her voice now full and passionate, beginning wordlessly with *Tra-hee-shala... Tra-shee-la-la...* and then:

Oh why oh why... Can't we live for evermore?
Instead of atom bombs and war...
Mass destruction everywhere....

My music follows the passion of Rose's words – which are influenced by what then were the tense early days of the Second Gulf War, as well as somehow merging with her own current personal conflicts. Her voice becomes increasingly declamatory:

I know the Lord God is very angry at the moment... there's war in the Middle East, they're bombing one another....

Then she changes back to singing again, and her voice softens into a benediction:

There should be peace and love, my brother,
Peace and love, my sister,
Peace and love to my father,
Peace and love to my mother,
Peace and love... like the dove... from above...
Tra-la-la-la-la....

The words fade, the tempo slackens, and our music finds a final transition into affirmation and celebration: 'Shall we have Swing High... "Swing Low, Sweet Chariot"? We used to do that one...', and with just a few minutes of the session left, we segue into this spiritual. She swings it, full throated – as musical, free, expressive and generously communicative as anyone could be – ending the song emphatically to include me too:

... coming for to carry us home!
'Thank you, Giri-Gary... I feel better now!'

My supervisor listens to this session and says, 'It's an epiphany!' I look puzzled and he explains that he hears Rose gathering and addressing those closest to her at this crisis point in her life. Ill though she is, she knows exactly how to deal with her grief and trouble by manifesting the souls of everyone and everything that's meaningful in order to gather her spiritual strength. She uses the music therapy situation as a quasi-ritual occasion to bring her worlds together – the visible and the invisible, the personal and the cultural, the here and now and the beyond. As well as this fluid and present interpenetration of realities, there are clear parallels with a ritual mourning process in the phases of the session: from evocation and grieving to regret and anger, then the transition to reparation, benediction and celebration. All of this is brought to an emotionally and aesthetically satisfying close through a known song that includes all those participating. In twenty minutes, Rose creates an island of integration and completion at a time of apparent dis-integration.

'Read James Joyce's "The Dead",' says my supervisor. 'It'll explain epiphany.'

ಐ

Joyce popularised the idea of secular epiphanies in several of his works. Stories like 'The Dead' in *Dubliners* revolve around manifestations and gatherings of souls at points of revelation in people's lives – points when inner and outer worlds merge in charged, numinous moments of epiphany. Suddenly something is realised, or newly makes sense (though such sense may not be sayable). In Joyce's abandoned novel *Stephen Hero*, the character Stephen talks about an epiphany as 'a sudden spiritual manifestation, whether in the vulgarity of speech or of gesture or in a memorable phase of the mind itself.' A writer's job, thought Joyce, was to record these epiphanies with extreme care, 'seeing that they themselves are the most delicate and evanescent of moments' (1963, p. 213).

ಐ

Roddy suddenly and unexpectedly does something he's never done before in his music therapy sessions.[2] He takes a drumstick and begins conducting us with it. I'm surprised, but I go with his gestures, improvising music on the piano to match his conducting. A ten-minute extended sequence of music emerges that wildly transcends what this forty-two-year-old man with Down's Syndrome has ever done before – and that my own prejudice imagined he could ever do. He uses precise and graceful gestures to compose out of myself and the co-therapist a slow Bruckner-style threnody of music that has precision, shape, and a carefully prepared cadence. It also has great solemnity and beauty. We're all shocked in

---

[2] Roddy is called 'Mathew' in my book Music for Life. He died many years ago and it feels right to call him by his proper name, now that his confidentiality will not be compromised. A fuller account of this episode can be found in chapters 25 and 26 of Ansdell 1995.

our own way at the end of this. Roddy never repeats this in subsequent sessions, but something changes in what we know about each other, inside and outside music. There is a transfiguration. For me, music therapy is never the same again.

Over the last twenty years, I've shown a video of this event many times when giving talks on music therapy. I often watch the audience watching the video. At almost precisely the same point each time, the same thing happens: there's a stillness and concentration in the room at the collective realisation that something special and unique is taking place – not only then (in the historical session), but also here and now in the room as people witness it. Some people weep; others later report 'chills and tingles'. It's difficult to say what happens, what manifests itself through a now-dated video to a current audience. But something is recognised, realised and revealed. Something is understood at this point – both about Roddy, and within many people who witness this happening, and who often bear witness to it afterwards.

୧୦

An *epiphany*[3] takes only a second (or less). It reveals, manifests, discloses, and often shocks. An illuminating realisation or discovery comes from the timely link between the call of an outer event and our inner answering response. A missing piece of a puzzle is delivered, and a broader picture emerges. Such glimpses of the whole are often experienced or interpreted from a spiritual perspective, and can precipitate a reorientation of thinking or action. Whilst the place of epiphany is very much in this world, it doesn't happen in the neutral clock-time of *chronos*, but in the eventful and opportune timing of *kairos*. *Why this, now?*, it questions. *Which star are you following?*

Epiphany is a word and concept more typically found in religious discourse, such as the Christian Epiphany where Christ is revealed to the wise men – who first followed the abstract theoretical evidence, but then sought out a concrete experience to complete their understanding. More recently, there has been an increase in the more secular use of the term 'epiphany', such as in the philosopher Charles Taylor's work:

> Realizing an epiphany is a paradigm case of what I called recovering contact with a moral source. The epiphany is our achieving contact with something, where this contact either fosters and/or constitutes a spiritually significant fulfilment or wholeness. (Taylor 1989, p. 425)

Taylor suggests how, in the modern West, art has increasingly functioned as an agent of epiphany, 'the locus of a manifestation which brings us into the presence of something which is otherwise inaccessible' (1989, p. 419). An artwork 'sets up a kind of frame or space or field within which there can be an epiphany' (p.

---

[3]   From the Greek *epiphaneia*: *epi* – 'upon' + *phaino* – 'shine', 'appear'.

477). This 'epiphanic field' draws together potential connections between people, things and emerging meanings, leading – either individually or communally – to transcendent experiences that are 'a revelation which at the same time defines and completes what it makes manifest' (p. 419). Something is understood.

Although Taylor talks in traditional ways about appreciating and understanding art objects, his thinking about aesthetic epiphany has an ecological dimension to it in its focus on reconnecting with the whole of life. As Taylor writes, the central issue of the nature of epiphany is not just our action, but 'a transaction between ourselves and the world' (1989, p. 482).

The psychotherapist Paul Gordon in turn suggests the parallel between Taylor's sense of artistic epiphany and similar experiences in therapy that involve an encounter 'that restores us to ourselves' (2009, p. 72) by similarly contacting a source of moral and spiritual value. To an extent, the arts therapies put these two potentials together, acknowledging how the 'source' can manifest through epiphanies that are both aesthetic and spiritual, and, because of this, healing.

In the vignettes above with Rose and Roddy, we see both an artistic and a therapeutic 'frame' setting the stage and the ritual-like context for musical epiphany to manifest. There's the sense of contacting something important, albeit the core of this is difficult to explain. Both events are nevertheless converted into stories too, and passed on to others. Such 'narratives of epiphany' (which can be potent through being shown rather than explained) also allow a further audience to 'recover contact with a moral source', in Taylor's sense (1989, p. 425). Continuing with religious terminology, we might think of how an epiphany manifests further through the telling of *musical parables* – exemplars or teaching stories that illuminate something of the whole through the lens of a particular case.[4] Like any parable, such examples may be inspiring, yet also troubling – causing cognitive dissonance or interruption to our settled beliefs and assumptions. As we've seen, moments of epiphany can simultaneously manifest beauty alongside suffering; transcendence within limitation; clarity within confusion. We are left struggling to understand high and low, dark and light at the same time. The temptation is to try to reconcile this apparent contradiction. But perhaps the key teaching of musical epiphany is just this: glimpses of beauty, wholeness, health and truth are often manifested *within* frailty, damage, illness and fragmentation. This is their message.

ဆ

Musical epiphanies also come through very personal manifestations in dreams and visions. In her interview, Rachel tells me how, since childhood, music has revealed things to her, both about its own nature, and its connection to people and the spiritual world:

---

[4]   *Parable* – from the Greek *paraballō*, 'I throw or set beside'. Hence a parable is a narrative story that illuminates by comparison and analogy, usually for moral or spiritual purpose. We are encouraged to see connections between a perennial story and our own current and local experience.

Rachel: I think my capacity for revelation is very personal to me. The way I perceive things as 'True' is something other people criticise. But what I mean is not just something personal, just to me... but the objective truth personally understood by me... here, in this instance, through musical sound. Yes, it's patterns, shapes of sounds... and that's how I began to dream about music. I think what I'd say is that there's a core experience I have of music... which is outside the doing of it, I think... and it's outside music as an earthly substance – it's music as a spiritual structure... or rather, it's physical–spiritual....

In illustration of this, Rachel tells me a significant dream about music that she had as an adult:

This dream, as they always are, was of the nature of a revelation. When I have these dreams, I always feel I'm being shown something of the truth of music. I had a dream where my spiritual teacher Mrs Tweedie disappeared into another world, she went on a journey... and she came back having been walking... and she came back to this world where I was, and she had notes of music stuck to her legs! Rather like when you walk through goose-grass and it sticks to you. The notes were like bars of light, not like music notes... but she'd just picked them up on her journey, because that was the world she'd been to... the spiritual world. I usually dream music like geometric shapes, but not ones I could draw, because they don't exist in this world, though they're related to the shapes of this world. Like I was once shown a triad in a dream – this was actually when I was studying with Paul Nordoff. I was shown that the tonic is like the self; and the fifth stands in relation to the tonic as the father does to the child; and the third as the mother does to the child... God knows what that means! But what I was shown was the shape of the triad, and that truth of it. In a way, what I felt when I woke up was that the father and the mother were in themselves a human way, a this-reality way of trying to say something about a truth of music. It doesn't literally mean the father to the mother to the self, but it's something like that! What's important to all of this overall is it's showing me something beyond the physical manifestation of music. It's a spiritual reality I've been shown. But it's also inside the physical reality... so we can partake in it. It's the inside-outsideness of music again.

A Musical Space for 'Spiritual Work'

Many people today will say that they are 'spiritual' but not religious. This often signals a broadly ecological sensibility, a sense of feeling part (or wanting to feel part) of a larger whole that transcends the narrow limits of the self. It also goes beyond just the need for community with others in how it centres on experiences of transcendence that involve imagining or experiencing connections to things 'higher' or beyond everyday life. As an orientation to such a spirituality, people increasingly turn not to established creeds and organisations but to more local and domestic resources, especially music:

> **Adam:** Music... I think it's all the things that you can't see, or touch, or pin down – that's what I think music is. Take this cup: it's got form and design... but music can't refer to this cup – what it refers to is nothing about what I can see... it's all those intangibles of life. It's in itself intangible... and it speaks, for me, about all those intangibles of life.
>
> I think it fits with the Buddhist small mind, big mind idea... there's a universality to human experience that goes beyond human experience. But for me the spiritual is about becoming as human as possible – really getting deeply into the human experience is what spiritual means to me. It's getting more into here, now – not thinking of spirituality as something removed. It's a paradox again: the more you get into it, the more you get lifted out of it... so it works both ways. There's something... I'm not sure I mean universal... but something that's common for all humans. And that's where I think music transcends, because it's always beyond all of the stuff that I just know. I don't separate music into either a human experience or a spiritual experience... it's not something that I'm interested in pursuing. My path is to really get into my own experience, then I feel like everyone else... it's a paradox again!

The 'locals' I interviewed usually began by talking about how music helped them with their identity, relationships, and everyday social life. But often the interviews ended in another territory (perhaps only after they knew it was safe to trust me with their thoughts and experiences): with how music and musicking also afforded them a sense of the trans-personal or the spiritual that was often inseparable from aesthetic experience. These people are, like Adam, using music as what Tia DeNora (2011, p. xvii) would call an everyday 'workspace' for orientating towards and contemplating another 'higher' or 'deeper' dimension of their lives. It seems that music's very intangibility as a phenomenon perhaps actively helps in creating this workspace for shaping up thoughts, feelings and personal 'theories' about the equally intangible and elusive quality of the spiritual or transcendent dimensions of life.

This is not to say that all such musical–spiritual work is verbal and conceptual. A 'spiritual' dimension might also include a strategy of accepting and coping with *not knowing* how to think or feel about the mysteries of life and death, suffering, joy, beauty and truth. DeNora (2003, chapter 3) reminds us that music's workspace is often a productive one exactly because of its essential grounding in largely non-verbal embodied and aesthetic understandings. We start off by using music's *non*-cognitive modes of experience and knowledge in order to feel our way towards more explicit new thoughts and states of consciousness. So there's a paradox here: by its seeming inability to 'talk of spiritual things', this is just what music often manages – if, and sometimes *only* if, it is allowed to remain 'just music'.

The process of musical–spiritual work trades on the same 'sideways' relationship between the musical and the *para*-musical that we've explored in other chapters. That is, there's seemingly a natural link between the musical and the spiritual, but without one being the explicit and direct cause of the other. Instead, musical materials, practices and situations can help us orientate towards certain experiences, feelings and apprehensions that could variously be labelled as existential, spiritual, sacred or transcendental (depending on the cultural context or favoured discourse). But again we need to remember that it is not music *creating* such spiritual experiences. Rather, by appropriating what music affords through its specific phenomenological properties and shareable cultural meanings, we ourselves can sometimes achieve transcendent shifts in feeling, thought and action. For some people, in some situations, music can be the only (or at least the strongest) channel for reaching spiritual forms of experience or knowledge. But it is not music itself doing the reaching.

> **Susanna:** For my Dad, who's a musician, teacher and conductor, he says music's the nearest he gets to an idea of God – because it has that sense of having always been there, yet always re-creating itself, and always being different. It's constant, unchanging, and yet is changing all the time! It has both of those paradoxical qualities... that's what I'm saying now, not him!... and this is how he links music to the divine.

For many people like Susanna's father, who are 'spiritual but not religious', music can provide a useful workspace for practice and reflection that sidesteps the languages of conventional religious institutions, which they find too explicit and restricting. This possibility can stand out especially clearly when there's a more urgent need for music's help with 'spiritual work', a situation in which music therapists often finding themselves involved:

> **Nigel:** As the music therapist at the hospice, people come to me who are dying, and somewhere they're asking, 'What's my life been about?', 'Why am I here?', 'Why do I have to die?' For me, these questions have this same resonance as those questions that come out of the often unexpected and powerful meetings that come through music, when we ask, 'What was that musical experience about?' It somehow belongs in the same place. That's for me why music and the 'Big Questions' people have when they are dying belong in this same space. Because the questions that people ask about life and about dying are, in my experience, the same questions they ask about those profound musical meetings, where, even when you're involved in doing it, you're feeling something that's bigger than yourself....

What is this 'something that's bigger than yourself', this 'sense of the whole' towards which music can orientate us? Why does music often lead to, or support, 'Big Questions' or 'Big Perspectives' – and how?

A useful starting perspective comes from Gregory Bateson (1988), who as an ecologist emphasised the unbroken unity of physical and mental processes across life. He thought of the *sacred* as 'that integrative dimension of experience'[5] that links the aesthetic, ethical and transcendental (or, to put it Platonically, that meets head on the Big Questions about Beauty, Goodness and Truth).[6] To be sensitive to the sacred is to recover contact with the whole integrated ecology of relationships that sustain our lives. The sacred gives us access to 'the pattern which connects', in Bateson's famous phrase. This is what spiritual experience and practice is when seen naturalistically, rather than supernaturally. It prepares the ground for those transcendent experiences that can give us a sense of purpose, meaning and beauty.

Bateson wrote few things about music to my knowledge, except mentioning that he abandoned the violin as a child because he couldn't grasp the relationship between individual notes and the piece as a whole. This comment could stand, however, as a metaphor for how he tried to link the aesthetic and the sacred in his mature theory. Bateson argued that biological (non-verbal) communication and meaning making is almost always done through implicit analogy and metaphor rather than through the explicit abstract logic of symbols (such as verbal and mathematical language). Biological connections start instead from perceived links between similar patterns (of design, or behaviour) in living things, from which comes an active coupling between one organism and another in order to form something more complex, or to do something together. Bateson suggested that the arts and sacred rituals use this same process in order for us to grasp this 'higher' sense of the whole. That is, the arts are not explicit or logical statements, but rather make and communicate meaning through gestural systems where patterns can be perceived and elaborated as metaphors, metonyms and analogies. This naturally leads to our making connections between the tangibles and the 'intangibles of life' that we sense yet often have trouble putting into words or understanding explicitly. Bateson's daughter Mary Catherine Bateson wrote that the sacred is 'a rich, internally structured model that stands in metaphorical relationship to the whole of life, and therefore can be used to think with' (in Bateson and Bateson 1988, p. 195).

I've pointed out many times in this book how music is fundamentally about this making and hearing of connections and relationships – as the gestures and forces of tone and rhythm mirror, elaborate or repeat on many levels, both within its internal structure and between musicking people. Music's aesthetic process is always striving to relate numerous parts to the whole, illustrating by analogy broader processes of integration beyond music. This metamusical metaphor – *as in music, so with the world* – has been used ever since the 'music of the spheres'

---

[5]   This quotation is Mary Catherine Bateson's characterisation of her father's theory from the book that they wrote together, *Angels Fear: An Investigation into the Nature and Meaning of the Sacred* (1988) (published after Bateson's death).

[6]   For another version of this naturalistic perspective on spirituality and transcendence, see Flanagan 2007, chapter 6, 'Spirituality Naturalized? "A Strong Cat without Claws"'.

theory was proposed by the Pythagoreans and Plato. Music's 'parallel track' to verbal and logical process helps lead from a bodily and felt sense towards a more explicit understanding (if we so desire), as further meaning emerges from mapping the relationships between the musical and the paramusical. Music provides a key example of this implicit 'seeing by analogy', using one complex aesthetic pattern to grasp and illuminate something more of the inclusive and holistic 'pattern which connects'.

Bateson also sounded a warning: since rationality and verbal language turn processes into things, talking about the sacred seldom matches people's basic experience of it – just as with music. We end up talking about gods and music as things, rather than both spiritual and musical experience being active, situated and personal.

This brings us back to musicking again, a concept for which Christopher Small acknowledges his debt to Bateson's ecological perspective. Small's account of music as a core human activity also ends up in the territory of the sacred:

> It is no wonder … that all of humanity uses musicking to call on the presence
> of the deities and summon them, since deities are the metaphorical embodiment
> of the pattern which connects, the pattern of proper relationships, and to invoke
> them is to affirm the pattern's sacred inviolability. (Small 1998, p. 142)

Small's book sets out a way of thinking about musicking as exactly the kind of ritual, metaphorical communication that Bateson suggested was the most convincing way of approaching the sacred in modern times. Indeed, there are many cultures (past and present) where the basic integration of ritual, sacred, aesthetic and social dimensions has not been lost, and whose shaman/musicians are what Small calls 'universal performance artists' whose function is to help 'all the members of the tribe to experience right, or ideal, relationships and thus to maintain their unity' (1998, p. 108). Unity suggests not only immediate social solidarity, but also that maintaining or restoring right relationships at *all* dimensions of the social ecology is key to the long-term health of the whole community. Many sacred rituals naturally incorporate health promotion and healing as part of their spiritual work.

Spiritual work is, of course, done not only in groups. We'll see how musicking can afford very personal and intimate spiritual experiences too. But an ecological perspective can show how this is based on how music helps us to transcend ourselves and connect to other material and non-material dimensions beyond the personal. Perhaps this is why we often turn to music when we feel dis-connected – personally, socially or spiritually. As Small suggests, music's overall purpose is

> the maintenance and restoring of relationships, so that humans may learn the
> shape of the pattern which connects, find their place in it, and be restored to right
> and harmonious relationship with it if they should lose their place and fall out of
> balance. (1998, p. 109)

Varieties of Musical Transcendence

People often talk now of 're-connecting with what matters', meaning variously the natural world, human values, or a more holistic balance of body–spirit–soul. They're often uncomfortable about separating out the spiritual from the everyday. Philosophers and theologians have been increasingly reporting this phenomenon of 'spirituality without religion' in the modern West. The theologian Don Cupitt (1999, 2003, p. 2) calls this 'the new religion of ordinary life' (or more technically, 'spiritual humanism'). We want not only guidance for personal meaning-of-life questions, but also access to spiritual experiences that take us beyond the narrow confines of the self. But we are no longer so convinced either by supernatural explanations or by the rigid separation of the sacred and the profane. This is why it is increasingly problematic to describe spiritual or sacred quests as for '*higher* things', given that there's been a reorientation between the 'higher' and the 'lower'. The search instead is for a more spiritual engagement with *this* world, an understanding that is usually defined humanistically and naturalistically through ordinary-language concepts such as 'life', which are given a newly transcendent weight.[7]

This new understanding has been termed 'horizontal' or 'ecological' spirituality in that it orientates us towards a further dimension of the everyday (Kalton 2000). As such, it gives an alternative to many traditional religious and metaphysical discourses that portray only a 'vertical transcendence' that rises above and beyond time, space and contingency. A 'horizontal transcendence' starts rather by grounding us in the here and now, within the messy contingency of time and chance as seen 'across' our lifeworld and the pattern of its interdependent connections with the world. It explores and celebrates this horizontal movement, this continual criss-crossing that might sometimes move 'up' or 'down', but will also involve a sideways bridging 'between' the everyday and the 'beyond', where 'beyond' is understood as a further, transcendent dimension of *this* life, here and now. As philosopher Mark Johnson writes,

> 'Horizontal transcendence' recognises the inescapability of human finitude and is compatible with the embodiment of meaning, mind, and personal identity. From this human perspective, transcendence is our happy ability to sometimes 'go beyond' our present situation in transformative acts that change both our world and ourselves. This is tied to a sense of ourselves as part of a broader human and more-than-human ongoing process in which change, creativity, and growth of meaning are possible ... Our aspirations for transcendence must be realised not in attempts to escape our bodily habitation, but rather by employing

---

[7] Don Cupitt defines 'spirituality' as 'a vague and contested word now. Perhaps, the collection of regular practices and forms of expression through which we may seek to get ourselves together, represent our feeling for the human condition, and find personal happiness' (1998, p. 105).

it in our ongoing efforts to transform ourselves and our world for the better. (Johnson 2007, p. 281/3)

ɞ

Part VI is concerned with *musical transcendence* understood largely in this sense of stepping over, beyond, or between the ordinary and the ordinarily extraordinary. By focusing on 'transcendence',[8] I outline the various ways in which the affordances of music and musicking can help move us beyond, over or through a variety of normal limits or thresholds – but without necessarily invoking any supernatural powers (musical or otherwise). 'Beyond' can stand for whatever is relevant to the particular case and context. It can mean music's help in finding ourselves 'outside' or 'besides' ourselves for seconds only, whilst for others the threshold that's crossed is life itself.

Musical epiphanies are manifestations of such transcendental possibility – not only evident through the experiences themselves, but also sometimes further understood, reinforced and communicated by the musical parables that we subsequently tell about them. The following two chapters suggest how music can (re)orientate us to two particular modes of transcendence: firstly, passing over the threshold of the limited self through a transcendence of person and space; and, secondly, passing through the limits of the usual modes of human time, where music points beyond, as a source of hope.

ɞ

This whole area of musical transcendence needs a very strict caveat or health warning attached to it. Musical talk of spiritual things needs discernment to keep its feet on the floor, and to preserve the authenticity of the phenomenon. Musical epiphanies cast a strong light, but there is always the risk of an equally powerful shadow accompanying them. This shadow manifests as distortion, inflation, manipulation and self-promotion. Equally risky is when a certain type of sentimental talk of spirituality artificially eclipses the darker side of people's experiences and situations. Musical epiphanies often emerge in situations that are complex and paradoxical, where they stand out in contrast to the grim realities of people's everyday lives, or alongside destructive situations. Because of this, we need to be cautious of a too-certain and too-literal concept of musical transcendence that presents wholeness, integration and unity as given, rather than as the possible outcome of the difficult human process of searching, struggling and only perhaps sometimes, and in some circumstances, finding. As we explore this area, it may be wise to heed music therapist Diane's warning to guard against limiting our view of music's spiritual help to some air-brushed angelic realm:

---

[8] Transcendence, from Latin *transcendere* ('to climb over', 'to step over', 'to surpass') – to pass beyond the limits of something.

Diane: There's something else too... in the tension and the darkness that's a quality of music too... it's all there... it's just that we never talk about all of this... it's the shadow of music, the missing piece... though this isn't just sex, it's the whole dark side of music and people. There's something in me that needs this 'edge' too. Whereas some of the New Age talk about music and angels does the opposite of this, it's sentimental and air-brushed. It makes me want to vomit!

Chapter 19
Musical Thresholds

Where are we when we listen to music?

Marcel Cobussen[1]

Who are we when we listen to music or when we trance?

Judith Becker[2]

Between Worlds

Adam: I feel there isn't a boundary between me and music – it's a kind of mysterious thing in that way: that music's not seen, just heard, yet I'm having this strong experience with it. I think it's magic! The inner and the outer fused... there's no boundary....

It's like when someone scores a movie. Before it has two dimensions, but then three when music's added. They could all act their hearts out, but films need this other dimension, which music adds. Music gets rid of the boundary, of the actors having their experience 'over there'... music connects me to them, it gets rid of the boundary between them and me... music makes it more permeable, I'm drawn into it... nothing between....

☙

Matthew: I think of music as somehow both in this world and as other-worldly. For instance, being a wind player, an oboist, I think of sound quite a lot... and sound quality. There are sounds... and this is hard to explain, that seem to come from another world. So I sometimes think of music as an other-worldly thing. This makes me think of when I was a child and I was given a record of Handel's Water Music. I remember being very pleased with this record, very attached to it... partly I think because it was an adult thing to be given. That's a memory that goes right back, and has followed me through... and I imagined at the time that it'd been recorded across an expanse of water, with horns drifting over water... coming from another world. But then equally, as an orchestral musician, there's a lot of mundanity too. You have set rehearsal times and tea breaks... and all

---

[1] Cobussen 2008, p. 139.
[2] Becker 2004, p. 87.

this is very much of this world. Perhaps that's what characterises music for me: it's a link, a thread between this world and another world....

‰

Ken: Music is the one area of my life when I believe in the unseen... or, rather, that I believe that there *are* things beyond those that we can hear, see, taste, touch and smell... that music emanates from somewhere... beyond....

These three accounts bear witness to music and musical experience as having something to do with the 'between' and the 'beyond', as a threshold between experiential worlds – where 'another world' may be experienced or defined as 'spiritual', sacred, non-material, or at the very least as 'non-ordinary'. The material in this chapter connects with this long and unbroken tradition of characterising music as transcendental. But we shall also explore how the experiences of Adam, Matthew, Ken and others exemplify something of the more contemporary 'horizontal' or 'ecological' understanding of transcendence that I suggested in the previous chapter. This involves seeing how music helps to bridge worlds of experience and consciousness – not losing hold of the everyday, but pointing towards quite another dimension of it.

‰

Traditional spiritual discourses often locate music (or music's origin or power) explicitly in another world. In mythic traditions, gods or sacred animals represent music's special powers, whilst sacred stories tell of how music emerges at special points of intersection between this world and the spiritual world. In the words of ethnomusicologist Philip Bohlman, 'it is as if music awaits encounter, the transcendence of humans through perception and representation of a divine order encoded by music' (2002, p. 2). The emerging Western philosophical tradition also had a foundational myth in Plato's 'music of the spheres', where an unsounded 'heavenly harmony' had a complex but mysterious connection with everyday human affairs.[3] Remnants of this theory have influenced Western beliefs about music and spirituality ever since, reinforcing the idea that music is fundamentally unworldly and ideal. As we saw in the Introduction, Platonic theory also provided some of the earliest conceptions of 'music therapy', where music was seen to balance and heal on earth through its heavenly influence.

This transcendent perspective continues through the Romantic and Modern eras. Musicologist Nicholas Cook (1998) writes of the cult of the 'spirit realm' in nineteenth-century high culture, where listeners begin to seek more than entertainment or social occasion from concert music. Beethoven himself

---

[3]   See Hamilton 2007, chapters 1 and 2 for a good account of the philosophical background of the Platonic theory of the harmony of the spheres.

characterises this well when he writes to a friend: 'Speak to Goethe, tell him about my symphonies, for then he will admit that music is the only entrance into that higher world of knowledge which, though it embraces a person, a person cannot grasp' (in Chanan 1994, p. xi). Cook suggests that this way of thinking about music remains in some form up to the present, certainly in art music, but arguably in aspects of rock and jazz too. Music is seen both as a form of *access* to the 'spirit realm', but also a form of removal or asylum from the mundanity of the modern world. 'Spiritual music' has also increasingly uncoupled itself from 'religious music', although it's somewhat paradoxical that musical venues seem increasingly to function as 'secular cathedrals', transporting people through music to a higher realm seemingly removed from everyday social functions and associations. This turning away from the world through music is perhaps tied to the increasing emphasis on individual experience and subjectivity that characterises the nineteenth and twentieth centuries. Music's role as something 'spiritual' is a logical part of this trend of retreating into and cultivating the inner world within certain sectors of society.

It's interesting how persistent this view of music is, despite all the religious, social and political changes of our own time. The otherworldly trope about music is still almost the norm in both popular and academic discourse – the latter perhaps most elegantly summed up by philosopher Roger Scruton:

> Music is heard as though breathed into the ear of the listener from another and higher sphere: it is not the here and now, the world of mere contingency that speaks to us through music, but another world, whose order is only dimly reflected in the empirical realm. Music fulfils itself as an art by reaching into this realm of pure abstraction and reconstituting there the movements of the human soul. (Scruton 1997, p. 489).

How Does Spirituality Sound?

However, does this rather generalised 'spiritualisation' of music not make us look for musical transcendence in the wrong place? Recent decades have seen the active marketing of 'spiritual music' – from recordings of 'New Age' music (often twinned with claims for vague therapeutic effects) through to the more serious postmodern idioms of the so-called 'New Spiritual Music' (or less reverentially, the 'Holy Minimalists' – Pärt, Tavener and Górecki). Is this what spirituality sounds like in music? If we listen to it, will we become more spiritual? Will it heal us?

Musicologist Marcel Cobussen tackles these questions directly in his book on music and spirituality, *Thresholds*. He concludes that 'there is no specific music that can bring us into contact with the spiritual. There are no intrinsic qualities which would legitimize ascribing the adjective "spiritual" to the noun "music". It is difficult, if not impossible, to compile the characteristics or parameters that would ensure the spiritual dimensions of certain music' (2008, p. 127). What, then, does it mean to talk of music and spirituality?

Christina's story (which we read in the Introduction and in Chapter 5) might help us to look at this question of where spirituality might stand in relation to music. Before her brain surgery, Christina selects music that she thinks will help her immediately afterwards. She chooses *Tabula Rasa* and *Fratres* by Arvo Pärt, and John Tavener's Blake setting *Eternity's Sunrise*. When Christina talks to me about how music helped her during this crisis in her life, she first describes how she appropriated the phenomenological properties of this deceptively simple music to help her with physical orientation and balance. But she also says that what was important to her at that time was something 'beyond the properties of the music itself – though I'm not sure you can distinguish this'. She describes how the recordings also communicated the expansive spaces in which they had been performed, 'like in a cathedral'. This in turn leads Christina to associating the music with the spirituality of the composers:

> **Christina:** I knew this was Orthodox religious music, and though I'm not a member of this faith I felt the music as benign. Its words were relating to some of the themes I'd been investigating before the operation, to do with spirituality. And it was this music that helped me feel something about people as wonderful and enabled. I don't want to put it into words really, just to say that it was a very good thing for me at that time. So I played the Tavener many times. I don't think it's great music actually... but it seemed to give me energy, like being in a hot country, soaking up the sun on the beach... it felt utterly benign... actually more than that. I was aware of Tavener's devotion and belief, and I wanted somewhere to participate in that. The question is, of course, how much you can wear someone else's belief! Not much perhaps, because when I put the same music on now it doesn't have the same effect. I think at the time of the operation I was much more open to... I don't know what... perhaps salvation [*laughs*]... certainly to *my* saving! And my soul was more open, like a big sponge which could absorb many things... though I don't know what the names of these things are!

How that particular music at that particular time afforded Christina transcendence seems quite different from how 'spiritual music' is often marketed as a general effect or panacea. The key difference is that it's Christina herself who does much of the transformative work. This matches how an eco-phenomenological perspective would see this, with music not primarily having a 'spiritual power' contained within it that does something *to* her, but rather by how Christina appropriates aspects of it for her particular situation. The Tavener has certain properties, qualities and associations that Christina draws into creating a spiritual experience that responds to her unique physical, psychological and spiritual needs. Her musicking involves not only direct listening, but also her use of the musical experience as a 'workspace for spiritual work' through inner reflection and narrative. Tellingly, she doesn't get the same response to this piece when she listens later on. Not only does one spiritual size not fit all, but when a situation changes, spirituality may sound quite different.

Dancing on the Threshold

Spirituality tends to emerge especially at times of crisis, change or threat – but also at points of joy and ecstasy. The edges of ordinary experience are its particular territory. Christina's crisis makes her soul, she says, 'open, like a big sponge which could absorb many things'. Perhaps what music does for challenging times is to bring what Cobussen calls 'an openness to otherness' (2008, p. 117) – something that can only be specified by each person in relation to a personal understanding connected within their cultural or religious tradition. In these circumstances, music can sometimes take us to, over, or through a *threshold*.[4] So when we ask, 'Where is music?', we are asking a similar elusive question to 'Where is spirituality?' Both questions point, Cobussen suggests, to *atopias* – non-spaces – that lack or perhaps elude being fixed by a specific location, and therefore transcend the usual physical parameters of space, time and person. An atopia characterises the experience of being betwixt and between, neither here nor there; neither entirely in nor out of the self. At any threshold, there's ambivalence as to whether we enter, retreat, hesitate, linger or dance.

So the seemingly natural link between music and spirituality perhaps comes from how both can be experienced as threshold phenomena in certain situations. A 'musical spirituality' can therefore afford an *atopia* – a 'no-place' that helps moving between; stepping out onto (or over) the edge; crossing a border; tentatively glimpsing beyond; flying out over in ecstasy. Whilst these are all metaphors, the experiences they describe are always phenomenologically grounded within specific sites and practices of everyday 'spiritual work'.

This links with a phenomenon we explored in terms of musical rituals in Chapter 17. We saw how liminality (from *limen*, Latin for 'threshold') is a quality of experience that is core to ritual. In-between spaces, times and status afford 'rites of passage' – where, in both concrete and metaphorical ways, people 'pass over' into other roles and realities. Notice how the liminal always suggests movement – not arriving and settling, but moving through, even if hesitantly and reluctantly. Interestingly, the anthropologist Victor Turner linked modern performance rituals in the arts to the liminal stage of traditional ceremonies. Separated out from the everyday, but still connected to it, there's a freedom to move temporarily into other qualities of time and space. 'You can call these "sacred" if you like,' states Turner (1987, p. 25).

---

[4]   A threshold is a hinge, a limit, bridge, entrance, boundary, margin, opening, interface, space between; it joins by separating, separates by joining; its reality is the 'between'; it affords crossing over. See Cobussen 2008, pp. 7ff.

Could this nebulous but real connection between music and spirituality be another example of the 'para-musical',[5] where music and musicking calls to, bridges and accompanies spiritual experience without directly containing or causing it? But equally, sometimes a quality of spirituality can only be called to or reached *by* music and musicking. Cobussen likewise suggests a *para-spirituality* (or 'ecological spirituality') as a way of sidestepping the fixing of the time, place and meaning of spirituality. This characterises the 'no-place' of spiritual experience that happens as a movement rather than a thing – an understanding that, as we may suspect, is itself a musical one:

> music can, at most, provide the opportunity for an experience which might be adorned with the adjective spiritual instead of being spiritual itself ... A musical work can offer [spirituality] the opportunity to appear ... [but] a spiritual experience is always mediated ... Spirituality occurs or happens in and through connections to the world, to other people, to music. (Cobussen 2008, p. 143)

Musical Ecstasy

Oksana: As a fourteen-year-old in the former Soviet Union, I was lucky to be at the opening of the Tchaikovsky piano competition in Moscow. I was very excited, they were playing the '1812' and it was such an incredible feeling – that piece, that performance, that occasion, surrounded by all those people also feeling this. I remember sitting there, tears just falling out of my eyes... the music moving me so intensely... the music moving inside me, inside my world, inside my feeling of what it's like to be me, and what it's like to live at this second. At the same time, I went into the music's world... I felt that wherever it went I went with it. I couldn't dis-attach myself from it. Now, this doesn't happen often! But at these points I forget myself, I dissolve. Sometimes this happens to me when I'm playing music, and very clearly when I'm dancing. I think there's something very erotic about this... when you don't think any more, when you're not there as *you* any more, there's just the *energy* there... and that's what I think I'm talking about. I always know *when* it happens, but before this I don't know whether it will happen, and I don't really know what triggers it, because you can't repeat it! I don't quite know how to say this, but it's when somehow *I* don't any longer exist for a time; but when this energy is 'I'. Sometimes people can misinterpret this and say I'm being overwhelmed by this. But in fact it doesn't scorch me, this energy; it shows me where I am. Normally I'm not entirely there, but at these moments, I'm there!

---

[5]   '*Para-*', you may recall, is a prefix indicating something that is beside, aside from, or beyond. It prevents or defers things becoming identical or too firmly associated in a rational or causal sense.

The cultural historian Barbara Ehrenreich (2007) asks what has happened in modern culture to what she calls the 'ecstatic possibility' previously provided by collective rituals, carnivals, or simply dancing in the streets. Ecstatic practices can be traced back to Greek Dionysian rites, where people would experience transcendence through a 'collective joy' that came through ritualised arts and conviviality. Dionysus, god of ecstasy, was born of fire, and became a musician, dancer, priest, healer and general hellraiser. He represents not only extremes of joy, but also madness and terror.[6] The Dionysian ceremonies included controlled ecstasy as part of the ritual, ceremonial practice that included forms of trancing. Interestingly, these rituals also often involved a healing function. Key to this 'ecstatic possibility', it seems, was the individual's submission to the collective extreme emotion that was generated by dancing to the music within a controlled ritual action.

The Dionysian rituals were distrusted and repressed by the Romans for the simple (and historically repeated reason) that ecstasy, as an 'extreme emotion', threatens political control. Ecstatic practices have nearly always been repressed eventually by authorities, missionaries and moralists. In modern times, some have claimed rock to be the new ecstatic tradition, and we are now left with a conventional association between 'ecstasy' and an illegal drug – be it still associated with music, dancing and collective events. But as Ehrenreich writes, 'It does not go away, this ecstatic possibility. Despite centuries of repression, despite the competing allure of spectacles, festivity keeps bubbling up, and in the most unlikely places' (2007, p. 258).

A musicking perspective would suggest that it's not the particular musical tradition that's important, but how personal and collective experience aligns in action and situation to afford experiential states that are the index of contacting the transcendent 'pattern which connects'.

ಬಿ

Jane: Recently I sang the soprano role in the Britten *War Requiem*. There were two orchestras and a huge choir and there I was above all of this, soaring over the top... and the feeling... not only the physiological flow... because it was very exciting and physically demanding... but also the *spiritual* union with everyone, the spiritual *sharing* within the music... this was extraordinarily powerful. It was like looking at yourself from above, not really being inside yourself any more. I don't know whether I can explain this, but I get these states when I'm performing; like being outside the body. Actually I'll tell you what it is... it's empathy with the emotion of the moment.... If I'd actually have had that emotion in that situation it would have meant complete abandon, and just

---

[6] For a psychological interpretation of the Dionysus myth and the function of joy and ecstasy, see Johnson 1987 and Eigen 2001.

start flying through the air... which I can't do! So you have to instead have an empathy with the emotion, so that the music can take you there....

It's partly to do with all the preparation you do with a scored piece. I know the ins and outs of the structure, and I know those structural effects that I can bring about in my performance – like the slowing at phrase boundaries and all of that – so then I can create things in performance that are transcendent... that are magical, that communicate with people very directly, that give me the shiver down the spine... that allow me to do things that perhaps I never could have done in the practice room.

So that's when I say that sometimes in performance I find myself *outside of myself!* You get rid of self in a way. Because when I'm *flying* and doing this, I'm not interested in the everyday mundane things about me... it's not *me, me, me!* So I've got music which both grounds me in my body, but it also takes me *out* of it! What I think is, 'Lucky me, lucky Jane!' – that I can experience all of that, across the spectrum. Many people at least have the grounded experience, which is fine. But to have the *other* experience too... to feel yourself go *beyond* those physical limits... I was thinking when I described it as 'flying' that I have a lot of flying dreams, and it's that sensation, certainly. How I can soar above three hundred people and a double orchestra.... What are the limits? It's also one of the most beautiful minutes... it adds beauty onto struggle....

And it wouldn't have been worth it to me if it hadn't taken a lot of struggle to get to that minute – the investment of years of refining skills to do it. So some of that comes into it too... it's not just the immediacy of being able to do it, it's all the context of what being able to do it means.... 'Yes, *now* I can do it... yes, now I can show these people, yes *now* I can fly!' As opposed to, 'Oh, look, I'm just doing it now!'

Oksana and Jane both illustrate a familiar paradox in cases of musical ecstasy: of simultaneously crossing a threshold of the self, but of also feeling *more* in themselves, more embodied and existentially orientated at the same time. The self is both dissolved and strengthened; identity is reinforced, but more shared with others; the self is transcended, but not lost. Oksana states that this ecstatic experience 'shows me where I am', whilst Jane says, 'I find myself outside of myself'. Their accounts include descriptions of intense emotion, erotic energy, transport, transcendence, magic, and the coupling of beauty and struggle.

We have here two fine examples of secular transcendence that comes through musical ecstasy: one just through listening, the other more actively performing. *Ecstasy*[7] is quite literally the 'standing outside oneself' that both women describe. Such experiences can be at once joyful, disturbing and potentially healing. Anthropologists and ethnomusicologists have increasingly appreciated that 'musical ecstasy' is a key to understanding how emotion, music, collective joy, spirituality and healing align – often centering on practices that induce trances. The

---

[7] From the Greek, *ekstasis* (*ek* – 'out' + *histanai* – 'to place').

ethnomusicologist Judith Becker usefully adds the category 'secular trancing' as one that relates more easily to the modern Western tradition. This is characterised by what she calls *deep listening*, which is 'divorced from religious practice but often carrying religious sentiments such as feelings of transcendence or a sense of communion with a power beyond oneself' (2004, p. 2). Becker sees such secular trances as part of a continuum of extraordinary states of musical consciousness:

> I believe that most of us have experienced 'near trance', or at least some of the characteristics of trance at certain times in our lives, especially in relation to musical listening or musical performing. Many of us have experienced sensations of nonself, out-of-body sensations, of closeness to forces that seem to be beyond ourselves, of momentary feelings of eternity … I define trance as a bodily event characterized by strong emotion, intense focus, the loss of the strong sense of self, usually enveloped by amnesia and a cessation of the inner language. Following [William] James, I wish to conclude that trance is an event that accesses types of knowledge and experience which are inaccessible in non-trance events, and which are felt to be ineffable, not easily described or spoken of. (2004, pp. 131 and 143)

There are clear similarities between Becker's description of 'secular trancing' and how Oksana and Jane talk about their 'strong' musical experiences. We could understand these in terms of three necessary dimensions of 'everyday' musical transcendence.[8]

Altered States

Jane experiences her singing as a demanding but exciting physiological flow, sending shivers down her spine, taking her beyond physical limits: 'I've got music which both grounds me in my body, but it also takes me *out* of it'. She explains that, although it feels like flying through the air, actually it's to do with how she aligns herself empathically to and with the music's flight. Since anthropologist Gilbert Rouget's (1985) famous study of trance onwards, the literature on musical ecstasy (whether sacred or secular) agrees on one point: it is not the music itself that directly causes the trance effect, but the 'total event' – how individual physiology becomes coupled to a psychological experience embedded within a particular cultural tradition and an immediate social/ritual event. Nevertheless, it seems that the catalytic agent is probably the intense emotion that musicking affords for some people at key times. As Becker explains:

> The arousal of emotion within the trancer, in part inspired by music, links trancers and deep listeners: trance consciousness and the transcendental experiences of deep listeners both rest on powerful emotional excitement … There is a joy in

---

[8]   I draw from both Ehrenreich 2007 and Becker 2004 in the following.

the pure bodily experiences of strong arousal, a life-affirming quality of feeling truly alive that both deep listening and trancing can enhance. Both are affectively akin to sexual arousal. (2004, pp. 45 and 67)

Oksana describes how 'there's something very erotic about this… when you don't think any more, when you're not there as *you* any more, there's just the *energy* there'. This link with the physiology of sexual arousal is due to the overlap in the body's arousal and reward systems for pleasurable, life-enhancing activities. Neuroscientific studies are showing how some participation in music is linked to high arousal of the Autonomic Nervous System and so-called 'musical emotions'.[9] Far from those mild feelings that people often associate with music ('peaceful', 'soothing', 'comforting'), the 'performative emotions' are 'primary' or Dionysian emotions such as joy, fear and anger, which are neurologically associated with high arousal. These are strongly embodied emotions involving changes in physiology (heart rate, breathing, muscle tone) and associated with tears, thrills and chills. There is a strong overlap between musical and sexual arousal within the brain systems, a fact that leads Jan Panksepp to call the 'musical chills' phenomenon a 'skin orgasm' (cited in Becker 2004, p. 63). It is an evolving hypothesis that high emotional arousal is the necessary precondition for tipping a person into the altered state of consciousness that characterises both trance and 'deep listening' or 'deep performing'. But equally important in all cases is that the extreme emotion is 'contained' within a cultural and social frame – regulating intense emotion as controlled abandon.

Altered Identities

Musical ecstasies are *trans*-personal. They help to loosen and sometimes to re-define identities, roles and relationships between people and their communities. 'Who are we when we listen to music or when we trance?', asks Judith Becker. Jane says, 'I find myself *outside* myself – you get rid of the self in a way', and this is accompanied by a feeling of spiritual union, of sharing with everyone in the concert. For Oksana, 'I forget myself, I dissolve … it's when somehow *I* don't exist any more for a time; but when this energy is "I"… it shows me *where I am*'. There's a relaxing of the boundaries of the physical and psychological self as they experience their ecstatic states as quite literally the 'being beside the self'. But importantly, this is not experienced as something risky and pathological, but rather as a healthy reorientation of their identity towards a more communal and transpersonal experience.

---

[9]   For more on the neurophysiology of musical experience, see MacDonald, Kreutz and Mitchell 2012.

Habits of Ecstasy

Part of why such experiences can be both extreme and relatively safe psychologically and socially for Oksana and Jane is that they are contained within a broader cultural and ritual event (albeit a secular one). Judith Becker talks of the 'habits' of musical ecstasy: 'Trancing is a learned bodily behaviour acted out within a culturally pregiven religious narrative' (2004, p. 42). Trances are collectively made, that is, not individually found. They are formed from and within the elements of the whole event, even if they seem to be manifested by single people. The extraordinary is prepared and controlled through the ordinary, with the overall ritual frame and script both guiding and grounding the experience. We've seen previously how a Western classical concert is no less a ritual event than any other occasion of musicking.

𝇍

Michael: If there was one defining musical experience I had, it was singing in the cathedral choir at Salisbury as a boy. It's to do with being in cathedral architecture... cathedrals are, as Goethe said, frozen music. If you look at the history of music, it's also the history of how contexts form the human being and his music. I was this star boy singer who made records, toured around, sang on TV. Frequently priests would come to me after I'd sung a solo, and say, 'That was divine – you sing like an angel!' This of course sounded ridiculous to a ten-year-old who liked kicking a football around! So where did my voice come from? For me singing was both an extraordinary experience, but also a spiritual one... because this voice just used to flow through me... it wasn't held or trapped. I used to ask myself, 'How did I get this voice? Where did it come from?' My standard reply to the priests was, 'It's not me singing sir, it's God singing through me'. The only thing I ever came up with – which I still think's profoundly true – is that it was to do with singing in that vast great gothic building. When you go in there, you're uplifted... your eyes literally go up... your soul expands into the space. When you look into how those gothic structures came to be built, there's the question of how you maintain a pointed arch. The cathedral's energy is actually flowing down, whilst from a human point of view we are drawn upwards into a state of ascension. So you've got this dual energy - one streaming up the pillars, with an equal and opposite energy flowing from above to below....

So when I stood there as a child, I could *feel* the pillars... to me, it was like my back was joined to these pillars. When I sang I felt more than this physical substance of my body... I felt I *was* the cathedral! I'd hear the cathedral sing *back* to me, the space would sing with you. So I felt the cathedral sing *through me* as I sang with the cathedral... and that dynamic relationship enabled the voice to be in a state of balanced freedom. So it was a unique experience of sacred music, and the feeling that I opened myself like a prayer. The music, the voice, would just flood through me as I offered myself as a vessel....

I remember an occasion when the queen's cousin was being married, and I had to do Mozart's *Laudate Dominum*, but I had horrendous tonsillitis! I went along to the rehearsal and nothing came out... but the choirmaster said, 'Royal wedding... got to be you, Michael!' Back at school after the rehearsal, I threw myself on the chapel floor and begged that my throat would open up... and when the moment arrived for me to sing, I leaned against the pillar, opened myself up, and it came: the voice just flooded through me....

So it transcended the physical, it reached beyond the limitations of my physical body, just for that moment. After the solo, my voice immediately gave up on me again. It reminds me of Kathleen Ferrier singing for the last time, when her pelvis cracked mid-performance... but she went on....

For me, this was the defining proof that music isn't just about the physical body... it was a transcendent experience for me – though, like a mystic, it's ruined me for life! [*laughs*] I *had* that experience, I can't deny it... it's enabled me to live in the openness of the listening... it's a prayer, you open yourself and it comes out: *Open wide the ears of your heart*, as the Benedictines say.

Michael's story powerfully illustrates a fourth potential feature of musical ecstasy: the transcendence of illness and pain. The physical, social and spiritual alchemy of a particular musical situation can lift a person up and through the threshold of normal limitations. In her study of communal ecstatic practices, Barbara Ehrenreich asks what has happened to the 'therapeutics of ecstasy', commenting, 'I know of no attempts in our own time to use festive behaviour as treatment for depression, if such an experiment is even thinkable in a modern clinical setting' (2007, p. 150). We've seen how something of this approach has been smuggled back into the clinic through music therapy, but often only with the requirement that its explicit goals are functional and controlled. The same anxiety is still there as has been throughout history: that musical ecstasy might 'tip people over the edge', that they might lose themselves or go out of (organisational) control.

But don't many of the examples in this book show that sometimes this is just what we all really need? Don't we all need ecstatic transcendence, where perhaps just for precious moments we can step beyond ourselves and the limits that we and others have imposed?

Music may still be our best help in both reaching and protecting such everyday transcendence.

Ken: For me, music's been a vehicle to enlarge my consciousness out of my own individual, personal sense of myself... to something broader, wider... *beyond*. When people's experiential worlds are often so narrow, the fact that music can be a vehicle for broadening that... I think it's a great way of mediating from the familiar to the unfamiliar. If we follow it, and trust it, it can surprise us, and help us experience things differently. It's not about a transcendent spiritual force, it's the being in it *completely* that's mind expanding. By music transforming where the person *is*... that opens up different possibilities....

Musical ecstasy is a phenomenon of spirit. Its essential qualities are lightness, freedom, abandon, and the unconditional offering of a self that can transcend the usual boundaries of possibility. As the poet Rilke wrote, 'The spirit wants only that there be flying'.[10]

---

[10] From a letter by Rilke, 27 December 1913.

Chapter 20
Musical Hope

Can only those hope who can talk?

Ludwig Wittgenstein[1]

If music is the most contemplative of the arts, it is *not* because it takes us into the timeless but because it obliges us to rethink time.

Rowan Williams[2]

The beyond is not what is infinitely remote, but what is nearest to hand.

Dietrich Bonhoeffer[3]

Playing with Hope

> **Nuri:** *What do I get from these music therapy sessions? It's some sort of hope... and something fresh is coming. I have to carry on... usually I feel this after the session....*

ဢ

> **David:** What's most important to me about music? I think it's *hope*. The old cliché stands, I suppose: life can't be too bad if it contains this beautiful piece of music. I'm interested that I find myself talking about hope, because I'm not aware of having conceptualised it like this before. Music's sustaining... on a higher level than just the bread-and-butter, as something necessary for one's wellbeing... one's soul. So perhaps hope's a development of that. Music has this hope-sustaining possibility....

Nuri suffers from chronic depression following experiences of political violence. Playing music in music therapy is one of the few things that helps to counter his despair. David's life experience has not been so extreme, but his ongoing relationship to music is also about sustaining everyday hope. I've noticed over the years as a music therapist that hope is perhaps the most common if mysterious

---

[1]   Wittgenstein 1953, p. 174.
[2]   Williams 1994, p. 248.
[3]   Bonhoeffer 1971, p. 376.

affordance of musicking – whether in everyday or more extreme situations. The philosopher Wittgenstein asked the provocative question, 'Can only those who can talk hope?' (1953, p. 174), and then answered this question through his own life, reporting to a friend that the slow movement of Brahms' Third String Quartet had pulled him back from the brink of suicide. But how does such 'musical hopefulness' come about?

One aspect of an answer probably has something to do with music's relationship to time. It's a commonplace to say that music is the 'art of time', but perhaps the more interesting question is, 'What *kind* of time?' This is a question that becomes particularly important to people whose struggle or suffering centres on time. Illness or spiritual anxiety can make time stand still or become empty and oppressive. For the terminally ill, it is simply that their biological time is running out. For a mother who sees her profoundly disabled child unexpectedly respond with joy in a music therapy session, there is the sudden hope of future possibility – of time opening out again. In all these different cases, people need to want or to believe in a future, and to experience time as flowing and fulfilling again. Music offers a particular form of help here, in how it can carry us forward hopefully, and can point to a future that is both possible and, despite all signs to the contrary, benign.

This last chapter of Part VI explores this final mode of musical transcendence, that of time. As with previous forms of music's help, there are two related aspects to this. Firstly, there are those direct experiences of music that can take us beyond everyday time and into the alternative quality of musical time. Secondly, reflecting on 'music's time' can provide material for 'spiritual work' – helping us to rethink what time is, or what it means to us in relation to our particular situation in life.

∞

Hope becomes important in our lives when we face a physical, psychological or spiritual threat. Hope counters despair. Whilst wishes can be just fantasy, hopes are orientations to things that *could* and often need to come about for us or for others. Our hopes are orientated to the future, in situations that are uncertain, and where positive outcomes can't be guaranteed, even if we act or pray more. We can hope for specific things, or hope simply that things will soon be different when we or others close to us are ill or distressed, or where conditions or situations are difficult. We hope for something better ahead; we hope that something will be possible. But there's also a paradox here: humans can also be anxious *because* they can look forward. We need, therefore, to think of hope as a particular benign orientation to the future – where 'all shall be well'.

Because hope is neither a thing nor a passive state, it's perhaps better to talk about *hoping* – an active psychological disposition that projects our minds forward to when things could be different, better, or, at best, fully resolved. In his book *Hope*, philosopher Stan Van Hooft suggests that our hoping bridges the gap between effort and outcome; between what we can do and what the stark forces of biology, causality and fate bring. 'Hope,' writes Van Hooft, 'is our existential response to the contingency that is a mark of all our actions and of the world we live in' (2011, p. 32).

A final dimension of this concept is *hopefulness*, which Van Hooft suggests is 'a fundamental existential structure of human existence' (p. 102). When hope is not directly for something, hopefulness is a more general attitude or disposition of our lives that is more like a character trait – though 'hopeful' can be the quality of an experience too. This is perhaps what makes Van Hooft call hopefulness a virtue, in that to a certain extent it can be cultivated as a means of living a good life.

Hope is therefore a complex human phenomenon. We can lose and find it, sometimes give it, and sustain it – both for ourselves and for others. Hoping and hopefulness are mostly interdependent with others' lives and actions, and with collective and cultural understandings that often overlap with religion and spirituality. Above all, hope is about *time*, but not time as we typically think about it. Because music gives us a way of experiencing and rethinking time in more nuanced ways, it also helps us to think about the parallel complexities of hoping and hopefulness.

Music's Hopeful Time[4]

People sometimes say things like, 'Music takes me somewhere else', or, 'Time stopped whilst I was listening to that music'. It's tempting to let such statements confirm the popular myth that music is somehow timeless, lifting us *out* of time into some ethereal, spiritual region. But is this really true? Zuckerkandl quipped that, if music really were timeless, then how could the angels in heaven be still singing and playing? More seriously, he argued against what he thought were equally unhelpful modern conceptual images of time – either as an hourglass with the sands of time flowing away, or of time as a big neutral container that we pour events into. Instead, Zuckerkandl suggested that we turn to music as a better guide to thinking about time. 'Music,' he writes, 'is a temporal art in the special sense that in it time reveals itself to experience' (1956, p. 200). An alternative image and understanding of time is before our ears.[5]

Music shows us that time is not a container that we fill with music, but rather that it is a core part of music's *content*. Music works *with* and *on* time, treating it as a force to be shaped and transformed. 'Tones are time become audible matter,' writes Zuckerkandl (p. 253). So, rather than simply moving *through* neutral time (though it does this too if we count the seconds), any music also 'has' an essential

---

[4]   This section follows on from the overall eco-phenomenological perspective on music outlined in Chapter 4. You may wish to refresh your memory with the section 'Aspect 3: Musical Space, Time and Motion', on pp. 70–72.

[5]   This section draws on Zuckerkandl's phenomenological analysis, 'The Musical Concept of Time', chapter 12 of *Sound and Symbol* (1956); and also from discussions of Zuckerkandl in Peacocke and Pederson 2006, and Begbie 2000.

time that is personal, qualitative, active and dynamic (and as such very little to do with the physical seconds of its duration). When a tone sounds, it summons time onto the scene, and draws us into that music's particular time world. Through musicking, we become *of* and *with* musical time.

Music also helps us to rethink the relationship between present, past and future. In particular, a musical time concept challenges the myth that the present moment is only a rather desperate, fleeting slither – gone before we can catch it. Instead, Zuckerkandl gives the image of a *sonic saddle* on which we can ride the fullness of the present musical moment, a comfortable 'now' within the musical flow, 'in which "now", "not yet" and "no more" are given together, in the most intimate interpenetration and with equal immediacy' (p. 227). This model shows us both the flow and the complex interpenetration of time modes (rather than the traditional and over-simplified succession of past→present→future). Think of listening to a melody, Zuckerkandl suggests: 'Hearing a melody is hearing, having heard, and being able to hear, all at once' (p. 235). The present is full and habitable, but also leans back towards the past and is pulled forwards from the future simultaneously – giving the alternative model: past←—→present←—→future. 'To hear music,' states Zuckerkandl, 'is to be flowing with time; is to know the past and the future only as characteristics of the flowing present, as its two directions, away from and toward' (p. 152).

Musical time therefore challenges the standard myths of time 'running out' (the hourglass) or 'standing still' (the neutral container). Instead, it gives us an audible understanding of the possibilities of our human time as something always alive, connected, habitable, purposeful and transcendent.

Scientist and priest Arthur Peacocke (in Peacocke and Pederson 2006, p. 20) usefully summarises the differences between a purely materialist view of time and a musical time concept:

Physical Time Concept	Musical Time Concept
Time is order, form of experience	Time is content of experience
Time measures events	Time produces events
Time is divisible into equal parts	Time knows no equality of parts
Time is perpetual transience	Time knows nothing of transience

For Peacocke, this alternative and counter-intuitive view revealed by 'musical time' communicates an important existential message:

> In music, we experience ordered change that is not futile or inferior because it is transient, a dynamic process that can attain its perfection only through and by the passage of time. In music, time is therefore experienced as 'very good' and

assures us that, in spite of much to the contrary in our immediate experience, even short times can be fulfilling and creative. (in Peacocke and Pederson 2006, p. 20)

Zuckerkandl writes that 'thanks to music we are able to *behold* time ... it finds the symbolic language in which we can apprehend, can view, can grasp becoming, flux, change' (1956, p. 200). This conclusion becomes even clearer if we move from the somewhat theoretical perspectives of those who only listen to pre-composed art music, and move instead to the messier, worldly practice of improvised everyday musicking, where time is also heard within human action and interaction, as *timing*. What more does this tell us about 'music's time'?[6]

Interestingly, the two ways to describe music that has not been pre-composed both specifically emphasise its time dimension. 'Improvisation' comes from the Latin *improvisus* ('unforeseen', 'unexpected'), whilst 'extemporisation' is from *extemporalis* ('arising from the moment'). The music emerges, that is, from people musicking – either from the relatively spontaneous musical actions of a single improviser or from a group of people bouncing off each other. Improvisations are, like our lives in general, a complex amalgam of habit and freedom. Players not only respond to and fit in with others, but also make spontaneous creative gestures that take themselves and others towards somewhere unexpected and new. Time is central to any improvising process, and I'd suggest that it reveals two key aspects. Firstly, there is the phenomenological process of 'music's time', as outlined above – where you can hear the active interpenetration of what *has* happened, what *is* happening and what *may* happen next as somehow all contained simultaneously in the *musical Now* (Zuckerkandl's 'sonic saddle'). But in improvisation – where music is always embodied and usually social – there's also a second dimension within the performative, relational, human timing that we've previously explored in Part IV, Musical Relationship, and Part V, Musical Community. Here, musical timing is about how people 'tune in' to each other and coordinate their actions within the 'musical Between'. The fruitful combination of these two time aspects helps to produce, I suggest, a uniquely *hopeful musical time* that is at the heart of musical improvisation broadly understood.

Key to music's hopeful time is the *musical future* that the players' musical actions prepare and instigate. Whilst this future is not predictable, retrospectively it's often possible to see how the flux of constant dynamic negotiation between people, events and materials shapes musical time – and the seemingly overlapping quality of what has happened, is happening, could happen, and will have happened in the music. Musicking is hopeful because anything is possible, and this possibility can often be kept open to a surprising degree. A non-determined musical present

---

[6] This section on improvisation, musical time and hope draws from Begbie 2000, Part III, 'Time to Improvise'; Love 2003; DeNora (unpublished paper), 'By the time we're finished with this, we will have played well; future perfect, retrospection and relationality as resources for "making good" improvised musical action'.

can flower into an infinity of musical futures, starting at the level of a single tone and its potential to lead *anywhere, anytime*.

Improvised musical action in this sense may not be different in kind from any other type of human social action that is spontaneously organised around current contingencies and future unknowns. It's perhaps just that hopeful musical time shows more clearly a view of human time that the assumptions of materialist modernity has obscured. Musicking shows that future action can emerge from a free present; that a future can unfold meaningfully even when we can't predict or guarantee where or how; and that what happens ahead is always to some extent in collaboration with others who help to project a future together.

In short, musical time is usually 'good time' – or, to use more religious language, music helps to redeem time. Musicking can help to show us what hope is by opening up the present moment and showing how we can live more comfortably *within it*, and then showing how a moment is constantly transcended as it gracefully gives itself up to the time to come. It shows us that the past can be fulfilled, not just lost; how the future can be entered with hope, not fear.

Chronos and *Kairos*: 'Bad Times', 'Good Times'

These complexities of time have been explored through myth, theology and philosophy since antiquity. Hugh Rayment-Pickard's book *The Myths of Time* (2004) presents a useful analysis of types of time and their effects on our experience of personal, social and spiritual life. The two most important types even have their own mythic figures. *Kronos* is the archetypal old man with a scythe, the grim reaper who devours his own children (each moment of time being symbolically 'killed' as it passes through the hourglass). His mood is depressed, haunted, anxious and paranoid as he reveals time as empty, meaningless and corrupted. In our culture, Kronos stands for profane, objective clock-time – usually the root of our 'time problems'. In short, Kronos is the god of bad time(s) and it is with him that the other times are forced to negotiate.

The description 'chronic' often refers to a health state today, where an illness extends indefinitely and without the possibility of complete healing. People are told that that they must 'learn to live' with their condition. As Kathy Charmaz's pioneering study, *Good Days, Bad Days: The Self in Chronic Illness and Time* (1997) shows, chronic illness often leads people to experience time quite differently and to rethink its meanings. In particular, chronic illness challenges the ideal of 'getting better' and the too-easy judgement of whether people are ill or healthy. Instead, a more complex view of time must be added to the equation, asking rather, '*When* are we ill/healthy?' Subjective wellbeing may fluctuate in all kinds of ways over an hour, a day or a month, and in relation to our physical, social and spiritual ecology (DeNora, 2013). Havi Carel, a philosopher with a chronic illness, remarks that the medical world often wrongly views chronic illness as a type of acute illness that is merely extended. But in contrast to the temporary disturbance of an acute episode, chronic illness can fundamentally transform a person's lifeworld (2008, p. 76).

This is why time as Kronos is often searching for its elusive twin, hope. This theme emerges from Louis's story of coping with his chronic mental illness, and its 'bad time(s)'.[7] After the acute stage passes, he finds himself anxious and depressed, stranded in a time that feels dead and flat:

> **Louis:** If you just sit there, doing nothing... time goes by, you just hear the clock tick. And usually nothing happens – you can sit there for hours. And I think that by the end of such hours, if you just sit there, you become very anxious about time passing by.

Time is 'chronic' for Louis within his illness. It feels dead, stuck and empty – provoking only anxiety about the future. But after ten sessions of music therapy, he tells me about the quite different experiences and thoughts he's had about time. 'Music,' Louis says, 'gives a person some insight into the past, the present and the future... I think in a sense music is like a brush with some paint – it paints a picture in time'. The way that Louis uses his experiences in music therapy to reflect on the broader connections between himself, his illness and time is a wonderful example of using music as a 'workspace' for personal and spiritual dilemmas. Louis tackles three inter-penetrating aspects of his 'time problems' with the aid of music:

Absorbed in the Present

Louis's anxiety stems from getting trapped either in the past, or in the emptiness of the present. He can't usually concentrate enough to get 'lost in the present' positively. Playing music helps him to do just this: to become absorbed into the musical moment. 'When I'm playing music,' says Louis, 'the brain just goes completely blank... except there is music! And I seem to have forgotten everything... everything else goes to the back of the brain – and I become focused, and I'm thinking only about music'. Playing music helps to free Louis from 'bad time', invites him into what Csikszentmihalyi (1992) famously called *flow* – the optimal state that comes when boredom and anxiety are balanced out through absorption in a skilled and pleasureable activity.[8]

Planning for the Future

Concentrated and absorbed in music, Louis is freed to think ahead again: '... in the past, when I was very ill... I could not think about what to do next. I was so occupied by the present and the past.... But by playing music – particularly in this

---

[7]   We met Louis earlier, in the Introduction and in Chapter 5. I've avoided repeating too much of his story here, so you may wish to look back at this point.

[8]   Csikszentmihalyi (1992) specifically talks of '[t]he flow of music' on p. 108.

environment – gives me a chance to quiet down... and then concentrate on planning the next note.' Here we see Louis finding himself capable of a different kind of experiential action, and thinking within action. In his musical improvisations with the therapist, there's a shared involvement in creating something spontaneously, helped by the particular qualities of musical time and timing that we discussed above.

Hoping for Good Times Again

Finally, Louis is able to use these experiences to reflect more generally on the relationship between himself, his illness and his ongoing recovery: 'So planning what the next note's going to be would in a sense lead me to think about planning the next step in my life... because there was a time when I thought there would not be a future... there was a time when I was so ill I thought, "That's it... that's the end". But I think basically I experience here the music painting a picture of the present and the future to me. And that picture basically is some light at the end of the tunnel!' In the earlier exploration of Louis's case in Chapter 5, we looked at the philosopher Mark Johnson's suggestion that more abstract or existential aspects of our personal life are often imagined and articulated through the SOURCE–PATH–GOAL schema. Louis is able to blend the experiential and reflective affordances of music to create an alternative reality of 'good time(s)' to stand up to Kronos for him, and to help clear a pathway to recovery.

୫

These moments of 'good time' are brought to Louis by a second mythological character, *Kairos* – a young man with winged feet and weighing scales in his hand, waiting for just the 'right time' to release the present moment. He's unconcerned with the past or the future, but totally focused on the quality of now. Kairos is present when we say something well at just the right time, or play a note just right, or take a photograph that captures the essence of a scene – calculating just how and when to act effectively. '*Kairos* is the epiphany of time ... a transcendence of *Kronos*,' writes Rayment-Pickard (2004, p. 89). As such, kairic time is subjective, non-linear, episodic and opportunistic – gathering our subjective experience into a richly textured point. Sacred, mystical, ethical and aesthetic experiences all need Kairos' help.

But how, asks the psychotherapist Daniel Stern, 'can we pry open *chronos* to create a present long enough to accommodate *kairos*?' (2004, p. 26) We explored in Chapter 12 how Stern's research shows that therapeutic change can often be traced to an unexpected event between client and therapist when a present moment suddenly opens out and thickens. The shared moment of presence that comes from this is experienced as a *meeting* in Buber's sense, often serving to break through a patient's limitations and resistances, or a blockage in the client-therapist relationship. Stern calls these moments 'micro-*kairos*', and his analogy for their size and character is a musical phrase, which he describes as 'a flowing whole occurring during a now' (2004, p. 26). Attending to a person at this level of a music-like phrase – with its up to ten seconds' window of expansive 'now' stitched into past and future – is a way that we can 'pry open chronos' enough to welcome kairos as a charged present that is long enough to allow something genuinely new to emerge and to be experienced.

When Stern comments that this 'happens in a moment of awareness', he brings up how kairic moments also need a further quality of time both to prepare for and to support them. This is a 'receptive time' or 'waiting time' that attends, listens or maintains a vigil in a relaxed but attentive way to what *may* or *could* happen. This form of time creates an expectant, potential present – a 'not-yet time' where the only option is to keep listening, following and exploring to see what might unfold. The theologian Rowan Williams suggests that music teaches us this further lesson about time: that 'there are things you will learn only by passing through this process, by being caught up in this series of relations and transformations' (1994, p. 247). Receptive time helps us to wait, to leave silence, and to allow things to come to pass. It can be experienced sometimes as 'treading water', but its mission is to remain in *potential time*, hoping for a breakthrough. This attention that we give to ourselves, or to another, takes the form of a careful listening or careful accompanying that midwives the arrival of Kairos. Such acute, active listening was exactly what Paul Nordoff and Clive Robbins brought to music therapy, showing how to liberate the kairic moment within the musical relationship – the 'Creative Now' that Clive Robbins was so fond of discussing.

ॐ

Fraser: One of the things music therapy's given me is a sense of being content to be in the present moment... and leave the future to take care of itself. It's to do with *trust*. And at quite a fundamental level in music therapy, I think what we're working with is enabling people to have an experience of trust....

ॐ

Matthew: I can remember those moments all these years later. You can *think* about 'being-here-now', but you *can't* think about it when you're *in it*! It's an experience that's different from a knowledge. I've thought many times, 'I can't *think* about this! I'm going to break this moment if I start thinking about what's going on...'.

It's this thing of *presence*.... Quite often one's mind can be split and spread out: some of it focusing on what's here, some on other things.... So somehow that experience of being *totally present* is really important to me. It's connected with an awareness of a spiritual dimension... it's when we stop thinking about everything else. This is part of this *absolute presence* within music making... it becomes so involving that you can realise the extraordinariness of the present moment....

Epiphanies of Beauty

One of the most common ways Kairos arrives is through moments of musical beauty that seem to slow time, or even stop it for a heartbeat. In Joyce's novel *Stephen Hero*, Stephen half-jokingly tells his friend Cranly that his glimpses of a Dublin clock are the 'gropings of a spiritual eye' that gradually adjust focus until 'then all at once I see it and know what it is: *epiphany*' (1963, p. 211). Stephen then goes on to summarise for his friend how the mediaeval philosopher–theologian St Thomas Aquinas' classical theory of aesthetics explains the occurrence of such an epiphany, where beauty 'arrests motion' through the way in which the independent and objective qualities of a thing such as proportion, unity and harmony afford pleasure when contemplated. Stephen's joke is that even the Dublin clock manages this.

This classical aesthetic theory has been challenged by modernists and post-modernists, who see it as conveniently repressing and downplaying the non-unified, imperfect, dissonant or contingent aspects of everyday reality and everyday beauty. Its ideal vision of beauty is seen to be as much about cultural politics as aesthetics. The philosophical arguments in this area tend to seesaw between those who believe in objective standards of beauty, and those for whom aesthetic judgements are mere subjective social constructions. I want to shortcut this binary argument by turning instead to how an ecological and pragmatist perspective might see experiences and meanings of beauty. As usual, we simply add in the factors of activity and context to the question – asking *when, where and how* beauty affords something to a particular situation, and is perceived and understood by the people there and then. An ecological aesthetics relocates experiences of beauty, from an exclusive focus on abstract objects to people, processes and occasions. After all, aesthetics comes from the Greek *aesthetikos* – meaning 'perceptible to the senses', and therefore to a person in action and situation. An aesthetic response is often the 'gasp' of inspiration – *aah!* – that stops us in our tracks and makes us notice, appreciate or reassess *this* moment, and what we value in it.

> **Susanna:** I think of a piece of music I love, like a bit of a favourite Mozart Piano Concerto... how you anticipate a melody coming... if you know the piece... and then physically you make a gesture as if you want to join in... then often I actually start singing it at that moment, and then I get a profound sense of satisfaction that it's happened – although I know that it's going to happen! And yet it never loses its breathtakingness – which it normally does when something's known to you. That's what's so peculiar about it – it's expected, you know what's coming, and yet every time there's physical tension and release. Then when it's gone, there's no disappointment! Pleasure doesn't quite put it strongly enough, there's an absolute rightness of things being in harmony I suppose – it's beauty!

ಬ

Sasha: Us playing music together... it's like completing a picture there... something beautiful there... that orchid we've made... and that's the twain of it. If I can keep my voice harmonious with the piano then you have a single thing... it's nice! It makes it like a circle rather than a mish-mash of different interwoven cloth. It makes it more a central thing for me. It's a bit like prayer... it has the same effect on me as prayer does for some people. It kind of centralises things – brings out one whole aspect, pure essence and soul to the thing....

Both Susanna, in her home, and Sasha, on the ward of a psychiatric hospital, have what John Dewey variously called '*an* experience', or a 'consummatory experience' (in Hildebrand 2008, p. 156). By this, he meant a particular kind of limited and heightened experience that he called 'aesthetic' because it often brings feelings of fulfilment, satisfaction or reassurance. In comparison to the chaotic flux of ordinary experience, a 'consummatory experience' is discrete and complete in itself. It typically has unity, clarity, character and drama, but unlike traditional aesthetics it's the *experience* rather than just the art object that has these satisfying qualities. This matches how Susanna and Sasha talk about the embodied, situational, and relational aspects of their aesthetic experiences as something lived through, not abstract. Later in her interview, Susanna tells me how such moments of aesthetic inspiration (the 'breathtakingly beautiful') reassure her of a fundamental rightness to things 'against all expectations, and all observations to the contrary'. The telling of this account (to me, to herself) is, of course, part also of what musical beauty affords her. For Sasha, any experience of integration and meaning that can be shared with another person is helpful to him in his disorientated state, and less than ideal surroundings.

This seemingly natural linking of the aesthetic and the spiritual makes good sense from an ecological perspective. As Gregory Bateson suggests, with appropriate ambiguity, 'The sacred (whatever that means) is surely related (somehow) to the beautiful (whatever that means)' (1985, p. 17). Both modes of experience, that is, sensitise us to the quality of our relationship to the things and people immediately around us. '"How are you related to this creature?" is an aesthetic question,' Bateson states (p. 17). Beauty is consequently the qualitative 'index' of things being well connected and 'true'. Hence Bateson's conclusion: 'by aesthetic I mean responsive to the pattern which connects' (p. 17), an idea that Christopher Small applies to musicking:

> the sensation of beauty is a sign that the gesture or object relates to the perceiver in such a way as to reveal the workings of the pattern which connects as it is conceived as a set of ideal relationships by the perceiver. It is as if the perceiver has in his or her mind a grid of relationships that appear as ideal and that the regularities in the perceived object or gesture are somehow mapped onto the regularities in the mental pattern; and where they fit, they create the sensation we call beauty. (Small 1998, p. 219)

Another way of saying this is that musical beauty often functions as an epiphany in the sense that we explored this earlier in Part VI – as something that restores and reassures by intimating a wholeness and connectedness that may not be apparent or accessible in other ways. Seen from a musicking perspective, this is *beauty in action*, where aesthetic musical experiences show up the wholeness potentially present within a situation. The 'pattern' can connect simultaneously within things or within people; between things and people; between people; between their values and their hopes; and so on. Musicking seems to provide an especially rich medium in which people can find or be surprised by beauty in a passing moment shared together, or in response to each other's creations and performances – and then sometimes, through this, expand their vision of the world around and beyond them.

ෂ

Strangely, the arts therapies have traditionally had a problem with beauty.[9] This began with the dilemma of fitting traditional 'objective' aesthetic theories with the aims and processes of therapeutic work. It's true that therapists do not aim *for* beauty as traditionally conceived. And how do you reconcile beauty in art or music therapy with the terrible suffering in people's lives? Whilst both of these dilemmas are real, the arts therapies for decades simply threw the aesthetic baby out with the therapeutic bathwater. Despite this, it's becoming increasingly acknowledged that beauty can't or won't be banished from the clinic. Clients will still welcome it, even if therapists won't – or haven't yet found a good theory to justify it, or work with it.

ෂ

A woman I'm working with in a psychiatric hospital will only let me play Mozart arias to her, each time saying, 'So beautiful!', as she visibly relaxes. I feel unsure about the therapeutic wisdom of just going with this and her refusal to do anything else, but I do so for the remaining weeks of her stay. On leaving the hospital, she tells her doctor: 'The Mozart took me away from my hell, into a world of beauty and freedom. It was the only thing that helped me survive here'.

ෂ

In *Smart Music*, Brenda comes up to the microphone to sing for the first time, having sat quietly listening to others for weeks. She's affectionately goaded by her friends, and sings 'Amazing Grace' with a small yet surprisingly steady and clear voice. The room hushes; people listen and will her on. At the end, someone says, 'That was really beautiful!' She smiles bashfully, and as she returns to her seat she looks beautiful too.

ෂ

---

[9] For accounts of the debate about aesthetics and therapeutics in music therapy, see Aigen 2007, 2008; Ruud 2010, chapter 5.

An answer to this dilemma that arts therapies have with beauty is simply to adopt a more performative and ecological aesthetic practice that is open to finding things, events and people beautiful because of how they rightly connect. Art therapist Cathy Moon calls such an expanded, inclusive notion of aesthetics a 'relational aesthetic':

> [this] is characterized by a concern for the capacity of art to promote healthy interactions within and amongst people and the created world. This emphasis prompts different questions than does an aesthetic concerned with the formal elements of art and their pleasurable effects ... [T]he concept of a relational aesthetic leads to a valuing of art based on its ability to foster and deepen relationships to the self, the art object, other people, and the environment. (2002, pp. 140 and 155)

Of course, thinking about beauty in therapy brings us up against the apparent dilemma that somebody put to me once as 'reconciling the shitty situations and the beautiful moments'. But often this is just what a therapist needs to do – to retain an 'ear for beauty', as music therapist Rachel Verney suggests:

> There's something here to do with our perception. If we are fine-tuned to the beautiful in people; if one of our basic beliefs is that people can be beautiful ... then in finding them beautiful we allow them to *be* beautiful. If I hear what a client is doing as beautiful, then in my loving response to that beauty, and to the client, perhaps it actually *becomes* beautiful, objectively. By 'objectively' I mean simply that someone else would also perceive that music as beautiful. And of course the other important thing to say is that it's often the contrast of this to the shit of people's lives that heightens it. (in Verney and Ansdell 2010, p. 88)

This 'hearing as' is an aesthetic perception that is both relational and ecological in the way we've previously discussed. The 'framing' of the beautiful event is not only within the context of that person and their situation, but also historically within a timeframe of what led up to the particular 'flowering' of beauty, and its significance for that person within that therapeutic relationship and that setting. This aesthetic framing might also include understanding and incorporating what might conventionally be thought *not* to be 'beautiful' – the sounds of the struggle that can happen in a music therapy relationship, the lack of the classical virtues of balance and moderation and closure. But a relational and ecological aesthetic can include all of this too, as it re-frames things as being heard *as* meaningful and potentially beautiful within the situation. Rachel concludes on this:

> So in the end what I want to say is: it's not that we run away from pain and ugliness – we often enter into it, but also find beauty coming *from* it! What we can perhaps say is that there's a hidden relationship between beauty and suffering – which most of the prevailing theories of music therapy don't encompass. (in Verney and Ansdell 2010, p. 97)

An ecological perspective can help to accommodate rather than compartmentalise different and potentially conflicting aesthetic manifestations – such as fragmentation in relation to integration; completion in relation to freedom; synchronisation in relation to discrepancy; and so on. It can appreciate too that real-life situations are always in transition and emergence – that beauty *can* emerge from suffering, if only for a moment. So rather than seeing the juxtaposition of momentary flowerings of musical beauty alongside the stark realities of people's everyday experience as problematic, we could instead see this as beauty's most important work within music's help.

Music's End-time

A critique of kairic moments of beauty might be that, whilst they can provide relief from the anxieties of chronic time, they can also turn sentimental or sensational, or can strand us in a blissed-out and isolated present. But it's clear, I hope, that moments of genuine beauty also initiate a momentum beyond themselves; that their epiphany is generative. We perhaps need, then, to ask the additional questions: What is 'now' *for*? What overall pattern of the whole do such epiphanic moments connect with and prepare for? – this is partly to ask, Where do they move *towards*? The fullest experience of transcendence needs to retain an active sense of reaching over, of getting somewhere beyond current limits. The state of 'being here now' is, both in life and in music, a necessary but not sufficient moment on the journey.

Kronos allows music's time to pass, whilst Kairos helps to expand its present moments. But it also needs a third temporal force, pulling it from the future. Here a final moderating time form enters the picture: 'end-time', described classically as *telos* or *eskhatos* (both meaning 'end' or 'purpose'). We saw in Louis's story that he finds 'good time' for himself not only by escaping Kronos through Kairos, but also by planning and hoping. Eschatological time (also called 'prophetic time' in theological writing) cultivates this hope towards a resolution, revelation or deliverance where time is positively fulfilled and redeemed.

At some point of our lives, we will enter 'end-time'. Kronos can invade then, invoking only anxiety and regret. But we can also invite in moments of Kairos, prepared for by 'waiting time' and leading into 'hopeful time'. Music provides a model of how these various times can interpenetrate and complement each other in challenging situations. Leonard Bernstein described the coda of Mahler's Ninth Symphony as 'the closest we have ever come, in any work of art, to experiencing the very act of dying, of giving it all up' (1976, p. 321). But he also said that paradoxically this very music 'reanimates us every time we hear it' (p. 321). A very different idiom, the 'New Spiritual Music' of Arvo Pärt, John Tavener and Henryk Górecki has also been helpful to people looking to music for 'hopeful time'.[10] Partly this is perhaps due to the explicit religiosity of the style, but also because of

---

[10]   Music critic Alex Ross reported that Pärt's music had turned up unexpectedly in places where people needed particular help, particularly in the worst time of AIDS in the

how its compositional structure somehow refuses to be entirely goal directed. In what Pärt calls his *tintinnabuli* style ('like bells'), he creates a ritual effect through the way static musical motifs both circle and progress in time. Tavener similarly describes his pieces as 'sounding icons' that are both static and moving, hinting at how this music provides a non-verbal parable of the mysteries of end-time.

Earlier, music therapist Nigel noted that the 'Big Questions' that people who are dying bring up about their lives are somehow matched by the mysteries of music. He goes on to describe his work in end-of-life care:

> **Nigel:** When we're in the normal flow of our lives, it's simply just happening. The average person isn't encouraged to ask many questions about life. Then you come to a point when it's *not* flowing... illness or whatever is stopping the flow of life. I meet people who are actually stopping the flow of life themselves because they don't want to get any further; because flowing means moving towards their death. Music can help people get back to that flow... they can be supported and held *within* it in music.... I think it can be quite a phenomenal experience to move back into the flow of life through music, but also somehow move beyond it. I wonder whether again it's something to do with this meeting in the music... where, even when you're involved in doing it, you're feeling something that's bigger than yourself... you're in time, living in time, but also you're sensing something of how it's possible to let go of time and *me*... but still feel OK.

Nigel brings the discussion to the further question, '*Whose* time?' Whilst some forms of time (such as kairic) seem to be more subjective and individual, music shows us how time – even our own 'end–time' – is something fundamentally shared and social as well. We've seen how we can create musical relationships and communities because we can share qualities of time and timing. This becomes especially poignant when personal time is scarce.

୫୬

I've been working with Gisela in music therapy for four weeks whilst she's been having further treatment. Yesterday she found that the cancer has spread again, and is inoperable. We both find ourselves lost for words, and after a few minutes' silence she goes to the second piano in the room. When we first met, Gisela told me that she was in a choir, but has not played the piano since she was a child.

She now plays tentative single notes on the piano, slow tones surrounded by stilled musical space. There's an awkwardness in her touch as she gets used to playing again, experimenting with sounds and silences. After a while I join her, playing on a second piano – at first supporting her tones, but then finding my playing more actively counterpointing hers. Soon our shared music seems to follow its natural course. There's no eye contact, but rather a strong musical

---

USA in the 1990s. See 'Consolations: The Uncanny Voice of Arvo Pärt', New Yorker, 2 December 2002.

rapport that creates a charged, concentrated atmosphere in the room. As we're playing, I look out of a big picture window onto a forest bathed in early-evening summer sun, and I gradually feel a shift into another time and space. The music still moves, but everything else seems suspended.

The twenty-minute improvisation that follows has a structure of several sections that seem naturally to unfold between us. A winding path of music is led by a modal melody Gisela plays mostly on single tones. At a mid-point, it twists into a chromatic melody, as if exploring another, darker side of the musical landscape. Then there's a musical breath that's like the sudden clearing of musical texture that sometimes happens in a Mahler symphony, and from this a clear and exquisite melody emerges from Gisela's fingers. Her tones step intently further and further forwards, gaining momentum, volume and intensity – which I support with thickening chords. But this melody doesn't climax, suddenly stepping back at the last moment, its cadence suspended, unresolved. An echo of the melody hangs in the air.

After the music, there's a long silence between us. Gisela says that the music had expressed what she couldn't say (which is true for me too). But it doesn't feel exactly right that our music 'said' something musically. If anything, the music articulated '?' – a question that couldn't be asked or answered.

At the time, this event disturbed me because I didn't understand what was happening. When I listen back to the tape of this session twenty years later, I'm not sure I understand much more, but I'm no longer disturbed – I'm more comfortable now with time's mysteries and life's mysteries, and how music sometimes allows us to contact them, but not answer them. As I listen again, I'm back in that experience we shared, where both of us are flowing towards somewhere – in the same time, if at different existential speeds.

છ

At one level, this improvisation was an elegy that could be interpreted as an expression of sadness and pain. But there is something more that I experienced then, and do so still twenty years later when I listen again. It seems as if the music travels, pauses, and then points towards somewhere. We stop at a threshold, unresolved – but something is glimpsed.

છ

Doctor and philosopher Raymond Tallis suggests the intriguing thesis that pointing is the human ability that most clearly indicates our human capacity for transcendence. In his remarkable book *Michelangelo's Finger* (2010), Tallis argues that this everyday human gesture is what progressively takes us beyond our everyday limits. As infants, we cultivate our conscious life by *pointing to* things that we want others to notice we notice, or help us name. From this developmental milestone onwards, we are increasingly motivated to share what we perceive and think, *pointing out* things to others, getting them to see what and how we are seeing and thinking. This everyday transcending of individuality inducts us into the social and cultural world and, tellingly, it's a sign of problems when people do not point or speak, or if they point to things that we can't collectively agree with or believe in.[11] 'See it my way' becomes a metaphor when what I'm pointing out is not physically there. Language and symbol take over as the 'pointers' when we cross over to the realm of abstractions or unobservables, aiming to engage another person's attention on what they can't themselves see beyond at that time (either physically or conceptually) and indicating its possibility or truthfulness. This form of 'beyond' – the possible being pointed out – has two dimensions, spatial and temporal: the 'out of sight' and the 'not yet'. Pointing is about sharing the possibility of something to come over there.

I'll jump now to the logical consequence of this fascinating human story of pointing, which Tallis wittily calls the *God Finger*. Here we transcend both sensory perception and causal logic, and glimpse possibilities 'beyond' that are spiritual rather than material. Tallis's important insight, however, is that this level of the transcendent has not been arrived at through a magical and discontinuous leap; rather, it is a logical continuity of the primary capability of pointing – which at each developmental stage takes us further in the process of 'crossing over'. At a spiritual level, transcendence is still concerned with the realm of *possibility*, but the pointing towards involves not the everyday forms of space and time but rather ideas of space and time that Tallis calls our 'intuition of the hidden' that we want to share with others:

> The transcendent, which is the most salient condition of our being able to point, and which is then enhanced by pointing, is rooted in the intuition of the hidden, in the presence or reality of that which is in the unobserved, absent, beyond … It is this – transcendence, the present of the absent that pointing, ultimately, points to. (Tallis 2010, p. 119)

This 'beyond pointed out by pointing' often involves our thinking about and thinking through our personal ending – and towards the ultimate and intractably hidden realm 'beyond' our own time and space on this earth. Tallis talks at the end of his book of witnessing a person close to death, whom he describes as occasionally making a gesture that he took to be 'pointing out the end of pointing' (p. 142).

છ

How does music 'point beyond' in this way?

Music does not operate in a visual, spatial field such that it can point *to* things, neither does it have discrete linguistic signs that can point *out* things.[12] But to

---

[11] Autistic children typically fail to point, not appreciating that the content of minds is shareable; whilst people with psychosis are frustrated when we cannot share the particular immediate reality that they perceive and point towards.

[12] Tallis takes the visual field as the basis for our being able to think beyond, to grasp the 'God finger'. For him, the visual field is privileged because it's always an intact and

state it negatively in this way is perhaps to get nearer to how music *can* indeed afford pointing *beyond*, to the 'present of the absent', making it somehow explicit and shared – even when ambiguous, as in the example above with Gisela. As we've previously explored, music is the transcendent medium *par excellence*. This begins with the 'everyday transcendence' of tone over sound. As soon as an acoustic sound is 'musicalised', it becomes a 'charged' symbol within a dynamic field of other tones, naturally pointing beyond itself in order to connect with other tones in musical motion and interaction. As Zuckerkandl suggests,

> At this point the audible breaks away ... from its correlation with visible–tangible things. As tone follows tone, as the tones become melody, in the midst of the audible world a door opens; we enter, as though in a dream or a fairy tale, not so much into another world as another mode of existence within our familiar world. (1973, p. 87)

In music we are able to 'hear the inaudible', and sometimes to metaphorically transfer our intuition of what is to come in music – its unique shaping of a temporal/spatial 'hidden dimension' – into our thinking about the transcendent, as yet unheard in other areas of our life. We use, that is, our aural senses of outer and 'inner' hearing to grasp something of the transcendent. But this is not because music has directly pointed *to* or pointed *out* something, but because of the process and quality of the musical gesturing itself as apprehended by us. Again, as Zuckerkandl explains:

> Tones ... *point to* something. The meaning of a tone, however, lies not in what it points to but *in* the pointing itself; more precisely, in the different way, in the individual gesture, with which each tone points toward the same place. The meaning is not the thing indicated but the manner of indicating .... (1973, p. 68)

Zuckerkandl wants us to appreciate that music gives a testimony to how the limits of our understanding of the external world are not defined only by what is physically perceptible. But the problem is that, as soon as we think of music 'as the voice of the "other" world', we distort music's potential spiritual lesson and its challenge to our assumptions about everyday reality. What music testifies to, rather, is the existence of an 'inner world' that is not just a property of our personal subjectivity, but also a property of the external world too – the world's 'interior', which is *our* 'exterior'. And it's *this* paradoxical dimension that is properly the

---

continuous field of perception: we see that there's something beyond (over the horizon), something hidden (within something else), and this experience allows us to see the unseen – or rather, to transfer this experience to our thinking about the 'beyond'/unseen. Tallis writes, however, that 'sounds are not linked by a continuous field of sound, and we do not hear the inaudible' (2010, p. 123). But – and, strangely, this is not noted by Tallis – music does have exactly this property of being a dynamic field of continuous linked sounds that become tonal pointers – as we've seen in Zuckerkandl's phenomenology of music. This affords the kind of 'transcendent pointing' that I'm discussing in this section.

spiritual realm of music. The real transcendence to which music opens the door for us is a 'further' audible world accessible through our 'second hearing' (a version of 'second sight'). But this need not be mystical or magical. It rests on the simple fact that music's phenomenology provides a medium that is free of the paradox inherent in the world of sight – of pointing towards nothing! Because in music, it's *the gesture of pointing itself* that affords and carries the transcendent experience: 'In musical tones, being, existence, is indistinguishable from, *is*, pointing-beyond-itself, meaning, saying' (1956, p. 371). We can climb onto the intentional arc of music's going-towards-somewhere with a confidence that the journey is real even if the destination is hidden. Something emerges from our encounters with music that can therefore be experienced as transcendent without feeling *other*-worldly:

> this kind of 'emergence' does not resemble the lifting of a veil, as when something hitherto invisible suddenly becomes visible. What happens, rather, is that something crosses the threshold of existence: something that never existed, save potentially, now is made actual. (Zuckerkandl 1973, p. 343)

ଚ

> **Ken:** To me, this is what music really is... it's *there*, it's telling us there's more in the world than we imagine... or more than our everyday walking-around consciousness points us to. So music for me, it's like a pointer... and it's similar to what Zuckerkandl says: that the presence of music proves to us that there's an existence beyond the material. That's why I emphasise the liminality of music – the whole thing music teaches us... that the purpose *isn't* the destination... the purpose of the theme isn't to get to the end, but *the process of getting there*! And this is music's profound lesson: we're all getting to the same place, but it's the transitions that are important, not the places!

How Music Speaks

Part VI has quite naturally gathered a religious or spiritual vocabulary in order to talk about its topics: *transcendence, epiphany, hope, beauty, ecstasy, manifestation, parable, revelation, threshold, the beyond....* I've not used this discourse to shoehorn musicking into a spiritual perspective, but have rather followed the phenomenon, allowing people and ideas to speak in the language that comes most easily. But this material has also circled around the paradox that, whilst music can seemingly speak to people so assuredly of the transcendental, they often find it impossible to speak about this outside the musical experience itself.

> **Susanna:** So music speaks to me very directly... but I'm not sure it's saying anything terribly specific. If I think it's saying *anything*, it's saying something to do with life having a value. It's not quite a meaning, because that gets you back into, 'What does it mean then?' It's rather that it points to a value that for me borders on a religious expression. There's something in music that demonstrates a fundamental *rightness* to things... against all expectations,

> and all observations to the contrary. It's so difficult to express, I can't think
> of a better word for 'rightness'… perhaps 'harmony', but then we're talking in
> circles, because this is a musical metaphor!

But perhaps we *should* stay with the musical metaphor, acknowledge that music and musicking is a valid non-verbal means of pointing towards and beyond. Music affords one of the best examples of the 'pattern which connects', the pattern that we intuitively transfer from music to a personal and often shared search, longing and appreciation for wholeness and transcendence.

Music therapist Rachel Verney remembers how, more than thirty years ago, Nordoff and Robbins developed the concept of the 'music child' to express the natural and responsive musicality of the damaged children they were working with then. Rather like Plato's *holon*,[13] this concept communicated an understanding that Nordoff and Robbins had come to through their work and that they believed was true for everyone: that there is a core wholeness and healthfulness to all of us that we can find particular access to through music. It's this region that we touch when we are touched by music; it's this region that we turn to when we return to music.

> **Rachel:** This idea of the 'music child' was an attempt to try to say how there's
> something about people which is whole and healthy and which responds to the
> call of music. But it's also *hope*, and its *love*, and it's *beauty*… and it promises
> the impossible! It's absolutely a spiritual concept… there's no question.
>
> You see for me this is why it's so important to say that when I talk about
> 'spiritual' I'm not talking about any other place, longing to leave this reality and
> go to another. I'm talking about the fullness of this reality. So I'm not saying
> that we need to fly along the beams of music into heaven. I just think that
> we become more wholly who we are when we recognise and live this spiritual
> reality. It feels 'other' because we exclude it so much. So I think this is where we
> have to be so careful when we talk about 'the spiritual', because people think
> we mean elsewhere, and it isn't! [*bangs table, laughs*] It's this *hope*, knowing
> the fullness of our reality, not just little bits of it, but the whole of it. And that
> in us which makes music… and longs for music… reaches out to it… is called
> by it… this aspect of us is *whole*… is capable of living wholly, and healthily and
> completely.

---

[13] In the *Phaedrus*, Socrates says that we can't know anything about the human body or soul without knowing the whole, the *holon* of nature. Gadamer writes: 'For *holon* is also that which is intact or undamaged, that which is sound and healthy' (1996, p. 88).

Conclusion
Musical Flourishing

- We love music because we need music.
- Music can help us because we are all musical.
- Musical experience is something done with others, not something that happens privately. Our musical experiences help us explore, create and enhance our lives.
- Musical experiences helpfully link music's world with the everyday world.
- Music helps by addressing our basic human needs - for recognition as persons, identity, relationship, community, transcendence.
- There is a musical core to these basic needs.
- Understanding how music helps is a way of understanding music, and people.
- This could help us value music and people more.
- Good music is music that does good.
- Bringing good music to those who need it is a matter of justice.
- When music flourishes, people flourish too.

ॐ

I hope that the complementary voices, stories and explorations of the 'voyagers', 'locals' and 'scholars' have made a convincing case to support these perhaps radical statements. The main point I've wanted to argue in this book is that there is no intrinsic difference between how music helps in everyday life and within the specialist area of music therapy. Where the examples from music therapy have been useful, however, is to bring more sharply into focus how unerringly music locates and then addresses our basic human needs and capabilities. A music therapist's specialist skill is to midwife music's help in situations where people can't necessarily access it for themselves. But I don't think this warrants the still-prevalent tendency to separate thinking about 'music in music therapy' from 'music in everyday life'. I've suggested instead how a more fruitful path will be to explore the basic continuity between them, and to see how they illuminate each other. Following this path has led me to a more ecological way of thinking about music, people and wellbeing that could in turn make us value music in ways that help us decide how best to use music in our society. In this conclusion, I'll summarise this perspective and suggest where it points.[1]

---

[1] This conclusion draws from material in Ansdell and DeNora 2012.

Figure C.1   Musical wellbeing matrix

In Need of Music

This book has taken us 'into the middle' of how music helps people and situations. From this perspective, we've seen that music helps not because it's a 'magic pill' – doing something *to* us – but rather because of how we manage to draw it towards us and actively work with what it offers. We are all, albeit in varying degrees, music lovers and music needers; we are attracted by music, and drawn into a relationship with it that can be supportive, sustaining, and even lifesaving. This relationship to music is possible because we are essentially musical persons. Music therapy shows up the need for rethinking and redefining what 'musicality' means. Rather than just a talent (though it can be this too), musicality is a natural sensitivity and responsiveness to music, perhaps better thought of as a faculty such as speech. We all have the capacity to musick, even if it's cultivated in different ways and engaged with at different levels.

A relationship with music is, however, seldom an exclusive personal relationship. Rather, to be a music lover is usually to extend and address your musical passion towards others – to become people lovers too, as music helps you to make a better relationship with yourself, with other people, with your community, and with the 'beyond'. Musicking helps us to come fully into a life with others and with the world, whilst at the same time serving as a way of stabilising and elaborating the self. Generally, music helps us to find what is good in our lives with others.

The 'wordle' matrix (Fig. C.1) presents the main core themes from this book. It portrays a complex blend of human needs, forms of life, values and 'virtues' [2]

---

[2]   By 'virtue' here, I mean a skill or attitude that guides our action to fit with the values we hold. For example, musical listening as a virtue affords recognition and communication;

These themes describe individual, relational and social qualities, activities and processes, and give a holistic picture of body, mind, spirit and soul. But tellingly, they give no indication that anyone linked with them is either sick or healthy in any objective sense. Rather, they portray what the sick, healthy, young and old share as core human needs: recognition and development as a person; good relationships; being in community with others; experiencing the transcendent. In Parts I to VI, many of these themes were preceded by the adjective 'musical' – where we explored how these human needs, forms of life, values and virtues were elicited, characterised, developed, supported, modified or transformed specifically in relation to situations involving music and musicking.

Wellbeing through Musicking

Overall, this pattern points towards a holistic and comprehensive territory of musical experience to which voyagers and locals bear equal witness. Here there's no separation of body, mind and spirit, or the personal and the social, or the everyday and the professional. The concept of wellbeing perhaps best characterises this territory. The matrix portrays the enabling conditions of wellbeing that can be cultivated or supported by music and musicking. Not all of the elements in the matrix will be significant to everyone all the time, but most will support our wellbeing at some stage of our lives.

Although the word 'wellbeing' has been distorted by its current commercial uses, its rich meanings are still helpful in exploring a more nuanced understanding of human needs (Vernon 2008; Webster 2002; Carel 2008). The origins of 'wellbeing' lie in Aristotle's concept *eudaimonia* – often translated as 'happiness', but more accurately 'higher flourishing'. To be *eudaimon* is to be a 'happy spirit' – someone who has a 'good life' by managing to balance aspects of health, contentment, social harmony, virtue, and an attention to what the philosopher Mark Vernon wittily calls the 'spirit level' (2008, p. 7).

In a sense, the conceptual move from health to wellbeing parallels that from music to musicking. That is, something that has become too objectified and thing-like in our thinking is re-imagined as a performed activity that takes place within a broader ecology. Western scientific medicine still clings to a concept of health that is largely mechanistic, individualistic and curative. Wellbeing, in contrast, can accommodate a more performative and ecological picture of being well. It can deal with some of the paradoxes we've come across in this book: of being well whilst being physically very ill or disabled, or even when dying; of defining health not just in material terms but also from relational, social and spiritual perspectives; and, lastly, of seeing how our being well is not necessarily specifiable just here and now, but is also a matter of past history, ongoing identity and future transcendence.

---

musical communication affords acceptance and cooperation.

For each of us, our wellbeing has a key subjective quality that is based on a complex combination of personal, social and existential factors, many of which are mapped by the pattern of themes in Fig. C.1. We do not 'have' wellbeing, but rather it emerges *between* us and the people, things, events, situations and processes of our lives. Wellbeing can often only be achieved indirectly, and only with the substantial help and support of the surrounding social ecology. 'Wellbeing' as a concept nudges us towards a more subtle appreciation of 'feeling good'.

In the Preface of this book, I quoted Cleo saying that, through singing again in a music therapy project, she had reached a level of wellbeing that she'd not experienced for thirty years. Cleo chooses the word 'wellbeing' intuitively, I think. But it matches how I've suggested that music (and especially music within music therapy) is not primarily a quick fix for specific problems or symptoms, but rather about finding a quality of wellness *within* illness, or, as Cleo also said, of finding through music that the wellness in her was a stronger force than her illness. So wellbeing is not just the absence of illness, or just an individual matter, or just the provision of 'health technologies'. The concept prompts us to consider instead how health and illness often exist together within a continuum, not as opposites; to attend more to when and how people can be well whilst 'ill' by medical definition; and to explore what offers the possibility of wellbeing – which may not be the same as what treats our sickness. This takes us back to Aristotle's original notion of *eudaimonia* – that flourishing is dependent on, and supported by, a range of 'goods' that blend material, ethical and aesthetic qualities, activities and processes. Together, these form the necessary ecology for wellbeing as human flourishing.

The matrix above characterises just such a pattern of conditions for human wellbeing that are afforded and helped by music and musicking. In short, it portrays *musical flourishing*.

The Magic of Music's Everyday Powers

People believe more than ever perhaps that music has powers to enhance health and wellbeing in this way. But whilst as a music therapist I'm only too happy to capitalise on this tide of enthusiasm and support, I've also wanted to explore more cautiously just *how* music's powers work. I believe them to be essentially worldly rather than magical – or perhaps, as Tia DeNora (2013) suggests, 'magic–realist'. That is, music's powers are essentially mirrors of *our* individual and social powers, and as such are dependent on our ongoing ability to realise and to cultivate them. Of course, with this qualification there's also the danger of going to the opposite extreme and explaining away music as a phantom, or simply an 'alibi' for a more mundane effect. So what I've looked for in this book is a middle ground where music's unique essence certainly shows up, but only in relation to our human activities and needs. DeNora's twinned concepts of musical affordance and musical appropriation are key here. Music's powers are related to its unique properties and affordances *as music* – but these are only realised in and through how we pick up and mobilise these affordances through situated musical experience and action. Musical affordances always need specifying, understanding and exploring in use and in context, not seen as a pre-designed stimulus or effect that is assumed to work for anyone, anywhere. All this is to say that music offers its help in specifically musical ways that match its phenomenology as this entangles with everyday life - its *eco*-phenomenology, that is. In the sense that a square wheel offers a poor affordance for mobility, so too sounds, gestures, things and situations become music – and musical help – only as they afford musicking that matches our particular and situated human projects and needs. Square music doesn't dig round holes.

Such musical offerings – and their everyday and specialist mediation – have been viewed with increasing enthusiasm by those looking for alternative solutions for personal and social problems. A current temptation, however, is to over-instrumentalise music's helpful effects – and in doing so, to reduce music to a useful tool that can be rapidly operationalised, and its effects measured for immediate cost–benefit analysis. Within this mechanistic understanding, music is seen to directly relax or stimulate, to decrease depression, or to increase intelligence. It may do all of these things indirectly, but such effects are mostly not what it does best, or indeed is primarily for. If anything, when music is turned into a hammer with a single nail as its focus, it loses its power. Musicking is seldom a single means to a single end, but rather a complex medium that has qualities that usually transcend any specific purpose. Music is not primarily just a way of getting something done, but a way of doing things, or rather an indication of *how* to do things – *musically*. As such, musicking has value and purpose as an end in itself. Paradoxically, this is exactly how it achieves other things. In this book, I've explored this 'adverbial quality' – the *musical* composition of personhood, identity, relationship, community and transcendence. But it seems that these subtle but powerful musical affordances only show up when music retains its wholeness as a phenomenon; when it remains musical.

As a way of clarifying this distinction, I've suggested thinking about the *para-musical*. Traditionally there has been a clear but false division between the 'purely musical' and the 'extra-musical' (that is, non-musical). Seeing music as more fluid and continuous within human experience and practice would rather suggest how *para*-musical phenomena accompany or work beside the musical, whilst not being purely musical themselves. Rather, the musical and the paramusical substantiate and transsubstantiate each other – the 'musicality' of a movement, communication or style of identity shows up for us within musicking. But these aspects are not necessarily separable *from* the music: they are an aspect *of* the musicking and not just a result of it (and as such are para-musical rather than 'extra-musical'). A paramusical phenomenon is always wrapped up in the immediate ecology and need of a situation, and is never an abstract entity that you could isolate – either during or afterwards. Take away the music, and the paramusical feature can also disappear – even if its echo often remains. This is perhaps no more than saying that overall we must preserve musicking for its own sake, not to achieve something else (even when it often does just this).

To show music active within the world of human projects and needs is to champion an ecological approach. In short, a 'musical ecology' describes how musical people, music things and musical occasions all support and flow creatively in and out of each other. This view perhaps helps with a problem that seems to have bedevilled thinking about music for decades: the temptation either to explain it away (as a tool for other social or psychological phenomena) or to isolate it and inflate it into an autonomous object. We need, instead, a different way of approaching the question, 'What is music?', by catching it within action and situation – which is where it best declares its identity, character and purpose. As John Blacking writes somewhat surprisingly (for an anthropologist) in *How Musical is Man?*, 'I am concerned primarily with what music is, and not what it is used for. If we know what it is, we might be able to use and develop it in all kinds of ways that have not yet been imagined, but which may be inherent in it' (1973, p. 26). Exploring how music helps could be a good way of furthering our understanding of music as a phenomenon – just as understanding people can be furthered by understanding them as musical.

The Conditions of Musical Flourishing

Cleo uses a spontaneous ecological metaphor to describe how she recovered her wellbeing during a difficult year with music's help. She characterises herself as 'a little shoot' appearing again and being nurtured: 'I'm developing a bit here and there... with a little bit of water and a little bit of sunshine... you know... it's part of a whole context'. Her 'musical flourishing' needs the whole context to create its optimal conditions. Firstly, there are the 'internal' conditions, which in Cleo's example are the intuition that her newfound wellbeing is linked to her reconnection to her musicality and to her musical capacities, and then that this somehow both contained and mobilised her wellness. But this inner resource also needed several external conditions to help it emerge, in what Cleo characterises as the 'little bit of water' and 'little bit of sunshine'. These conditions for her included the support of the music therapists, her peers in the music group, other professional staff, and the physical availability of a 'stage' on which to sing the performance of her newly emerging wellness during the weekly café music group. If health is a performance then we need to give attention to its necessary 'rehearsal process', props, staging, and its witnessing 'audience'. We also need to attend to the layers of the ecological system that ripple outwards and inwards to the immediate person or event: the material, attitudinal and political dimensions that create either the facilitating or limiting factors to musical performances of health. The following interdependent conditions for musical flourishing become usefully more visible the more extreme the situation.

Musical Access

Music has power and benefit only to the extent that we can appropriate what it affords. What music offers is always in a reciprocal and complementary relationship to what we need of it, how its properties show up in terms of this need, and how we are able to access, grasp and do something with it in a given situation for ourselves, or with others. For most of us, the resources and processes of culture, technology and social life bring music effortlessly into our world – for us to experience, shape, and pass on again. But when there are barriers, what is previously relatively invisible comes starkly into view. The practice of music therapy forefronts in a useful way how musical access is at once a material, relational and ecological concern – and how a helpful musical experience is related to where you are, what you can do, and who assists.

I've suggested how the process of musical appropriation relies on two factors within music therapy situations (and in other forms of music work). Firstly, access often stems from people's core attraction to music, and their motivation to make music sometimes leads to heroic feats of appropriation. But secondly, there's the therapist's craft and discernment in facilitating or mediating this appropriation – through a variety of skilled ways of bringing music and musicking within reach, such that its affordances show up and are useable by someone. We've seen how the flexibility of improvisation helps here – underpinned by the therapist's art of 'listening musically' to a person, and for their potential for participation. It's also based on the music therapist's knowledge of how the musical affordances of a variety of resources match a particular need and situation. This includes appraising how technology and formats of musicking[3] elicit musicality, cultivate musicianship, and provide satisfactory occasions for musicking. This might also involve the practical matter of 'assistive technologies', where access routes to musicking are the equivalent to providing ramps for wheelchairs or hearing loops. We've seen how wellbeing is a situational and environmental achievement, and so when the local ecology is re-formed and adapted, certain inabilities can recede and abilities and opportunities can be supported.

Musical Ethics

However, disabling doesn't only come from problems with practical or material access. The barriers to inclusion and participation are also ethical and relational. Social and cultural exclusions based on thoughts, attitudes, values, judgements and relations can be equally disabling and disempowering. This is the province of practical (or 'virtue') ethics – by which I mean how the choices we make about

---

[3] By 'formats', I mean the difference between how a one-to-one session, a group, workshop, rehearsal, performance event, instrument lesson or concert visit offers specific affordances that relate to specific needs or capability building. See Wood 2006.

what is good and what helps further or limit our mutual flourishing.[4] The necessary parallel strategy to re-forming material access to musicking is the re-forming of ethical and aesthetic relationships as necessary conditions for musical flourishing.

We've seen in this book how an attention to musicking in the service of human needs naturally brings in ethical concerns. This often begins within musicking itself, rather than with words and concepts. The core of this area can be summed up by the simple question, 'What is good musicking?' Notice how this is different from the time-honoured philosophical conundrum, 'What is good *music*?' We all have personal and culturally based ideas about the latter question if it's thought about in terms of a specific musician, piece of music, style or format. Focus, rather, on the process of musicking and it leads us to think more about aspects of human relatedness, conduct, values and virtues (as summarised in the matrix above). Exploring musical personhood, identity, relationship, community, and transcendence leads to the core but more elusive question: *What are the values of musicking?* This puts ethics and aesthetics back into closer proximity.

My suggestion of an answer is that musicking helps to orientate us to the general conditions of human flourishing. This includes a sometimes messy but productive interlinking of: (i) *human needs* – e.g. for recognition, self-definition, vitality, creativity, communication, companionship, belonging, transcendence; (ii) *forms of life, action and conduct* that help address these – e.g. listening, ritual, collaborating; (iii) *values* that motivate these – uniqueness, freedom, dignity, care, beauty, etc.; and (iv) *virtues* that help orientate such action – love, hope, attention, trust, hospitality, etc.

Musicking is an enactment of such an ethical system during the time of its performance, and after. It's an ethical practice before it's a theory. Yes, there are of course those much-quoted, glaring counter-examples of string quartets played in concentration camps, or rock music used for torture or to motivate tank crews. But ethical conversations need such anomalies and complexities to help to define the broader, commonsense consensus. Tia DeNora (2013) suggests that, from an ecological perspective, aesthetic judgements about 'musical goodness' are always necessarily relational, temporal and situational. We always need to ask, that is, 'good for *whom*?', and follow this up with *When? Where? How?* Further, we are always balancing the two dimensions of what '*is* good' (in terms of properties, affordances and cultural preferences) alongside what '*does* good' in any specified time, place and circumstance. As in life in general, a shadow often falls between these two factors, alerting us to the difficulties of thinking ethically about particular situations and their unique moral dilemmas.

However, I maintain overall that the uncorrupted examples are the more instructive: that 'good musicking' is at root an ethical practice that both focuses human needs and provides a way of addressing them through an orientation to what is good, beautiful and true. Here, the processes, values and virtues that are

---

[4]   This perspective draws from the tradition of 'virtue ethics' and the more recent trend of 'citizen ethics'.

called out and cultivated by the demands, pleasures and potentials of musicking are ultimately in the service of human flourishing.

Musical Justice

Because of its non-verbal nature, it's easy for music to slip under the radar of politics – despite its increasingly acknowledged power as a medium of both benign and more questionable social influence (Brown and Volgsten 2006). Music therapy has likewise traditionally downplayed its political dimension – perhaps because of the individualism and medicalism of its main adoptive theories. This situation is changing as broader psycho-sociocultural approaches are cultivating a much-needed political dimension. Stige and Aarø, for example, describe Community Music Therapy as a 'rights-based practice' that emerges 'where human rights challenges and socio-musical possibilities meet' (2012, p. 199). But this movement is only pointing out what has always been implicitly true for music therapy, and for any use of music that addresses human needs: that political values such as justice, dignity, equality, respect and solidarity are really core, not peripheral to any practice that works towards human flourishing.

Do we all have a right to musick? Surely so – if we follow the case that musicking helps, enhances, and perhaps even sometimes saves, lives. But such 'rights to musick' go beyond ensuring the conditions of practical access and ethical relations we've already discussed. Rather, behind the basic freedom to pursue 'good musicking' in any way that nurtures and furthers wellbeing surely stands a more fundamental virtue: *justice.*

A traditional, liberal rights-based perspective would situate its talk of social justice in terms of broad values of equal opportunity and equal access to resources, where human needs and human rights are as well balanced as possible for everyone. Entitlement is not earned but deserved, following from core values such as fairness, equality, dignity, and respect. In the name of these values, we work to remove barriers to others' social and cultural participation. A related way of thinking attends to human *capabilities,* focusing on the core question, 'What are people actually able to do and to be?' (Nussbaum 2011, p. x). This aligns with ecological thinking well in stressing how full human potential or capability always calls to be nurtured and supported, and that this is often a matter of the quality of the surrounding conditions (material, relational and spiritual). This not only takes in human needs but also acknowledges our 'higher flourishing' – our need and right to develop, extend and make a 'good life' for ourselves.

However, there is also a third way of thinking about justice in relation to a social resource such as music. Political theorist Michael Sandel uses Aristotle's musical analogy in a discussion of a more challenging principle of justice. A test for deciding how to distribute limited resources according to this approach is to think of purpose. Aristotle asks his pupils who should receive the best flutes, and the answer they give is that the best musicians should have them. The reason is that the *telos* or purpose of flutes is to create the best sound – this is what they are *good* for. And the best players are needed to make the best sounds, whatever the needs or virtues of the others who would also like a flute. Whilst this logic might seem a little strange to us today, Sandel explains how it leads to a useful conversation on values in relation to justice. 'Justice,' he writes, 'is not only about the right way to distribute things. It is also about the right way to value things' (2010, p. 261).

You may think that I'm leading down a contradictory path here given the very liberal argument of this book – that at the end I'm suddenly arguing that music should be available only to those who can make the best sound (albeit that it's clear that this judgement is inevitably relative). Rather, Aristotle and Sandel's argument is helpful for rethinking our basic musical values – which is where I think the argument in this book is pointing towards.

The Value of Music

Pam wanted to talk to me about the cutbacks in the hospital that will probably threaten services such as music therapy. 'I know the managers think it's a luxury,' she said, 'but it's not for me – it's a lifesaver'.

∞

How do we value music in our society? What is music for? Who gets it? This depends. In the music industry, music still has high value as a commodity to be produced and marketed. For consumers of these musical products, it has entertainment value. For a smaller group of connoisseurs across several styles, there are 'great works' that have transcendent value as almost museum pieces to be preserved and treasured, and both amateur and professional performances are evaluated on the shifting sands of fashion and reputation, often looping back into market forces and fashion trends.

In this book, I've tried to show that a focus on how music offers help and care highlights a radical and alternative way of valuing music and seeing what it's really for – and even perhaps for understanding what it really 'is'. My experiences as a music therapist have convinced me that the most valuable use of music is to maintain and enrich the quality of our personal, social and spiritual lives. This has been common knowledge and practice in many other times and places, but needs renewing in our culture today.

Aristotle and Sandel propose the analogy of symbolic flutes and flautists as a way of exploring core value and purpose. If we keep this within the realm of music and society (rather than the broader moral territory they expand into), we can ask the simple question, *Who should get music?* Our answer depends, of course, on how we value music, and this in turn relates to how we link music's purpose with people and their needs. If we have a wider understanding of its purpose (as I hope has come out of this book) then we also need to have a different understanding of the value of music, and consequently what 'musical justice' might mean. If music can be so helpful (or in some cases, crucial) to having and maintaining a good life, then is this not what music is *good for* overall? If we take this question seriously, how we distribute those symbolic flutes will need to be very different in the future. And having distributed them, we shall also need to have a very different idea about how to cultivate the capacities of our symbolic flute players and their various opportunities for good musicking. Music's powers must be justly deployed if they're to empower.

The world could sound different.

The Love of Music

This book has shown how loving music and needing music often belong fruitfully together. As Rachel explained, it's 'that in us which makes music... and longs for music... reaches out to it... is called by it... this aspect of us is *whole*... is capable of living wholly, and healthily and completely'. A perfect description of *eudaimonia* incarnated as *musical flourishing*.

We've also seen how wellbeing as flourishing rests on what's good in itself, a thing done for its own sake, because you love doing it. *Love*: is this the true core of musicking, and its strong yet mysterious link to wellbeing? This is not primarily love as *eros* (though this often accompanies musicking), nor even the friendship-type love of *philia* that lights up musical companionship and community, but perhaps yet another distinctive form of sensibility that the Greeks identified as *kalos*. As Mark Vernon explains,

> the primary concern, if the goal is wellbeing ... is what you love ... because love is desire for the good, and wellbeing is living alongside the good. There is a synthesis here, reflected in the Greek word for beauty, *kalos*, which also means good and honourable, and, as an adverb, rightly and happily. (Vernon 2008, pp. 124 and 125)

The love of doing something that brings recognition of beauty as goodness can provide an 'education' in loving. Music does not, of course, make people love each other – but it helps with this. This was the conclusion that John Blacking also came to from his long-term immersion into the musical culture of the Venda tribe of South Africa. 'Problems in human societies begin when people learn less about love,' wrote Blacking (1973, p. 28). 'The hard task is to love, and music is a skill that prepares man for this most difficult task' (1973, p. 103). This highlights a final distinction that we've been gradually building up to through this book: that when we say that music helps, what we are really saying is that music helps us to help each other.

When music flourishes, people flourish too. People love music, and they love musicking together. It is not difficult to understand why. This is how music helps.

Appendix
A Note on Method

The appreciation of any phenomenon calls for a phenomenological method …
Our approach tries to penetrate the phenomenon itself. We walk around it from
many sides (circumambulation), expand it by turning up its volume (amplification),
distinguish amongst its everyday appearances (differentiation). We want more of its
character to shine forth; epiphanies, revelations.

James Hillman[1]

… it is the obersver's first duty to discover every condition under which a
phenomenon may occur, and to aim at the completeness of the phenomena, since
they actually form a series, or rather are forced to interpenetrate, so that they will
present themselves to one's observation as an organisation manifesting an inner life
of its own.

Johann Wolfgang von Goethe[2]

This book was not intended primarily as a research study, though it is certainly
informed and inspired by research (my own, my colleagues', and current
interdisciplinary scholarship), and its explorative methods draw from several
research traditions. Equally, it is not just a work of theory, or a straightforward
guide to practice. Rather, as it took shape, I came to think of this book as an
appreciative exploration of 'music's help', a complex phenomenon that is not only
highlighted by the specialist area of music therapy, but is also prevalent within
everyday life situations. Understanding the continuity of this phenomenon across
both these domains needed more than a conventional phenomenology of music,
and my aim differed from many traditional approaches to inquiry within music
therapy, music sociology, musicology, and music psychology (though it drew from
all of these). In the text, I've called my perspective an 'eco-phenomenology of
music's help', stressing the ecological sensitivity I've attempted. I've explored the
central phenomenon through a variety of methods – aiming to listen, watch, take
witness statements, and to follow in a variety of empirically grounded ways the
complex manifestations of music *in helpful action* in people's lives. I've tried to
track where, when and how it helps them in specific situations. The characteristics
and processes of music's help tend to retreat or turn inert within the laboratory, or in

---

[1]   Hillman 1999, p. 43.
[2]   Goethe, in Naydler 1996, p. 83.

armchair theorising, or when not actively working within the immediate activities and needs of our everyday lives, or more specialist contexts. This dimension of music and musicking needs then a particular kind of exploration that ensures that the method is adequate to the phenomenon.

I took inspiration for such an adequate method from a lesser-known aspect of the Nordoff–Robbins music therapy tradition, one that has provided it with a particular approach to practice-based theory and research. This originated in Nordoff and Robbins's personal and professional association with Anthroposophy, a philosophical–spiritual tradition that developed a 'qualitative science' with epistemological and methodological approaches deriving largely from Rudolf Steiner's study and editing of Goethe's scientific works (Steiner 1886/2008; Bortoft 1996). Nordoff and Robbins used this style of practical theorising to help them to develop and research their approach to music therapy (Ansdell and Pavlicevic 2010). Key to this is a methodological attitude stemming from Goethe and Steiner that has been termed *gentle empiricism*[3] (Naydler 1996). This emphasises that understanding in both natural and human realms should first strive to 'save the phenomenon' – that is, the thing being explored should not be damaged, abstracted or reduced in the attempt to grasp and understand it. Equally, when theorising, the qualitative phenomenon should not be replaced by an abstract explanation that omits either human experience or the ecological situation of its typical occurrence.[4] As Nigel Hoffmann puts it, Goethe's aim with 'gentle empiricism' was 'to let the phenomena speak. To this end, he knew he had to be most delicate in the way he applied concepts – so that pre-formed mental grooves did not force the phenomena into particular conceptual frameworks' (2007, p. x).

Mercédès Pavlicevic and I have summarised the key methodological aspects of such a gentle empiricism in relation to exploring music therapy in the following sequence of suggested commitments:

- Following a 'gentle empiricism' means allowing the emergent phenomena (of people-in-music, therapy-in-music, music-and-health) to show themselves.
- Exploring a phenomenon within its natural setting as far as possible.
- Devoted to detail: 'listening through a microscope' to the micro-level particularity of the phenomenon of people-in-musical-relationship.
- Reverential – allowing love and will to guide the work and its exploration.
- Idiographic – attending to the individuality of each case, and of each manifestation of a phenomenon.

---

[3] Sometimes also translated as 'delicate empiricism'.

[4] There are fascinating if seldom-acknowledged connections between this intellectual/research tradition and the more contemporary traditions of qualitative research in the social sciences. Equally, many key figures in the humanities, such as Wittgenstein, Zuckerkandl, Freud and Schenker, were also influenced by Goethe's scientific philosophy.

- Seriated – building a collection of exemplary cases for demonstration and comparison.
- Theoretically 'agnostic' – allowing theory to emerge and demonstrate its fit, rather than fitting phenomena to extant theory.
- Holistic: searching for the varying circumstances in which the same phenomenon occurs. (Ansdell and Pavlicevic 2010, p. 134)

Most of these commitments can be seen in the range of methods I've utilised in preparing and presenting this book. My overall intention has been to allow the phenomenon of 'music's help' to show and sound itself through its varying aspects, and their consistencies and variations across cases and contexts. This represents the 'circumambulation' aspect of the phenomenological method, as described by the psychologist James Hillman (1999). Key here is that music's help is both presented and theorised in action, and in situation. In particular, the following methods and theoretical approaches were used in order to generate the three key perspectives – from 'voyagers', 'locals', and 'scholars':

Case Series

The 'voyagers' are represented by a series of case studies and vignettes that I've collected from my own practice and from that of my colleagues over the last twenty-five years. It's a commonplace of therapeutic disciplines (from Freud to Oliver Sacks) that some cases seem almost to present themselves to therapists for detailed scrutiny. Importantly, the 'exemplary case' is not seen as atypical, but one that because of its clarity and particular narrative force presents the key elements and principles that underlie the more mundane. A phenomenological inquiry utilises this 'amplification', letting the exemplary case show us more through how its key features sound out and guide further scrutiny.

However, good case study method needs more than narrative: it also needs a high level of empirical detail to tease below the surface, to explore the fine grain of the case, and to guard against ungrounded interpretation. Here I've been influenced both by how Nordoff and Robbins interrogated the detail of their cases observationally through careful description and microanalysis of audio (and later video) recordings of music therapy, and by the detailed grounded empiricism of the case study approach deriving from the ethnographic tradition, as presented in an exemplary way in Tia DeNora's (2000, 2003) studies of music in everyday life.

The 'voyager' cases gradually form an accumulating and developing series throughout this book, providing a more 'synoptic' view of the overall phenomenon of 'music's help'. Each case necessarily presents its uniqueness, as well as mirroring aspects of the others, helping to show what aspects are common.

Qualitative Ethnographic Interviewing

The data from the 'locals' forms a second strand to the book. Face-to-face interviewing is a mainstay of qualitative research, and the style and attitude towards this method informed my approach.. I interviewed twenty-one people in depth over the course of more than ten years, selecting them simply when the opportunity presented itself. They were a 'purposive sample', in the jargon – that is, they were selected because of how well I thought they could answer the questions that I had for them – i.e., about how helpful music was in their and other people's lives. I made no attempt to find people for whom this was not the case. As I explain in the Preface, it does not discredit an exploration of a phenomenon to say that it is only operative at certain times and places, and with certain people. I talked to people who were informed by experience in one way or another such that they could tell me interesting things about the subject. To some extent, there is a range of ages, types of people, musical experience, and life experience – but I did not sample strategically to obtain such a range. Unsurprisingly, many of my interviewees were also professional music therapists – they are, after all, experts in the territory. They talked about music's help from both personal and professional perspectives – which, of course, mirrored the key argument of this book that there is a smooth continuum between personal and professional knowledge in this area.

The 'locals' were as follows:[5]

- **Adam** is a music therapist
- **Alan** is a music therapist
- **Ben** is a musician
- **Christina** is a former journalist and amateur musician
- **David** is a music lover and psychotherapist
- **Diane** is a music therapist
- **Fraser** is a music therapist
- **Jane** is an academic music psychologist and singer
- **Ken** is a music therapist
- **Matthew** is a music therapist
- **Mercédès** is a music therapist
- **Michael** is a community musician and teacher based in the anthroposophical tradition
- **Nigel** is a senior manager in healthcare and music therapist
- **Oksana** is a music therapist
- **Oliver** is a passionate amateur listener to all kinds of music
- **Peter** is an academic and semi-professional pianist
- **Rachel** is a music therapist

---

[5]   A few of the names are pseudonyms. The music therapists listed all have a host of other attributes, both as musicians and in terms of other professional and non-professional dimensions. Here, the purpose is simply to indicate their professional identity.

- **Richard** is a journalist, popular music biographer and music lover
- **Simon** is a senior manager of an international symphony orchestra
- **Susanna** is an amateur musician and social worker
- **Tony** is a music lover and former music therapy client

The interviews with these people were detailed and semi-structured, in that I attempted to cover similar areas through asking similar overall questions. But I generally followed where people wanted to go in their accounts of music and its help for them and others. I took inspiration both from ethnographic interviewing and from techniques such as Daniel Stern's (2004) 'breakfast interview' – trying to get interviewees to tell me what actually happens in their everyday experience and (inter-)action (rather than their *ideas* about this, or what they thought they should say). It's often better, that is, to ask someone what music they heard over breakfast than ask them, 'How does music help you?' The interviews were transcribed, themed and coded in a conventional way in order to explore both idiographic detail and cross-case associations and patterns. What is the factual status of this material? What people tell you in interviews is, of course, their *account* of their experience and action, not an objective record of such action and experience itself. But as such, it can be juxtaposed and compared with that of others 'in parallel', and with aspects of the cases of the 'voyagers'.

Emergent and Abductive Theorising

A more synoptic perspective began to emerge as the voices of the diverse material was 'triangulated' (or perhaps, to use a more musical metaphor, began to 'attune'). The discipline at this point is to listen to what is emerging, and not to shoehorn the 'evidence' into an extant and neat theoretical framework. At the same time, I certainly intended to differentiate, compare and contrast the material in order to see new connections, and old continuities. The Goethean, phenomenological stance on theory building is first to bear personal witness, then to gather, lay out comparatively, gently probe and explore – to the point that the holistic phenomenon begins to show itself in terms of itself. Theory is thus the uncovering, displaying and arranging of 'facts' such that they *become* theory – rather than starting with a prepared view and fitting the facts to the theory. As Goethe wrote, 'Theory, in and of itself, is useless unless it leads us to believe in the interrelationship of phenomena' (in Naydler 1996, p. 86).

'Looking' within, between and amongst the rich mass of data, and waiting for theory in this sense is also typical of the inductive stance of much contemporary qualitative research. I've been influenced in styles of data analysis and interpretation by such approaches as Grounded Theory and Interpretive Phenomenological Analysis (Smith and Osborn 2003).

A useful complement to inductive theory building is abduction – the disciplined but imaginative movement of thinking outwards towards extant ideas in other domains: looking there for a good match, similarities of observation, and suggestions of explanation for phenomena. This is different from assimilating, or being assimilated by, a single theoretical position from another discipline, in that abduction begins resolutely from your own territory, and then reaches out. In this book, the third group of informants – the 'scholars' – represent abducted theory. Their ideas are entertained in relation to the emerging ideas I have from my own sources. A model here for me was the perspective of the ecological interdisciplinary scholar Gregory Bateson, who was always looking out imaginatively for the relational 'pattern which connects'. Finally, more recent socio-ecological theory from Bruno Latour, Tia DeNora and Antoine Hennion has been influential in the way that I came to think about connecting together things, people, situations, histories and futures. I came to realise in a very Goethean way, that a fairly simple broadening shift in one's mental perspective or framework allows an ecology to reveal itself. It was always there, of course, but it requires a particular acuity of perception for it to become visible, audible and knowable.

I hope that together these methods of data identification, gathering, interpretation and theory building have allowed me to present a particular yet accurate picture of the phenomenon of music's help. As I say in the Preface, my aim is primarily to map this territory rather than to give a comprehensive explanatory framework for it. More work needs doing on almost all of the aspects that are highlighted throughout this book. But without a larger-scale synoptic view of the territory, these more specialist investigations can find themselves disoriented in relation to the richness and breadth of the phenomenon as a whole. This book has, I hope, helped the broad and rich phenemenon of music's help to come further into plain view.

Bibliography

Agassi, Judith Buber (ed.) (1999). *Martin Buber on Psychology and Psychotherapy: Essays, Letters, and Dialogues*. Syracuse, NY: Syracuse University Press.

Ahmed, Sarah (2006). *Queer Phenomenology: Orientations, Objects, Others*. Durham, NC: Duke University Press.

Aigen, Kenneth (1996). *Being in Music: Foundations of Nordoff–Robbins Music Therapy*. Gilsum, NH: Barcelona Publishers.

Aigen, Kenneth (2002/2005). *Playin' in the Band: A Qualitative Study of Popular Music Styles as Clinical Improvisation*. Gilsum, NH: Barcelona Publishers.

Aigen, Kenneth (2004). Conversations on Creating Community: Performance as Music Therapy in New York City. In: Mercédès Pavlicevic and Gary Ansdell (eds), *Community Music Therapy*. London: Jessica Kingsley.

Aigen, Kenneth (2005). *Music-centered Music Therapy*. Gilsum, NH: Barcelona Publishers.

Aigen, Kenneth (2007, 2008). In Defense of Beauty: A Role for the Aesthetic in Music Therapy Theory. *Nordic Journal of Music Therapy*, Part 1, 16(2), pp. 112–128; Part 2, 17(1), pp. 3–18.

Aigen, Kenneth (2009). Verticality and Containment in Song Improvisation: An Application of Schema Theory to Nordoff–Robbins Music Therapy. *Journal of Music Therapy*, 46(3), pp. 238–267.

Aldridge, David (2004). *Health, the Individual & Integrated Medicine*. London: Jessica Kingsley.

Anderson, Rob and Cissna, Kenneth (1997). *The Martin Buber–Carl Rogers Dialogue: A New Transcript with Commentary*. New York: State University of New York Press.

Ansdell, Gary (1995). *Music for Life*. London: Jessica Kingsley.

Ansdell, Gary (1997). Musical Elaborations: What has the New Musicology to Say to Music Therapy? *British Journal of Music Therapy*, 11(2), pp. 36–44.

Ansdell, Gary (2001). Musicology: Misunderstood Guest at the Music Therapy Feast? In: David Aldridge, Gianluigi DiFranco, Even Ruud and Tony Wigram (eds), *Music Therapy in Europe*. Rome: Ismez.

Ansdell, Gary (2002). Community Music Therapy and the Winds of Change – A Discussion Paper. Voices: A World Forum for Music Therapy, Vol 2, No 2 (2002). Retrieved 4 August 2013, from https://normt.uib.no/index.php/voices/article/view/83/65

Ansdell, Gary (2003). The Stories We Tell: Some Metatheoretical Reflections on Music Therapy. *Nordic Journal of Music Therapy*, 12(2), pp. 152–159.

Ansdell, Gary (2004). Rethinking Music and Community: Theoretical Perspectives in Support of Community Music Therapy. In: Mercédès Pavlicevic and Gary Ansdell (eds), *Community Music Therapy*. London: Jessica Kingsley.

Ansdell, Gary (2005a). Being Who You Aren't; Doing What You Can't: Community Music Therapy and the Paradoxes of Performance. *Voices: A World Forum for Music Therapy*. Retrieved 14 September 2008, from http://www.voices.no/mainissues/mi40005000192.html

Ansdell, Gary (2005b). Community Music Therapy: A Plea for 'Fuzzy Recognition' Instead of Final Definition [contribution to moderated discussions]. *Voices: A World Forum for Music Therapy*. Retrieved 28 October 2005, from http://voices.no/discussions/discm4_07.html

Ansdell, Gary (2010a). Belonging Through Musicing: Explorations of Musical Community. In: Brynjulf Stige, Gary Ansdell, Cochavit Elefant and Mercédès Pavlicevic (eds), *Where Music Helps: Community Music Therapy in Action and Reflection*. Farnham: Ashgate.

Ansdell, Gary (2010b). Can Everything Become Music? *Scrap Metal* in Southern England. In: Brynjulf Stige, Gary Ansdell, Cochavit Elefant and Mercédès Pavlicevic (eds), *Where Music Helps: Community Music Therapy in Action and Reflection*. Farnham: Ashgate.

Ansdell, Gary (2010c). Musicing on the Edge: *Musical Minds* in East London, England. In: Brynjulf Stige, Gary Ansdell, Cochavit Elefant and Mercédès Pavlicevic (eds), *Where Music Helps: Community Music Therapy in Action and Reflection*. Farnham: Ashgate.

Ansdell, Gary (2010d). Where Performing Helps: Processes and Affordances of Performance in Community Music Therapy. In: Brynjulf Stige, Gary Ansdell, Cochavit Elefant and Mercédès Pavlicevic (eds), *Where Music Helps: Community Music Therapy in Action and Reflection*. Farnham: Ashgate.

Ansdell, Gary and DeNora, Tia (2012). Musical Flourishing: Community Music Therapy, Controversy, and the Cultivation of Wellbeing. In: Raymond MacDonald, Gunther Kreutz and Laura Mitchell (eds), *Music, Health, and Wellbeing*. Oxford: Oxford University Press.

Ansdell, Gary and DeNora, Tia (in preparation). *Musical Pathways for Mental Health*. Farnham: Ashgate.

Ansdell, Gary and Meehan, John (2010). 'Some Light at the End of the Tunnel': Exploring Users' Evidence for the Effectiveness of Music Therapy in Adult Mental Health Settings. *Music and Medicine*, 2(1), pp. 41–47.

Ansdell, Gary and Pavlicevic, Mercédès (2005). Musical Companionship, Musical Community: Music Therapy and the Process and Values of Musical Communication. In: Dorothy Miell, Raymond MacDonald and David Hargreaves (eds), *Musical Communication*. Oxford: Oxford University Press.

Ansdell, Gary and Pavlicevic, Mercédès (2010). Practising 'Gentle Empiricism': The Nordoff–Robbins Research Heritage. *Music Therapy Perspectives*, 28(2), pp. 131–139.

Ansdell, Gary and Stige, Brynjulf (in press). Community Music Therapy. In: Jane Edwards (ed.), *The Oxford Handbook of Music Therapy*. Oxford: Oxford University Press.

Ansdell, Gary, Davidson, Jane, Magee, Wendy, Meehan, John and Procter, Simon (2010). From 'This ****ing Life' to 'That's Better'... in Four Minutes: An Interdisciplinary Study of Music Therapy's 'Present Moments' and their Potential for Affect Modulation. *Nordic Journal of Music Therapy*, 19(1), pp. 3–28.

Avnon, Dan (1998). *Martin Buber: The Hidden Dialogue*. Oxford: Rowman & Littlefield.

Baldwin, Clive and Capstick, Andrea (2007). *Tom Kitwood on Dementia: A Reader and Critical Commentary*. Maidenhead: Open University Press.

Bamberger, Jeanne (2006). What Develops in Musical Development? In: Gary McPherson (ed.), *The Child as Musician: A Handbook of Musical Development*. Oxford: Oxford University Press.

Barenboim, Daniel (2008). *Everything is Connected*. London: Weidenfeld & Nicolson.

Barenboim, Daniel and Said, Edward (2002). *Parallels and Paradoxes: Explorations in Music & Society*. London: Bloomsbury.

Barrett, Margaret (2005). Musical Communication and Children's Communities of Musical Practice. In: Dorothy Miell, Raymond MacDonald and David Hargreaves (eds), *Musical Communication*. Oxford: Oxford University Press.

Barrington, Alison (2008). Challenging the Profession. *British Journal of Music Therapy*, 22(2), pp. 65–72.

Bateson, Gregory (1985). *Mind and Nature: A Necessary Unity*. London: Flamingo.

Bateson, Gregory and Bateson, Mary Catherine (1988). *Angels Fear: An Investigation into the Nature and Meaning of the Sacred*. London: Rider.

Bauman, Zygmunt (2001). *Community: Seeking Safety in an Insecure World*. Cambridge: Polity Press.

Bauman, Zygmunt (2004). *Identity*. Cambridge: Polity Press.

Becker, Howard (2000). The Etiquette of Improvisation. *Mind, Culture, and Activity*, 7(3), pp. 171–176.

Becker, Judith (2004). *Deep Listeners: Music, Emotion, and Trancing*. Bloomington, IN: Indiana University Press.

Beckles Willson, Rachel (2009). Whose Utopia? Perspectives on the West-Eastern Divan Orchestra. *Music & Politics*, 3(2), pp. 1–21.

Begbie, Jeremy (2000). *Theology, Music and Time*. Cambridge: Cambridge University Press.

Benson, Bruce Ellis (2003). *The Improvisation of Musical Dialogue: A Phenomenology of Music*. Cambridge: Cambridge University Press.

Benson, Bruce Ellis (2011). Improvising Texts, Improvising Communities: Jazz, Interpretation, Heterophony, and the *Ekklesia*. In: Jeremy Begbie and Steven Guthrie (eds), *Resonant Witness: Conversations Between Music & Theology*. Grand Rapids, MI: Eerdmans Publishing Company.

Bergh, Arild (2010). I'd Like to Teach the World to Sing: Music and Conflict Transformation. Unpublished PhD thesis, University of Exeter, UK.

Bergh, Arild and Sloboda, John (2010). Music and Conflict Transformation: A Review. *Music and Arts in Action*, 2(2), pp. 2–18.

Bernstein, Leonard (1976). *The Unanswered Question: Six Talks at Harvard.* Cambridge, MA: Harvard University Press.

Blacking, John (1973). *How Musical is Man?* Seattle, WA: University of Washington Press.

Blacking, John (1985). Versus Gradus Novos Ad Parnassum Musicum: Exemplum Africum. In: D.P. McAllester (ed.), *Becoming Human through Music.* Reston, VA: MENC, The Western Symposium 1984, Connecticut.

Blacking, John (1987). *A Common-sense View of all Music.* Cambridge: Cambridge University Press.

Bohlman, Philip V. (2002). *World Music: A Very Short Introduction.* Oxford: Oxford University Press.

Bollas, Christopher (1993). *Being a Character: Psychoanalysis and Self Experience.* London: Routledge.

Bollas, Christopher (1995). *Cracking Up: The Work of Unconscious Experience.* New York: Hill & Wang.

Bonde, Lars Ole (2011). Health Musicing – Music Therapy or Music and Health? A Model, Empirical Examples and Personal Reflections. *Music and Arts in Action*, 3(2), pp. 120–140. Retrieved 1 July 2012, from http://musicandartsinaction. net/index.php/maia/article/view/healthmusicingmodel

Bonhoeffer, Dietrich (1971). *Letters & Papers from Prison*, ed. Eberhard Bethge. New York: Collier Books.

Bortoft, Henri (1996). *The Wholeness of Nature: Goethe's Way of Science.* Edinburgh: Floris Books.

Bowman, Wayne (1998). *Philosophical Perspectives on Music.* Oxford: Oxford University Press.

Bradley, Benjamin (2005). *Psychology and Experience.* Cambridge: Cambridge University Press.

Brown, Steven and Volgsten, Ulrik (2006). *Music and Manipulation: On the Social Uses and Social Control of Music.* New York: Berghahn Books.

Buber, Martin (1937/1958). *I and Thou*, trans. Ronald Gregor Smith. Edinburgh: T. & T. Clark.

Buber, Martin (1947/2002). *Between Man & Man.* London: Routledge.

Buber, Martin (1949). *Paths in Utopia.* London: Routledge & Kegan Paul.

Buber, Martin (1967/2002). *Meetings: Autobiographical Fragments.* London: Routledge.

Buber, Martin (1999a). Dialogue on the Unconscious. In: Judith Buber Agassi (ed.), *Martin Buber on Psychology and Psychotherapy: Essays, Letters, and Dialogues.* Syracuse, NY: Syracuse University Press.

Buber, Martin (1999b). Healing through Meeting. In: Judith Buber Agassi (ed.), *Martin Buber on Psychology and Psychotherapy: Essays, Letters, and Dialogues*. Syracuse, NY: Syracuse University Press.

Cage, John (1981). *For The Birds: In Conversation with Daniel Charles*. London: Marion Boyars.

Capra, Fritjof (1997). *The Web of Life: A New Synthesis of Mind and Matter*. London: Flamingo.

Caputo, John (1997). *Deconstruction in a Nutshell: A Conversation with Jacques Derrida*. New York: Fordham University Press.

Carel, Havi (2008). *Illness*. London: Acumen.

Chanan, Michael (1994). *Musica Practica*. London: Verso.

Charmaz, Kathy (1997). *Good Days, Bad Days: The Self in Chronic Illness and Time*. New Brunswick, NJ: Rutgers University Press.

Clarke, Eric (2003). Music and Psychology. In: Martin Clayton, Trevor Herbert and Richard Middleton (eds), *The Cultural Study of Music: A Critical Introduction*. New York and London: Routledge.

Clarke, Eric (2005). *Ways of Listening: An Ecological Approach to the Perception of Musical Meaning*. Oxford: Oxford University Press.

Clarke, Eric (2011). Music Perception and Musical Consciousness. In: David Clarke and Eric Clarke (eds), *Music and Consciousness: Philosophical, Psychological, and Cultural Perspectives*. Oxford: Oxford University Press.

Clarke, Eric and David Clarke (eds) (2011). *Music and Consciousness: Philosophical, Psychological, and Cultural Perspectives*. Oxford: Oxford University Press.

Clayton, Martin, Trevor Herbert and Richard Middleton (eds) (2003). *The Cultural Study of Music: A Critical Introduction*. New York and London: Routledge.

Clifton, Thomas (1983). *Music as Heard: A Study in Applied Phenomenology*. New Haven, CT: Yale University Press.

Cobussen, Marcel (2008). *Thresholds: Rethinking Spirituality through Music*. Farnham: Ashgate.

Cook, Nicholas (1998). *Music: A Very Short Introduction*. Oxford: Oxford University Press.

Cook, Nicholas (2003). Music as Performance. In: Martin Clayton, Trevor Herbert and Richard Middleton (eds), *The Cultural Study of Music: A Critical Introduction*. New York and London: Routledge.

Csikszentmihalyi, Mihaly (1992). *Flow: The Psychology of Happiness*. London: Rider.

Cupitt, Don (1998). *The Revelation of Being*. London: SCM Press.

Cupitt, Don (1999). *The New Religion of Life in Everyday Speech*. London: SCM Press.

Cupitt, Don (2003). *Life, Life*. Santa Rosa, CA: Polebridge Press.

Czubaroff, Jeanine and Friedman, Maurice (2000). A Conversation with Maurice Friedman. *Southern Communication Journal*, 65, pp. 243–254.

Darnley-Smith, Rachel and Patey, Helen M. (2003). *Music Therapy*. London: Sage.

Delanty, Gerard (2003). *Community*. London: Routledge.

Dileo, Cheryl and Bradt, Joke (2005). *Medical Music Therapy: A Meta-analysis of the Literature and an Agenda for Future Research*. Cherry Hill, NJ: Jeffrey Books.

Deliège, Irene and Sloboda, John (eds) (1996). *Musical Beginnings: Origins and Development of Musical Competence*. Oxford: Oxford University Press.

DeNora, Tia (2000). *Music in Everyday Life*. Cambridge: Cambridge University Press.

DeNora, Tia (2003). *After Adorno: Rethinking Music Sociology*. Cambridge: Cambridge University Press.

DeNora, Tia (2011a). *Music-in-action: Selected Essays in Sonic Ecology*. Farnham: Ashgate.

DeNora, Tia (2011b). Practical Consciousness and Social Relation in *MusEcological* Perspective. In: David Clarke and Eric Clarke (eds), *Music and Consciousness: Philosophical, Psychological, and Cultural Perspectives*. Oxford: Oxford University Press.

DeNora, Tia (2013). *Music Asylums: Wellbeing through Music in Everyday Life*. Farnham: Ashgate.

Dewey, John (1934). *Art as Experience*. New York: Perigee Books.

Dissanayake, Ellen (2000). *Art and Intimacy: How the Arts Began*. Seattle, WA: University of Washington Press.

Dissanayake, Ellen (2006). Ritual and Ritualization: Musical Means of Conveying and Shaping Emotion in Humans and Other Animals. In: Steven Brown and Ulrik Volsten (eds), *Music and Manipulation: On the Social Uses and Social Control of Music*. New York: Berghahn Books.

Edwards, Jane (2008). The Use of Music in Healthcare Contexts: A Select Review of Writings from the 1890s to the 1940s. *Voices: A World Forum for Music Therapy*, 8(2). Retrieved 24 July 2013, from https://normt.uib.no/index.php/voices/article/viewArticle/428/352

Ehrenreich, Barbara (2007). *Dancing in the Streets: A History of Collective Joy*. London: Granta.

Eigen, Michael (2001). *Ecstasy*. Middletown, CT: Wesleyan University Press.

Elliott, David J. (1995). *Music Matters: A New Philosophy of Music Education*. New York: Oxford University Press.

Elliott, David J., and Silverman, Marissa (2012). Why Music Matters: Philosophical and Cultural Foundations. In: Raymond MacDonald, Gunther Kreutz and Laura Mitchell (eds), *Music, Health, and Wellbeing*. Oxford: Oxford University Press.

Esposito, Roberto (2010). *Communitas: The Origin and Destiny of Community*. Stanford, CA: Stanford University Press.

Ferrara, Lawrence (1991). *Philosophy & the Analysis of Music*. Excelsior Springs, MO: Excelsior Publishing Company.

Flanagan, Owen (2007). *The Really Hard Problem: Meaning in a Material World.* Cambridge, MA: MIT Press.

Frank, Arthur W. (2004). *The Renewal of Generosity: Illness, Medicine, and How to Live.* Chicago, IL: University of Chicago Press.

Friedman, Maurice (1955/2002). *Martin Buber: The Life of Dialogue.* London: Routledge.

Friedman, Maurice (1992). *Dialogue and the Human Image: Beyond Humanistic Psychology.* London: Sage.

Friedman, Maurice (2003). Buber and Dialogical Psychotherapy. In: Roger Frie (ed.), *Understanding Experience: Psychotherapy & Postmodernism.* New York: Routledge.

Gadamer, Hans-Georg (1996). *The Enigma of Health.* Stanford, CA: Stanford University Press.

Gibson, James J. (1979/1986). *The Ecological Approach to Visual Perception.* Hillsdale, NJ: Lawrence Erlbaum Associates, Publishers.

Giddens, Anthony (1991). *Modernity and Self-identity: Self and Society in the Late Modern Age.* Cambridge: Polity Press.

Gioia, Ted (2006). *Healing Songs.* Durham, NC, and London: Duke University Press.

Godlovitch, Stan (1998). *Musical Performance: A Philosophical Study.* London: Routledge.

Goffman, Erving (1959/1990). *The Presentation of Self in Everyday Life.* London: Penguin Books.

Gordon, Paul (1999). *Face to Face: Therapy as Ethics.* London: Constable.

Gordon, Paul (2009). *The Hope of Therapy.* Ross-on-Wye: PCCS Books.

Gouk, Penelope (2000). *Musical Healing in Cultural Contexts.* Aldershot: Ashgate.

Gratier, Maya, and Apter-Danon, Gisèle (2009). The Improvised Music of Belonging: Repetition and Variation in Mother–Infant Vocal Interaction. In: Stephen Malloch and Colwyn Trevarthen (eds), *Communicative Musicality.* Oxford: Oxford University Press.

Green, Lucy (2008). *Music, Informal Learning and the School: A New Classroom Pedagogy.* Farnham: Ashgate.

Hagberg, Garry (2011). Jazz Improvisation and Ethical Interaction: A Sketch of the Connections. In: Garry Hagberg (ed.), *Art and Ethical Criticism.* Chichester: Wiley-Blackwell.

Hamilton, Andy (2007). *Aesthetics and Music.* London: Continuum.

Hennion, Antoine (2001). Music Lovers: Taste as Performance. *Theory, Culture, Society,* 18(5), pp. 1–22.

Hennion, Antoine (2003). Music and Mediation. In: Martin Clayton, Trevor Herbert and Richard Middleton (eds), *The Cultural Study of Music: A Critical Introduction.* New York and London: Routledge.

Hesmondhalgh, David (2013). *Why Music Matters.* Chichester, UK: Wiley-Blackwell.

Hesser, Barbara and Heinemann, Harry (eds) (2010). *Music as a Natural Resources: Solutions for Social & Economic Issues*. New York: United National Headquarters [paper and online editions].

Higgins, Lee (2008). The Creative Music Workshop: Event, Facilitation, Gift. *International Journal of Music Education*, 26(4), pp. 326–338.

Higgins, Lee (2012). *Community Music: In Theory and in Practice*. Oxford: Oxford University Press.

Hildebrand, David (2008). *Dewey*. Oxford: Oneworld.

Hillman, James (1983). *Inter Views*. New York: Harper & Row.

Hillman, James (1996). *The Soul's Code: In Search of Character and Calling*. New York: Random House.

Hillman, James (1999). *The Force of Character and the Lasting Life*. New York: Random House.

Hodges, Donald (2006). The Musical Brain. In: Gary McPherson (ed.), *The Child as Musician: A Handbook of Musical Development*. Oxford: Oxford University Press.

Hoffmann, Nigel (2007). *Goethe's Science of Living Form: The Artistic Stages*. Hillsdale, NY: Adonis Press.

Horden, Peregrin (2000). *Music as Medicine: The History of Music Therapy since Antiquity*. Aldershot: Ashgate.

Hunt, Stephen (2005). *The Life Course: A Sociological Introduction*. London: Palgrave.

Husserl, Edmund (1935/1970). *The Crisis of European Sciences and Transcendental Phenomenology*. Evanston, IL: Northwestern University Press.

Ihde, Don (2009). *Postphenomenology and Technoscience*. Albany, NY: State University of New York Press.

Jankélévitch, Vladimir (2003). *Music and the Ineffable*, trans. Carolyn Abbate. Princeton, NJ: Princeton University Press.

Johnson, Mark (2007). *The Meaning of the Body: Aesthetics of Human Understanding*. Chicago, IL: University of Chicago Press.

Johnson, Robert A. (1987). *Ecstasy: Understanding the Psychology of Joy*. San Francisco, CA: Harper & Row.

Joyce, James (1963). *Stephen Hero*. New York: New Directions.

Kalton, Michael (2000). Green Spirituality: Horizontal Transcendence. In: Melvin Miller (ed.), *Paths of Integrity, Wisdom, and Transcendence: Spiritual Development in the Mature Self*. New York: Routledge.

Keil, Charles (1994). Participatory Discrepancies and the Power of Music. In: Charles Keil and Steven Feld (eds), *Music Grooves*. Chicago, IL: University of Chicago Press.

Kittay, Jeffrey (2008). The Sound Surround: Exploring How One Might Design the Everyday Soundscape for the Truly Captive Audience. *Nordic Journal of Music Therapy*, 17(1), pp. 41–54.

Kitwood, Tom (1997). *Dementia Reconsidered: The Person Comes First*. Buckingham: Open University Press.

Kramer, Kenneth Paul (2003). *Martin Buber's I and Thou: Practicing Living Dialogue*. New York: Paulist Press.

Kramer, Lawrence (2011). *Interpreting Music*. Berkeley, CA: University of California Press.

Lakoff, George and Johnson, Mark (1980). *Metaphors We Live By*. Chicago, IL: University of Chicago Press.

Lakoff, George and Johnson, Mark (1999). *Philosophy in the Flesh: The Embodied Mind and its Challenge to Western Thought*. New York: Basic Books.

Latour, Bruno (2005). *Reassembling the Social: An Introduction to Actor-Network-Theory*. Oxford: Oxford University Press.

Lievegoed, Bernard (1979/2003). *Phases: The Spiritual Rhythms of Adult Life*. London: Rudolf Steiner Press.

Levinas, Emmanuel (2006). *Entre Nous: Thinking-of-the-Other*. London: Continuum.

Love, Andrew Cyprian (2003). *Musical Improvisation, Heidegger, and the Liturgy: A Journey to the Heart of Hope*. Lewiston, ME: The Edwin Mellor Press.

MacDonald, Raymond, Hargreaves, David and Miell, Dorothy (eds) (2002). *Musical Identities*. Oxford: Oxford University Press.

MacDonald, Raymond, Kreutz, Gunter and Mitchell, Laura (eds) (2012). *Music, Health, and Wellbeing*. Oxford: Oxford University Press.

Malloch, Stephen (1999). Mothers and Infants and Communicative Musicality. *Musicae Scientiae*, special issue 1999–2000, pp. 29–53.

Malloch, Stephen and Trevarthen, Colwyn (eds) (2009a). *Communicative Musicality*. Oxford: Oxford University Press.

Malloch, Stephen and Trevarthen, Colwyn (2009b). Musicality: Communicating the Vitality and Interests of Life. In: Stephen Malloch and Colwyn Trevarthen (eds), *Communicative Musicality*. Oxford: Oxford University Press.

Maratos, Anna, Crawford, Mike and Procter, Simon (2011). Music for Depression: It Seems to Work, But How? *British Journal of Psychiatry*, 199(2), pp. 92–93.

Mattern, Mark (1998). *Acting in Concert: Music, Community, and Political Action*. New Brunswick, NJ: Rutgers University Press.

McFerran, Katrina (2010). *Adolescents, Music and Music Therapy: Methods and Techniques for Clinicians, Educators and Students*. London: Jessica Kingsley.

McGuiness, Andy and Overy, Katie (2011). Music, Consciousness and the Brain: Music as Shared Experience of an Embodied Present. In: David Clarke and Eric Clarke (eds), *Music and Consciousness: Philosophical, Psychological, and Cultural Perspectives*. Oxford: Oxford University Press.

McPherson, Gary (ed.) (2006). *The Child as Musician: A Handbook of Musical Development*. Oxford: Oxford University Press.

McPherson, Gary, Davidson, Jane and Faulkner, Robert (2012). *Music in Our Lives: Rethinking Musical Ability, Development and Identity*. Oxford: Oxford University Press.

Mead, George Herbert (1934). *Mind, Self, and Society*. Chicago, IL: University of Chicago Press.

Moon, Catherine Hyland (2002). *Studio Art Therapy*. London: Jessica Kingsley.

Naydler, Jeremy (1996). *Goethe on Science: An Anthology of Goethe's Scientific Writings*. Edinburgh: Floris Books.

Nelson, Geoffrey and Prilleltensky, Isaac (eds) (2005). *Community Psychology: In Pursuit of Liberation and Well-being*. New York: Palgrave Macmillan.

Newlands, George and Smith, Allen (2010). *Hospitable God: The Transformative Dream*. Farnham: Ashgate.

Newman, Fred (1999). A Therapeutic Deconstruction of the Illusion of Self. In: Lois Holzman, *Performing Psychology: A Postmodern Culture of the Mind*. London: Routledge.

Noë, Alva (2010). *Out of Our Heads: Why You Are Not Your Brain, and Other Lessons from the Biology of Consciousness*. New York: Hill & Wang.

Noë, Alva (2012). *Varieties of Presence*. Cambridge, MA: Harvard University Press.

Nordoff, Paul and Robbins, Clive (1971/2004). *Therapy in Music for Handicapped Children*. Gilsum, NH: Barcelona Publishers.

Nordoff, Paul and Robbins, Clive (1977/2007). *Creative Music Therapy*. Gilsum, NH: Barcelona Publishers.

North, Adrian and Hargreaves, David (2008). *The Social and Applied Psychology of Music*. Oxford: Oxford University Press.

Nussbaum, Martha (2011). *Creating Capabilities: The Human Development Approach*. Cambridge, MA: The Belknap Press of Harvard University Press.

Osborne, Nigel (2009). Towards a Chronobiology of Musical Rhythm. In: Stephen Malloch and Colwyn Trevarthen (eds), *Communicative Musicality*. Oxford: Oxford University Press.

Parncutt, Richard (2006). Prenatal Development. In: Gary McPherson (ed.), *The Child as Musician: A Handbook of Musical Development*. Oxford: Oxford University Press.

Pavlicevic, Mercédès and Ansdell, Gary (eds) (2004). *Community Music Therapy*. London: Jessica Kingsley.

Pavlicevic, Mercédès and Ansdell, Gary (2009). Between Communicative Musicality and Collaborative Musicing. In: Stephen Malloch and Colwyn Trevarthen (eds), *Communicative Musicality*. Oxford: Oxford University Press.

Peacocke, Arthur and Pederson, Ann (2006). *The Music of Creation*. Minneapolis, MN: Fortress Press.

Phillips, Adam (1988). *Winnicott*. London: Fontana.

Pieslak, Jonathan (2009). *Sound Targets: American Soldiers and Music in the Iraq War*. Bloomington, IN: Indiana University Press.

Pitts, Stephanie (2012). *Chances and Choices: Exploring the Impact of Music Education*. Oxford: Oxford University Press.

Procter, Simon (2004). Playing Politics: Community Music Therapy and the Therapeutic Redistribution of Music Capital for Mental Health. In: Mercédès

Pavlicevic and Gary Ansdell (eds), *Community Music Therapy*. London: Jessica Kingsley.

Procter, Simon (2006). What Are We Playing at? Social Capital and Music Therapy. In: Rosalind Edwards, Jane Franklin and Janet Holland (eds), *Assessing Social Capital: Concept, Policy & Practice*. Newcastle: Cambridge Scholars Press.

Procter, Simon (2011). Reparative Musicing: Thinking on the Usefulness of Social Capital Theory within Music Therapy. *Nordic Journal of Music Therapy*, 20(3), pp. 242–262.

Procter, Simon (2013). 'Music therapy: what is it for whom? An ethnography of music therapy in a community mental health resource centre'. University of Exeter Doctoral thesis, available online at http://hdl.handle.net/10871/11101

Rayment-Pickard, Hugh (2004). *The Myths of Time*. London: Darton, Longman & Todd.

Raw, Anni, Lewis, Sue, Russell, Andrew and Macnaughton, Jane (2012). A Hole in the Heart: Confronting the Drive for Evidence-based Impact Research in Arts and Health. *Arts & Health*, 4(2), pp. 97–108.

Riiser, Solveig (2010). National Identity and the West-Eastern Divan Orchestra. *Music and Arts in Action*, 2(2), pp. 19–37.

Robbins, Clive (2005). *A Journey into Creative Music Therapy*. Gilsum, NH: Barcelona Publishers.

Robbins, Clive and Robbins, Carol (eds) (1998). *Healing Heritage: Paul Nordoff Exploring the Tonal Language of Music*. Gilsum, NH: Barcelona Publishers.

Rolvsjord, Randi (2010). *Resource-oriented Music Therapy in Mental Health Care*. Gilsum, NH: Barcelona Publishers.

Rouget, Gilbert (1985). *Music and Trance: A Theory of the Relations between Music and Possession*, trans. Brunhilde Biebuyck. Chicago, IL: Chicago University Press.

Ruud, Even (1998). *Music Therapy: Improvisation, Communication, and Culture*. Gilsum, NH: Barcelona Publishers.

Ruud, Even (2010). *Music Therapy: A Perspective from the Humanities*. Gilsum, NH: Barcelona Publishers.

Sacks, Oliver (1995). *An Anthropologist on Mars*. London: Picador.

Sacks, Oliver (2007). *Musicophilia*. London: Picador.

Sandel, Michael J. (2010). *Justice: What's the Right Thing to Do?* London: Penguin Books.

Sawyer, Keith (2003). *Group Creativity: Music, Theater, Collaboration*. Hillsdale, NJ: Lawrence Erlbaum Associates, Publishers.

Sawyer, Keith (2005). Music and Conversation. In: Dorothy Miell, Raymond MacDonald and David Hargreaves (eds), *Musical Communication*. Oxford: Oxford University Press.

Schore, Allan (2003). Minds in the Making: Attachment, the Self-organising Brain, and Developmentally-oriented Psychoanalytic Psychotherapy. In: Jenny Corrigall and Heward Wilkinson (eds), *Revolutionary Connections: Psychotherapy and Neuroscience*. London: Karnac Books.

Schütz, Alfred (1964). Making Music Together: A Study in Social Relationship. In: Arvid Brodersen (ed.), *Collected Papers, vol. 2: Studies in Social Theory*. The Hague: Martinus Nijhoff.

Schütz, Alfred (1976). Mozart and the Philosophers. In: Arvid Brodersen (ed.), *Collected Papers, vol. 2. Studies in Social Theory*. The Hague: Martinus Nijhoff.

Scruton, Roger (1997). *The Aesthetics of Music*. Oxford: Clarendon Press.

Scruton, Roger (2009). *Understanding Music: Philosophy & Interpretation*. London: Continuum.

Scruton, Roger (2012). *The Face of God*. London: Continuum.

Sennett, Richard (2004). *Respect: The Formation of Character in an Age of Inequality*. London: Allen Lane.

Sennett, Richard (2007). *The Craftsman*. London: Allen Lane.

Sennett, Richard (2012). *Together: The Rituals, Pleasures and Politics of Cooperation*. London: Allen Lane.

Shotter, John (1999). Life Inside Dialogically Structured Mentalities: Bakhtin's and Voloshinov's Account of our Mental Activities as Out in the World Between Us. In: John Rowan and Mick Cooper (eds), *The Plural Self*. London: Sage.

Shusterman, Richard (2000). *Performing Live: Aesthetic Alternatives for the Ends of Art*. Ithaca, NY: Cornell University Press.

Shusterman, Richard (2008). *Body Consciousness: A Philosophy of Mindfulness and Somaesthetics*. Cambridge: Cambridge University Press.

Simanowitz, Valerie and Pearce, Peter (2003). *Personality Development*. Oxford: Open University Press.

Small, Christopher (1998). *Musicking: The Meanings of Performing and Listening*. Hanover, NH: Wesleyan University Press.

Small, Christopher (2010). Misunderstanding and Reunderstanding. *Peace & Policy*, 15, pp. 4–12.

Smith, Jonathan and Osborn, M. (2003). Interpretative Phenomenological Analysis. In Jonathan A. Smith (ed.), *Qualitative Psychology: A Practical Guide to Research Methods*. London: Sage.

Solomon, Maynard (2003). *Late Beethoven: Music, Thought, Imagination*. Berkeley, CA: University of California Press.

Steiner, Rudolf (1886/2008). *Goethe's Theory of Knowledge: An Outline of the Epistemology of his Worldview*. Great Barrington, MA: Steiner Books.

Stensæth, Karette (2007). Musical Answerability: A Theory on the Relationship between Music Therapy Improvisation and the Phenomenon of Action. Unpublished PhD thesis, Norwegian Academy of Music, Oslo.

Stern, Daniel (2004). *The Present Moment in Psychotherapy and Everyday Life*. New York: Norton.

Stern, Daniel (2010a). *Forms of Vitality: Exploring Dynamic Experience in Psychology, the Arts, Psychotherapy, and Development*. Oxford: Oxford University Press.

Daniel (2010b). The Issue of Vitality. *Nordic Journal of Music Therapy*, 19 (2), pp. 88–103.

Stige, Brynjulf (2002). *Culture Centered Music Therapy*. Gilsum, NH: Barcelona Publishers.

Stige, Brynjulf (2003/2012). *Elaborations towards a Notion of Community Music Therapy*. Gilsum, NH: Barcelona Publishers.

Stige, Brynjulf (2010). Musical Participation, Social Space, and Everyday Ritual. In: Brynjulf Stige, Gary Ansdell, Cochavit Elefant and Mercédès Pavlicevic (eds), *Where Music Helps: Community Music Therapy in Action and Reflection*. Farnham: Ashgate.

Stige, Brynjulf and Aarø, Leif Edvard (2012). *Invitation to Community Music Therapy*. New York: Routledge.

Stige, Brynjulf, Ansdell, Gary, Elefant, Cochavit and Pavlicevic, Mercédès (eds) (2010). *Where Music Helps: Community Music Therapy in Action and Reflection*. Farnham: Ashgate.

Tallis, Raymond (2010). *Michelangelo's Finger: An Exploration of Everyday Transcendence*. London: Atlantic Books.

Tallis, Raymond (2011). *Aping Mankind: Neuromania, Darwinitis and the Misrepresentation of Humanity*. Durham: Acumen.

Taylor, Charles (1989). *Sources of the Self: The Making of Modern Identity*. Cambridge: Cambridge University Press.

Thompson, Mel (2009). *Me*. Stocksfield: Acumen.

Trehub, Sandra (2006). Infants as Musical Connoisseurs. In: Gary McPherson (ed.), *The Child as Musician: A Handbook of Musical Development*. Oxford: Oxford University Press.

Trevarthen, Colwyn (1999). Musicality and the Intrinsic Motive Pulse: Evidence from Human Psychobiology and Infant Communication. *Musicae Scientiae*, special issue 1999–2000, pp. 155–215.

Trevarthen, Colwyn (2002). Origins of Musical Identity: Evidence from Infancy for Musical Social Awareness. In: Raymond MacDonald, David Hargreaves and Dorothy Miell (eds), *Musical Identities*. Oxford: Oxford University Press.

Turino, Thomas (2008). *Music as Social Life: The Politics of Participation*. Chicago, IL: University of Chicago Press.

Turner, Victor (1969a). Communitas: Model and Process. In: *The Ritual Process*. London: Penguin Books.

Turner, Victor (1969b). *The Ritual Process*. London: Penguin Books.

Turner, Victor (1982). *From Ritual to Theatre: The Human Seriousness of Play*. New York: PAJ Publications.

Turner, Victor (1987). *The Anthropology of Performance*. New York: PAJ Publications.

Tyler, Helen (2000). The Music Therapy Profession in Modern Britain. In: Peregrin Horden (ed.), *Music as Medicine: The History of Music Therapy since Antiquity*. Aldershot: Ashgate.

Tyler, Helen (2002). Frederick Kill Harford – Dilettante Dabbler or Man of our Time? *Nordic Journal of Music Therapy*, 11(1), pp. 39–42.

Urbain, Olivier (2010). Inspiring Musical Movements and Global Solidarity. *Peace & Policy*, 15, pp. 25–35.

Uy, Michael (2012). Venezuela's National Music Education Program *El Sistema*: Its Interactions with Society and its Participants' Engagement in Praxis. *Music and Arts in Action*, 4(1), pp. 5–21.

Van Hooft, Stan (2011). *Hope*. Durham: Acumen.

Verney, Rachel and Ansdell, Gary (2010). *Conversations on Nordoff–Robbins Music Therapy*. Gilsum, NH: Barcelona Publishers.

Vernon, Mark (2008). *Wellbeing*. Stocksfield: Acumen.

Vygotsky, Lev (1978). *Mind in Society: The Development of Higher Psychological Processes*, ed. Michael Cole, Vera John-Steiner, Sylvia Scribner and Ellen Souberman. Cambridge, MA: Harvard University Press.

Vygotsky, Lev (1989). Concrete Human Psychology. *Soviet Psychology*, 27(2), pp. 53–77.

Webster, Alison (2002). *Wellbeing*. London: SCM Press.

Wenger, Etienne (1998). *Communities of Practice: Learning, Meaning and Identity*. New York: Cambridge University Press.

Wenger, Etienne, McDermott, Richard and Snyder, William M. (2002). *Cultivating Communities of Practice*. Boston, MA: Harvard Business School Press.

Williams, Rowan (1994). Keeping Time, in *Open to Judgement: Sermons and Addresses*. London: Darton, Longman & Todd.

Windsor, Luke (2012). Music and Affordances. *Musicae Scientiae*, 16(1), pp. 102–120.

Wittgenstein, Ludwig (1953). *Philosophical Investigations*, ed. G.E.M. Anscombe and Rush Rees. Oxford: Blackwell.

Wood, Stuart (2006). 'The Matrix': A Model of Community Music Therapy Processes. *Voices: A World Forum for Music Therapy*. Retrieved 20 October 2012, from: https://normt.uib.no/index.php/voices/article/view/279/204

Zharinova-Sanderson, Oksana (2004). Promoting Integration and Socio-cultural Change: Community Music Therapy with Traumatised Refugees in Berlin. In: Mercédès Pavlicevic and Gary Ansdell (eds), *Community Music Therapy*. London: Jessica Kingsley.

Zuckerkandl, Victor (1956). *Sound and Symbol: Music and the External World*. Princeton, NJ: Princeton University Press.

Zuckerkandl, Victor (1973). *Man the Musician*. Princeton, NJ: Princeton University Press.

Index

DATE DUE